nancy

BY OLIVIA JAIMES

Andrews McMeel
PUBLISHING®

Introduction

Last winter, at her insistence, I played basketball with Olivia Jaimes.

Olivia Jaimes is not very good at basketball. Let's get that out of the way right now. She's definitely getting better, but right now, if you had to choose teams for some pickup games, I would strongly encourage you to pick other people first. What Olivia Jaimes is good at, however, is comics.

The process of finding a new cartoonist to take over *Nancy* was daunting. How do you find someone to breathe new life into a strip that is literally one hundred years old? When I saw the samples that Olivia sent, I said (out loud, to the fire hazard that is my desk), "This is it. This is Nancy." Many of the strips that were included in those first samples made it to newspapers untouched. Olivia's handle on the character, the art, the humor . . . everything, was perfect. Like Cinderella, if instead of a glass slipper, the item in question was a series of digital files containing line drawings of an iconic little girl being difficult and solving problems in a hilarious manner. So, exactly like Cinderella.

The production schedule for a syndicated comic strip is grueling. Cartoonists have to create a new comic every day for years. Papers need strips weeks in advance. It's not a career for the dilettante. I got the first batch of samples from Olivia in January of 2018. The new *Nancy* by Olivia Jaimes launched on April 9, 2018, for dailies and May 6, 2018, for Sundays. No one ever really understands what I do, and I never really feel like going into it, but trust me when I say, as a person who has worked in this industry for years and years, this is an incredibly compressed timeline for a feature launch. It involves a tremendous amount of work on the part of the cartoonist, and a great deal of trust on the part of the syndicate, because the quality of a strip will have to be maintained day in and day out for YEARS.

There was no hesitation on my part whatsoever on handing the *Nancy* keys to the *Nancy* kingdom over to Olivia Jaimes, and as you will see in this book, she is crushing it. I will repeat: CRUSHING IT.

These are some of the funniest comics anywhere. Not just in newspapers. Not just on the internet. This is an all-time take on an all-time comic strip, and though Olivia is, again, very bad at basketball, it is an honor to get to work with her on this comic.

I hope you will enjoy reading this selection of *Nancy* comic strips. To say that I am fond of them would be a tremendous understatement.

Shena Wolf, editor of *Nancy*

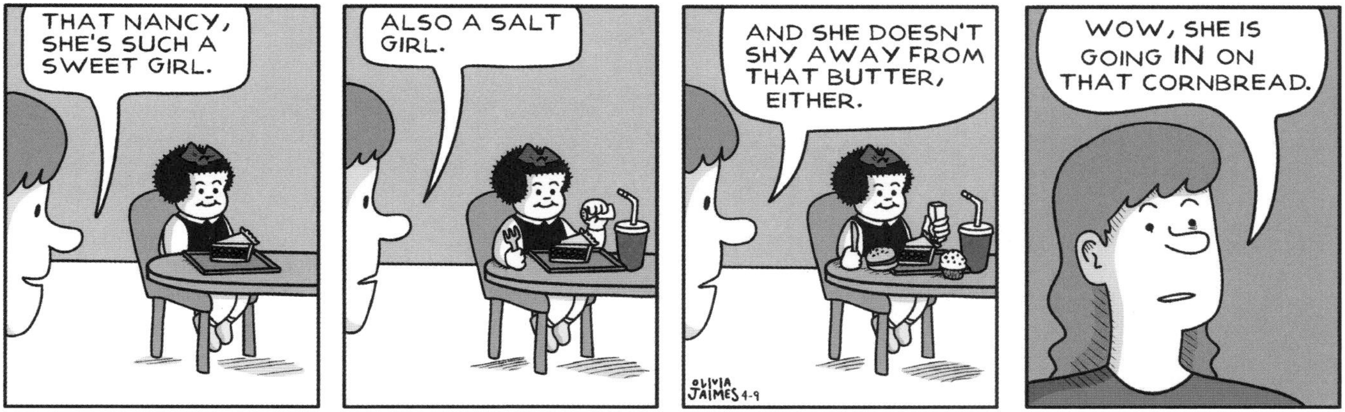
THAT NANCY, SHE'S SUCH A SWEET GIRL.
ALSO A SALT GIRL.
AND SHE DOESN'T SHY AWAY FROM THAT BUTTER, EITHER.
WOW, SHE IS GOING IN ON THAT CORNBREAD.
OLIVIA JAIMES 4-9

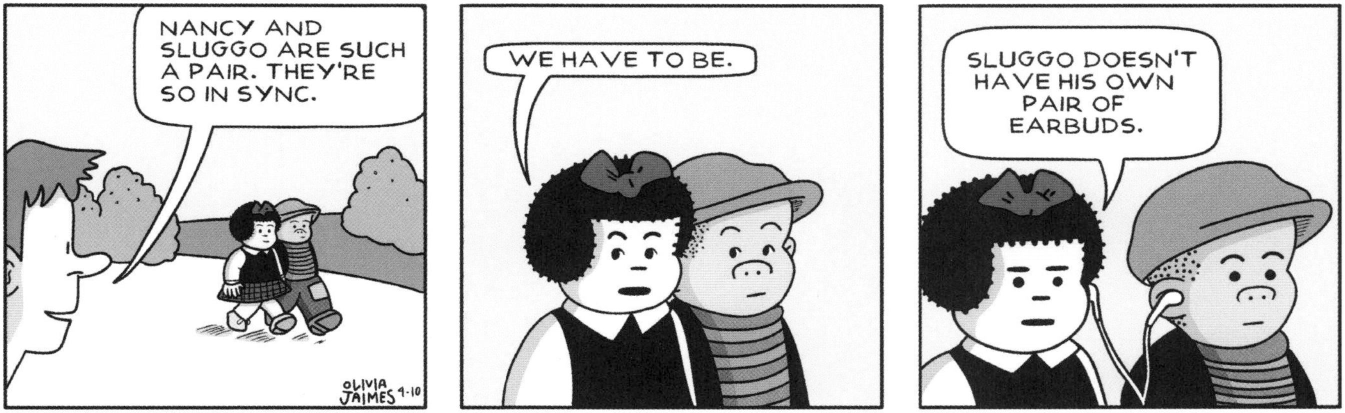
NANCY AND SLUGGO ARE SUCH A PAIR. THEY'RE SO IN SYNC.
OLIVIA JAIMES 4-10
WE HAVE TO BE.
SLUGGO DOESN'T HAVE HIS OWN PAIR OF EARBUDS.

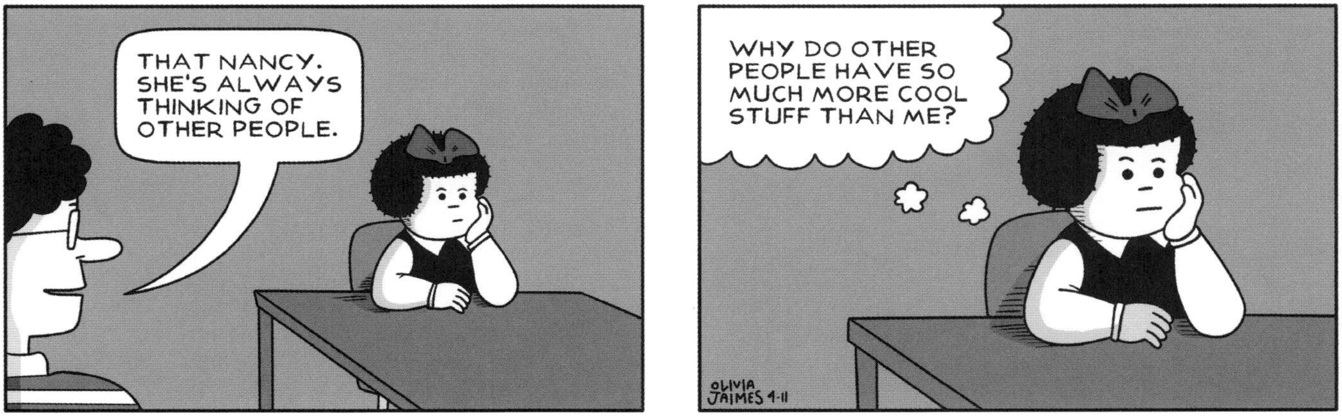
THAT NANCY. SHE'S ALWAYS THINKING OF OTHER PEOPLE.
WHY DO OTHER PEOPLE HAVE SO MUCH MORE COOL STUFF THAN ME?
OLIVIA JAIMES 4-11

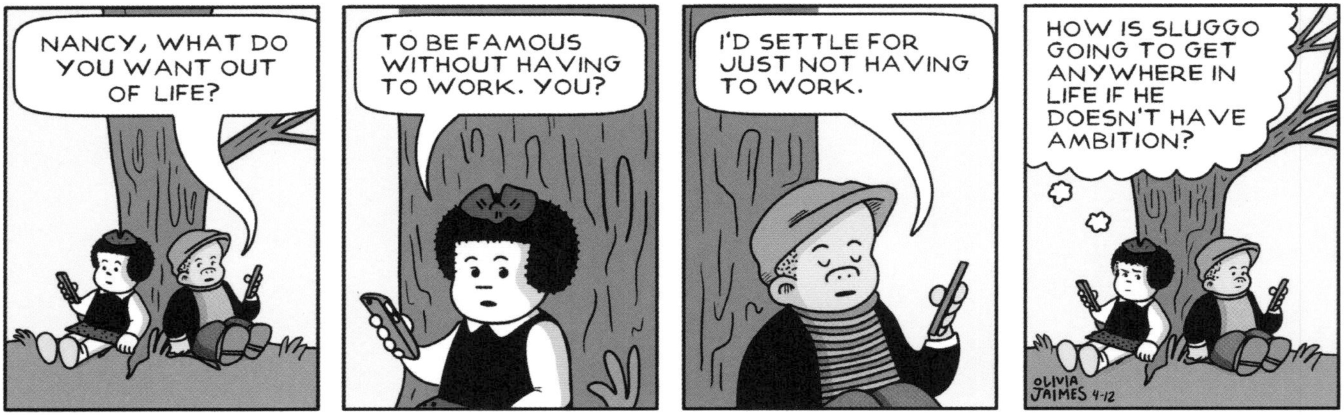
NANCY, WHAT DO YOU WANT OUT OF LIFE?
TO BE FAMOUS WITHOUT HAVING TO WORK. YOU?
I'D SETTLE FOR JUST NOT HAVING TO WORK.
HOW IS SLUGGO GOING TO GET ANYWHERE IN LIFE IF HE DOESN'T HAVE AMBITION?
OLIVIA JAIMES 4-12

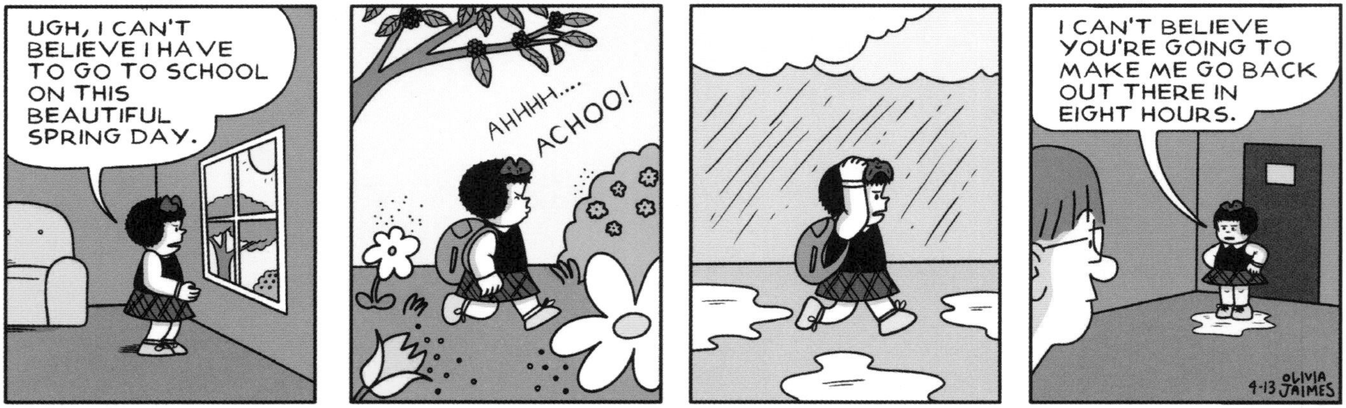
UGH, I CAN'T BELIEVE I HAVE TO GO TO SCHOOL ON THIS BEAUTIFUL SPRING DAY.
AHHHH.... ACHOO!
I CAN'T BELIEVE YOU'RE GOING TO MAKE ME GO BACK OUT THERE IN EIGHT HOURS.
4-13 OLIVIA JAIMES

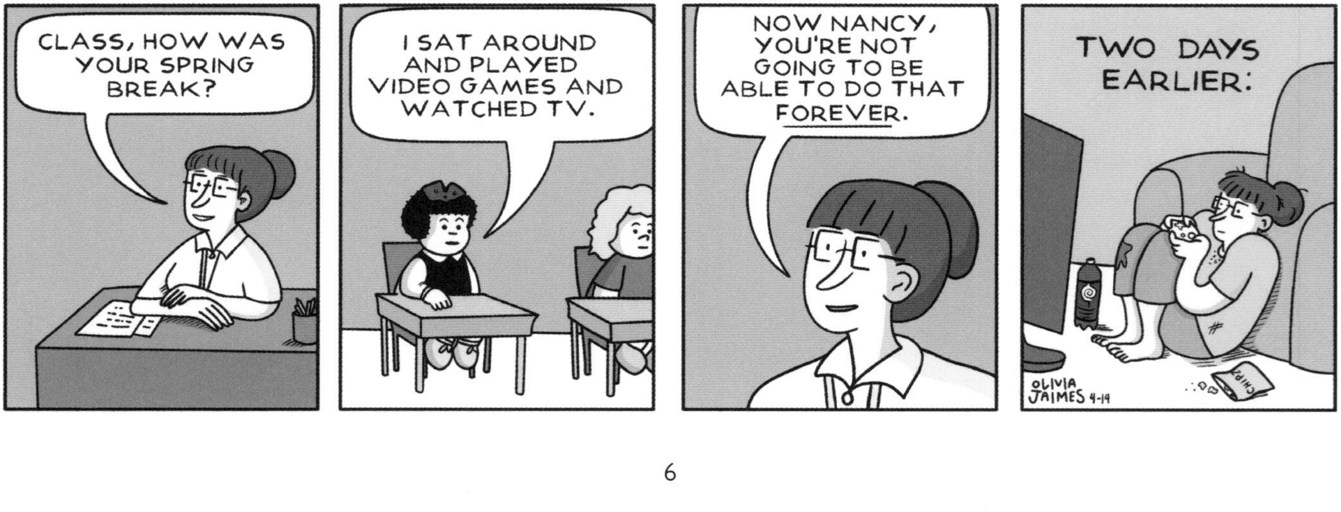
CLASS, HOW WAS YOUR SPRING BREAK?
I SAT AROUND AND PLAYED VIDEO GAMES AND WATCHED TV.
NOW NANCY, YOU'RE NOT GOING TO BE ABLE TO DO THAT FOREVER.
TWO DAYS EARLIER:
OLIVIA JAIMES 4-14

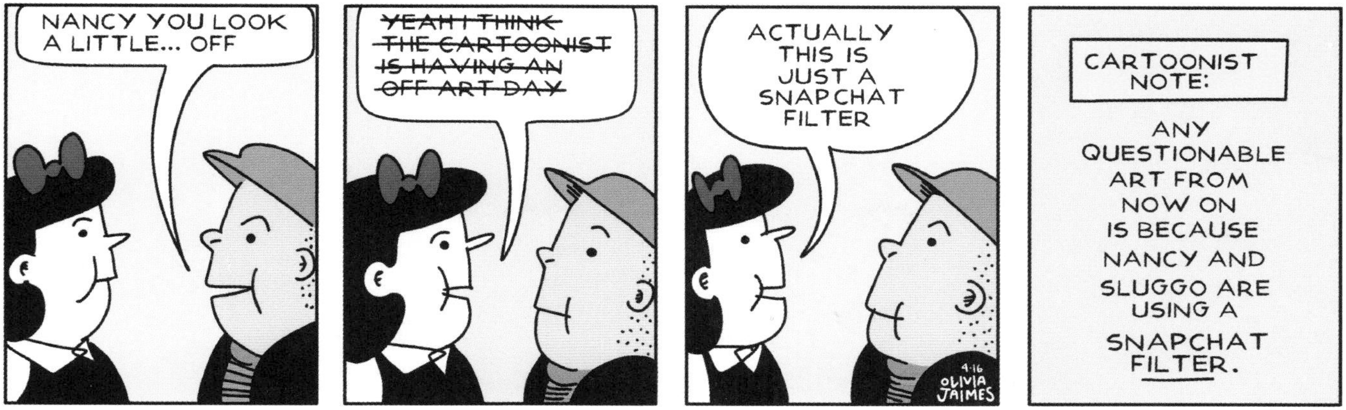
NANCY YOU LOOK A LITTLE... OFF
~~YEAH I THINK THE CARTOONIST IS HAVING AN OFF ART DAY~~
ACTUALLY THIS IS JUST A SNAPCHAT FILTER
4-16 OLIVIA JAIMES
CARTOONIST NOTE:
ANY QUESTIONABLE ART FROM NOW ON IS BECAUSE NANCY AND SLUGGO ARE USING A SNAPCHAT FILTER.

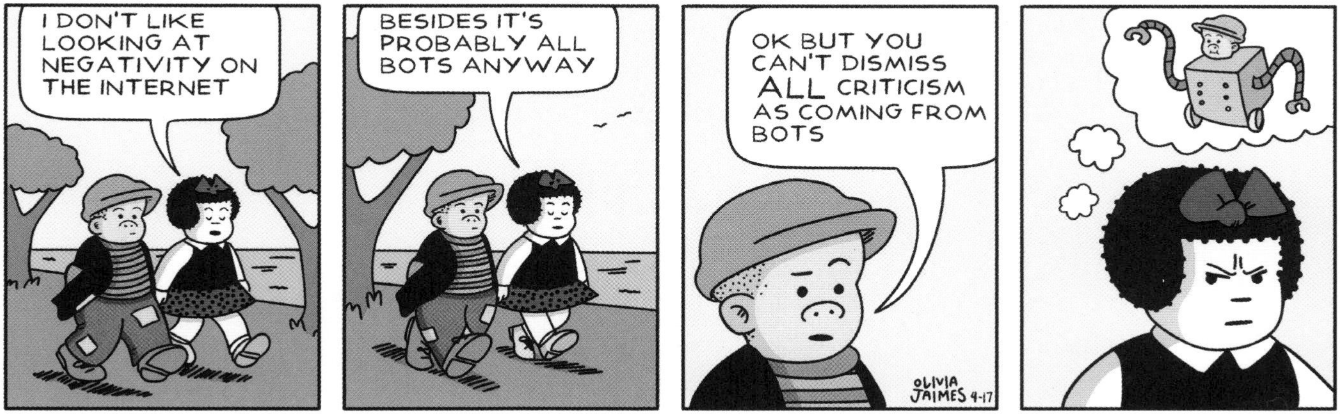
I DON'T LIKE LOOKING AT NEGATIVITY ON THE INTERNET
BESIDES IT'S PROBABLY ALL BOTS ANYWAY
OK BUT YOU CAN'T DISMISS ALL CRITICISM AS COMING FROM BOTS
OLIVIA JAIMES 4-17

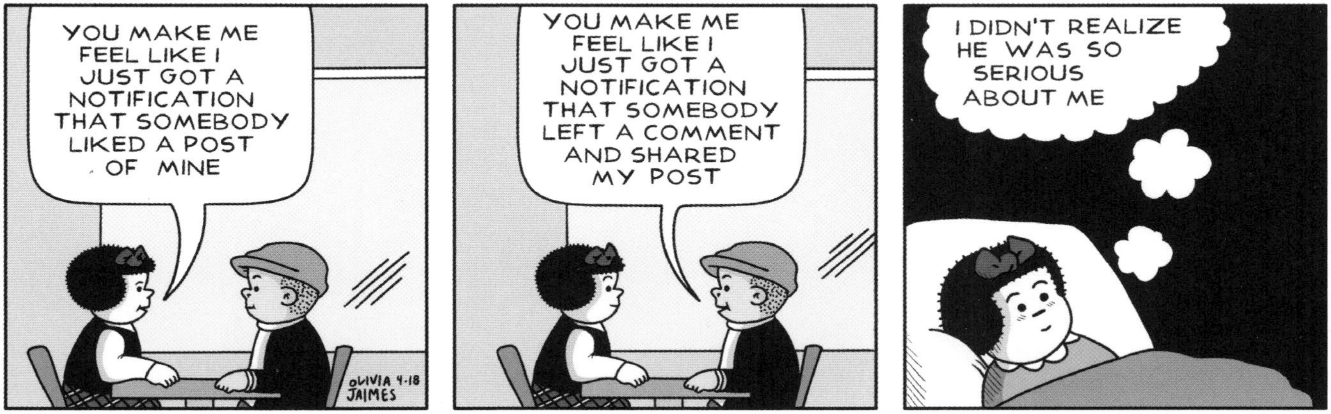
YOU MAKE ME FEEL LIKE I JUST GOT A NOTIFICATION THAT SOMEBODY LIKED A POST OF MINE
OLIVIA 4-18 JAIMES
YOU MAKE ME FEEL LIKE I JUST GOT A NOTIFICATION THAT SOMEBODY LEFT A COMMENT AND SHARED MY POST
I DIDN'T REALIZE HE WAS SO SERIOUS ABOUT ME

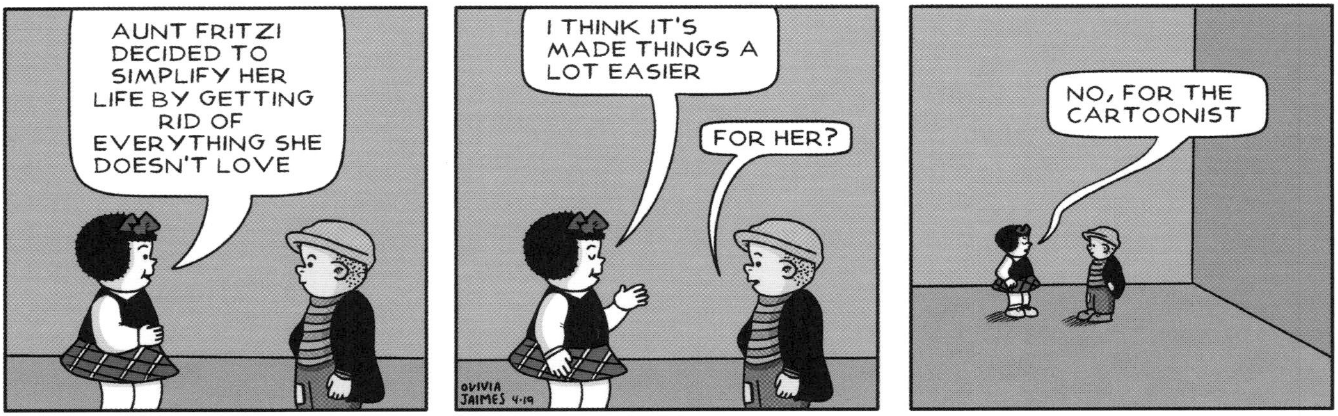
AUNT FRITZI DECIDED TO SIMPLIFY HER LIFE BY GETTING RID OF EVERYTHING SHE DOESN'T LOVE
I THINK IT'S MADE THINGS A LOT EASIER
FOR HER?
NO, FOR THE CARTOONIST
OLIVIA JAIMES 4·19

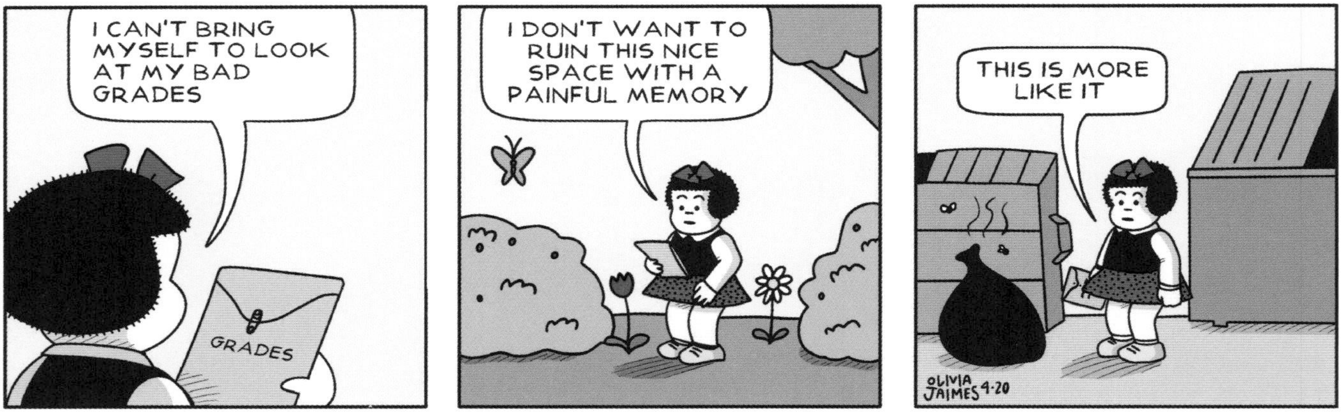
I CAN'T BRING MYSELF TO LOOK AT MY BAD GRADES
GRADES
I DON'T WANT TO RUIN THIS NICE SPACE WITH A PAINFUL MEMORY
THIS IS MORE LIKE IT
OLIVIA JAIMES 4·20

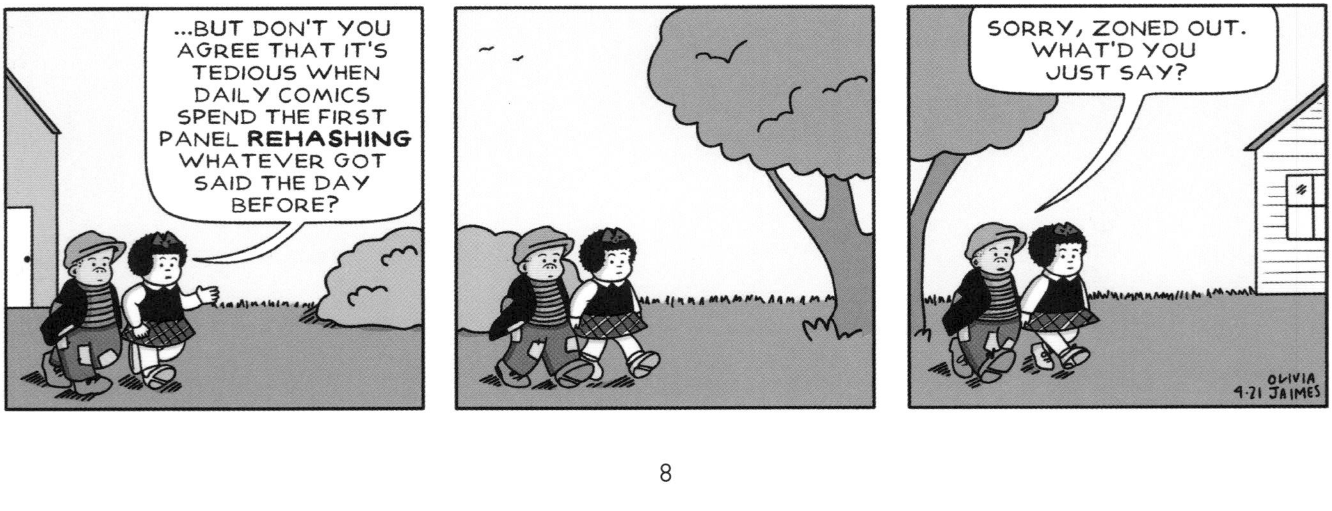
...BUT DON'T YOU AGREE THAT IT'S TEDIOUS WHEN DAILY COMICS SPEND THE FIRST PANEL **REHASHING** WHATEVER GOT SAID THE DAY BEFORE?
SORRY, ZONED OUT. WHAT'D YOU JUST SAY?
OLIVIA 4·21 JAIMES

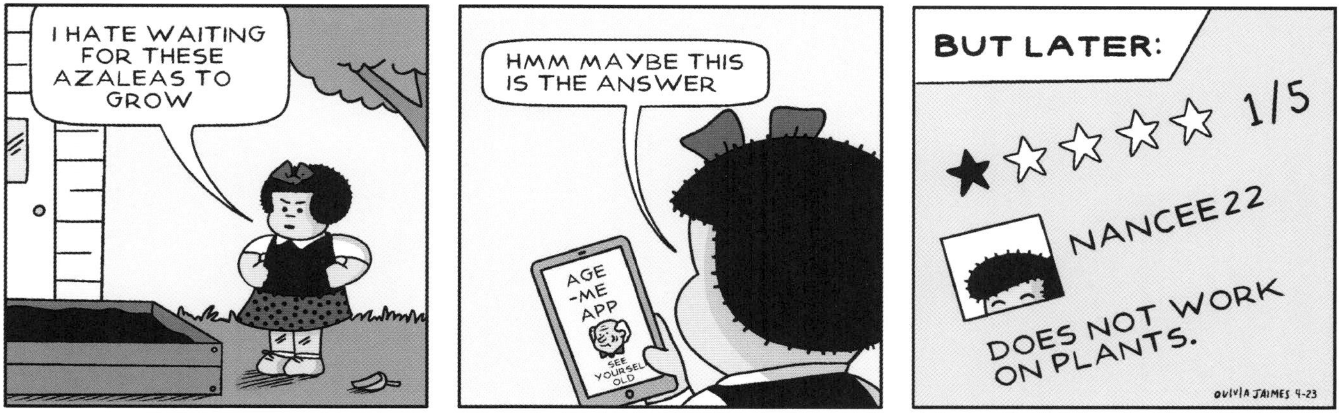
I HATE WAITING FOR THESE AZALEAS TO GROW
HMM MAYBE THIS IS THE ANSWER
AGE -ME APP
BUT LATER:
1/5
NANCEE22
DOES NOT WORK ON PLANTS.
OLIVIA JAIMES 4-23

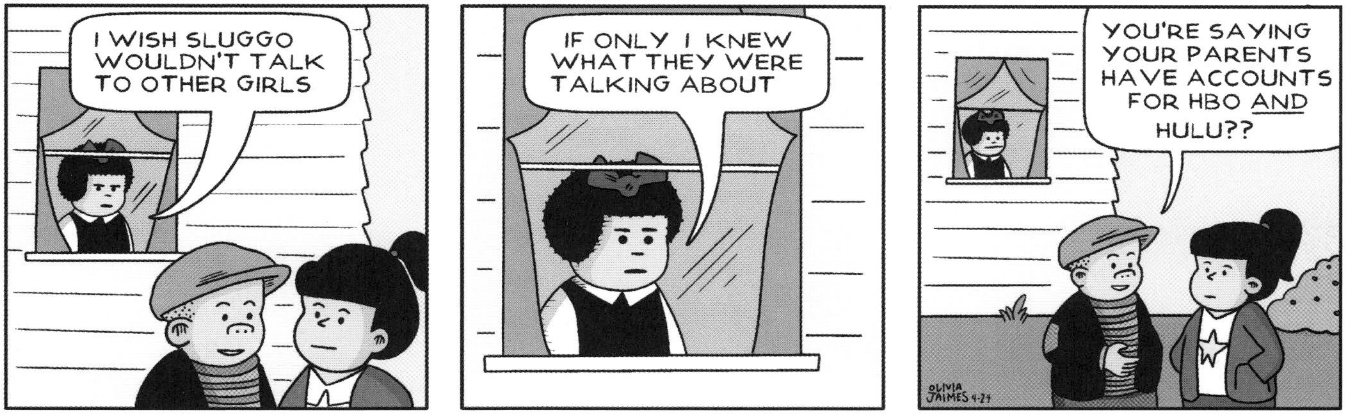
I WISH SLUGGO WOULDN'T TALK TO OTHER GIRLS
IF ONLY I KNEW WHAT THEY WERE TALKING ABOUT
YOU'RE SAYING YOUR PARENTS HAVE ACCOUNTS FOR HBO AND HULU??
OLIVIA JAIMES 4-24

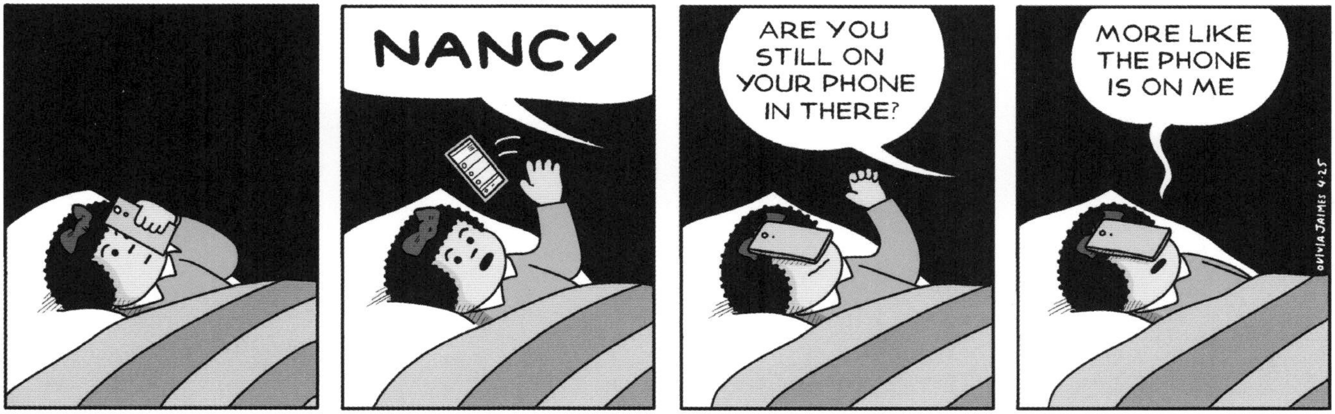
NANCY
ARE YOU STILL ON YOUR PHONE IN THERE?
MORE LIKE THE PHONE IS ON ME
OLIVIA JAIMES 4-25

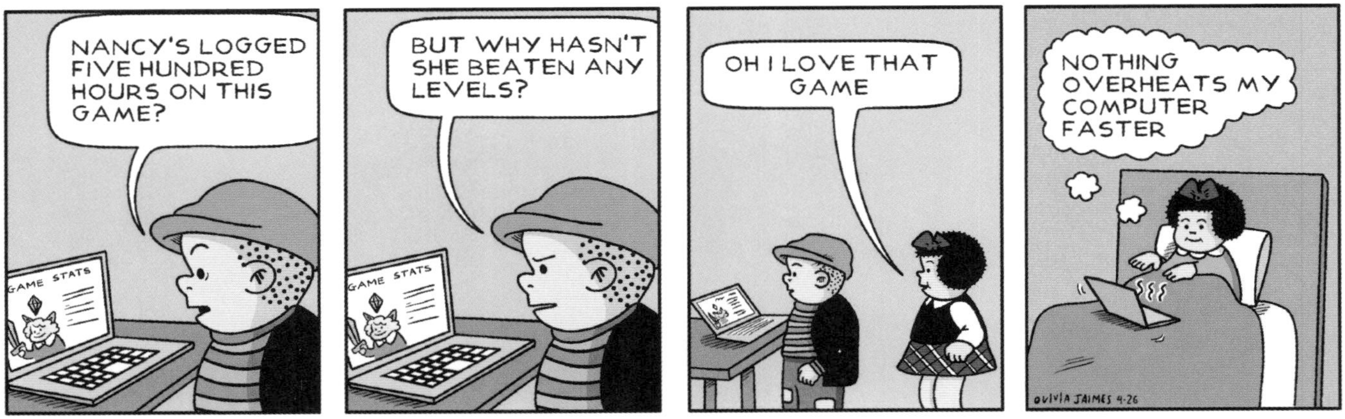
NANCY'S LOGGED FIVE HUNDRED HOURS ON THIS GAME?
GAME STATS
BUT WHY HASN'T SHE BEATEN ANY LEVELS?
GAME STATS
OH I LOVE THAT GAME
NOTHING OVERHEATS MY COMPUTER FASTER
OLIVIA JAIMES 4-26

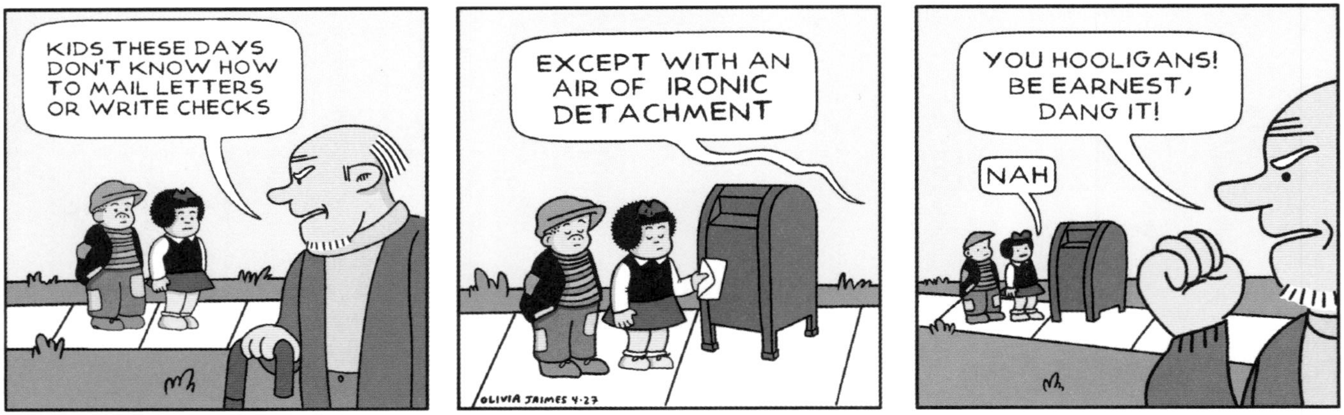
KIDS THESE DAYS DON'T KNOW HOW TO MAIL LETTERS OR WRITE CHECKS
EXCEPT WITH AN AIR OF IRONIC DETACHMENT
OLIVIA JAIMES 4-27
YOU HOOLIGANS! BE EARNEST, DANG IT!
NAH

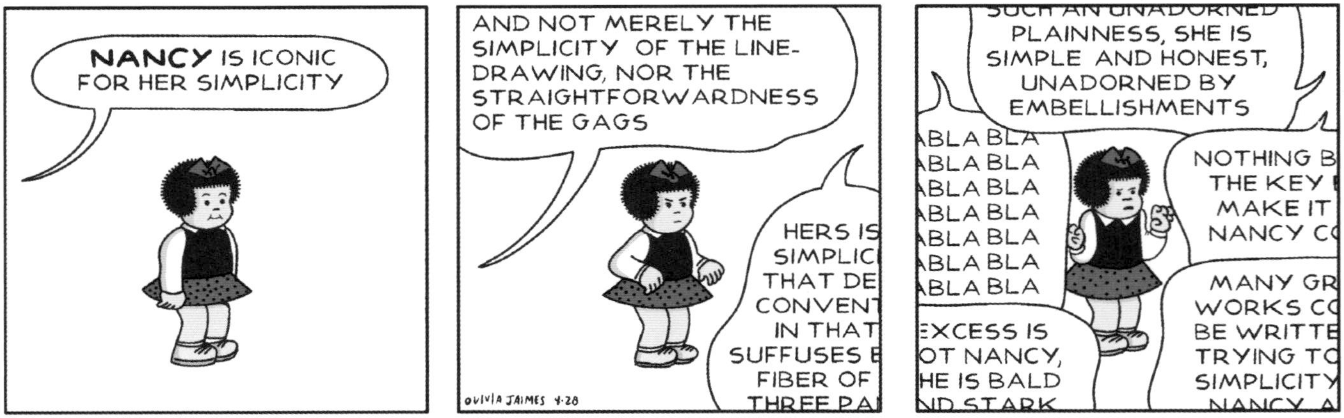
NANCY IS ICONIC FOR HER SIMPLICITY
AND NOT MERELY THE SIMPLICITY OF THE LINE-DRAWING, NOR THE STRAIGHTFORWARDNESS OF THE GAGS
HERS IS SIMPLIC THAT DE CONVENT IN THAT SUFFUSES E FIBER OF
OLIVIA JAIMES 4-28
PLAINNESS, SHE IS SIMPLE AND HONEST, UNADORNED BY EMBELLISHMENTS
ABLA BLA ABLA BLA ABLA BLA ABLA BLA ABLA BLA ABLA BLA ABLA BLA
NOTHING B THE KEY MAKE IT NANCY C
EXCESS IS OT NANCY, HE IS BALD
MANY GR WORKS C BE WRITTE TRYING TO SIMPLICITY

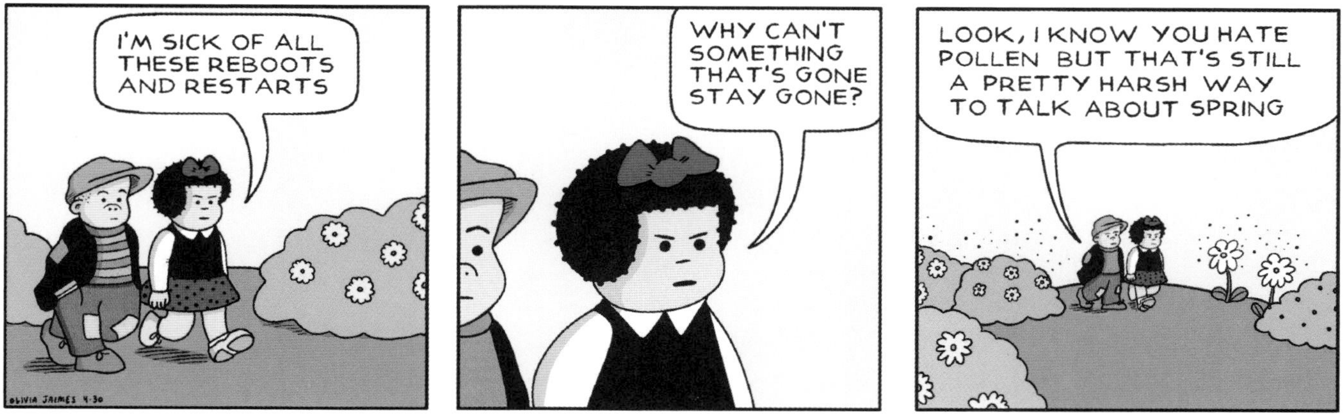
I'M SICK OF ALL THESE REBOOTS AND RESTARTS
OLIVIA JAIMES 4-30
WHY CAN'T SOMETHING THAT'S GONE STAY GONE?
LOOK, I KNOW YOU HATE POLLEN BUT THAT'S STILL A PRETTY HARSH WAY TO TALK ABOUT SPRING

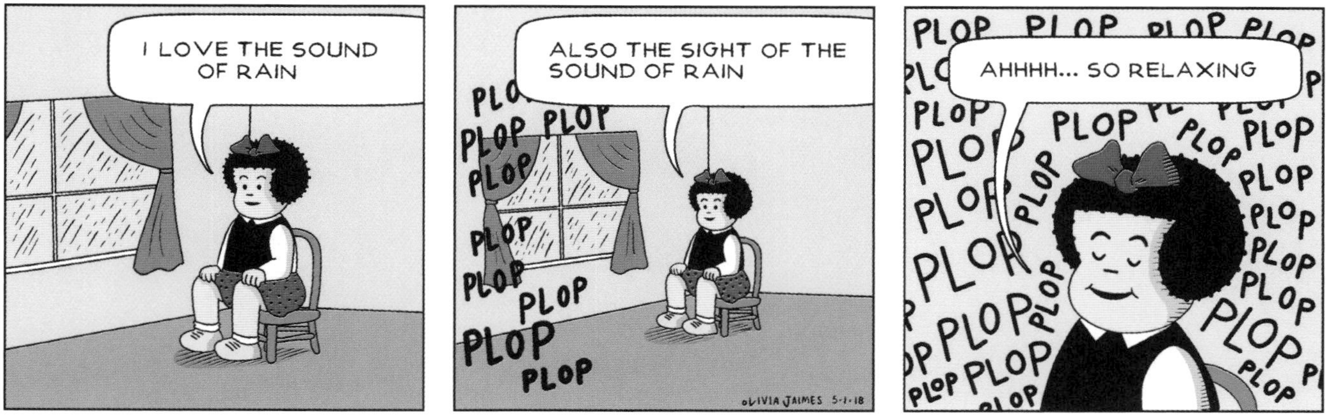
I LOVE THE SOUND OF RAIN
ALSO THE SIGHT OF THE SOUND OF RAIN
PLOP PLOP PLOP PLOP PLOP PLOP PLOP PLOP
OLIVIA JAIMES 5-1-18
AHHHH... SO RELAXING
PLOP PLOP PLOP PLOP PLOP PLOP PLOP PLOP

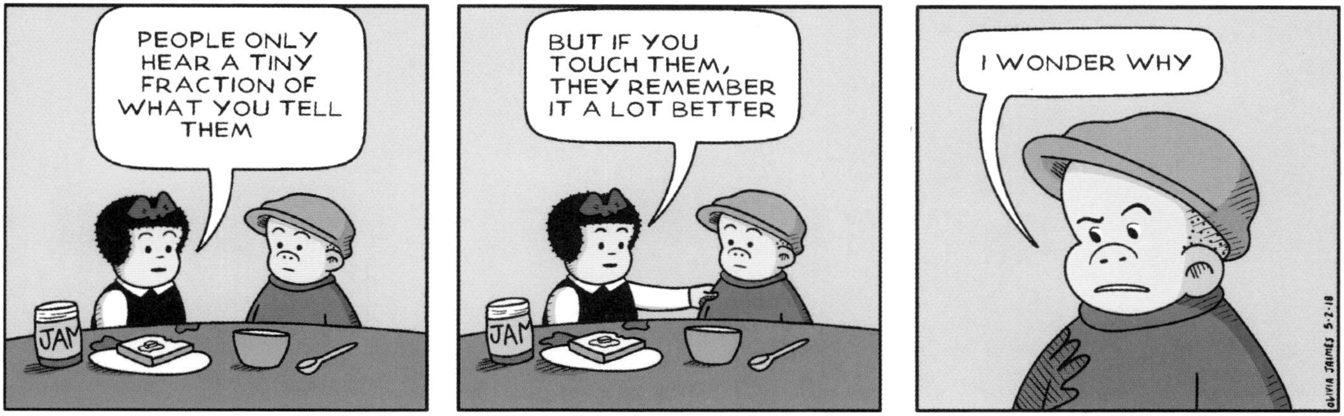
PEOPLE ONLY HEAR A TINY FRACTION OF WHAT YOU TELL THEM
JAM
BUT IF YOU TOUCH THEM, THEY REMEMBER IT A LOT BETTER
JAM
I WONDER WHY
OLIVIA JAIMES 5-2-18

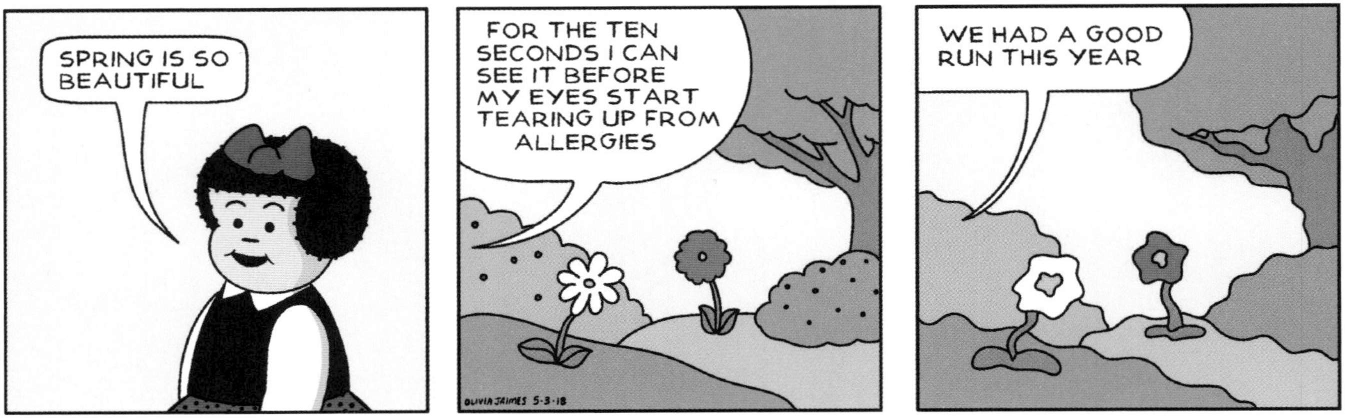
SPRING IS SO BEAUTIFUL
FOR THE TEN SECONDS I CAN SEE IT BEFORE MY EYES START TEARING UP FROM ALLERGIES
OLIVIA JAIMES 5-3-18
WE HAD A GOOD RUN THIS YEAR

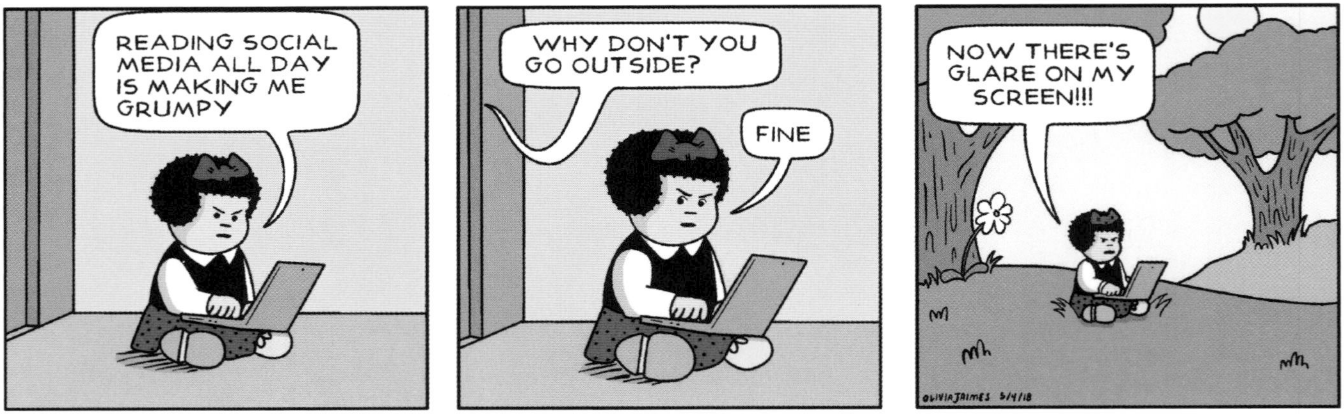
READING SOCIAL MEDIA ALL DAY IS MAKING ME GRUMPY
WHY DON'T YOU GO OUTSIDE?
FINE
NOW THERE'S GLARE ON MY SCREEN!!!
OLIVIA JAIMES 5/4/18

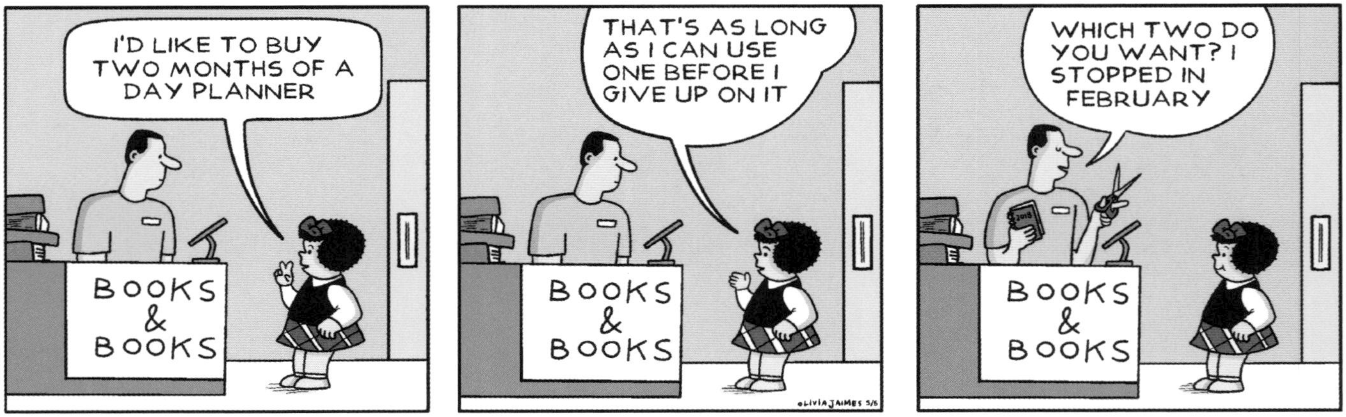
I'D LIKE TO BUY TWO MONTHS OF A DAY PLANNER
BOOKS & BOOKS
THAT'S AS LONG AS I CAN USE ONE BEFORE I GIVE UP ON IT
BOOKS & BOOKS
OLIVIA JAIMES 5/5
WHICH TWO DO YOU WANT? I STOPPED IN FEBRUARY
BOOKS & BOOKS

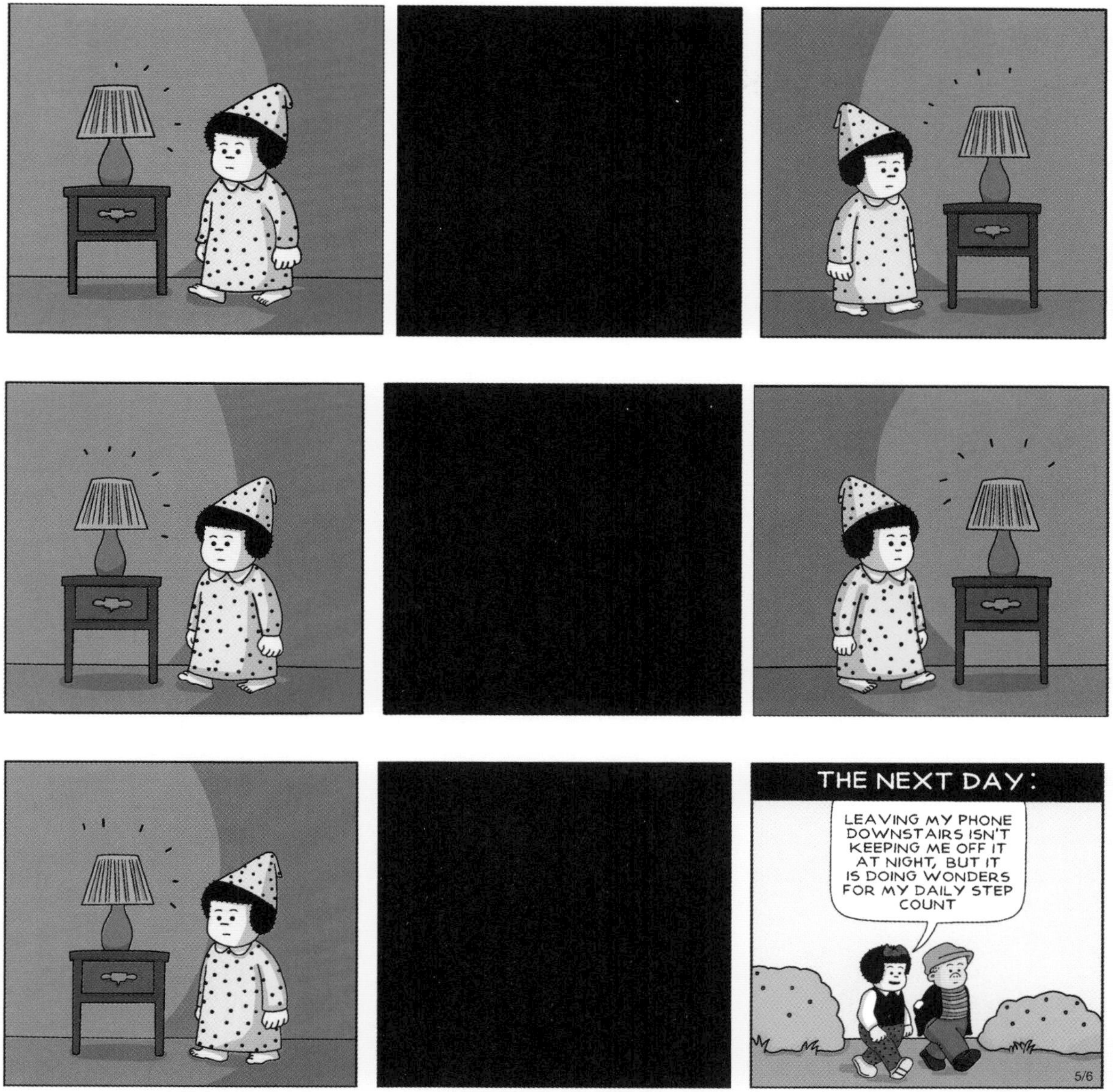
THE NEXT DAY:
LEAVING MY PHONE DOWNSTAIRS ISN'T KEEPING ME OFF IT AT NIGHT, BUT IT IS DOING WONDERS FOR MY DAILY STEP COUNT
5/6

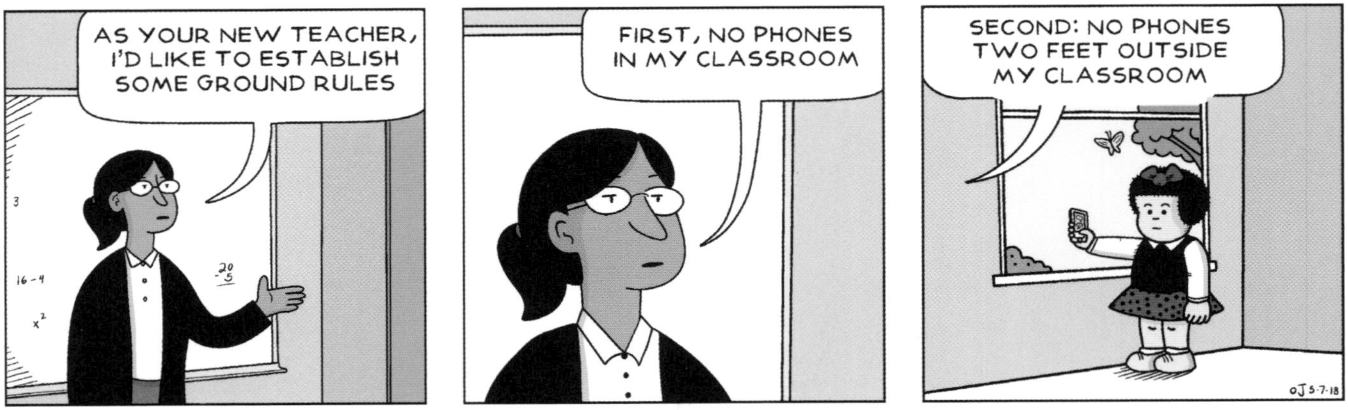
AS YOUR NEW TEACHER, I'D LIKE TO ESTABLISH SOME GROUND RULES
FIRST, NO PHONES IN MY CLASSROOM
SECOND: NO PHONES TWO FEET OUTSIDE MY CLASSROOM
OJ 5·7·18

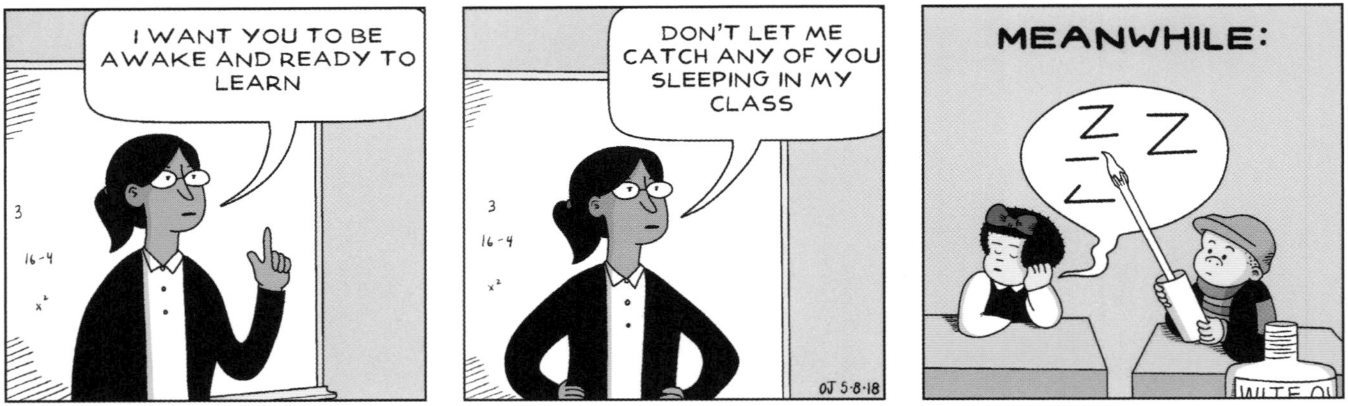
I WANT YOU TO BE AWAKE AND READY TO LEARN
DON'T LET ME CATCH ANY OF YOU SLEEPING IN MY CLASS
OJ 5·8·18
MEANWHILE:
Z Z Z

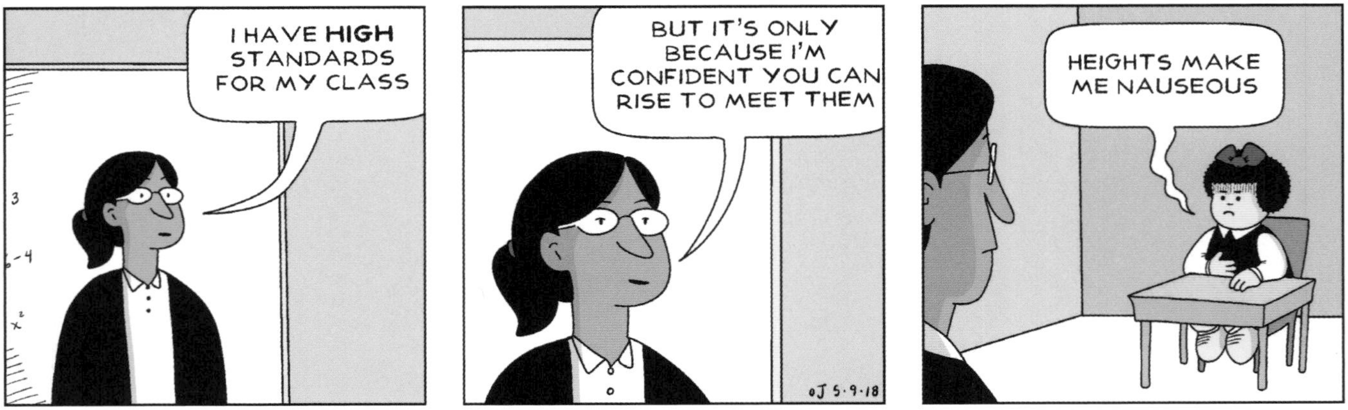
I HAVE **HIGH** STANDARDS FOR MY CLASS
BUT IT'S ONLY BECAUSE I'M CONFIDENT YOU CAN RISE TO MEET THEM
OJ 5·9·18
HEIGHTS MAKE ME NAUSEOUS

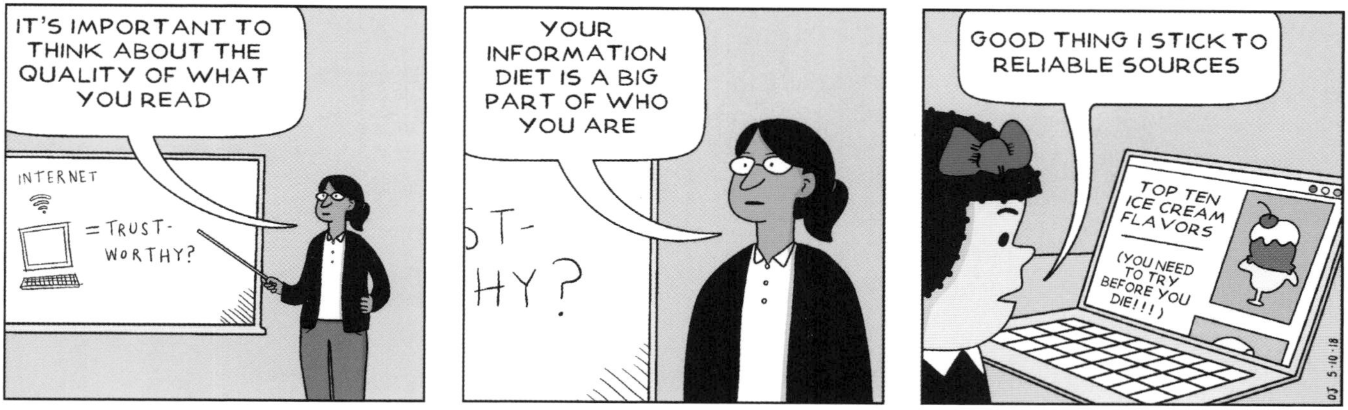
IT'S IMPORTANT TO THINK ABOUT THE QUALITY OF WHAT YOU READ
INTERNET
= TRUST-WORTHY?
YOUR INFORMATION DIET IS A BIG PART OF WHO YOU ARE
GOOD THING I STICK TO RELIABLE SOURCES
TOP TEN ICE CREAM FLAVORS
(YOU NEED TO TRY BEFORE YOU DIE!!!)
OJ 5·10·18

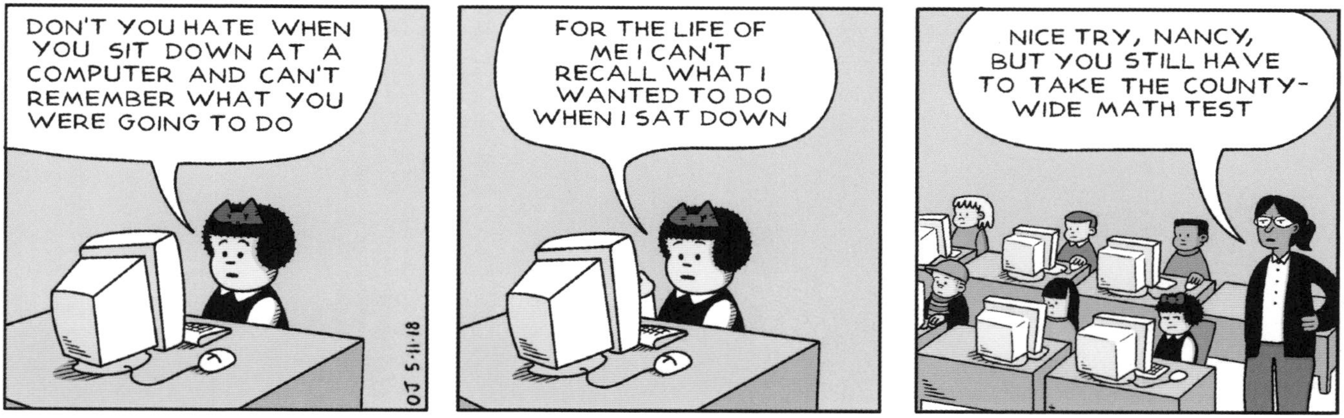
DON'T YOU HATE WHEN YOU SIT DOWN AT A COMPUTER AND CAN'T REMEMBER WHAT YOU WERE GOING TO DO
OJ 5·11·18
FOR THE LIFE OF ME I CAN'T RECALL WHAT I WANTED TO DO WHEN I SAT DOWN
NICE TRY, NANCY, BUT YOU STILL HAVE TO TAKE THE COUNTY-WIDE MATH TEST

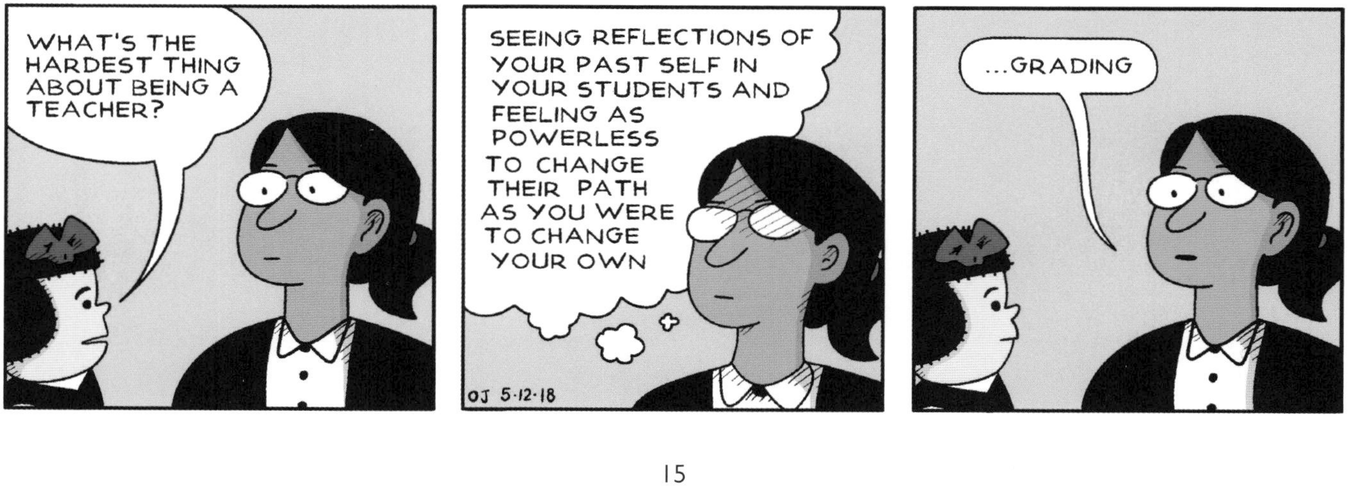
WHAT'S THE HARDEST THING ABOUT BEING A TEACHER?
SEEING REFLECTIONS OF YOUR PAST SELF IN YOUR STUDENTS AND FEELING AS POWERLESS TO CHANGE THEIR PATH AS YOU WERE TO CHANGE YOUR OWN
OJ 5·12·18
...GRADING

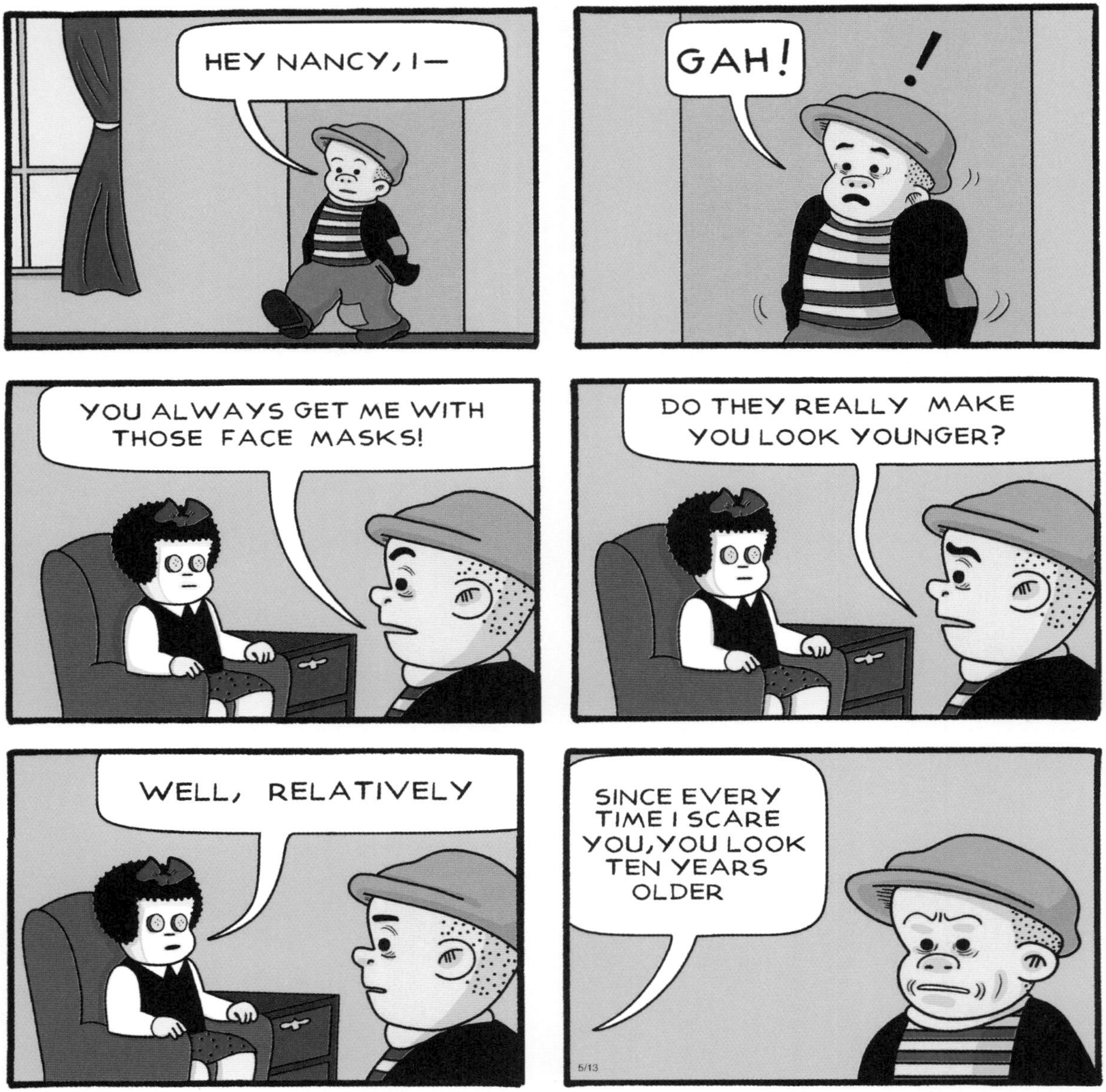
HEY NANCY, I—
GAH!
!
YOU ALWAYS GET ME WITH THOSE FACE MASKS!
DO THEY REALLY MAKE YOU LOOK YOUNGER?
WELL, RELATIVELY
SINCE EVERY TIME I SCARE YOU, YOU LOOK TEN YEARS OLDER
5/13

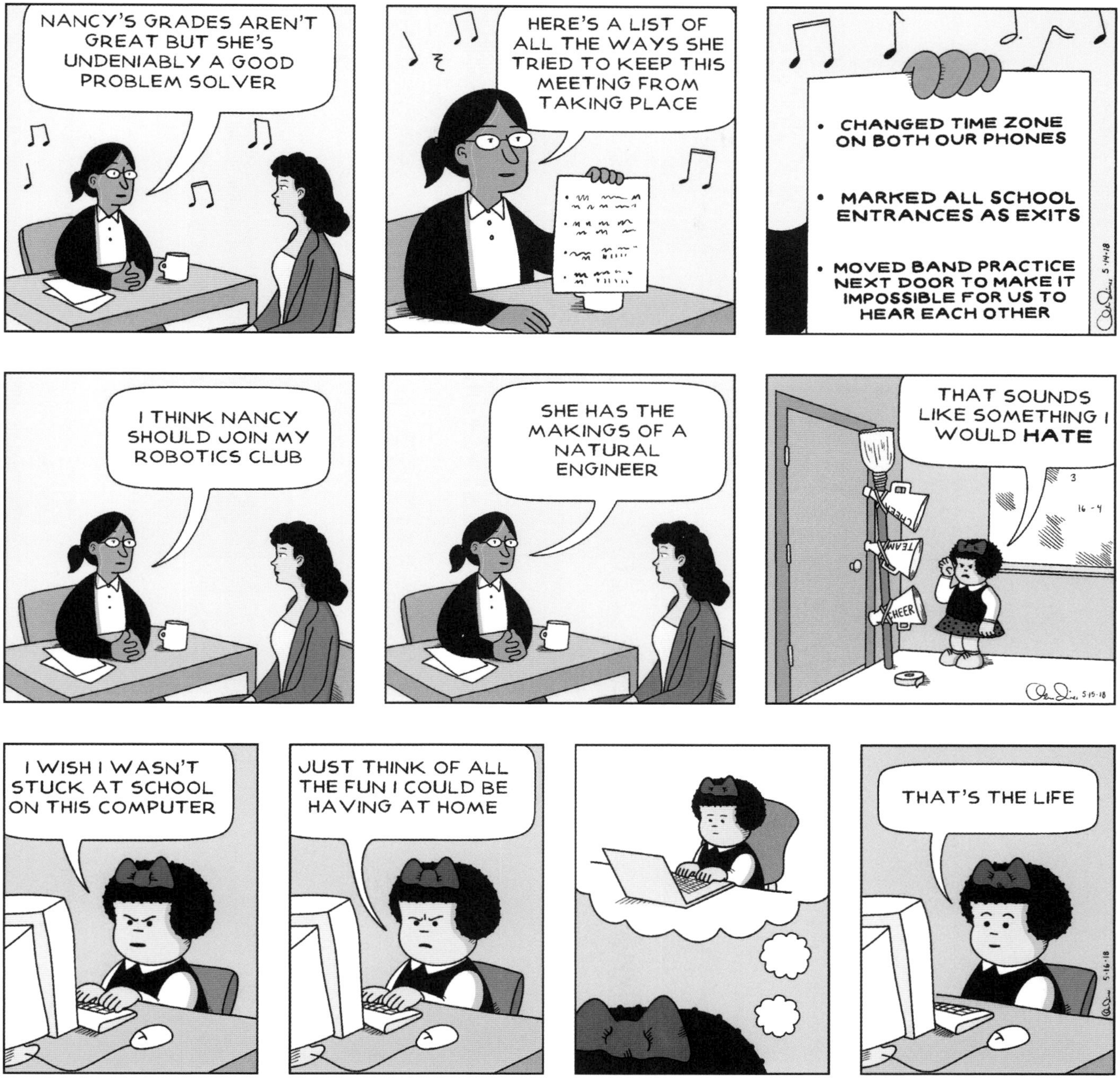
NANCY'S GRADES AREN'T GREAT BUT SHE'S UNDENIABLY A GOOD PROBLEM SOLVER
HERE'S A LIST OF ALL THE WAYS SHE TRIED TO KEEP THIS MEETING FROM TAKING PLACE
• CHANGED TIME ZONE ON BOTH OUR PHONES
• MARKED ALL SCHOOL ENTRANCES AS EXITS
• MOVED BAND PRACTICE NEXT DOOR TO MAKE IT IMPOSSIBLE FOR US TO HEAR EACH OTHER
5·14·18
I THINK NANCY SHOULD JOIN MY ROBOTICS CLUB
SHE HAS THE MAKINGS OF A NATURAL ENGINEER
THAT SOUNDS LIKE SOMETHING I WOULD **HATE**
CHEER
TEAM
CHEER
5·15·18
I WISH I WASN'T STUCK AT SCHOOL ON THIS COMPUTER
JUST THINK OF ALL THE FUN I COULD BE HAVING AT HOME
THAT'S THE LIFE
5·16·18

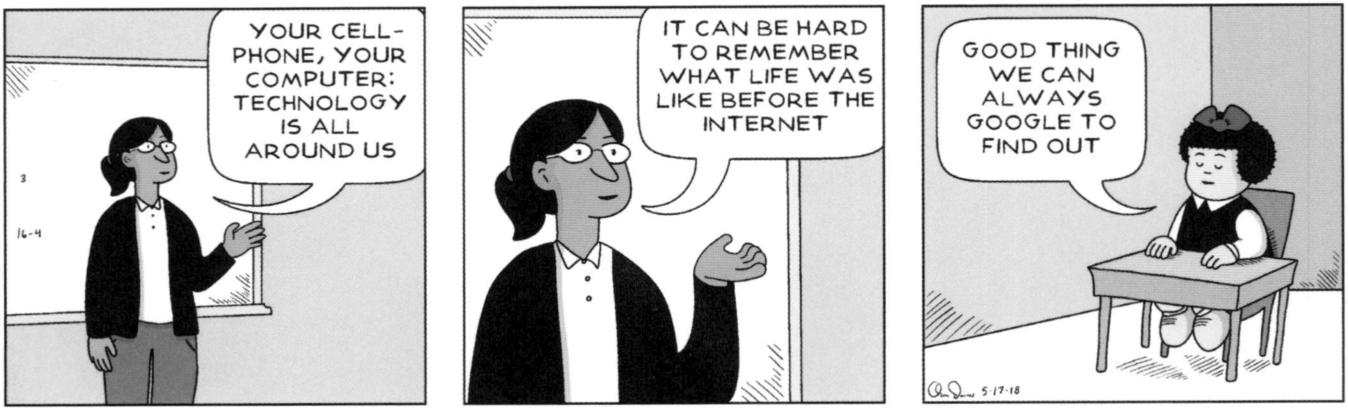
YOUR CELL-PHONE, YOUR COMPUTER: TECHNOLOGY IS ALL AROUND US
IT CAN BE HARD TO REMEMBER WHAT LIFE WAS LIKE BEFORE THE INTERNET
GOOD THING WE CAN ALWAYS GOOGLE TO FIND OUT
5·17·18

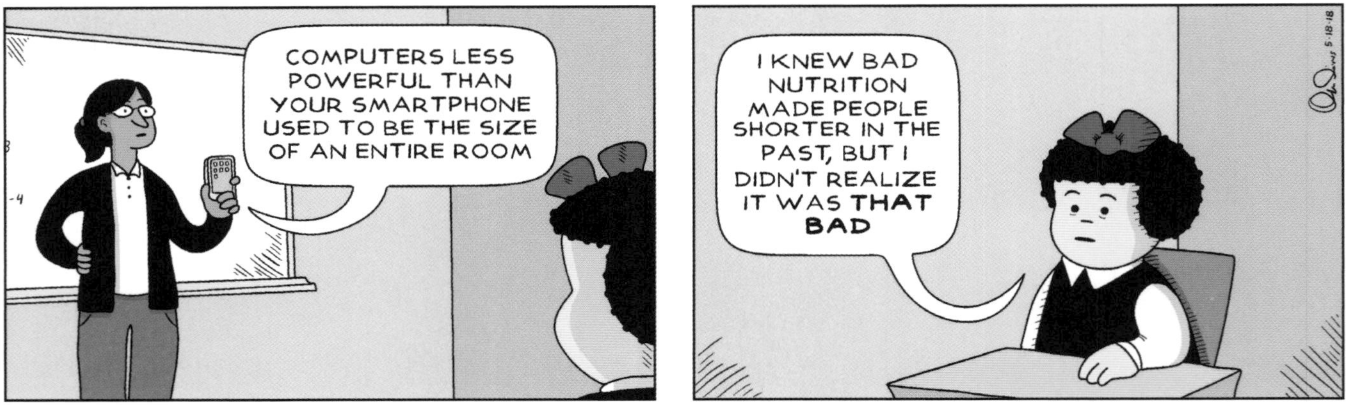
COMPUTERS LESS POWERFUL THAN YOUR SMARTPHONE USED TO BE THE SIZE OF AN ENTIRE ROOM
I KNEW BAD NUTRITION MADE PEOPLE SHORTER IN THE PAST, BUT I DIDN'T REALIZE IT WAS **THAT BAD**
5·18·18

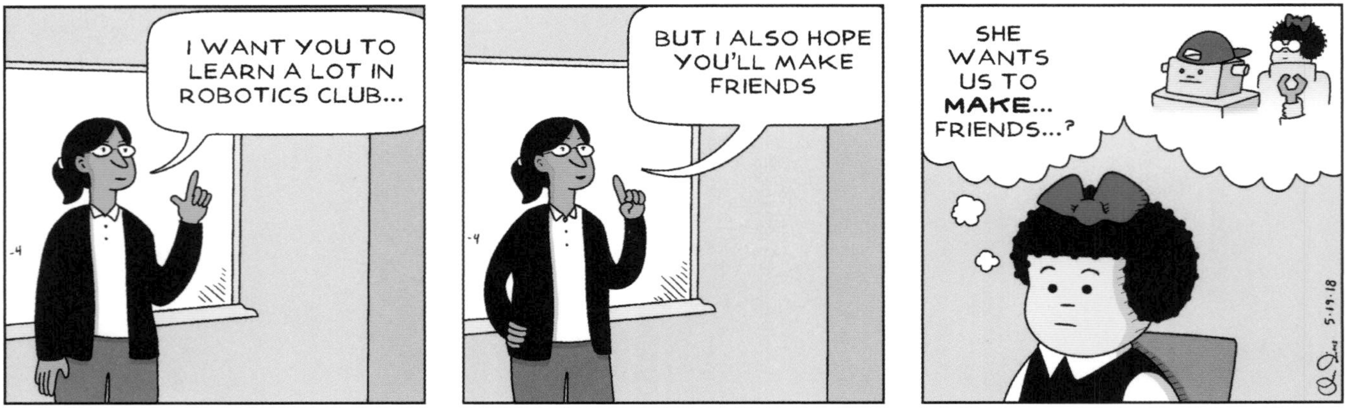
I WANT YOU TO LEARN A LOT IN ROBOTICS CLUB...
BUT I ALSO HOPE YOU'LL MAKE FRIENDS
SHE WANTS US TO **MAKE...** FRIENDS...?
5·19·18

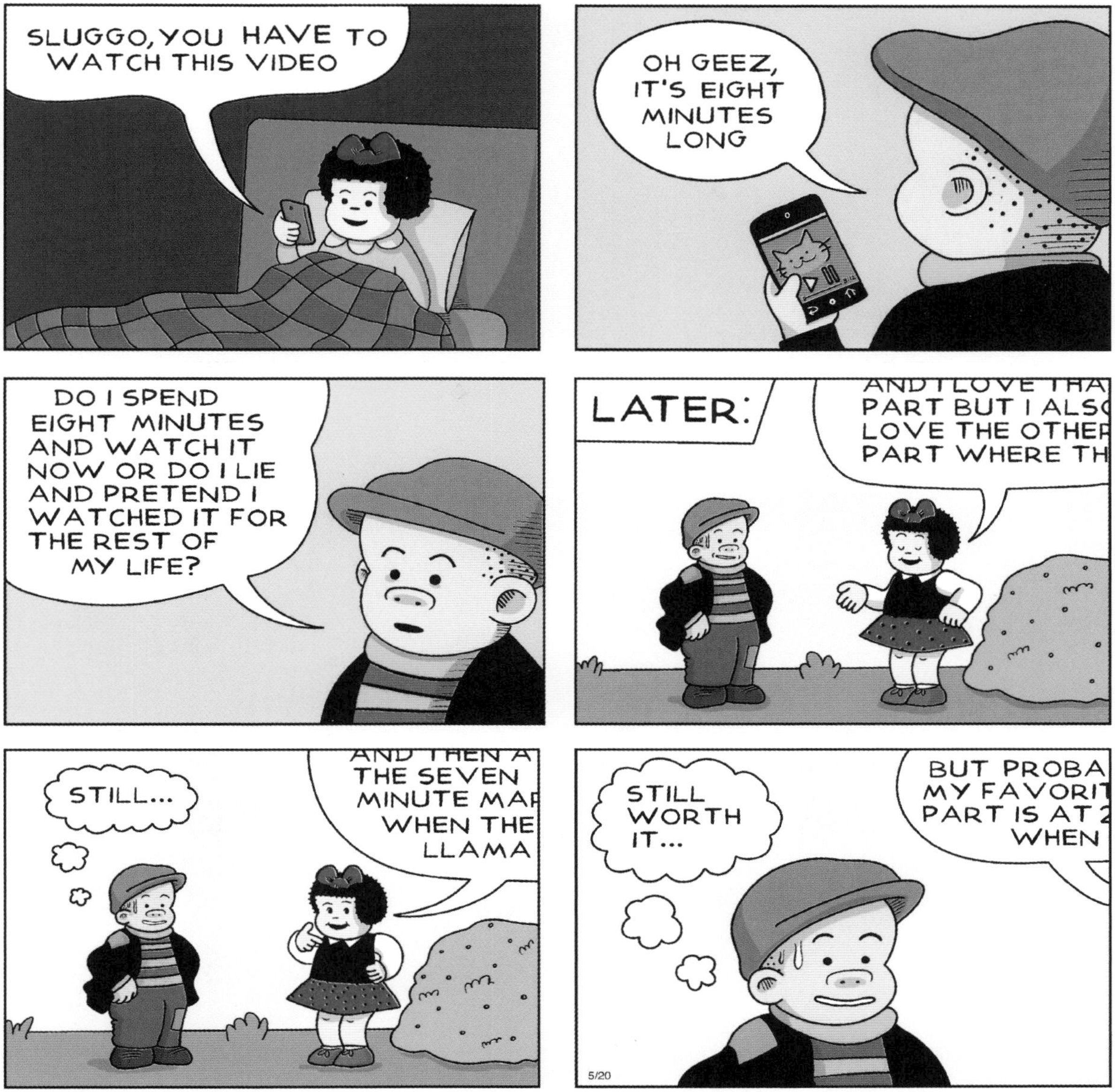
SLUGGO, YOU HAVE TO WATCH THIS VIDEO
OH GEEZ, IT'S EIGHT MINUTES LONG
DO I SPEND EIGHT MINUTES AND WATCH IT NOW OR DO I LIE AND PRETEND I WATCHED IT FOR THE REST OF MY LIFE?
LATER:
PART BUT I ALS
LOVE THE OTHE
PART WHERE TH
STILL...
THE SEVEN
MINUTE MA
WHEN THE
LLAMA
STILL WORTH IT...
BUT PROBA
MY FAVORIT
PART IS AT
WHEN
5/20

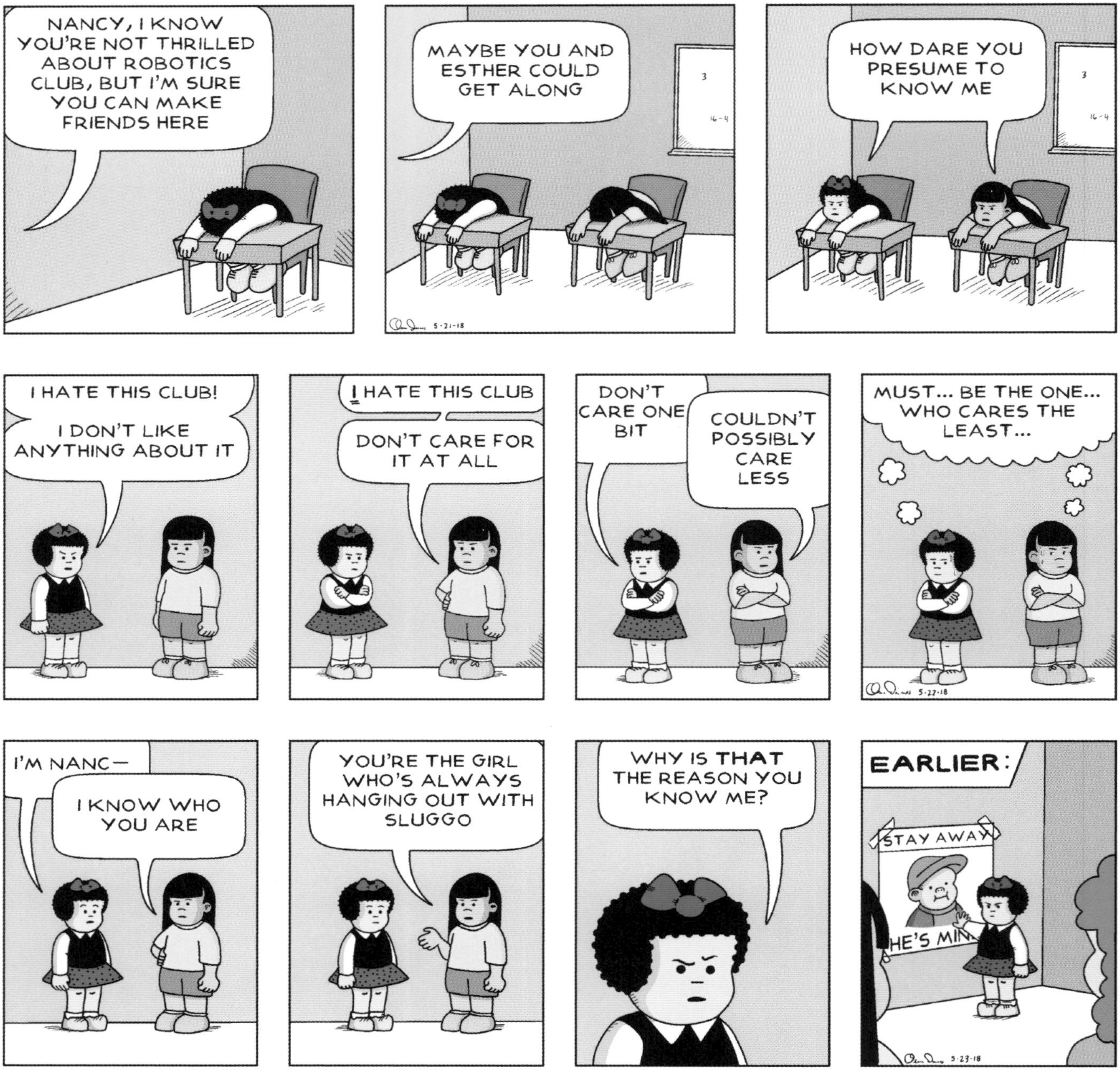
NANCY, I KNOW YOU'RE NOT THRILLED ABOUT ROBOTICS CLUB, BUT I'M SURE YOU CAN MAKE FRIENDS HERE
MAYBE YOU AND ESTHER COULD GET ALONG
3
16 - 4
5-21-18
HOW DARE YOU PRESUME TO KNOW ME
I HATE THIS CLUB!
I DON'T LIKE ANYTHING ABOUT IT
I HATE THIS CLUB
DON'T CARE FOR IT AT ALL
DON'T CARE ONE BIT
COULDN'T POSSIBLY CARE LESS
MUST... BE THE ONE... WHO CARES THE LEAST...
5-22-18
I'M NANC—
I KNOW WHO YOU ARE
YOU'RE THE GIRL WHO'S ALWAYS HANGING OUT WITH SLUGGO
WHY IS THAT THE REASON YOU KNOW ME?
EARLIER:
STAY AWAY
HE'S MIN
5-23-18

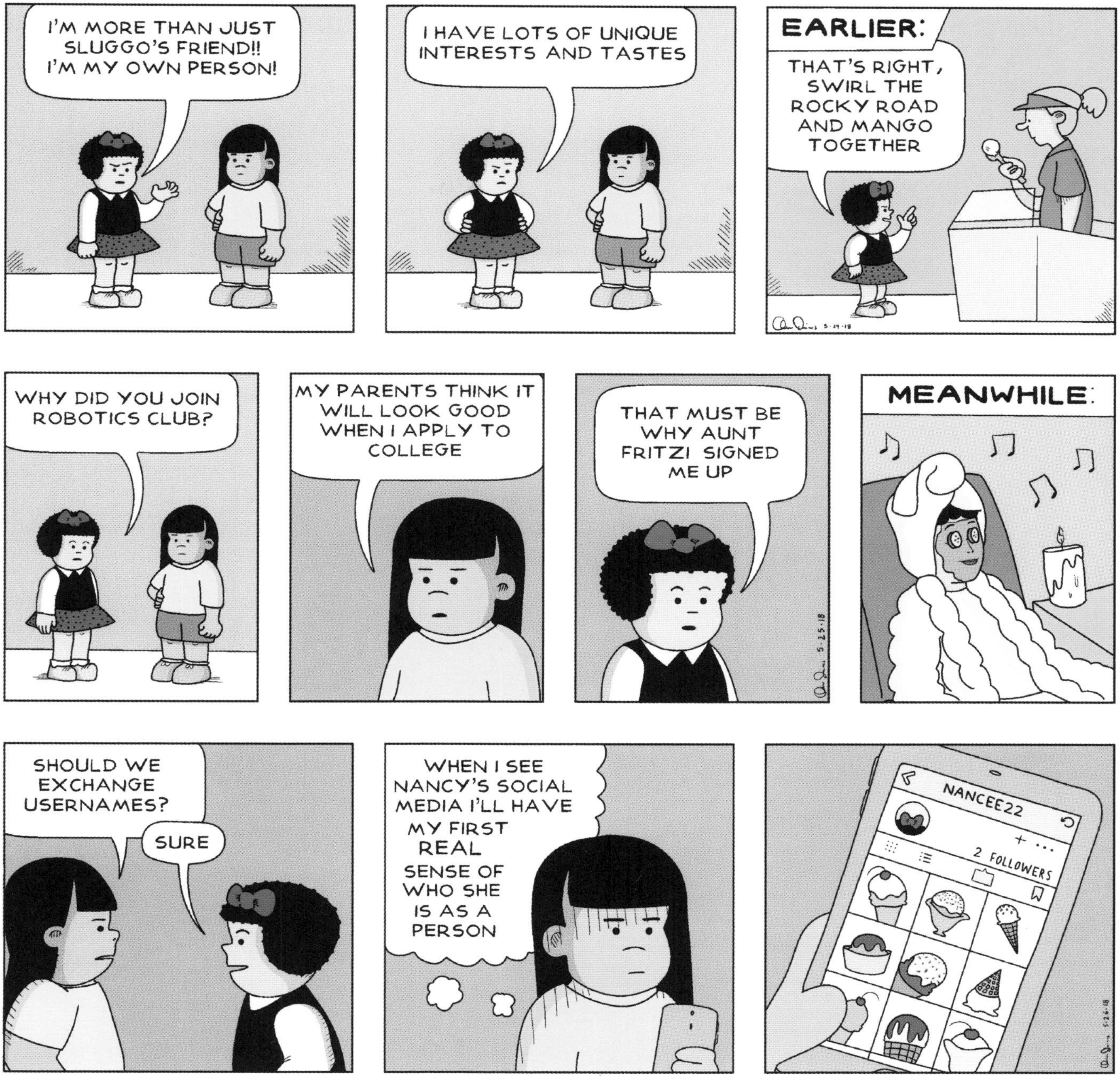
I'M MORE THAN JUST SLUGGO'S FRIEND!! I'M MY OWN PERSON!
I HAVE LOTS OF UNIQUE INTERESTS AND TASTES
EARLIER:
THAT'S RIGHT, SWIRL THE ROCKY ROAD AND MANGO TOGETHER
WHY DID YOU JOIN ROBOTICS CLUB?
MY PARENTS THINK IT WILL LOOK GOOD WHEN I APPLY TO COLLEGE
THAT MUST BE WHY AUNT FRITZI SIGNED ME UP
MEANWHILE:
SHOULD WE EXCHANGE USERNAMES?
SURE
WHEN I SEE NANCY'S SOCIAL MEDIA I'LL HAVE MY FIRST REAL SENSE OF WHO SHE IS AS A PERSON
NANCEE22
2 FOLLOWERS

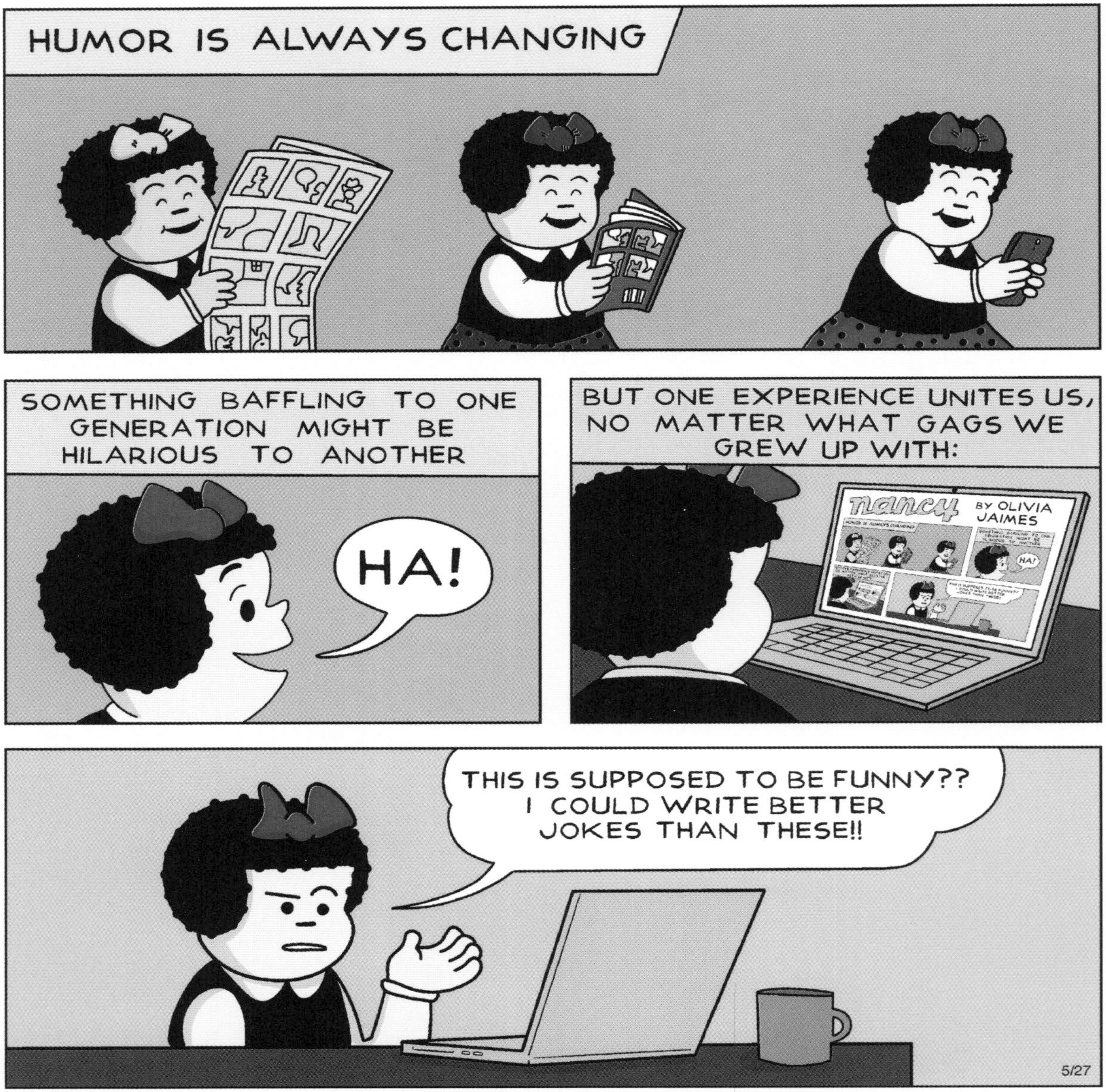
HUMOR IS ALWAYS CHANGING
SOMETHING BAFFLING TO ONE GENERATION MIGHT BE HILARIOUS TO ANOTHER
HA!
BUT ONE EXPERIENCE UNITES US, NO MATTER WHAT GAGS WE GREW UP WITH:
nancy
BY OLIVIA JAIMES
THIS IS SUPPOSED TO BE FUNNY?? I COULD WRITE BETTER JOKES THAN THESE!!
5/27

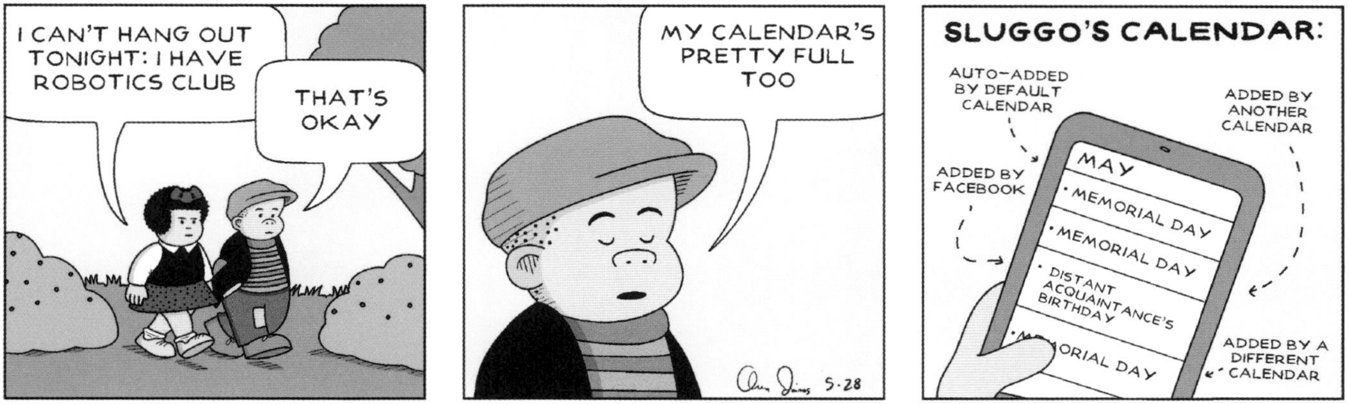
I CAN'T HANG OUT TONIGHT: I HAVE ROBOTICS CLUB
THAT'S OKAY
MY CALENDAR'S PRETTY FULL TOO
5·28
SLUGGO'S CALENDAR:
AUTO-ADDED BY DEFAULT CALENDAR
ADDED BY FACEBOOK
ADDED BY ANOTHER CALENDAR
MAY
• MEMORIAL DAY
• MEMORIAL DAY
• DISTANT ACQUAINTANCE'S BIRTHDAY
ORIAL DAY
ADDED BY A DIFFERENT CALENDAR

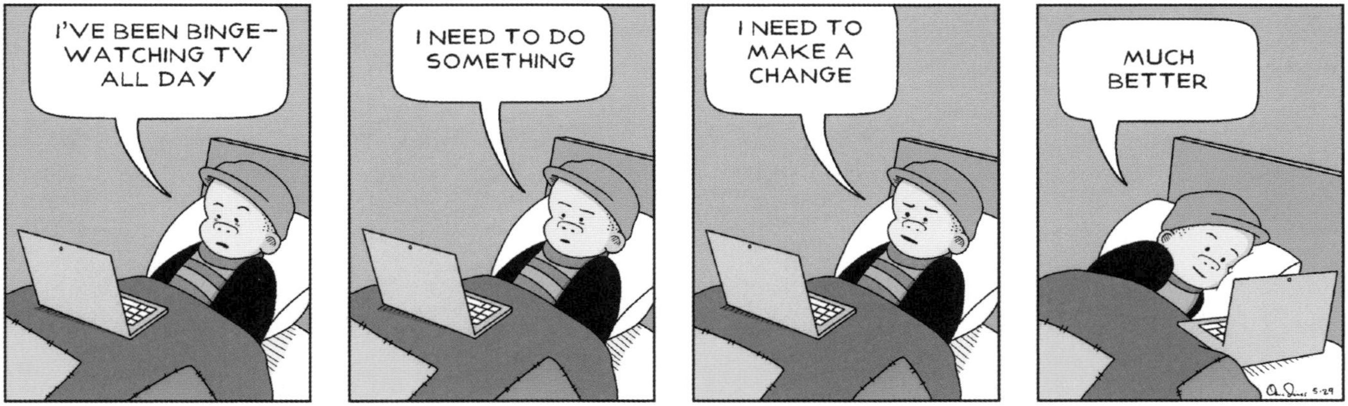
I'VE BEEN BINGE-WATCHING TV ALL DAY
I NEED TO DO SOMETHING
I NEED TO MAKE A CHANGE
MUCH BETTER

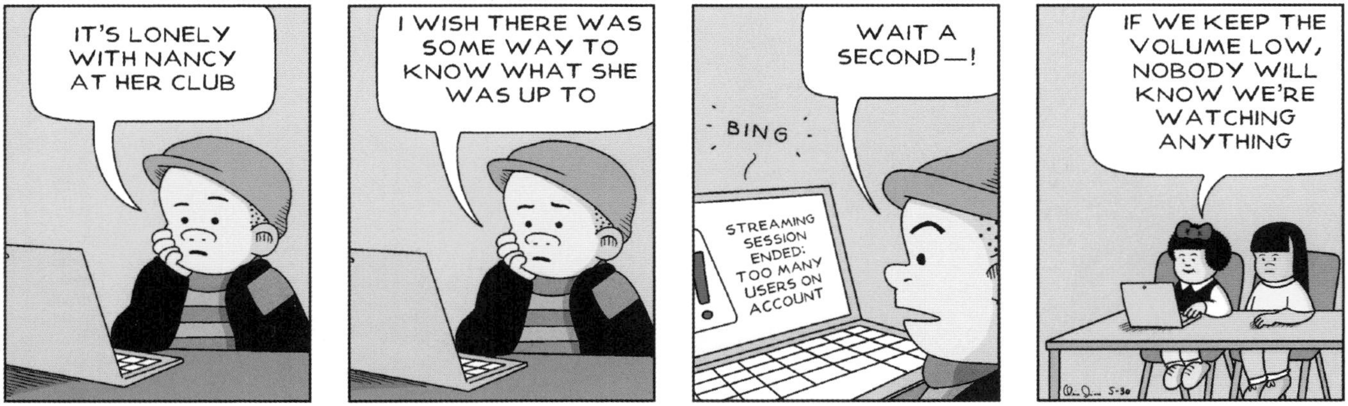
IT'S LONELY WITH NANCY AT HER CLUB
I WISH THERE WAS SOME WAY TO KNOW WHAT SHE WAS UP TO
BING
STREAMING SESSION ENDED: TOO MANY USERS ON ACCOUNT
WAIT A SECOND—!
IF WE KEEP THE VOLUME LOW, NOBODY WILL KNOW WE'RE WATCHING ANYTHING

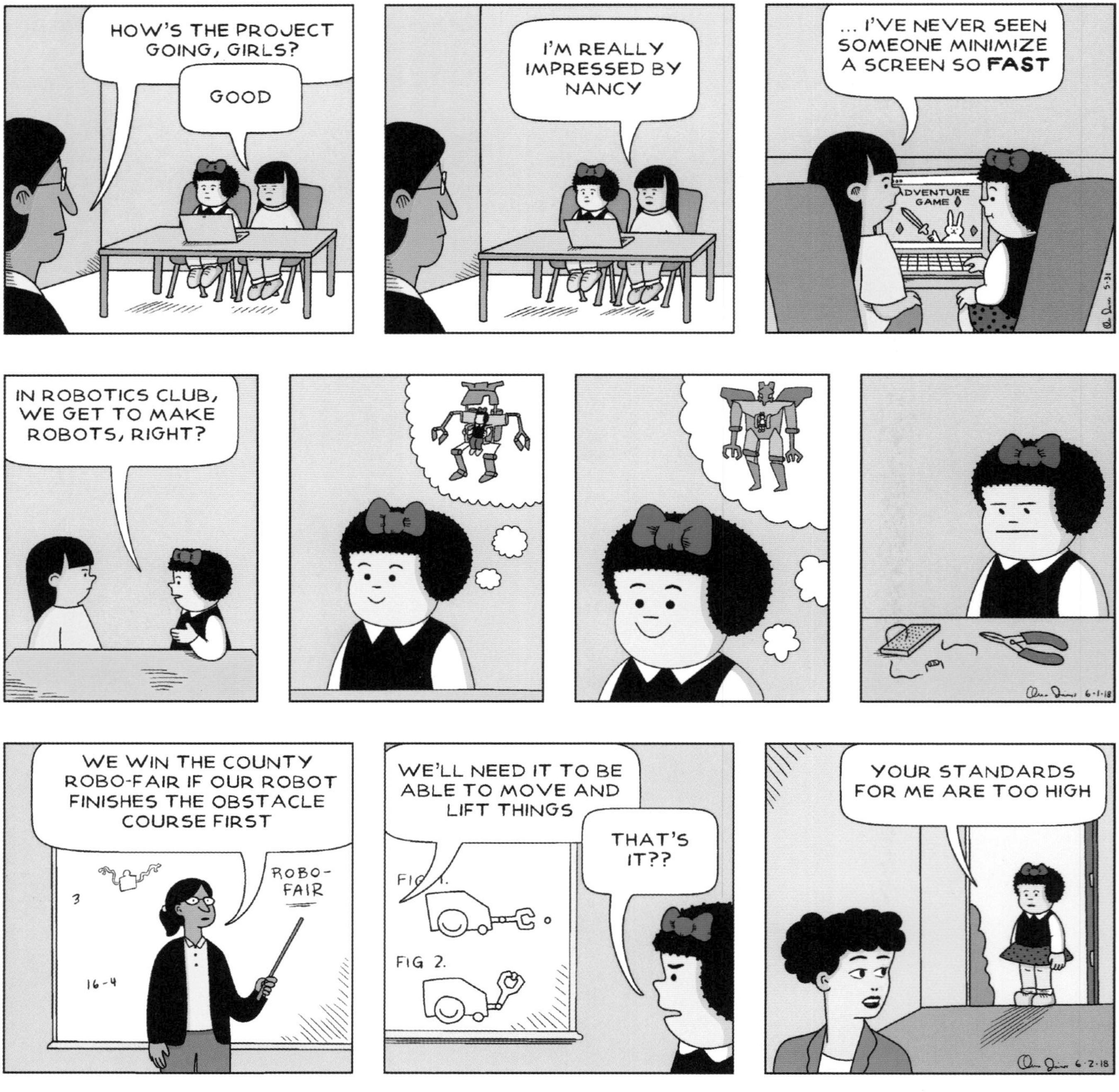
HOW'S THE PROJECT GOING, GIRLS?
GOOD
I'M REALLY IMPRESSED BY NANCY
... I'VE NEVER SEEN SOMEONE MINIMIZE A SCREEN SO **FAST**
ADVENTURE GAME
IN ROBOTICS CLUB, WE GET TO MAKE ROBOTS, RIGHT?
WE WIN THE COUNTY ROBO-FAIR IF OUR ROBOT FINISHES THE OBSTACLE COURSE FIRST
ROBO-FAIR
WE'LL NEED IT TO BE ABLE TO MOVE AND LIFT THINGS
THAT'S IT??
FIG 2.
YOUR STANDARDS FOR ME ARE TOO HIGH

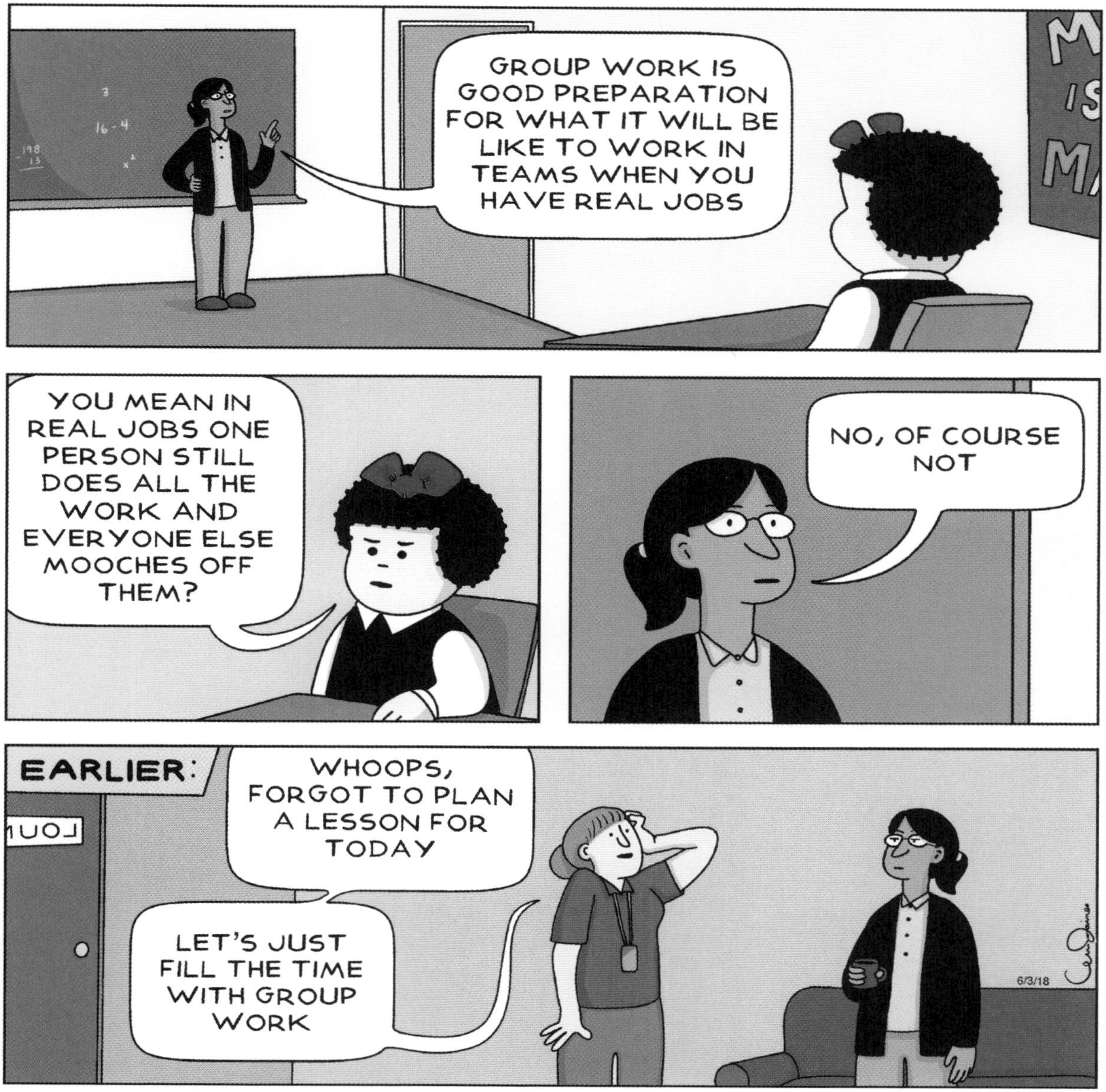
GROUP WORK IS GOOD PREPARATION FOR WHAT IT WILL BE LIKE TO WORK IN TEAMS WHEN YOU HAVE REAL JOBS
YOU MEAN IN REAL JOBS ONE PERSON STILL DOES ALL THE WORK AND EVERYONE ELSE MOOCHES OFF THEM?
NO, OF COURSE NOT
EARLIER:
WHOOPS, FORGOT TO PLAN A LESSON FOR TODAY
LET'S JUST FILL THE TIME WITH GROUP WORK
6/3/18

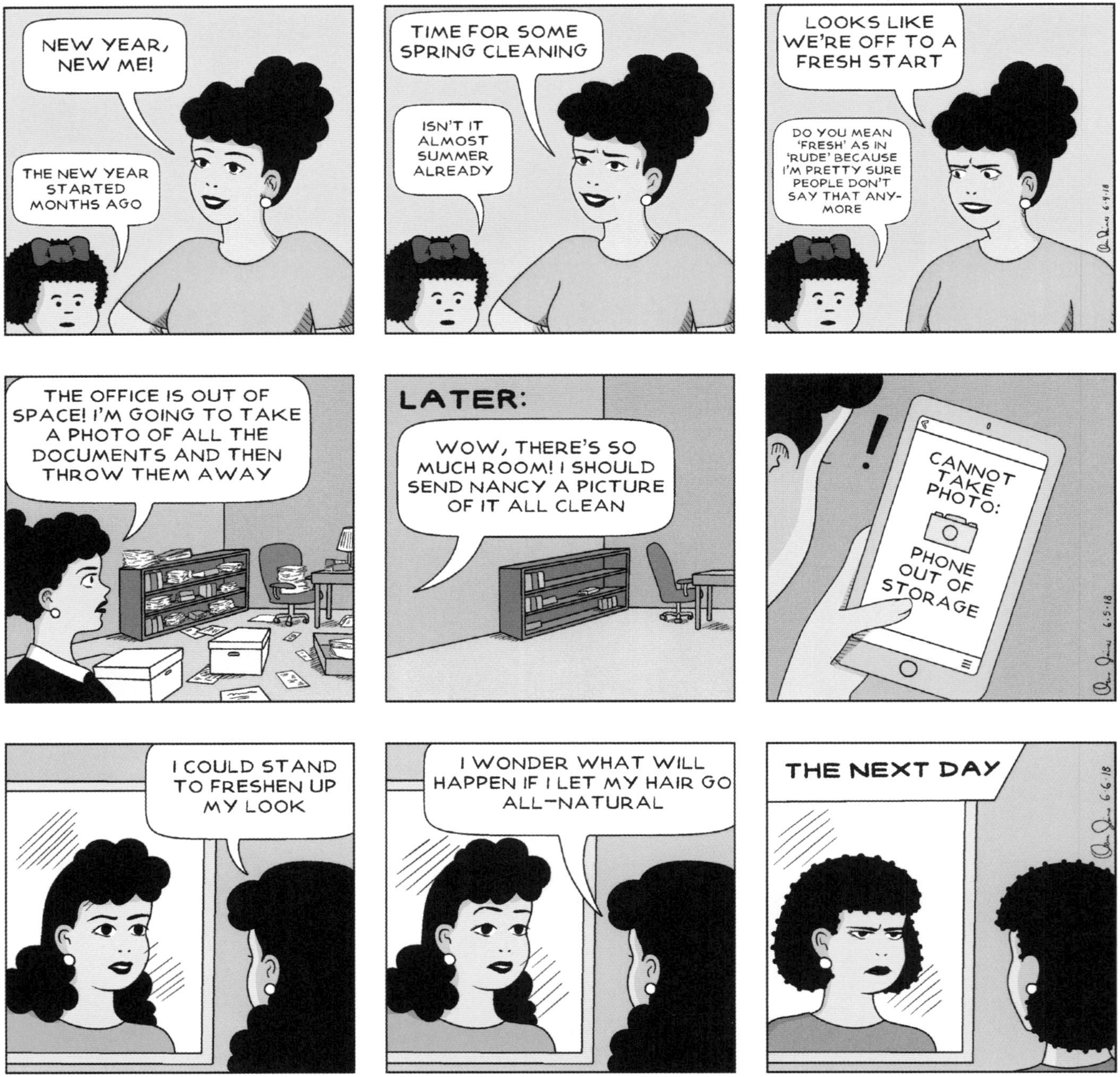
NEW YEAR, NEW ME!
THE NEW YEAR STARTED MONTHS AGO
TIME FOR SOME SPRING CLEANING
ISN'T IT ALMOST SUMMER ALREADY
LOOKS LIKE WE'RE OFF TO A FRESH START
DO YOU MEAN 'FRESH' AS IN 'RUDE' BECAUSE I'M PRETTY SURE PEOPLE DON'T SAY THAT ANY-MORE
THE OFFICE IS OUT OF SPACE! I'M GOING TO TAKE A PHOTO OF ALL THE DOCUMENTS AND THEN THROW THEM AWAY
LATER:
WOW, THERE'S SO MUCH ROOM! I SHOULD SEND NANCY A PICTURE OF IT ALL CLEAN
!
CANNOT TAKE PHOTO:
PHONE OUT OF STORAGE
I COULD STAND TO FRESHEN UP MY LOOK
I WONDER WHAT WILL HAPPEN IF I LET MY HAIR GO ALL-NATURAL
THE NEXT DAY

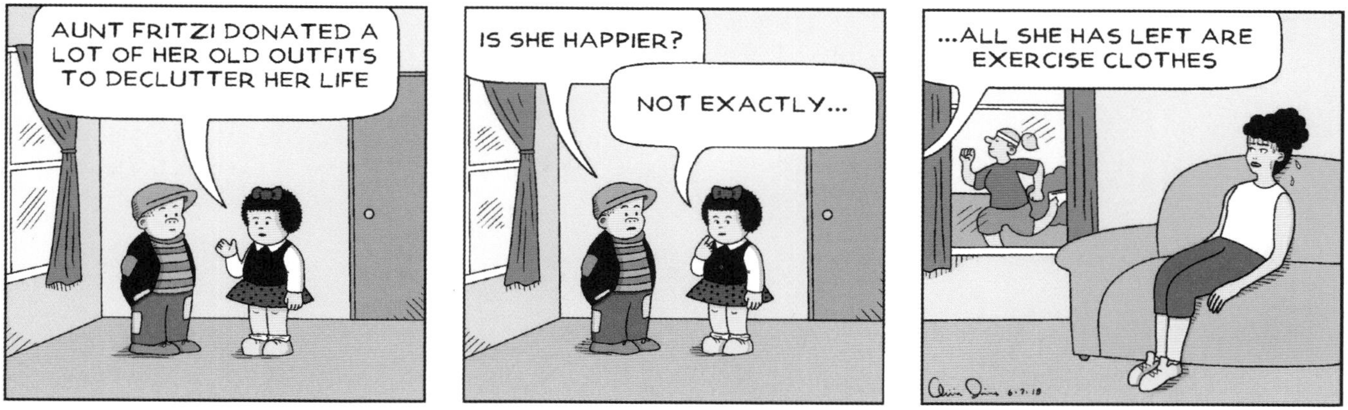
AUNT FRITZI DONATED A LOT OF HER OLD OUTFITS TO DECLUTTER HER LIFE
IS SHE HAPPIER?
NOT EXACTLY...
...ALL SHE HAS LEFT ARE EXERCISE CLOTHES

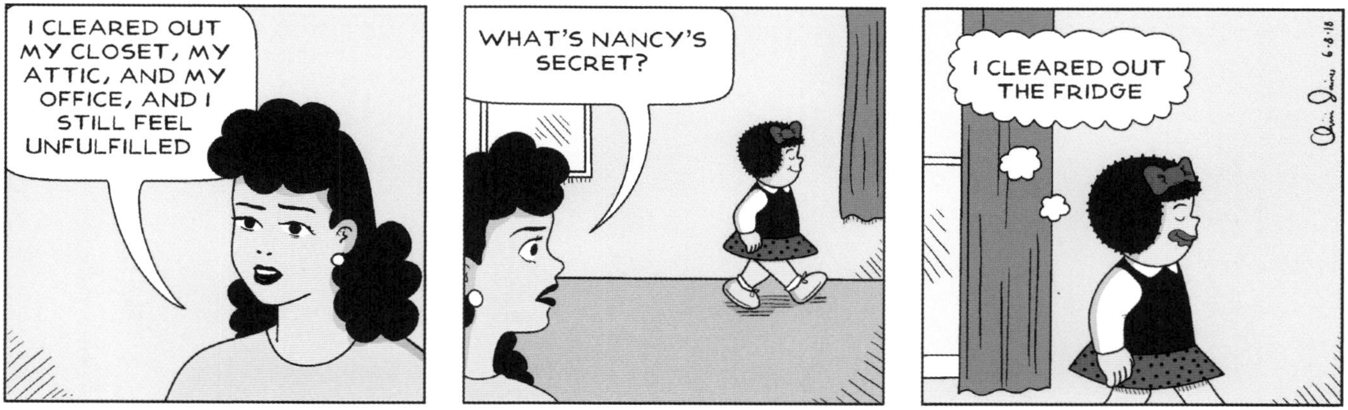
I CLEARED OUT MY CLOSET, MY ATTIC, AND MY OFFICE, AND I STILL FEEL UNFULFILLED
WHAT'S NANCY'S SECRET?
I CLEARED OUT THE FRIDGE

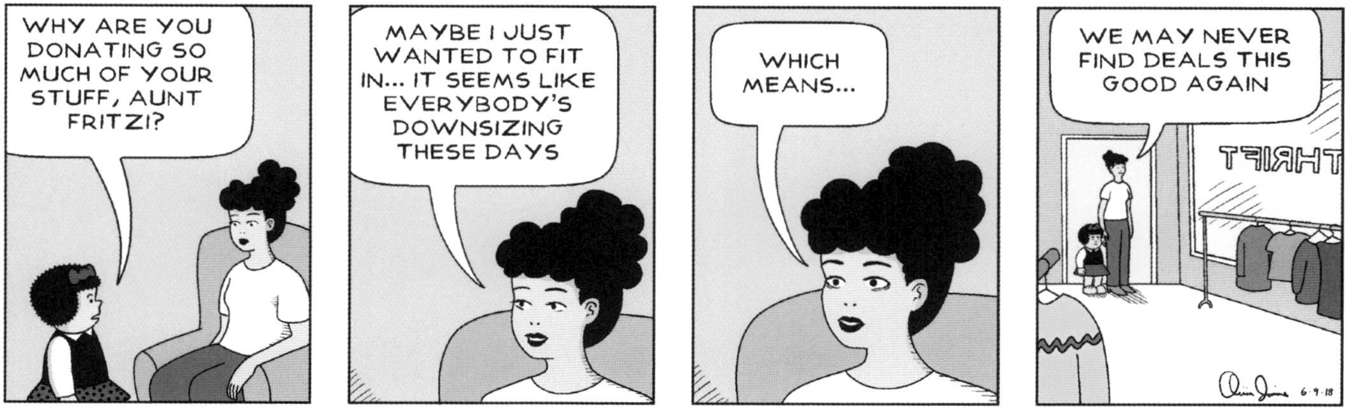
WHY ARE YOU DONATING SO MUCH OF YOUR STUFF, AUNT FRITZI?
MAYBE I JUST WANTED TO FIT IN... IT SEEMS LIKE EVERYBODY'S DOWNSIZING THESE DAYS
WHICH MEANS...
WE MAY NEVER FIND DEALS THIS GOOD AGAIN
THRIFT

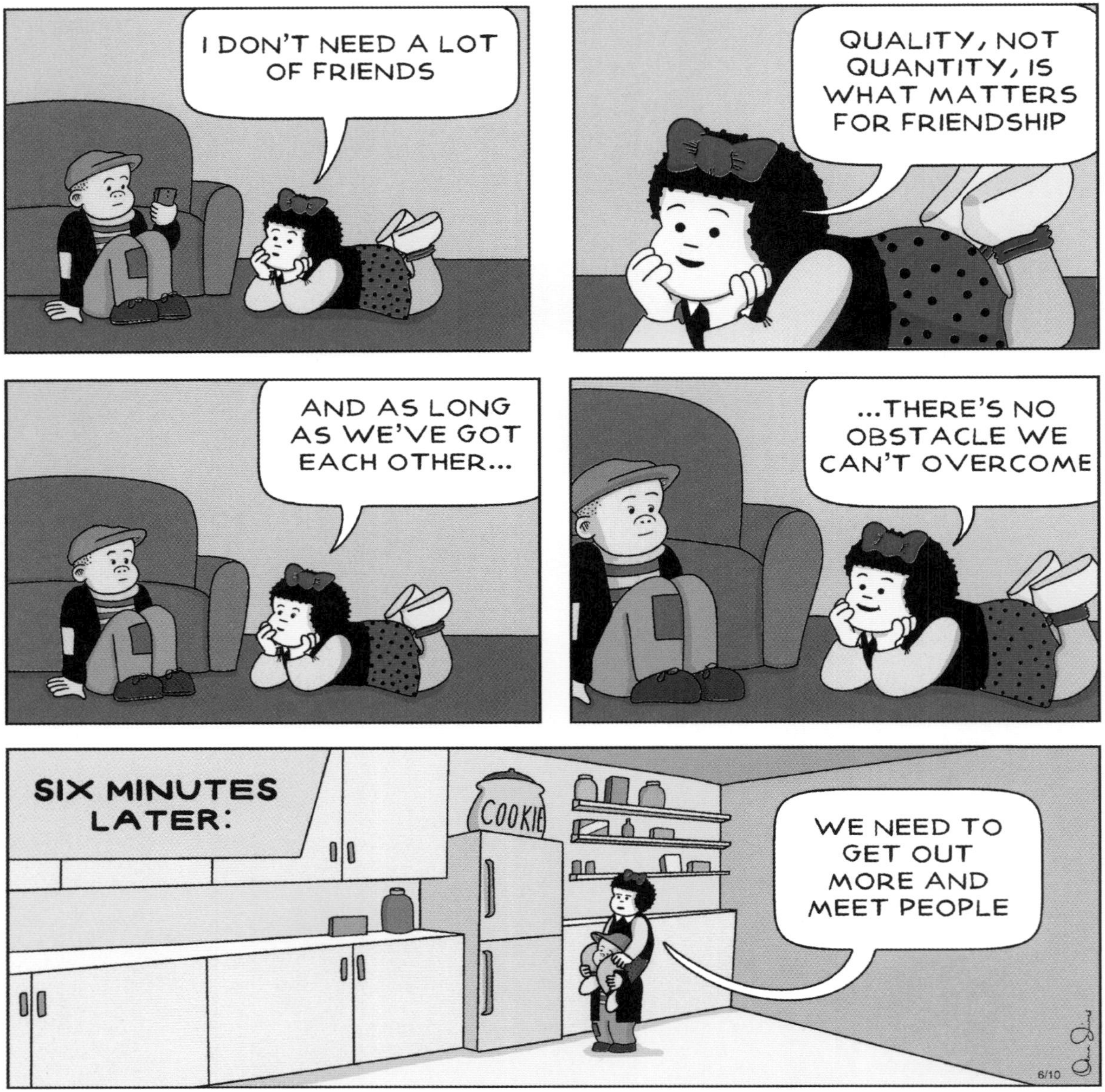
I DON'T NEED A LOT OF FRIENDS
QUALITY, NOT QUANTITY, IS WHAT MATTERS FOR FRIENDSHIP
AND AS LONG AS WE'VE GOT EACH OTHER...
...THERE'S NO OBSTACLE WE CAN'T OVERCOME
SIX MINUTES LATER:
COOKIE
WE NEED TO GET OUT MORE AND MEET PEOPLE
6/10

NANCY, IF YOU APPLY YOURSELF I THINK YOU CAN ACHIEVE GREAT THINGS

BUT UNTIL YOU DO, I'LL KEEP APPLYING PRESSURE

IS IT TOO LATE TO APPLY TO A DIFFERENT SCHOOL?

THE FIRST STEP OF THE ASSIGNMENT IS TO FIND A PARTNER

WHAT'S THE SECOND STEP?

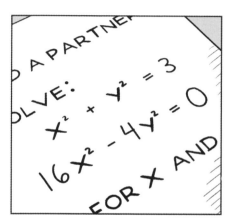

A PARTNER

LVE:
$$x^2 + y^2 = 3$$
$$16x^2 - 4y^2 = 0$$

FOR X AND

NEITHER OF US COULD FIND A PARTNER

THIS PROBLEM IS **SO EASY**

WHAT A **SIMPLE** ASSIGNMENT

THE ANSWER IS **OBVIOUS**

IF EVERYONE WASTES THE NEXT FEW MINUTES FEELING DISCOURAGED, I THINK WE CAN CATCH UP

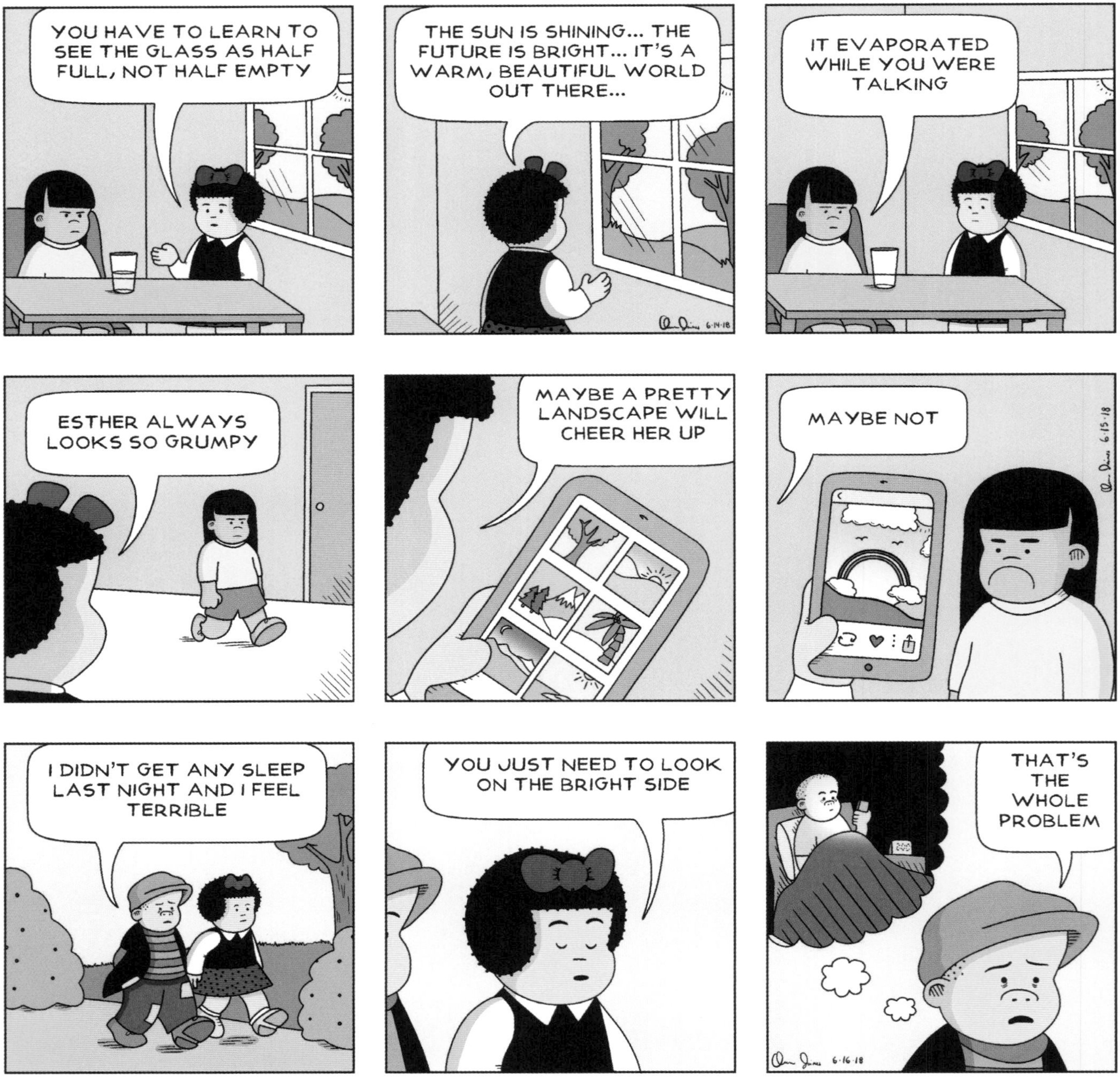
YOU HAVE TO LEARN TO SEE THE GLASS AS HALF FULL, NOT HALF EMPTY
THE SUN IS SHINING... THE FUTURE IS BRIGHT... IT'S A WARM, BEAUTIFUL WORLD OUT THERE...
6-14-18
IT EVAPORATED WHILE YOU WERE TALKING
ESTHER ALWAYS LOOKS SO GRUMPY
MAYBE A PRETTY LANDSCAPE WILL CHEER HER UP
MAYBE NOT
6-15-18
I DIDN'T GET ANY SLEEP LAST NIGHT AND I FEEL TERRIBLE
YOU JUST NEED TO LOOK ON THE BRIGHT SIDE
THAT'S THE WHOLE PROBLEM
6-16-18

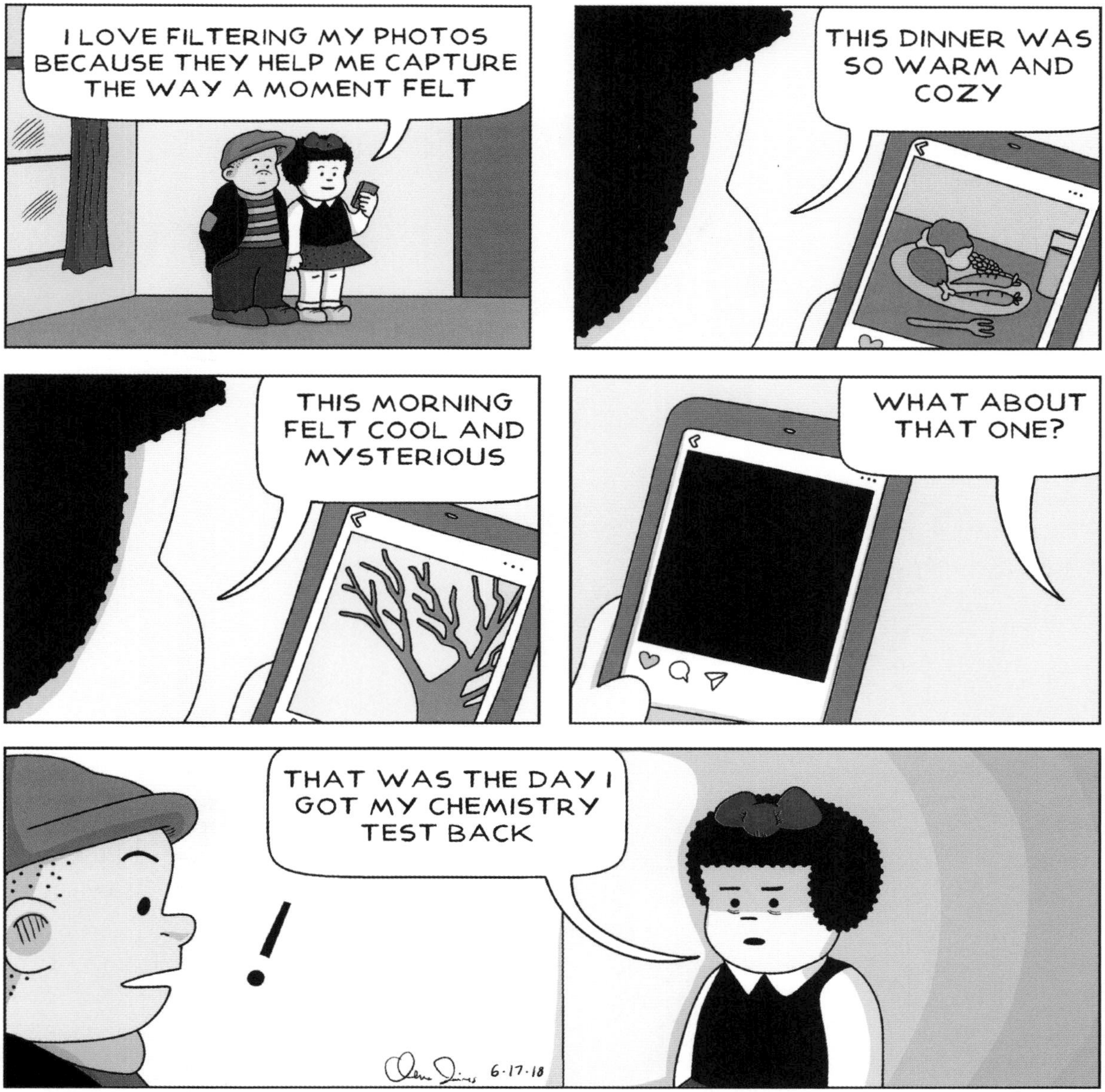
I LOVE FILTERING MY PHOTOS BECAUSE THEY HELP ME CAPTURE THE WAY A MOMENT FELT
THIS DINNER WAS SO WARM AND COZY
THIS MORNING FELT COOL AND MYSTERIOUS
WHAT ABOUT THAT ONE?
THAT WAS THE DAY I GOT MY CHEMISTRY TEST BACK
!
6-17-18

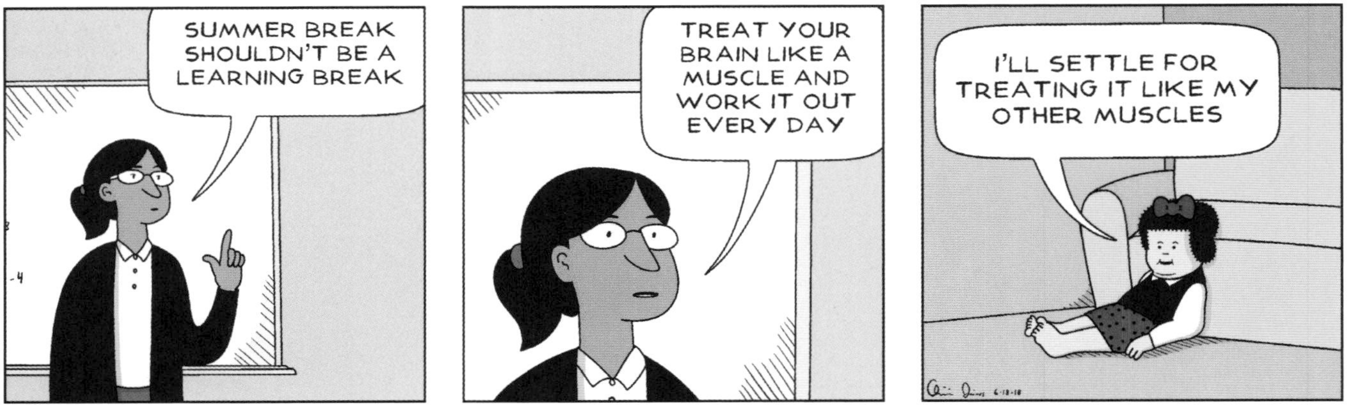
SUMMER BREAK SHOULDN'T BE A LEARNING BREAK
TREAT YOUR BRAIN LIKE A MUSCLE AND WORK IT OUT EVERY DAY
I'LL SETTLE FOR TREATING IT LIKE MY OTHER MUSCLES

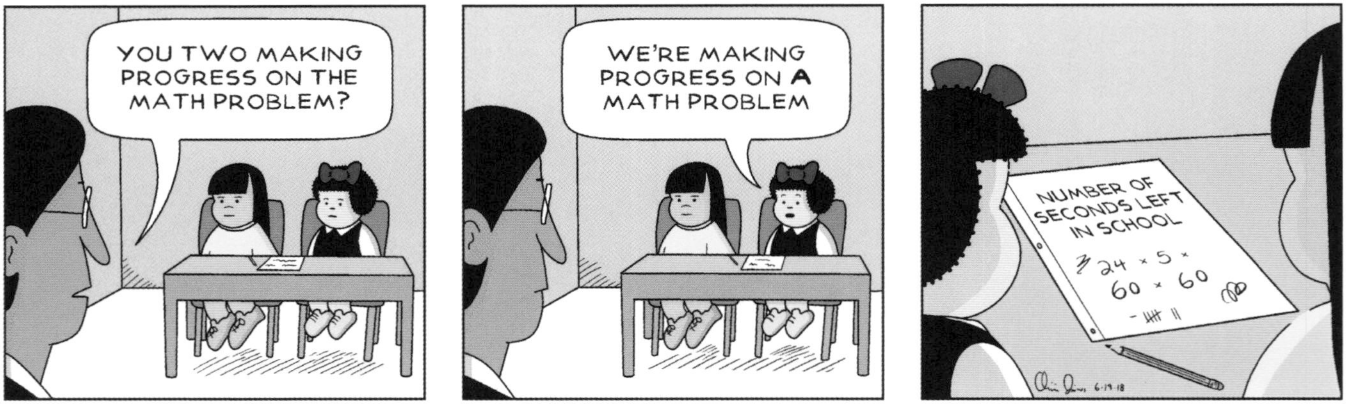
YOU TWO MAKING PROGRESS ON THE MATH PROBLEM?
WE'RE MAKING PROGRESS ON **A** MATH PROBLEM
NUMBER OF SECONDS LEFT IN SCHOOL
24 × 5 × 60 × 60

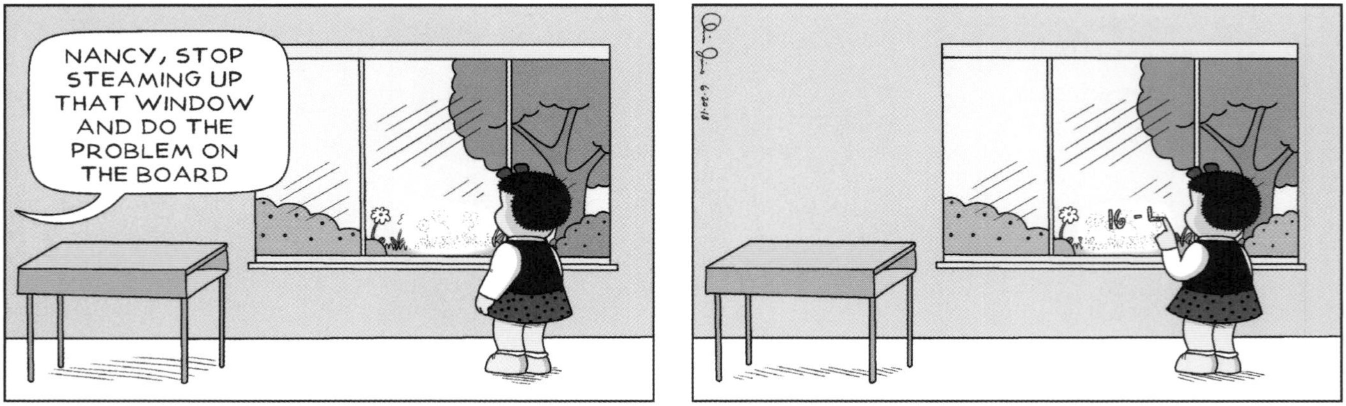
NANCY, STOP STEAMING UP THAT WINDOW AND DO THE PROBLEM ON THE BOARD

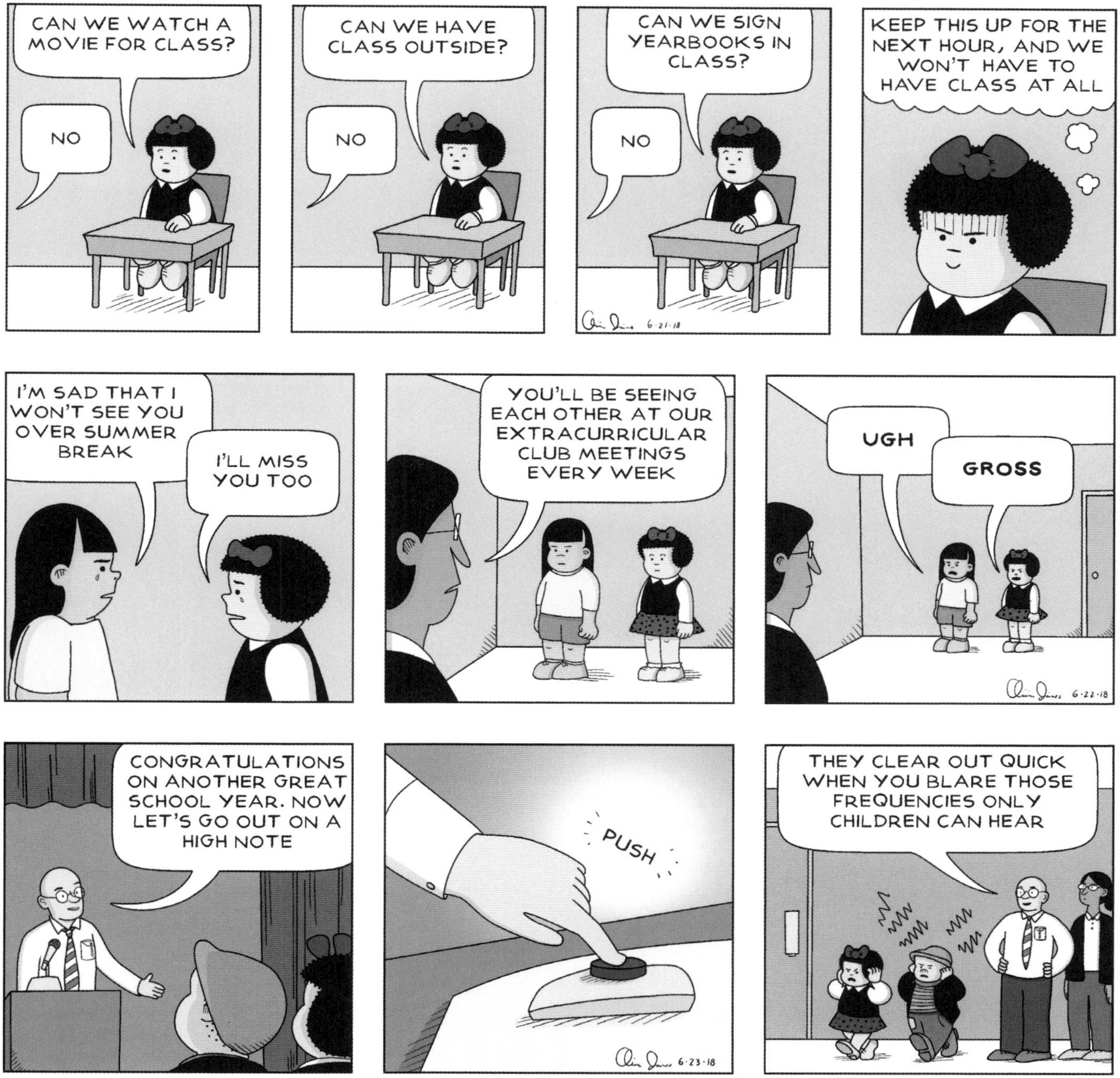
CAN WE WATCH A MOVIE FOR CLASS?
NO
CAN WE HAVE CLASS OUTSIDE?
NO
CAN WE SIGN YEARBOOKS IN CLASS?
NO
KEEP THIS UP FOR THE NEXT HOUR, AND WE WON'T HAVE TO HAVE CLASS AT ALL
I'M SAD THAT I WON'T SEE YOU OVER SUMMER BREAK
I'LL MISS YOU TOO
YOU'LL BE SEEING EACH OTHER AT OUR EXTRACURRICULAR CLUB MEETINGS EVERY WEEK
UGH
GROSS
CONGRATULATIONS ON ANOTHER GREAT SCHOOL YEAR. NOW LET'S GO OUT ON A HIGH NOTE
PUSH
THEY CLEAR OUT QUICK WHEN YOU BLARE THOSE FREQUENCIES ONLY CHILDREN CAN HEAR

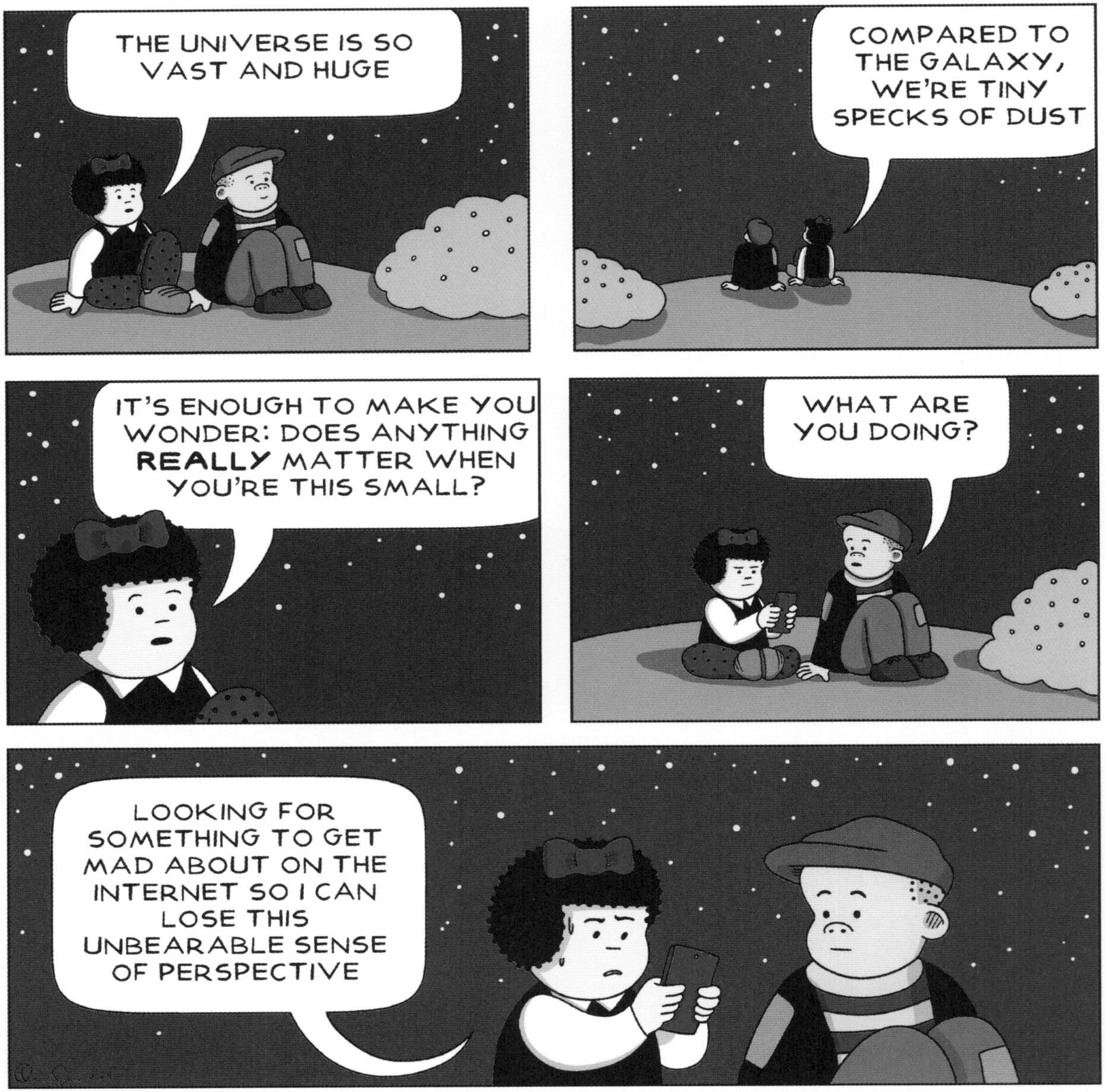
THE UNIVERSE IS SO VAST AND HUGE
COMPARED TO THE GALAXY, WE'RE TINY SPECKS OF DUST
IT'S ENOUGH TO MAKE YOU WONDER: DOES ANYTHING **REALLY** MATTER WHEN YOU'RE THIS SMALL?
WHAT ARE YOU DOING?
LOOKING FOR SOMETHING TO GET MAD ABOUT ON THE INTERNET SO I CAN LOSE THIS UNBEARABLE SENSE OF PERSPECTIVE

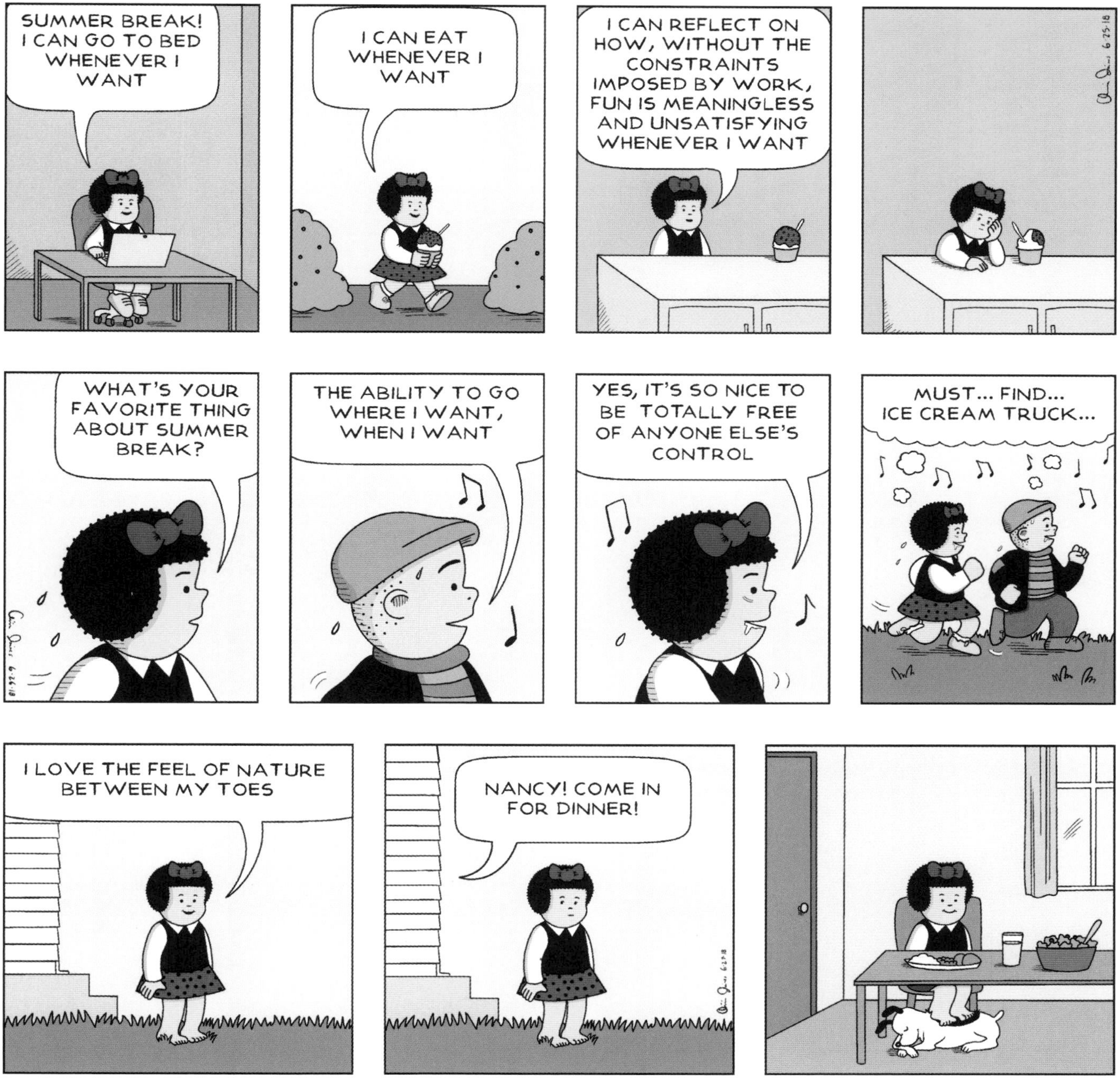
SUMMER BREAK! I CAN GO TO BED WHENEVER I WANT
I CAN EAT WHENEVER I WANT
I CAN REFLECT ON HOW, WITHOUT THE CONSTRAINTS IMPOSED BY WORK, FUN IS MEANINGLESS AND UNSATISFYING WHENEVER I WANT
WHAT'S YOUR FAVORITE THING ABOUT SUMMER BREAK?
THE ABILITY TO GO WHERE I WANT, WHEN I WANT
YES, IT'S SO NICE TO BE TOTALLY FREE OF ANYONE ELSE'S CONTROL
MUST... FIND... ICE CREAM TRUCK...
I LOVE THE FEEL OF NATURE BETWEEN MY TOES
NANCY! COME IN FOR DINNER!

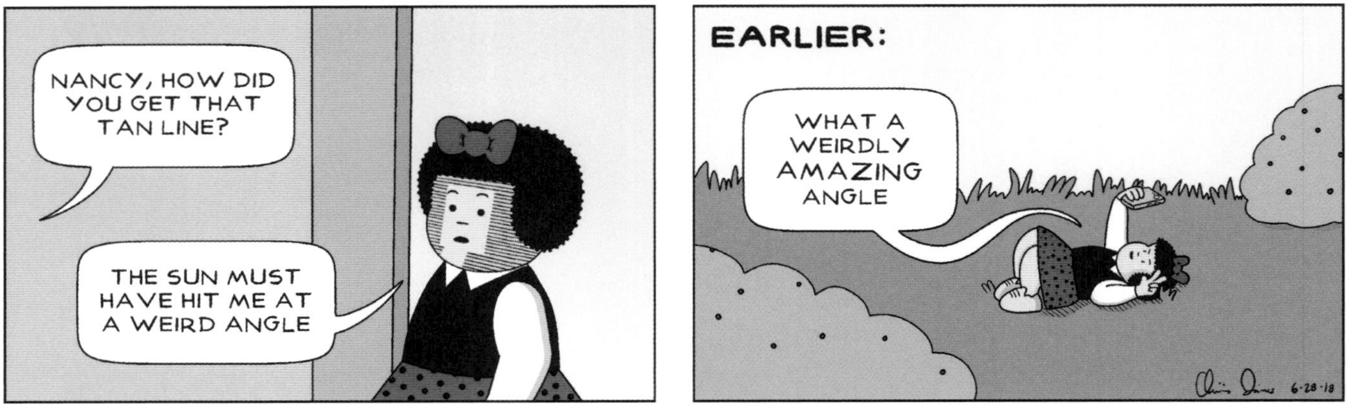
NANCY, HOW DID YOU GET THAT TAN LINE?
THE SUN MUST HAVE HIT ME AT A WEIRD ANGLE
EARLIER:
WHAT A WEIRDLY AMAZING ANGLE

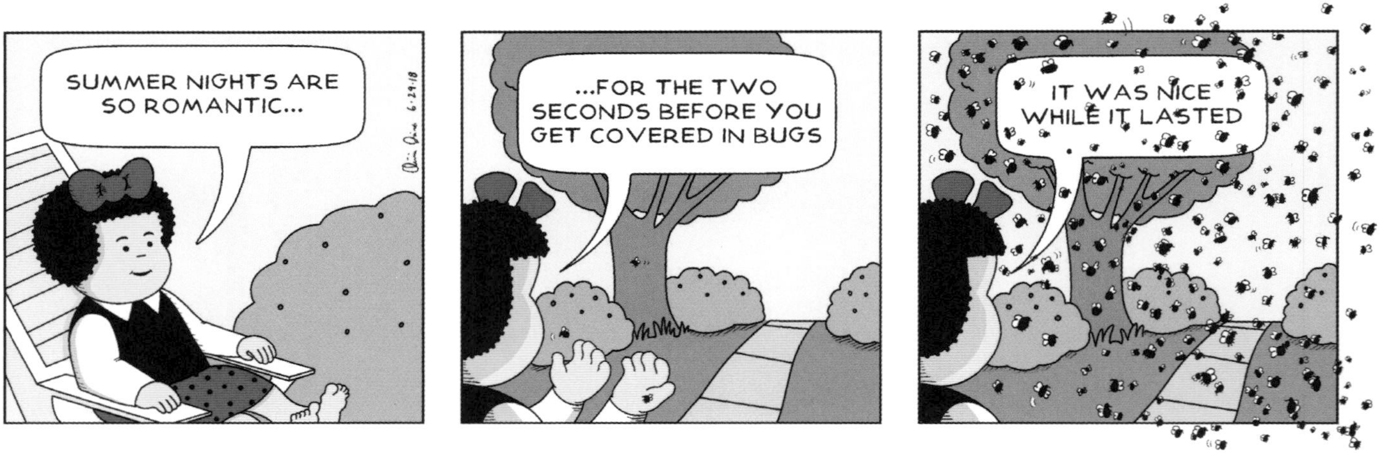
SUMMER NIGHTS ARE SO ROMANTIC...
...FOR THE TWO SECONDS BEFORE YOU GET COVERED IN BUGS
IT WAS NICE WHILE IT LASTED

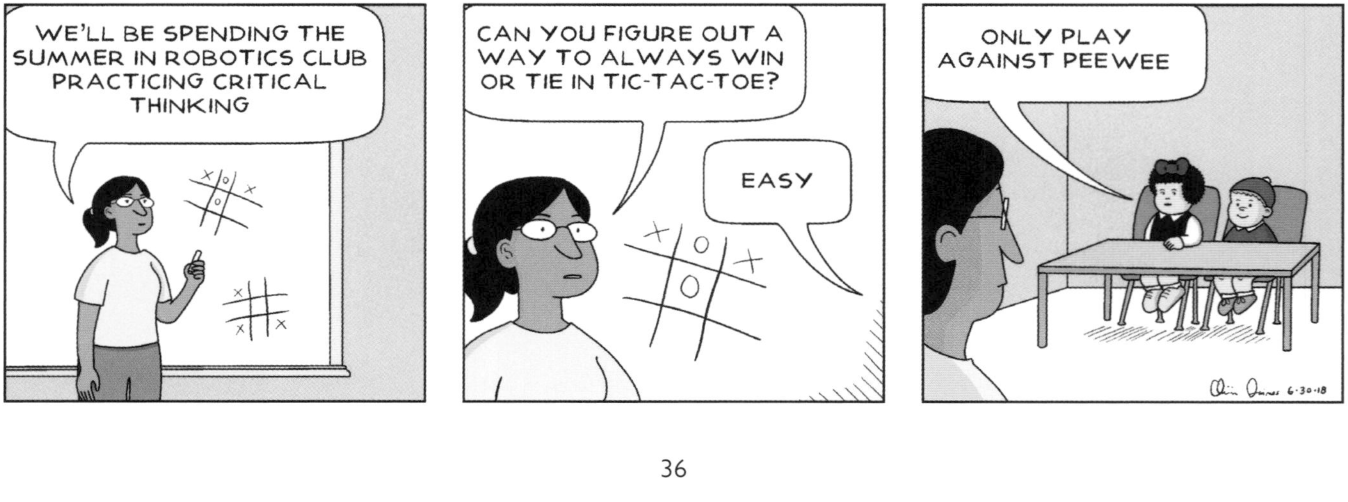
WE'LL BE SPENDING THE SUMMER IN ROBOTICS CLUB PRACTICING CRITICAL THINKING
CAN YOU FIGURE OUT A WAY TO ALWAYS WIN OR TIE IN TIC-TAC-TOE?
EASY
ONLY PLAY AGAINST PEEWEE

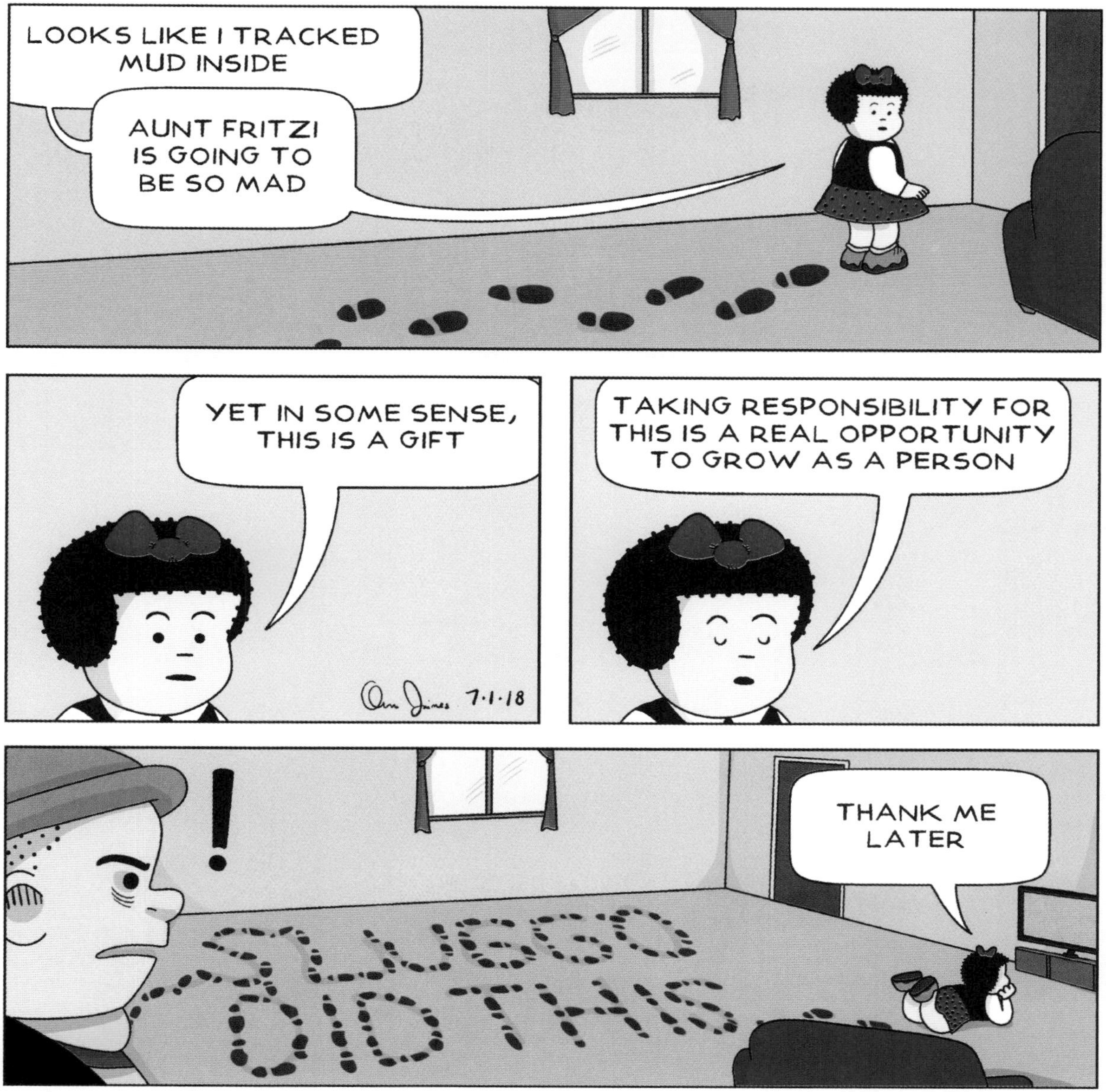
LOOKS LIKE I TRACKED MUD INSIDE
AUNT FRITZI IS GOING TO BE SO MAD
YET IN SOME SENSE, THIS IS A GIFT
7·1·18
TAKING RESPONSIBILITY FOR THIS IS A REAL OPPORTUNITY TO GROW AS A PERSON
!
SLUGGO DID THIS
THANK ME LATER

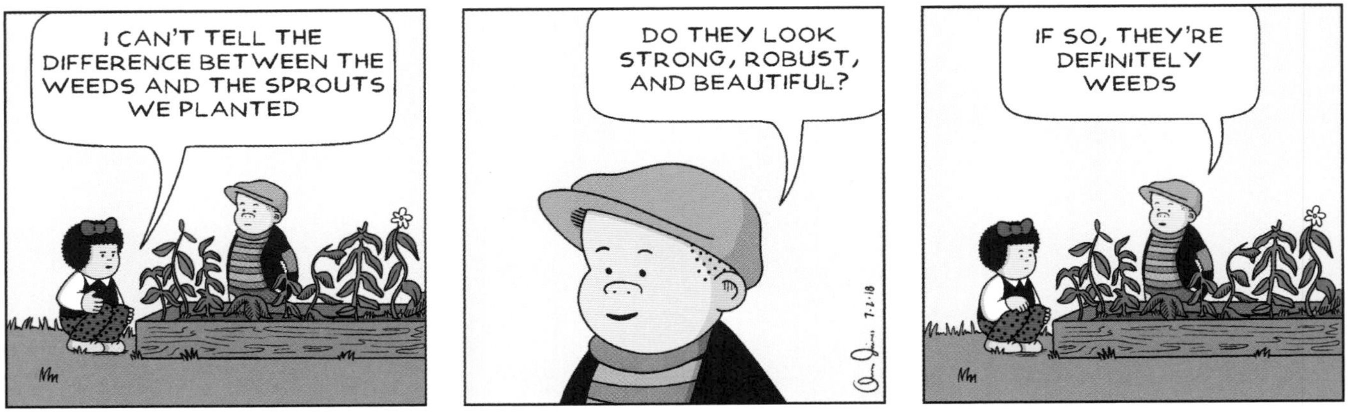
I CAN'T TELL THE DIFFERENCE BETWEEN THE WEEDS AND THE SPROUTS WE PLANTED
DO THEY LOOK STRONG, ROBUST, AND BEAUTIFUL?
IF SO, THEY'RE DEFINITELY WEEDS
7.2.18

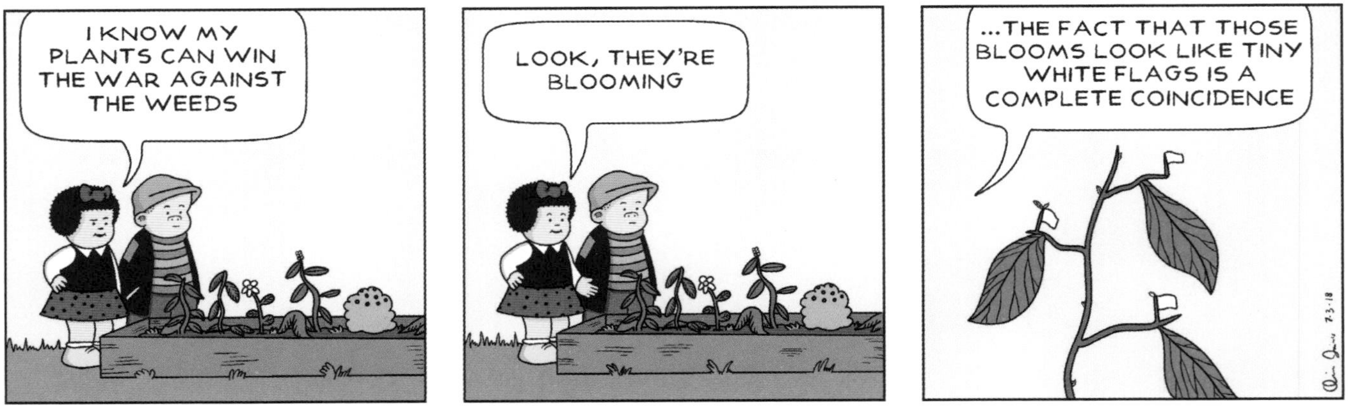
I KNOW MY PLANTS CAN WIN THE WAR AGAINST THE WEEDS
LOOK, THEY'RE BLOOMING
...THE FACT THAT THOSE BLOOMS LOOK LIKE TINY WHITE FLAGS IS A COMPLETE COINCIDENCE
7.3.18

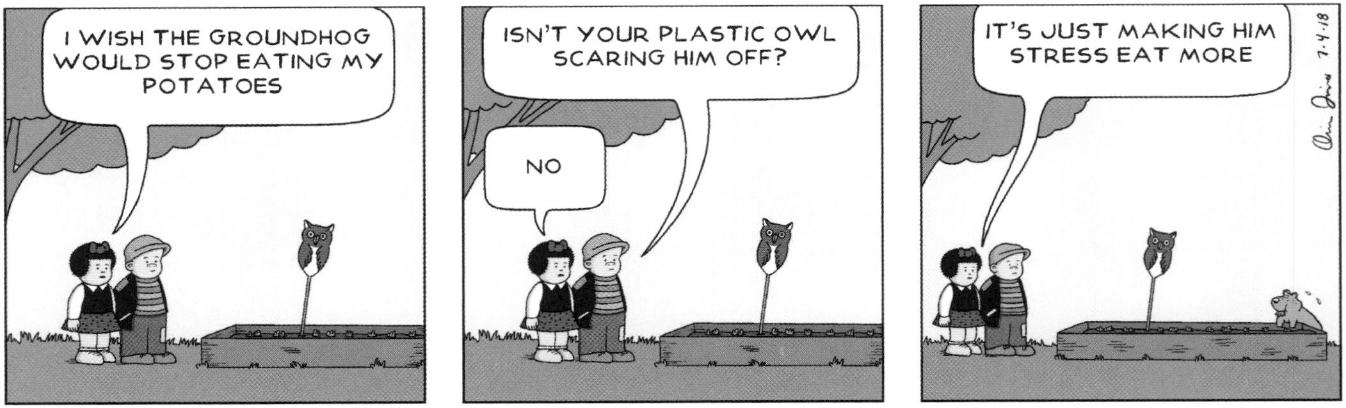
I WISH THE GROUNDHOG WOULD STOP EATING MY POTATOES
ISN'T YOUR PLASTIC OWL SCARING HIM OFF?
NO
IT'S JUST MAKING HIM STRESS EAT MORE
7.4.18

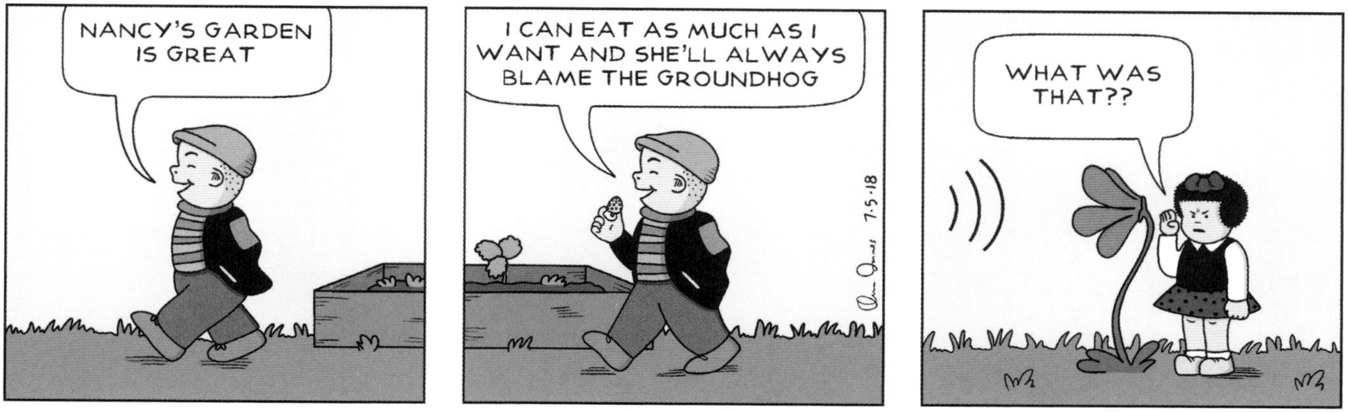
NANCY'S GARDEN IS GREAT
I CAN EAT AS MUCH AS I WANT AND SHE'LL ALWAYS BLAME THE GROUNDHOG
7-5-18
WHAT WAS THAT??

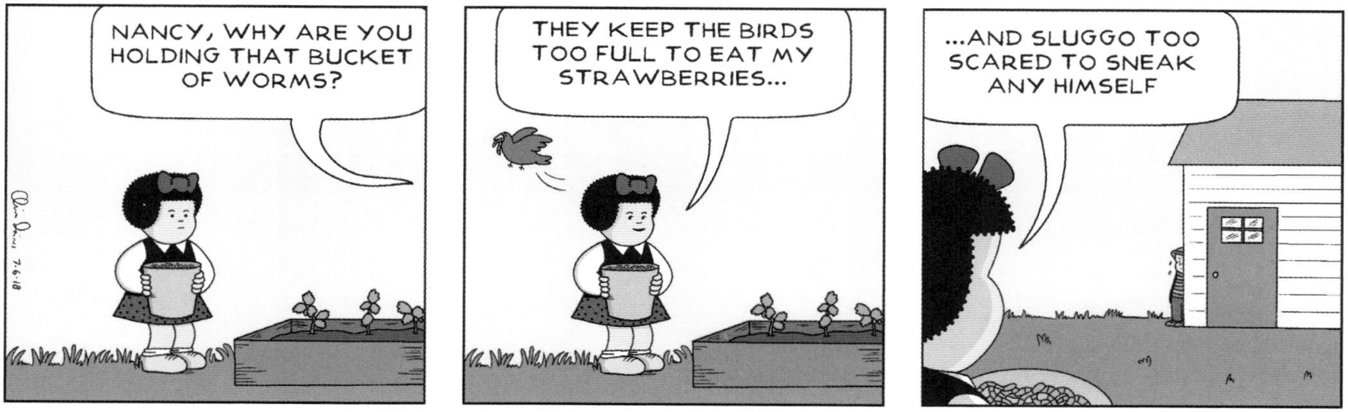
7-6-18
NANCY, WHY ARE YOU HOLDING THAT BUCKET OF WORMS?
THEY KEEP THE BIRDS TOO FULL TO EAT MY STRAWBERRIES...
...AND SLUGGO TOO SCARED TO SNEAK ANY HIMSELF

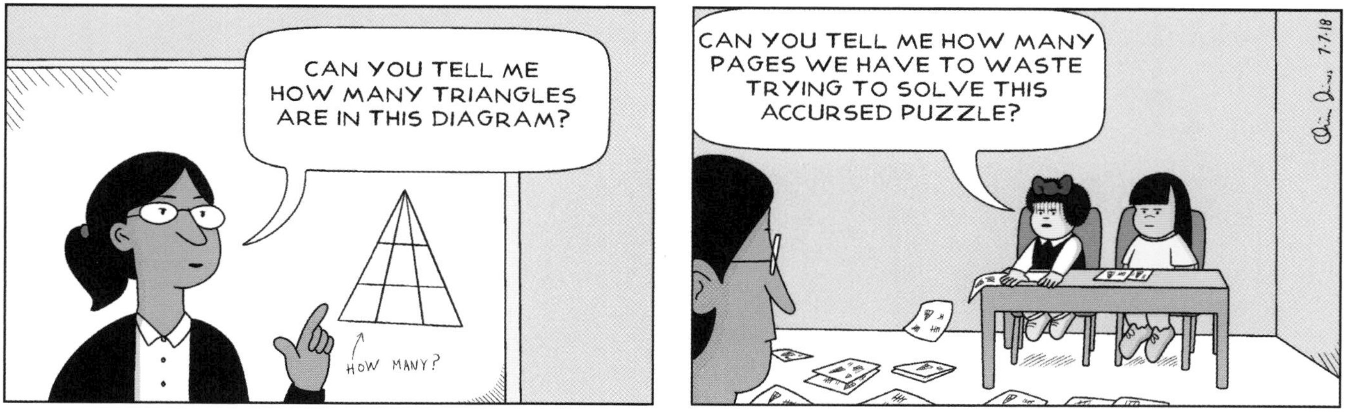
CAN YOU TELL ME HOW MANY TRIANGLES ARE IN THIS DIAGRAM?
HOW MANY?
CAN YOU TELL ME HOW MANY PAGES WE HAVE TO WASTE TRYING TO SOLVE THIS ACCURSED PUZZLE?
7-7-18

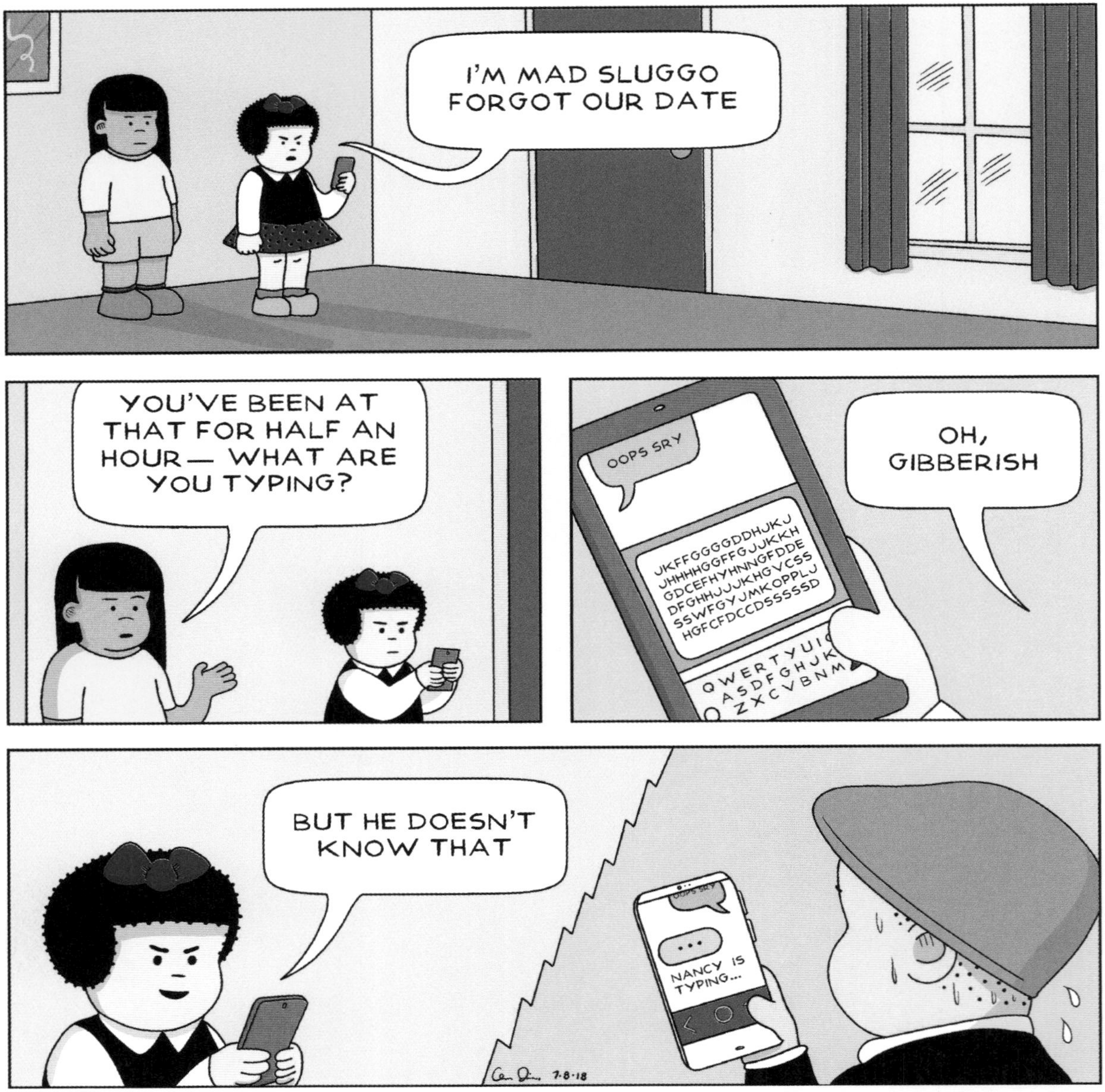
I'M MAD SLUGGO FORGOT OUR DATE
YOU'VE BEEN AT THAT FOR HALF AN HOUR— WHAT ARE YOU TYPING?
OOPS SRY
UKFFGGGGDDHJKJ UHHHHGGFFGJJKKH GDCEFHYHNNGFDDE DFGHHJJJKHGVCSS SSWFGYJMKOPPLJ HGFCFDCCDSSSSSD
OH, GIBBERISH
BUT HE DOESN'T KNOW THAT
NANCY IS TYPING...

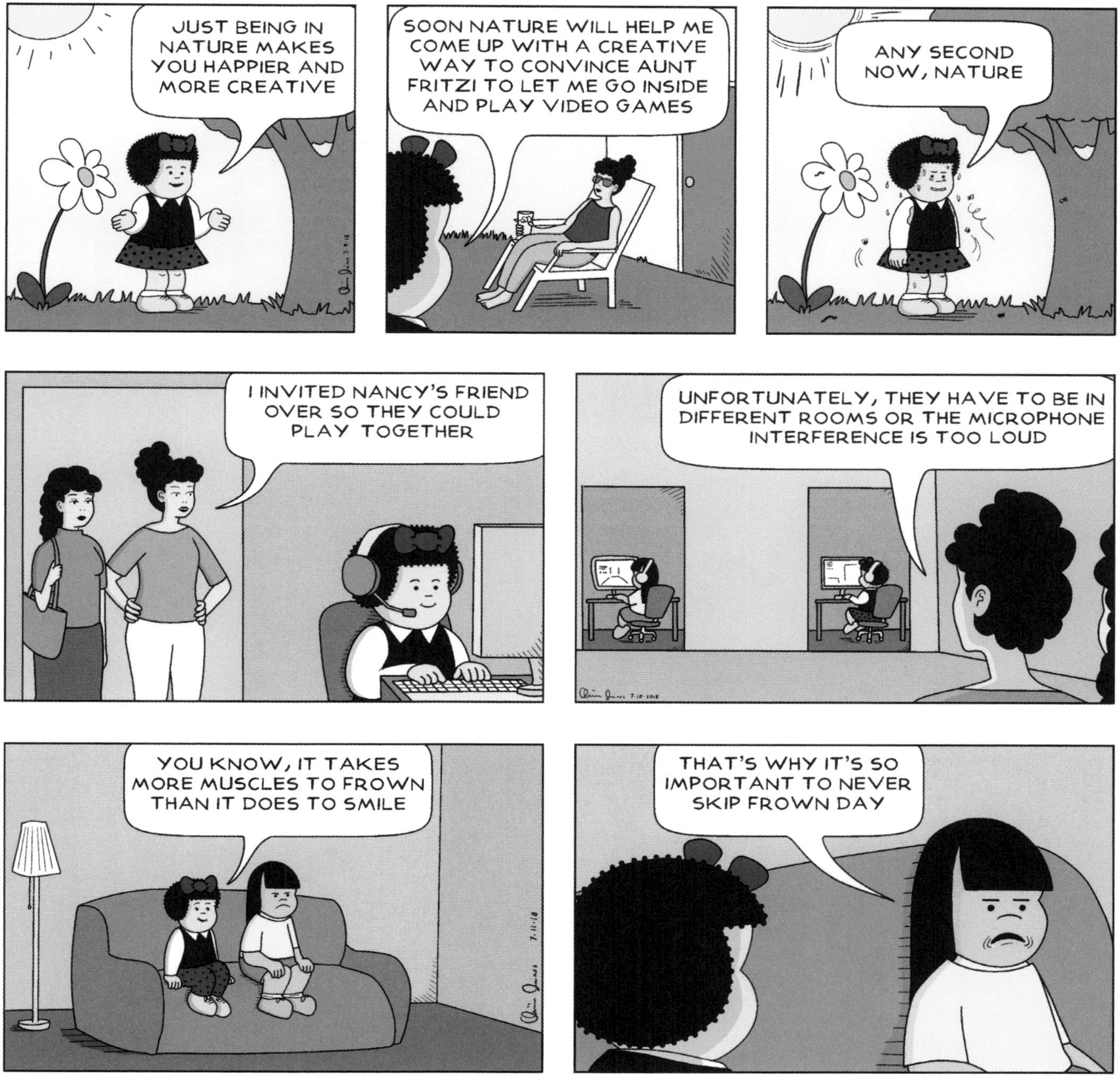
JUST BEING IN NATURE MAKES YOU HAPPIER AND MORE CREATIVE
SOON NATURE WILL HELP ME COME UP WITH A CREATIVE WAY TO CONVINCE AUNT FRITZI TO LET ME GO INSIDE AND PLAY VIDEO GAMES
ANY SECOND NOW, NATURE
I INVITED NANCY'S FRIEND OVER SO THEY COULD PLAY TOGETHER
UNFORTUNATELY, THEY HAVE TO BE IN DIFFERENT ROOMS OR THE MICROPHONE INTERFERENCE IS TOO LOUD
YOU KNOW, IT TAKES MORE MUSCLES TO FROWN THAN IT DOES TO SMILE
THAT'S WHY IT'S SO IMPORTANT TO NEVER SKIP FROWN DAY

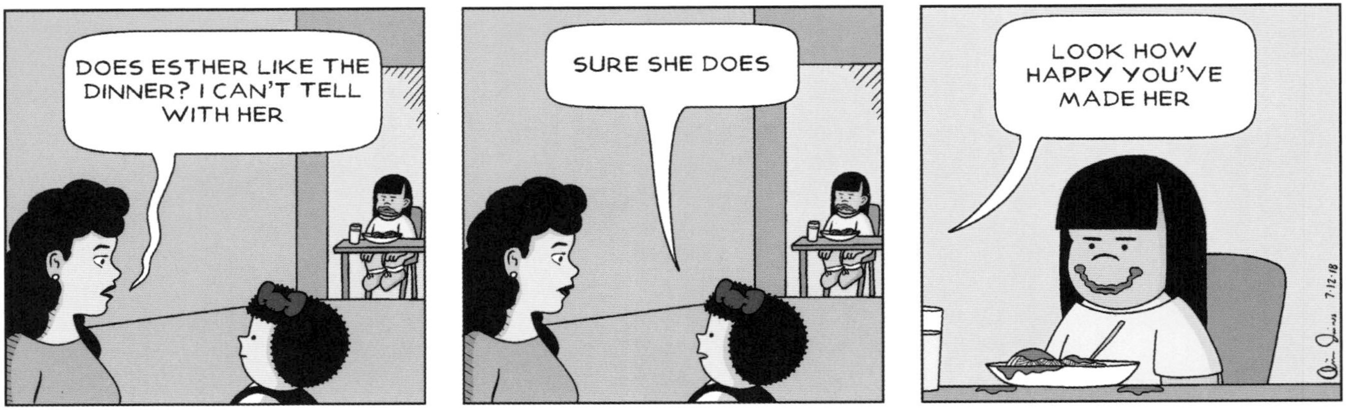
DOES ESTHER LIKE THE DINNER? I CAN'T TELL WITH HER
SURE SHE DOES
LOOK HOW HAPPY YOU'VE MADE HER
7-12-18

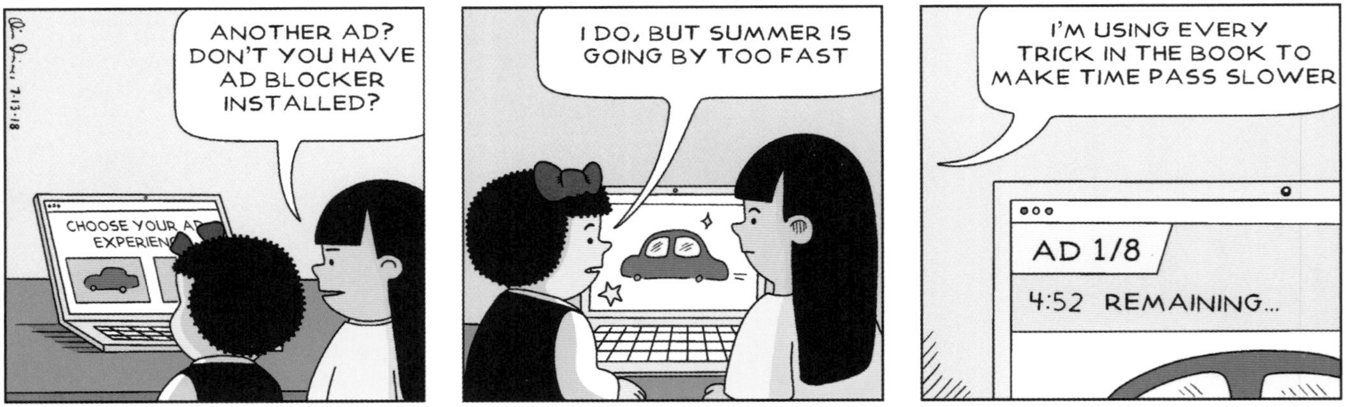
7-13-18
ANOTHER AD? DON'T YOU HAVE AD BLOCKER INSTALLED?
CHOOSE YOUR AD EXPERIENCE
I DO, BUT SUMMER IS GOING BY TOO FAST
I'M USING EVERY TRICK IN THE BOOK TO MAKE TIME PASS SLOWER
AD 1/8
4:52 REMAINING...

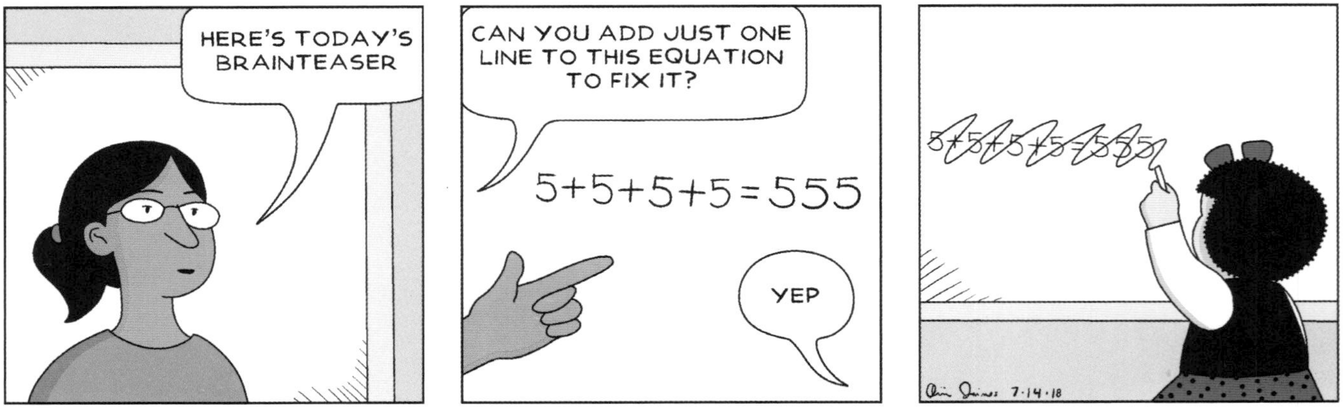
HERE'S TODAY'S BRAINTEASER
CAN YOU ADD JUST ONE LINE TO THIS EQUATION TO FIX IT?
5+5+5+5=555
YEP
7-14-18

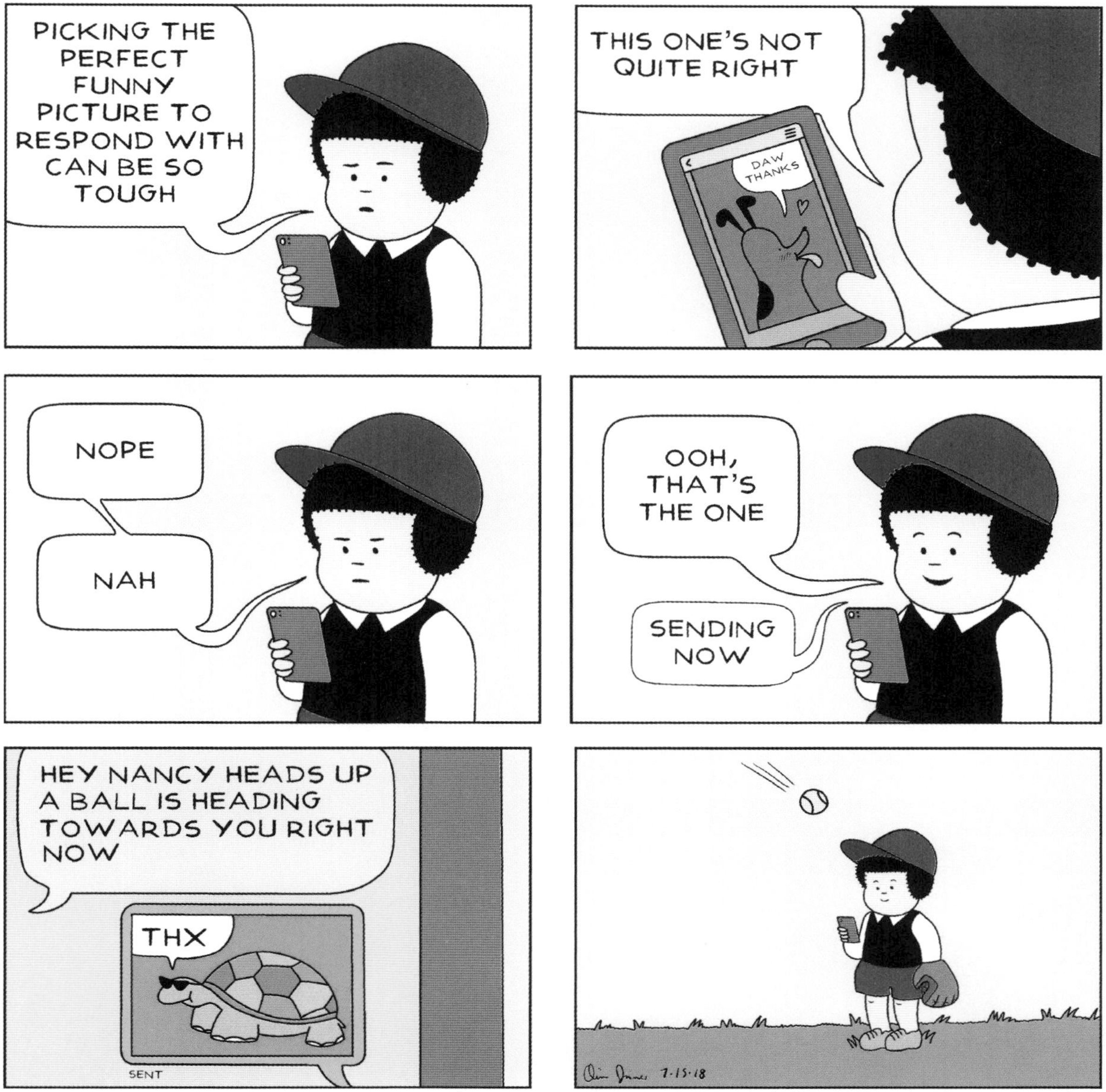
PICKING THE PERFECT FUNNY PICTURE TO RESPOND WITH CAN BE SO TOUGH
THIS ONE'S NOT QUITE RIGHT
DAW THANKS
NOPE
NAH
OOH, THAT'S THE ONE
SENDING NOW
HEY NANCY HEADS UP A BALL IS HEADING TOWARDS YOU RIGHT NOW
THX
SENT
7·15·18

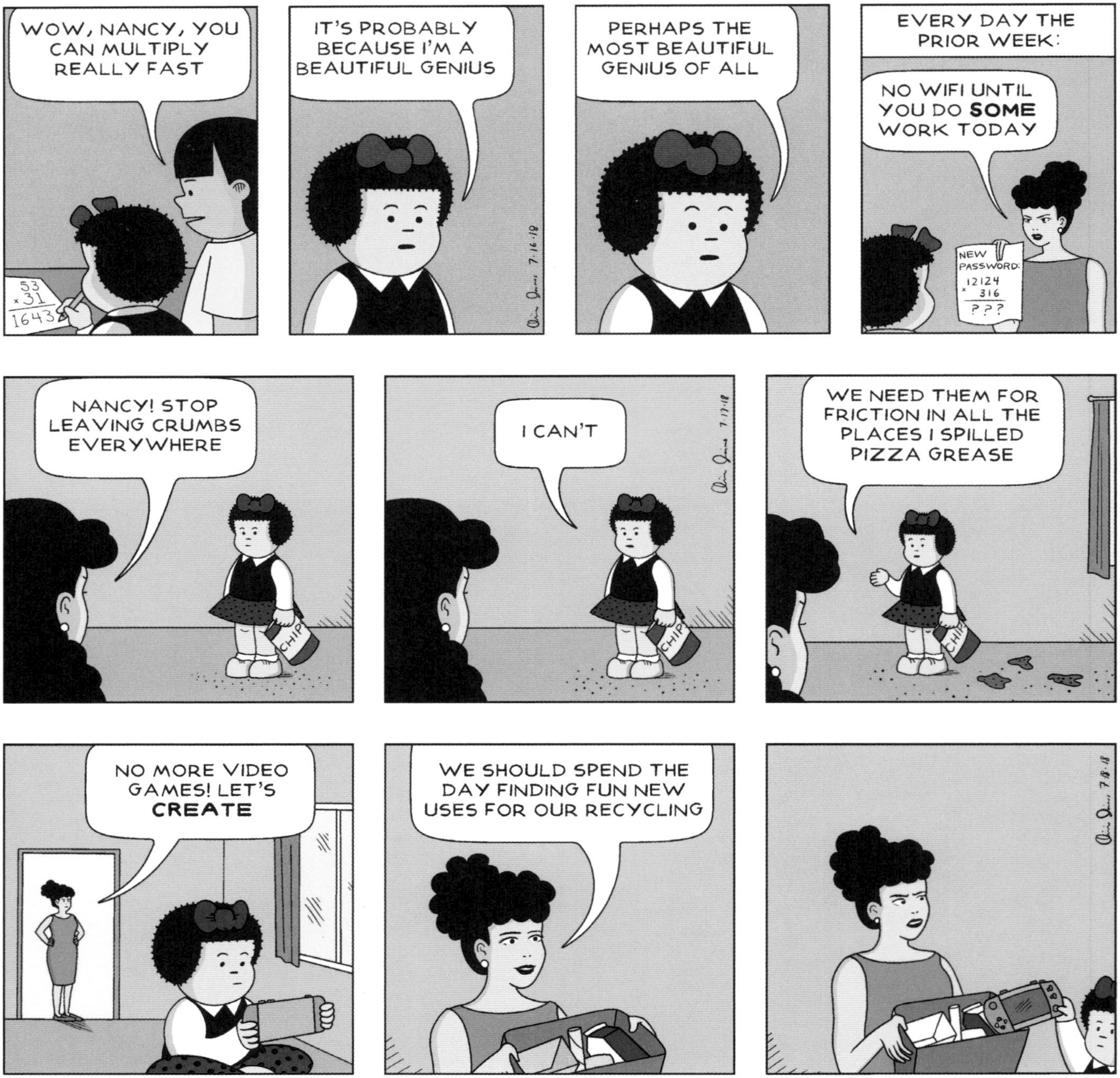
WOW, NANCY, YOU CAN MULTIPLY REALLY FAST
53
×31
1643
IT'S PROBABLY BECAUSE I'M A BEAUTIFUL GENIUS
7.16.18
PERHAPS THE MOST BEAUTIFUL GENIUS OF ALL
EVERY DAY THE PRIOR WEEK:
NO WIFI UNTIL YOU DO **SOME** WORK TODAY
NEW PASSWORD:
12124
× 316
???
NANCY! STOP LEAVING CRUMBS EVERYWHERE
CHIPS
I CAN'T
7.17.18
WE NEED THEM FOR FRICTION IN ALL THE PLACES I SPILLED PIZZA GREASE
NO MORE VIDEO GAMES! LET'S **CREATE**
WE SHOULD SPEND THE DAY FINDING FUN NEW USES FOR OUR RECYCLING
7.18.18

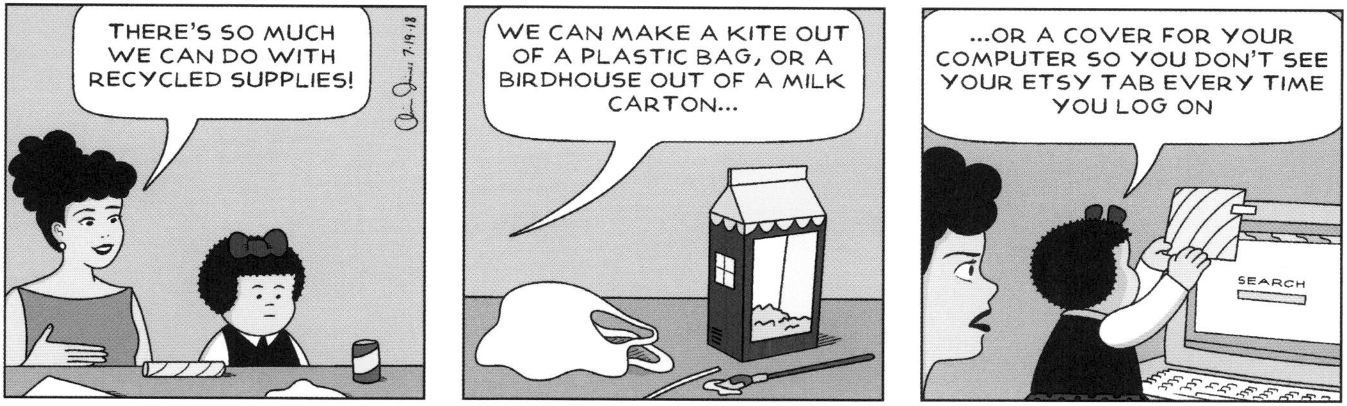
THERE'S SO MUCH WE CAN DO WITH RECYCLED SUPPLIES!
WE CAN MAKE A KITE OUT OF A PLASTIC BAG, OR A BIRDHOUSE OUT OF A MILK CARTON...
...OR A COVER FOR YOUR COMPUTER SO YOU DON'T SEE YOUR ETSY TAB EVERY TIME YOU LOG ON
SEARCH

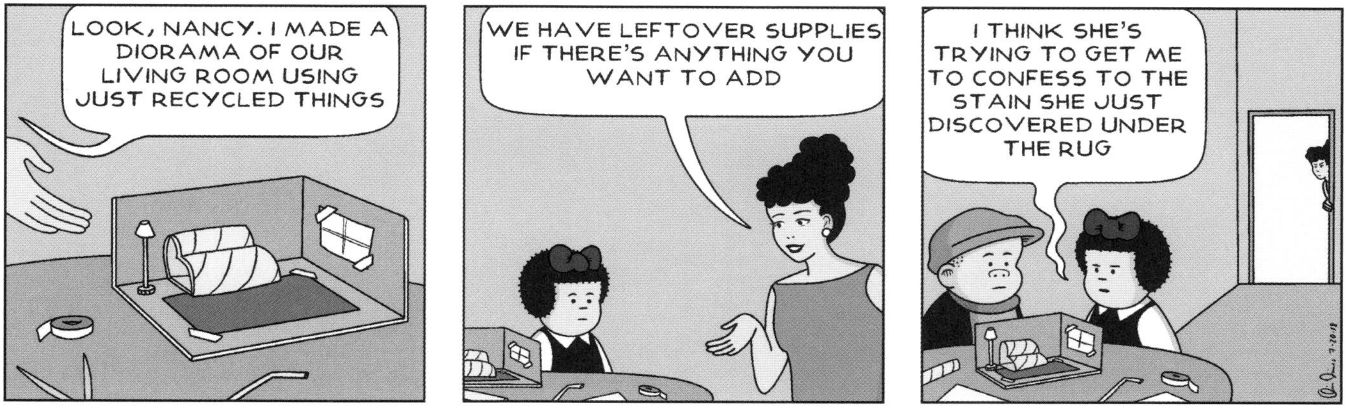
LOOK, NANCY. I MADE A DIORAMA OF OUR LIVING ROOM USING JUST RECYCLED THINGS
WE HAVE LEFTOVER SUPPLIES IF THERE'S ANYTHING YOU WANT TO ADD
I THINK SHE'S TRYING TO GET ME TO CONFESS TO THE STAIN SHE JUST DISCOVERED UNDER THE RUG

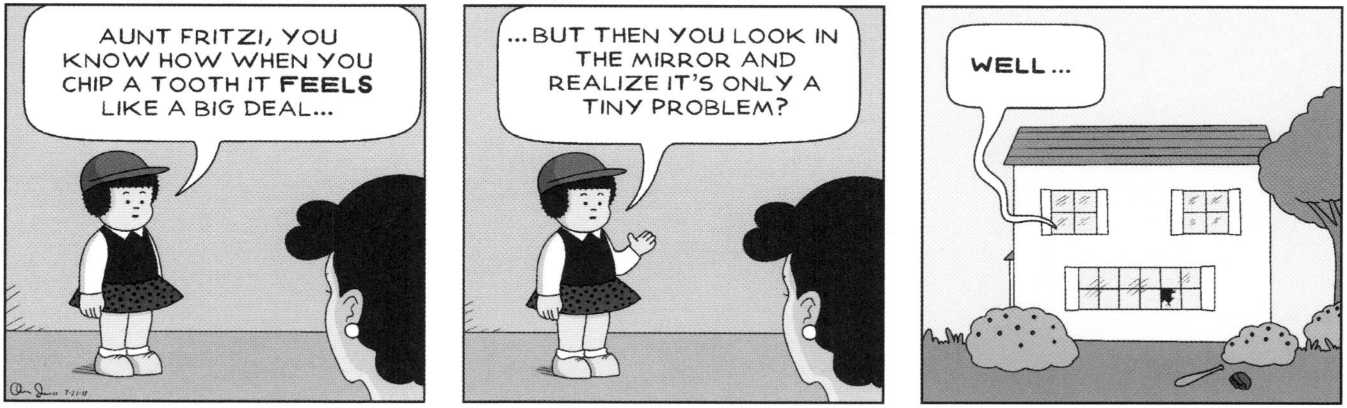
AUNT FRITZI, YOU KNOW HOW WHEN YOU CHIP A TOOTH IT **FEELS** LIKE A BIG DEAL...
...BUT THEN YOU LOOK IN THE MIRROR AND REALIZE IT'S ONLY A TINY PROBLEM?
WELL...

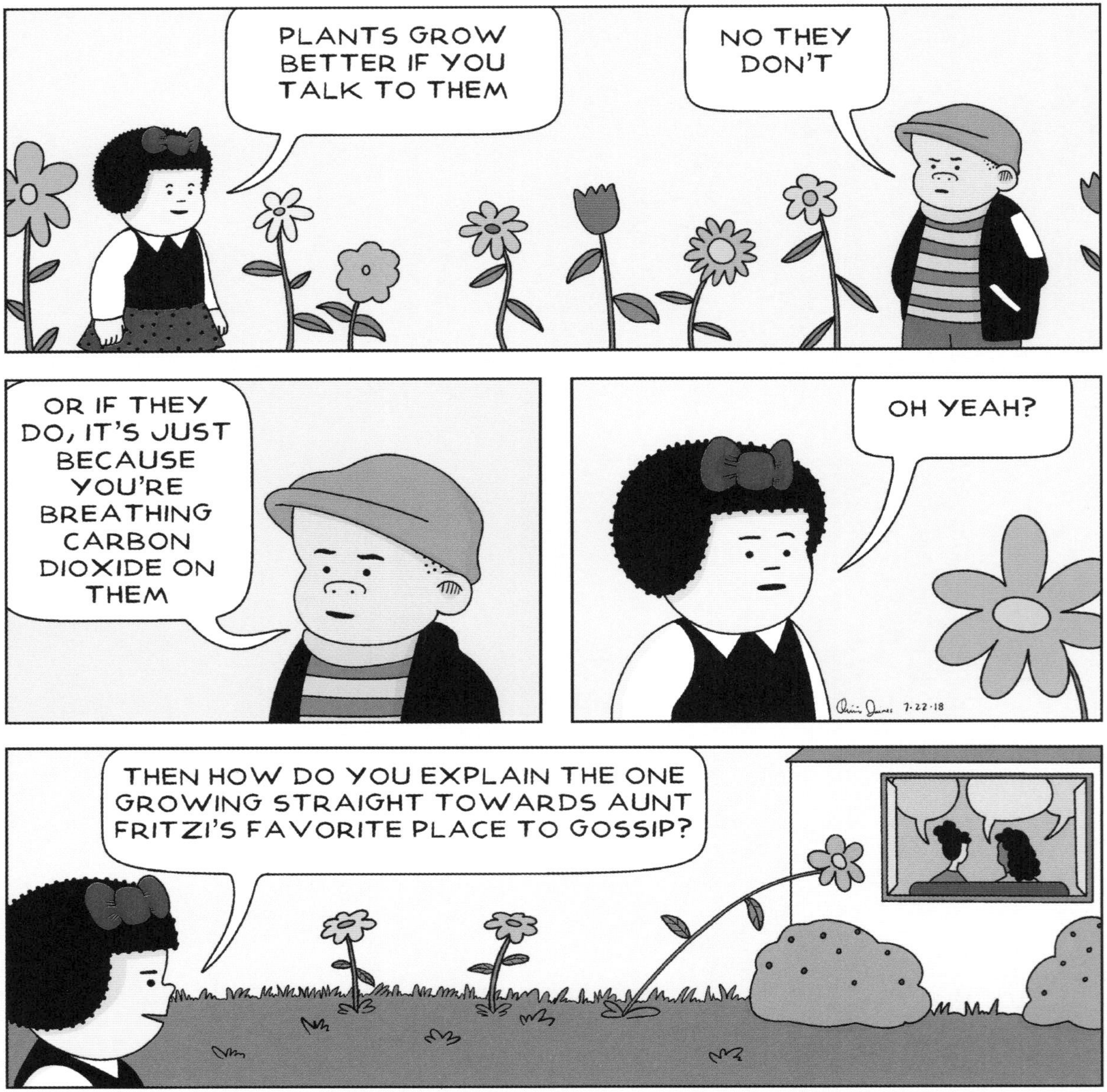
PLANTS GROW BETTER IF YOU TALK TO THEM
NO THEY DON'T
OR IF THEY DO, IT'S JUST BECAUSE YOU'RE BREATHING CARBON DIOXIDE ON THEM
OH YEAH?
7-22-18
THEN HOW DO YOU EXPLAIN THE ONE GROWING STRAIGHT TOWARDS AUNT FRITZI'S FAVORITE PLACE TO GOSSIP?

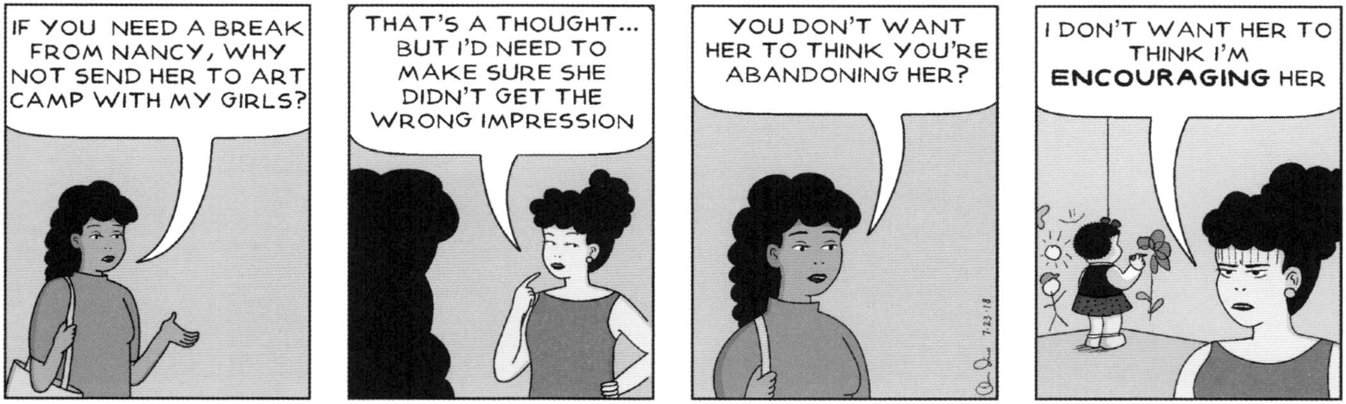
IF YOU NEED A BREAK FROM NANCY, WHY NOT SEND HER TO ART CAMP WITH MY GIRLS?
THAT'S A THOUGHT... BUT I'D NEED TO MAKE SURE SHE DIDN'T GET THE WRONG IMPRESSION
YOU DON'T WANT HER TO THINK YOU'RE ABANDONING HER?
I DON'T WANT HER TO THINK I'M **ENCOURAGING** HER

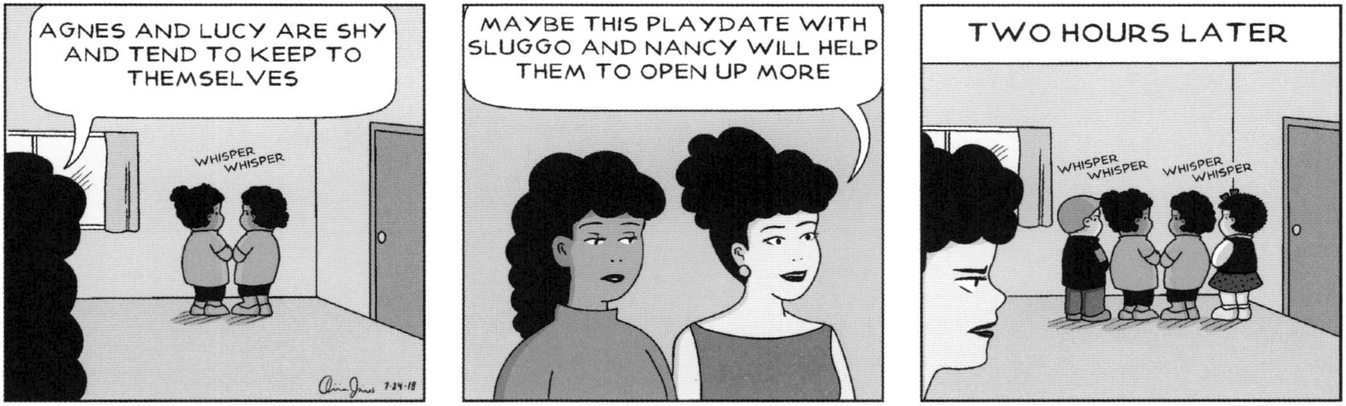
AGNES AND LUCY ARE SHY AND TEND TO KEEP TO THEMSELVES
WHISPER WHISPER
MAYBE THIS PLAYDATE WITH SLUGGO AND NANCY WILL HELP THEM TO OPEN UP MORE
TWO HOURS LATER
WHISPER WHISPER
WHISPER WHISPER

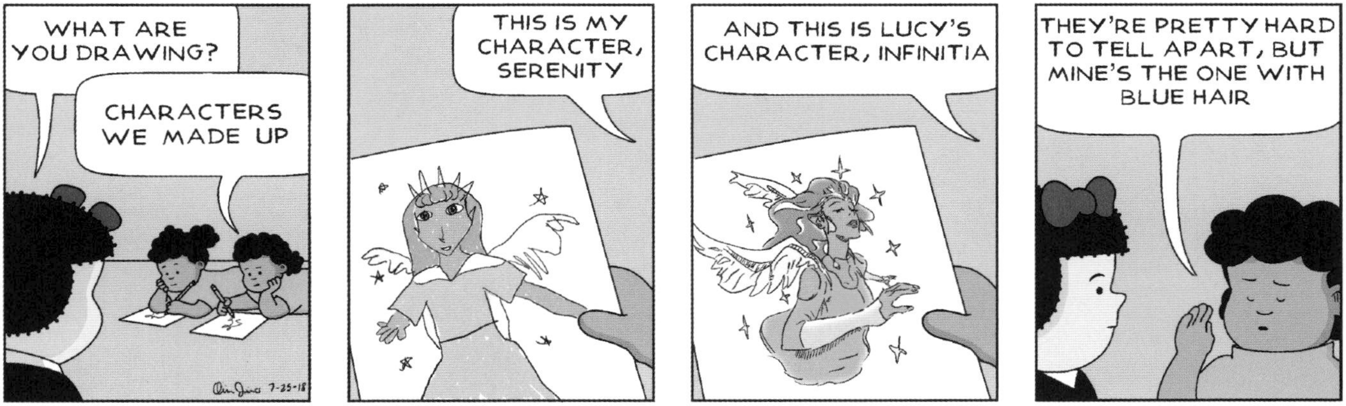
WHAT ARE YOU DRAWING?
CHARACTERS WE MADE UP
THIS IS MY CHARACTER, SERENITY
AND THIS IS LUCY'S CHARACTER, INFINITIA
THEY'RE PRETTY HARD TO TELL APART, BUT MINE'S THE ONE WITH BLUE HAIR

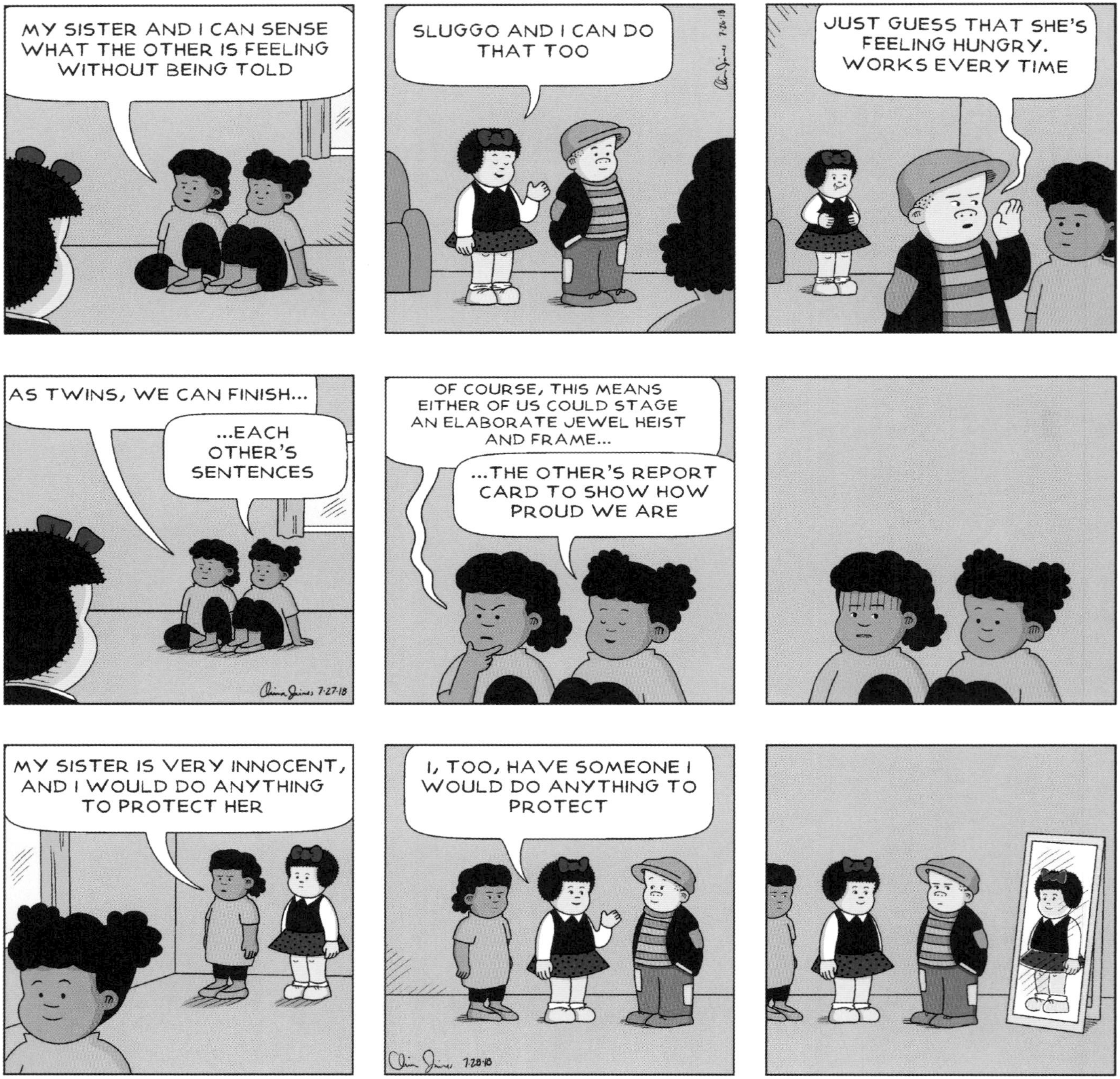
MY SISTER AND I CAN SENSE WHAT THE OTHER IS FEELING WITHOUT BEING TOLD
SLUGGO AND I CAN DO THAT TOO
JUST GUESS THAT SHE'S FEELING HUNGRY. WORKS EVERY TIME
AS TWINS, WE CAN FINISH...
...EACH OTHER'S SENTENCES
OF COURSE, THIS MEANS EITHER OF US COULD STAGE AN ELABORATE JEWEL HEIST AND FRAME...
...THE OTHER'S REPORT CARD TO SHOW HOW PROUD WE ARE
MY SISTER IS VERY INNOCENT, AND I WOULD DO ANYTHING TO PROTECT HER
I, TOO, HAVE SOMEONE I WOULD DO ANYTHING TO PROTECT

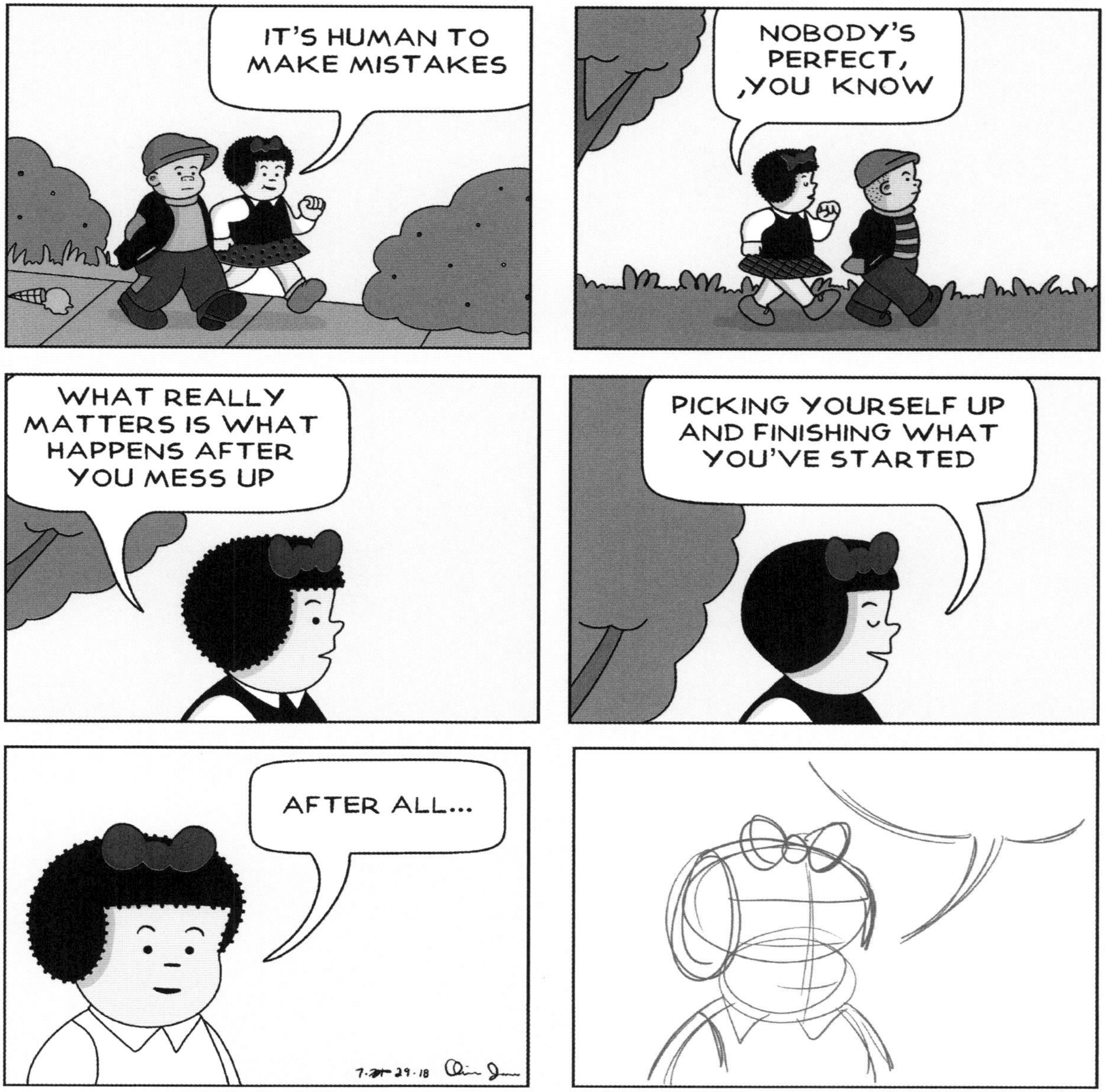
IT'S HUMAN TO MAKE MISTAKES
NOBODY'S PERFECT, ,YOU KNOW
WHAT REALLY MATTERS IS WHAT HAPPENS AFTER YOU MESS UP
PICKING YOURSELF UP AND FINISHING WHAT YOU'VE STARTED
AFTER ALL...

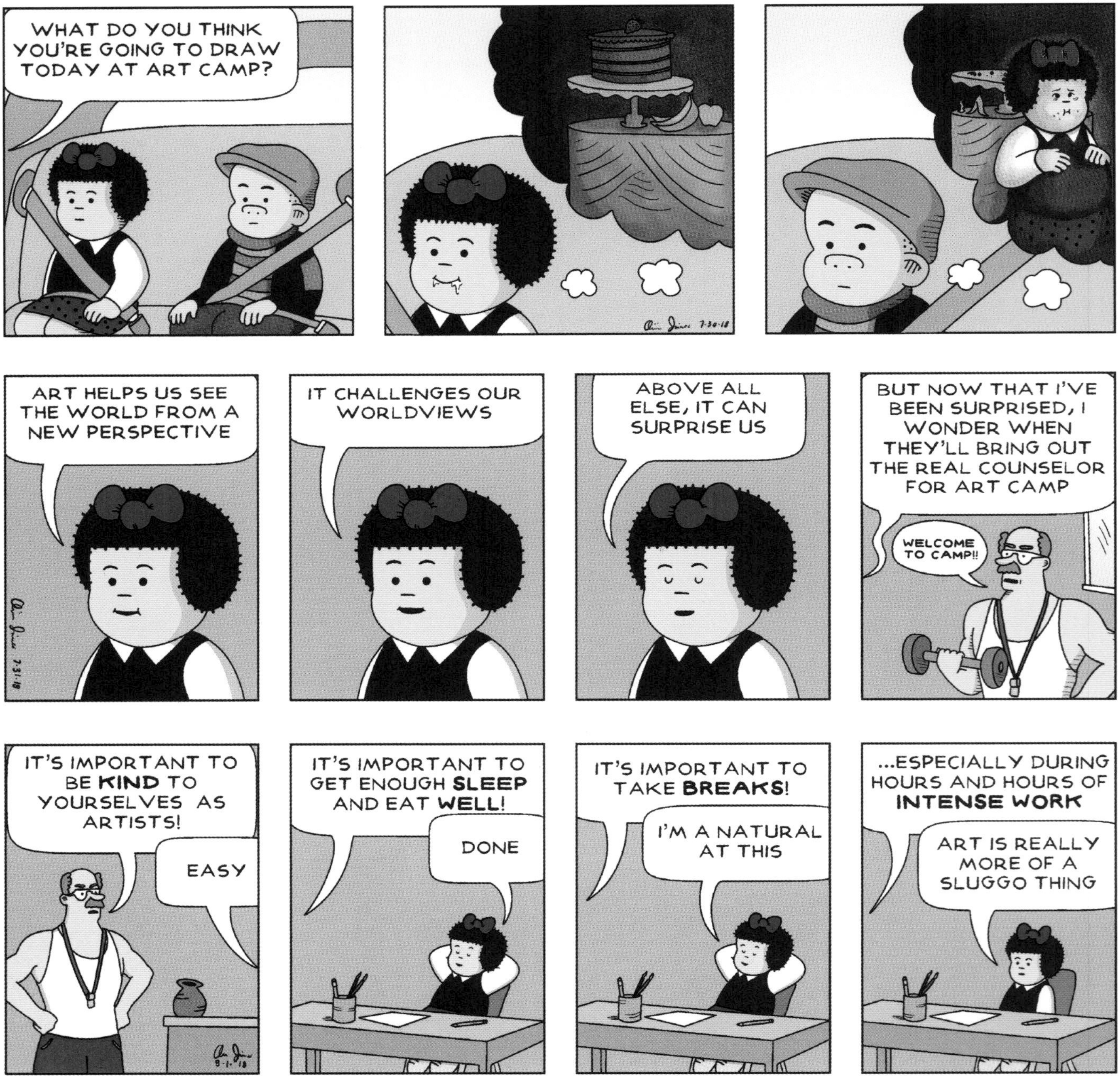

WHAT DO YOU THINK YOU'RE GOING TO DRAW TODAY AT ART CAMP?
ART HELPS US SEE THE WORLD FROM A NEW PERSPECTIVE
IT CHALLENGES OUR WORLDVIEWS
ABOVE ALL ELSE, IT CAN SURPRISE US
BUT NOW THAT I'VE BEEN SURPRISED, I WONDER WHEN THEY'LL BRING OUT THE REAL COUNSELOR FOR ART CAMP
WELCOME TO CAMP!!
IT'S IMPORTANT TO BE KIND TO YOURSELVES AS ARTISTS!
EASY
IT'S IMPORTANT TO GET ENOUGH SLEEP AND EAT WELL!
DONE
IT'S IMPORTANT TO TAKE BREAKS!
I'M A NATURAL AT THIS
...ESPECIALLY DURING HOURS AND HOURS OF INTENSE WORK
ART IS REALLY MORE OF A SLUGGO THING

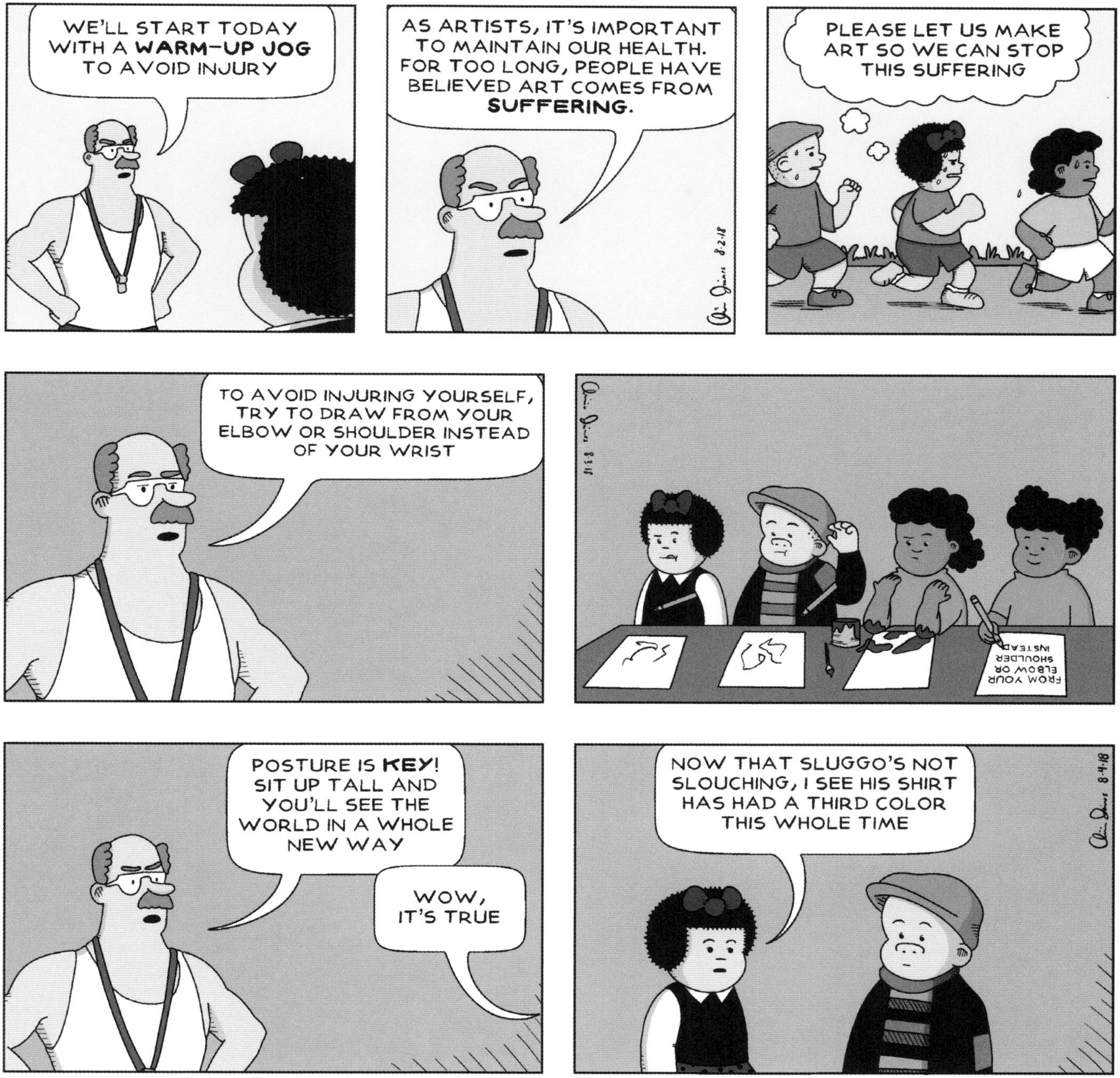
WE'LL START TODAY WITH A **WARM-UP JOG** TO AVOID INJURY
AS ARTISTS, IT'S IMPORTANT TO MAINTAIN OUR HEALTH. FOR TOO LONG, PEOPLE HAVE BELIEVED ART COMES FROM **SUFFERING**.
8-2-18
PLEASE LET US MAKE ART SO WE CAN STOP THIS SUFFERING
TO AVOID INJURING YOURSELF, TRY TO DRAW FROM YOUR ELBOW OR SHOULDER INSTEAD OF YOUR WRIST
8-3-18
FROM YOUR ELBOW OR SHOULDER INSTEAD
POSTURE IS **KEY**! SIT UP TALL AND YOU'LL SEE THE WORLD IN A WHOLE NEW WAY
WOW, IT'S TRUE
NOW THAT SLUGGO'S NOT SLOUCHING, I SEE HIS SHIRT HAS HAD A THIRD COLOR THIS WHOLE TIME
8-4-18

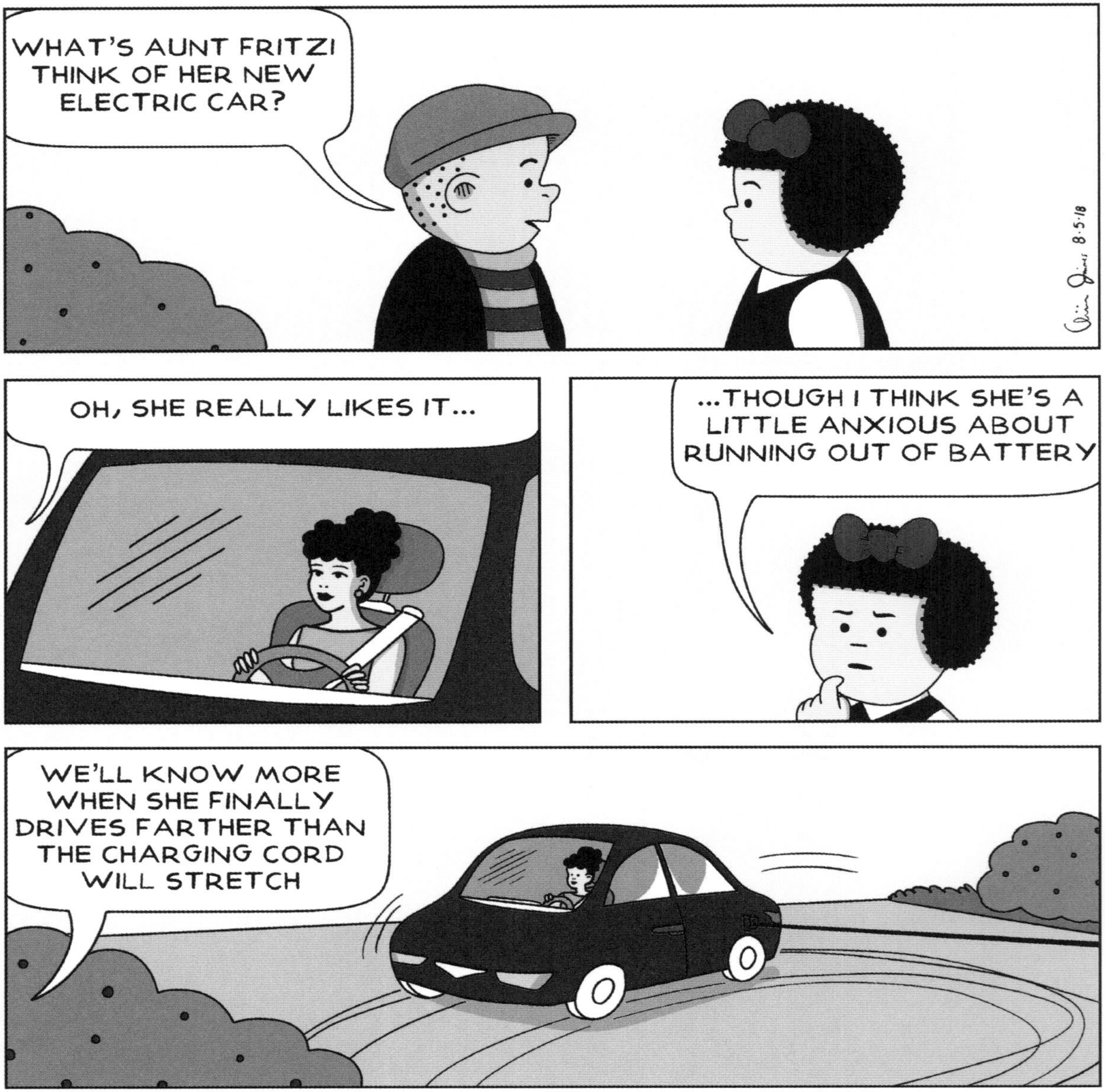
WHAT'S AUNT FRITZI THINK OF HER NEW ELECTRIC CAR?
OH, SHE REALLY LIKES IT...
...THOUGH I THINK SHE'S A LITTLE ANXIOUS ABOUT RUNNING OUT OF BATTERY
WE'LL KNOW MORE WHEN SHE FINALLY DRIVES FARTHER THAN THE CHARGING CORD WILL STRETCH

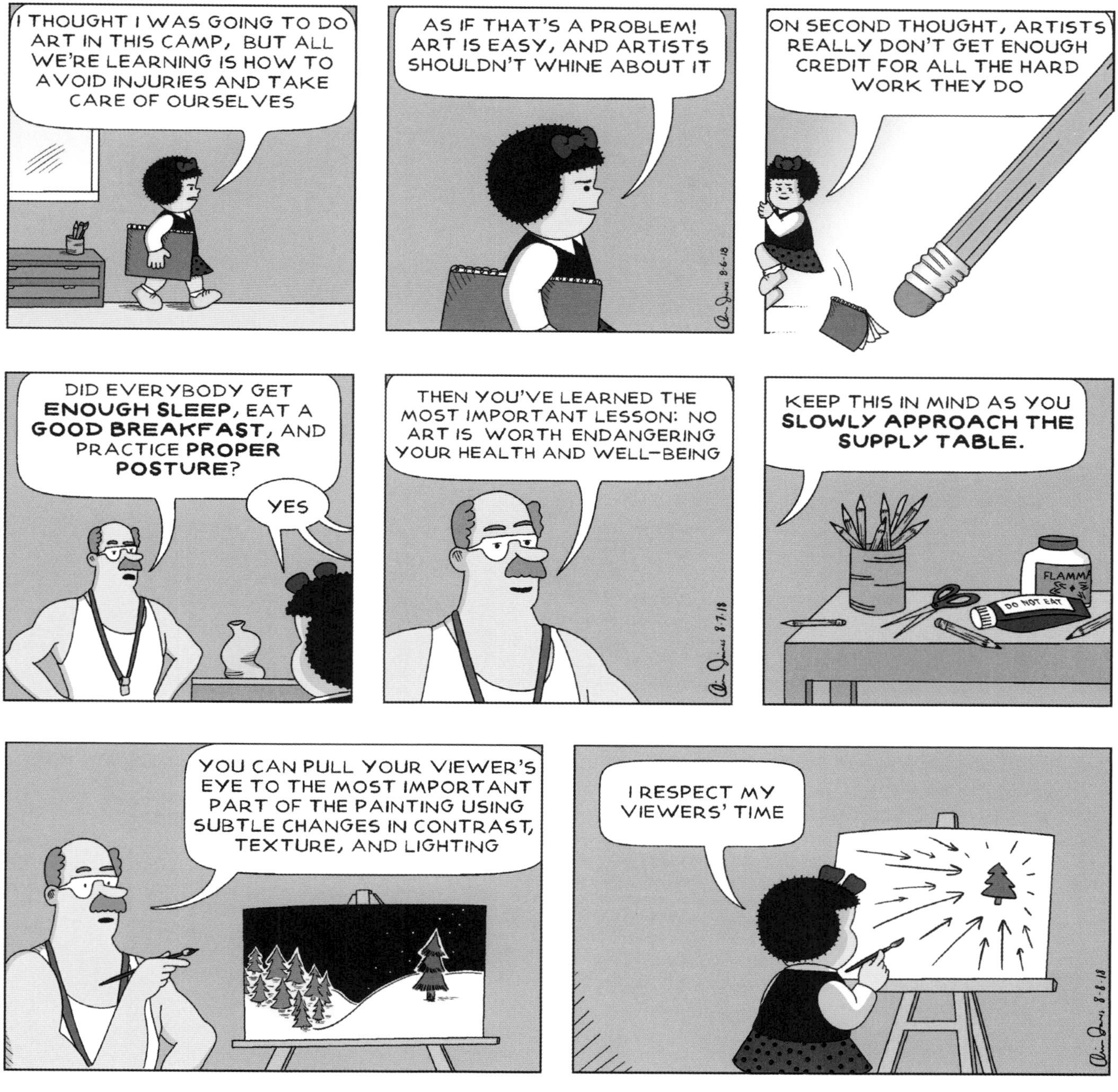
I THOUGHT I WAS GOING TO DO ART IN THIS CAMP, BUT ALL WE'RE LEARNING IS HOW TO AVOID INJURIES AND TAKE CARE OF OURSELVES
AS IF THAT'S A PROBLEM! ART IS EASY, AND ARTISTS SHOULDN'T WHINE ABOUT IT
ON SECOND THOUGHT, ARTISTS REALLY DON'T GET ENOUGH CREDIT FOR ALL THE HARD WORK THEY DO
DID EVERYBODY GET ENOUGH SLEEP, EAT A GOOD BREAKFAST, AND PRACTICE PROPER POSTURE?
YES
THEN YOU'VE LEARNED THE MOST IMPORTANT LESSON: NO ART IS WORTH ENDANGERING YOUR HEALTH AND WELL-BEING
KEEP THIS IN MIND AS YOU SLOWLY APPROACH THE SUPPLY TABLE.
FLAMMA
DO NOT EAT
YOU CAN PULL YOUR VIEWER'S EYE TO THE MOST IMPORTANT PART OF THE PAINTING USING SUBTLE CHANGES IN CONTRAST, TEXTURE, AND LIGHTING
I RESPECT MY VIEWERS' TIME

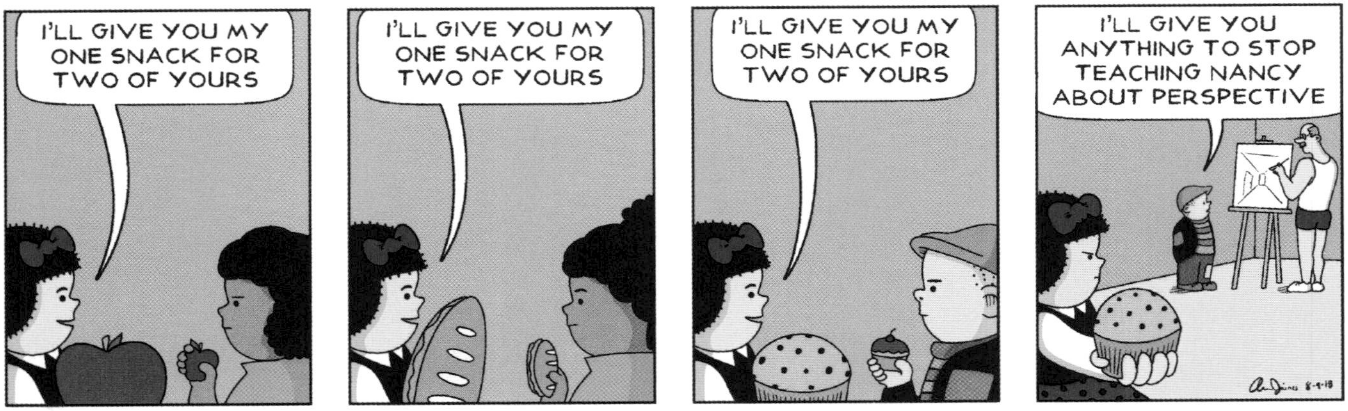
I'LL GIVE YOU MY ONE SNACK FOR TWO OF YOURS
I'LL GIVE YOU MY ONE SNACK FOR TWO OF YOURS
I'LL GIVE YOU MY ONE SNACK FOR TWO OF YOURS
I'LL GIVE YOU ANYTHING TO STOP TEACHING NANCY ABOUT PERSPECTIVE

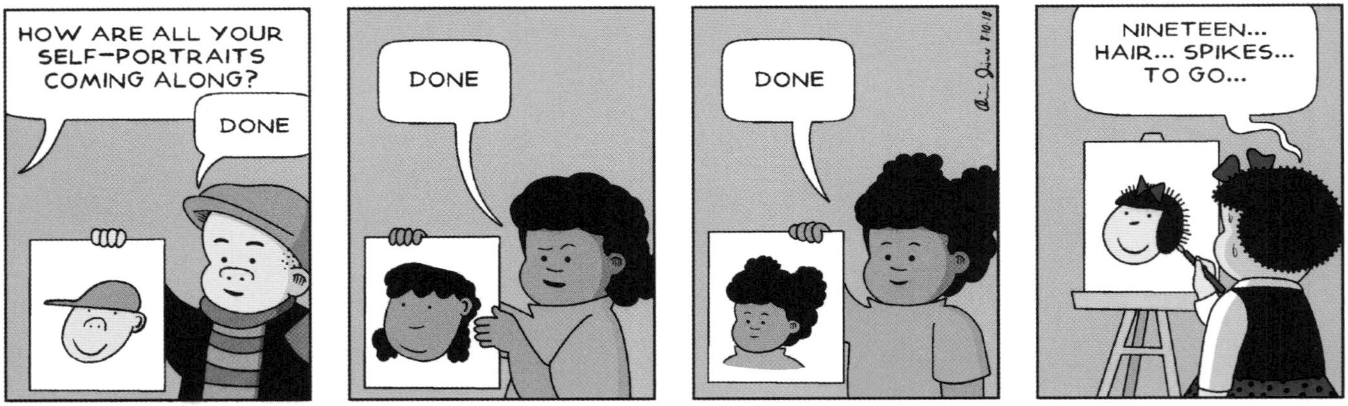
HOW ARE ALL YOUR SELF–PORTRAITS COMING ALONG?
DONE
DONE
DONE
NINETEEN... HAIR... SPIKES... TO GO...

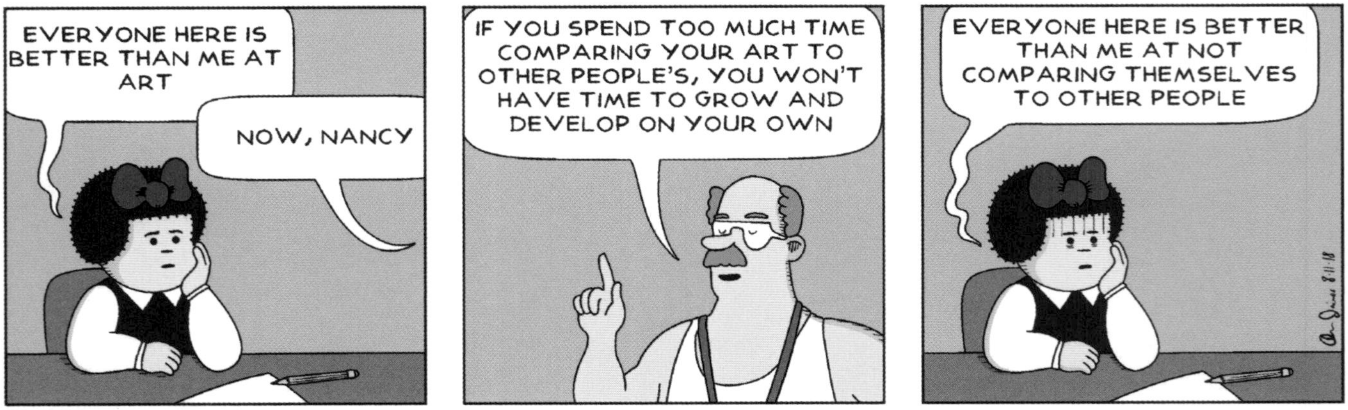
EVERYONE HERE IS BETTER THAN ME AT ART
NOW, NANCY
IF YOU SPEND TOO MUCH TIME COMPARING YOUR ART TO OTHER PEOPLE'S, YOU WON'T HAVE TIME TO GROW AND DEVELOP ON YOUR OWN
EVERYONE HERE IS BETTER THAN ME AT NOT COMPARING THEMSELVES TO OTHER PEOPLE

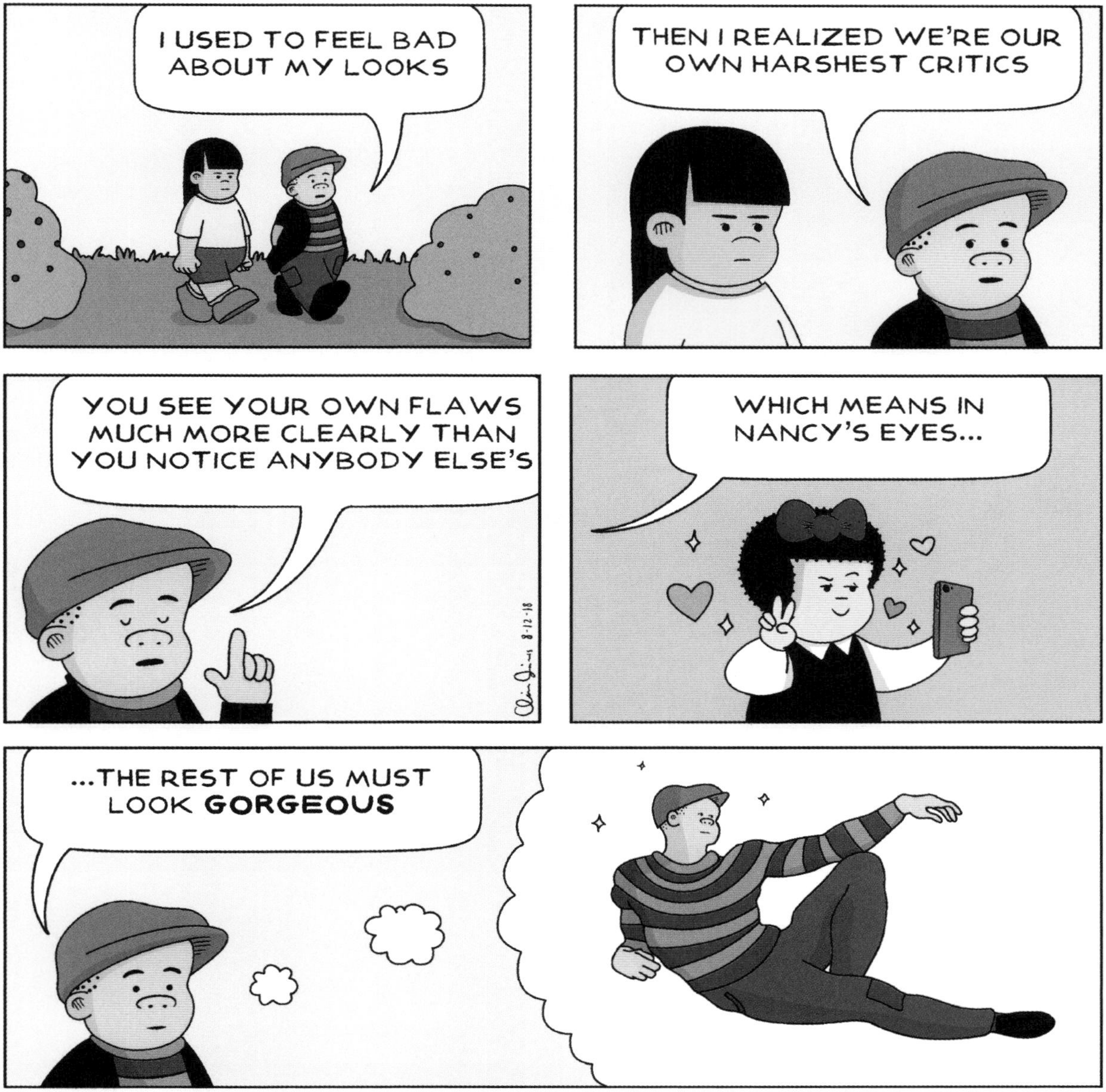
I USED TO FEEL BAD ABOUT MY LOOKS
THEN I REALIZED WE'RE OUR OWN HARSHEST CRITICS
YOU SEE YOUR OWN FLAWS MUCH MORE CLEARLY THAN YOU NOTICE ANYBODY ELSE'S
8-12-18
WHICH MEANS IN NANCY'S EYES...
...THE REST OF US MUST LOOK **GORGEOUS**

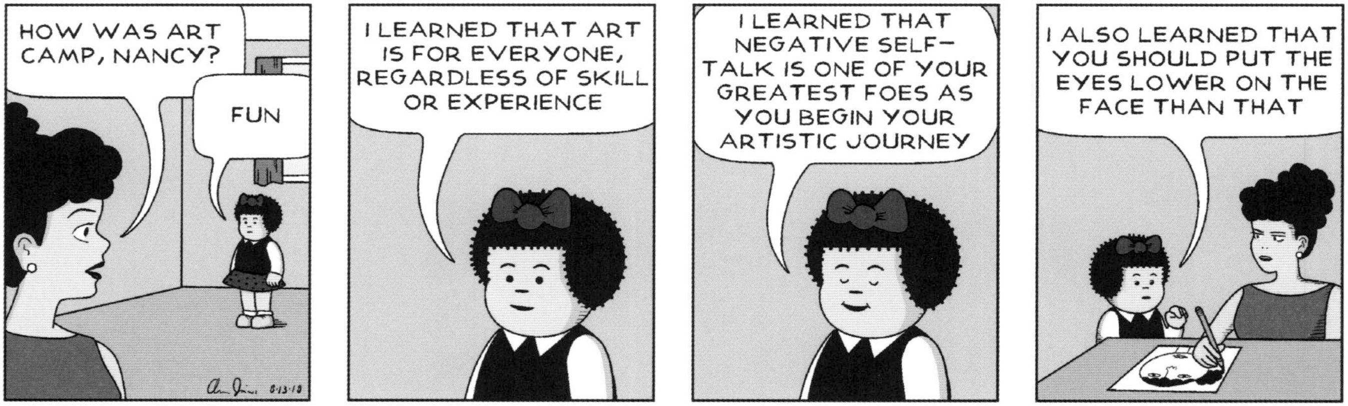
HOW WAS ART CAMP, NANCY?
FUN
I LEARNED THAT ART IS FOR EVERYONE, REGARDLESS OF SKILL OR EXPERIENCE
I LEARNED THAT NEGATIVE SELF-TALK IS ONE OF YOUR GREATEST FOES AS YOU BEGIN YOUR ARTISTIC JOURNEY
I ALSO LEARNED THAT YOU SHOULD PUT THE EYES LOWER ON THE FACE THAN THAT

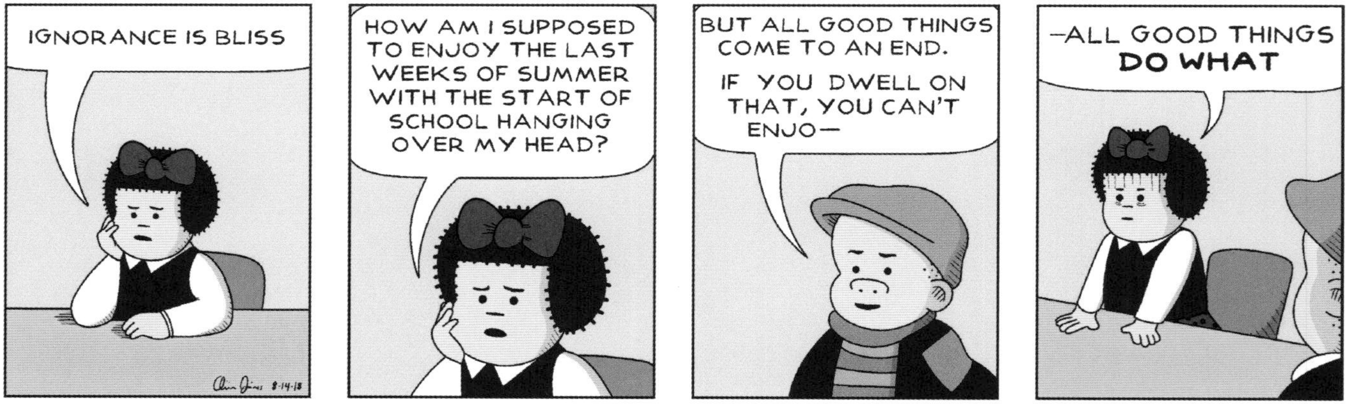
IGNORANCE IS BLISS
HOW AM I SUPPOSED TO ENJOY THE LAST WEEKS OF SUMMER WITH THE START OF SCHOOL HANGING OVER MY HEAD?
BUT ALL GOOD THINGS COME TO AN END.
IF YOU DWELL ON THAT, YOU CAN'T ENJO—
—ALL GOOD THINGS **DO WHAT**

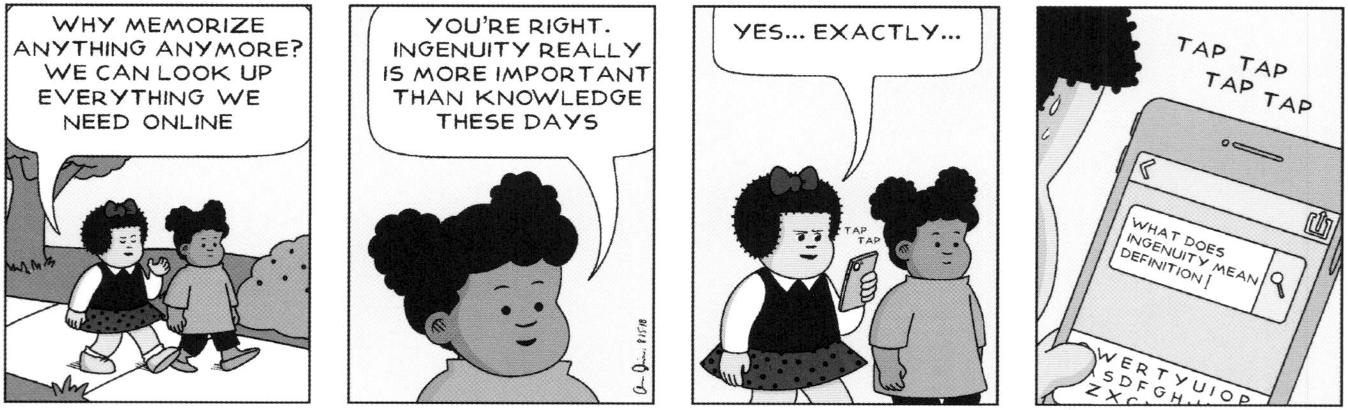
WHY MEMORIZE ANYTHING ANYMORE? WE CAN LOOK UP EVERYTHING WE NEED ONLINE
YOU'RE RIGHT. INGENUITY REALLY IS MORE IMPORTANT THAN KNOWLEDGE THESE DAYS
YES... EXACTLY...
TAP TAP
TAP TAP TAP TAP
WHAT DOES INGENUITY MEAN DEFINITION!

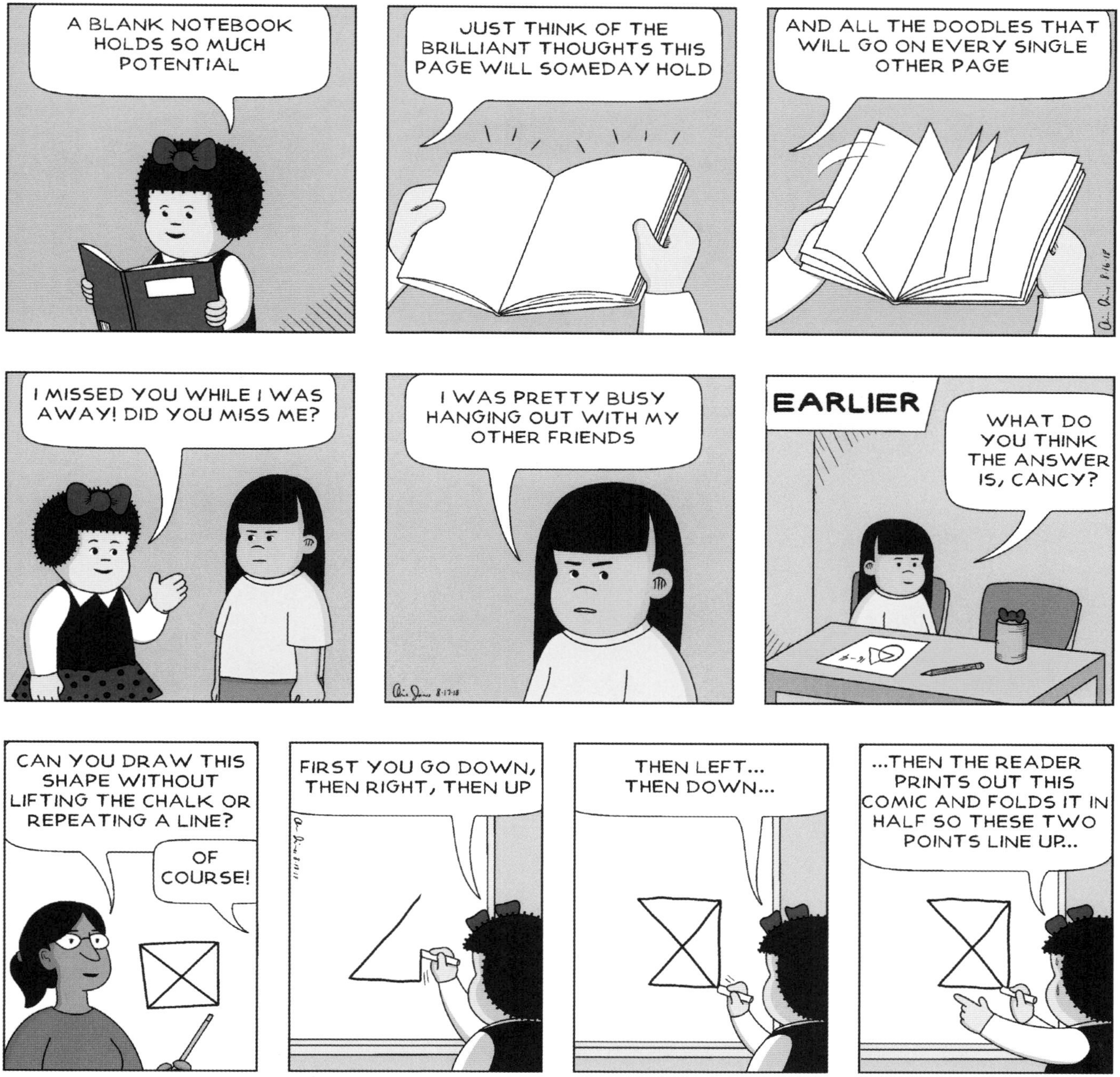

A BLANK NOTEBOOK HOLDS SO MUCH POTENTIAL
JUST THINK OF THE BRILLIANT THOUGHTS THIS PAGE WILL SOMEDAY HOLD
AND ALL THE DOODLES THAT WILL GO ON EVERY SINGLE OTHER PAGE
I MISSED YOU WHILE I WAS AWAY! DID YOU MISS ME?
I WAS PRETTY BUSY HANGING OUT WITH MY OTHER FRIENDS
EARLIER
WHAT DO YOU THINK THE ANSWER IS, CANCY?
CAN YOU DRAW THIS SHAPE WITHOUT LIFTING THE CHALK OR REPEATING A LINE?
OF COURSE!
FIRST YOU GO DOWN, THEN RIGHT, THEN UP
THEN LEFT... THEN DOWN...
...THEN THE READER PRINTS OUT THIS COMIC AND FOLDS IT IN HALF SO THESE TWO POINTS LINE UP...

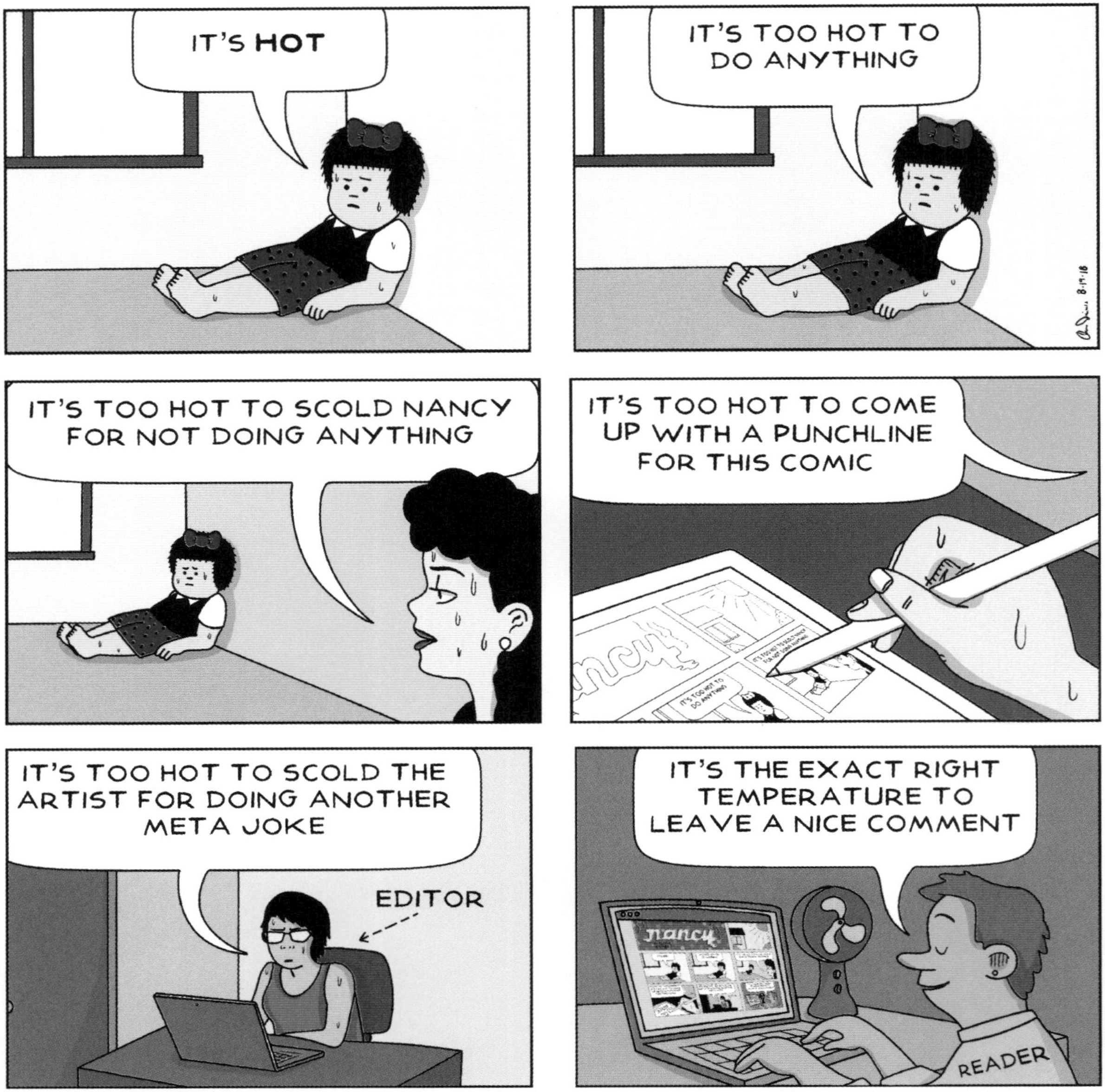
IT'S HOT
IT'S TOO HOT TO DO ANYTHING
IT'S TOO HOT TO SCOLD NANCY FOR NOT DOING ANYTHING
IT'S TOO HOT TO COME UP WITH A PUNCHLINE FOR THIS COMIC
IT'S TOO HOT TO SCOLD THE ARTIST FOR DOING ANOTHER META JOKE
EDITOR
IT'S THE EXACT RIGHT TEMPERATURE TO LEAVE A NICE COMMENT
READER

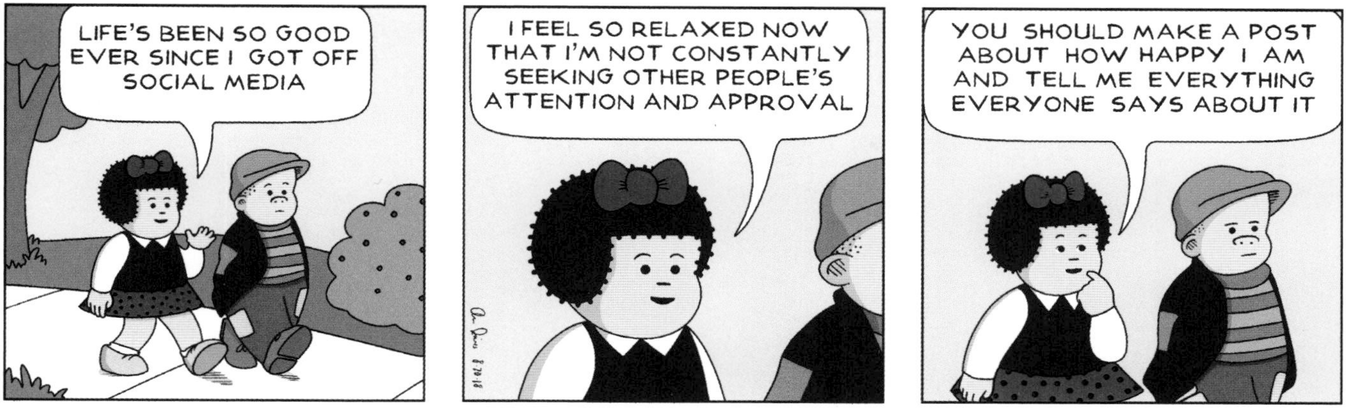
LIFE'S BEEN SO GOOD EVER SINCE I GOT OFF SOCIAL MEDIA
I FEEL SO RELAXED NOW THAT I'M NOT CONSTANTLY SEEKING OTHER PEOPLE'S ATTENTION AND APPROVAL
YOU SHOULD MAKE A POST ABOUT HOW HAPPY I AM AND TELL ME EVERYTHING EVERYONE SAYS ABOUT IT

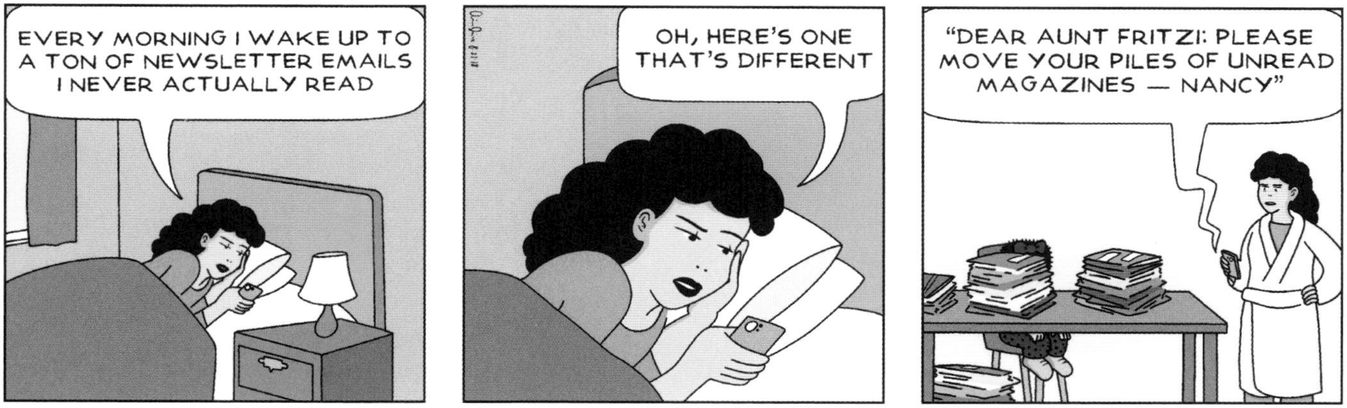
EVERY MORNING I WAKE UP TO A TON OF NEWSLETTER EMAILS I NEVER ACTUALLY READ
OH, HERE'S ONE THAT'S DIFFERENT
"DEAR AUNT FRITZI: PLEASE MOVE YOUR PILES OF UNREAD MAGAZINES — NANCY"

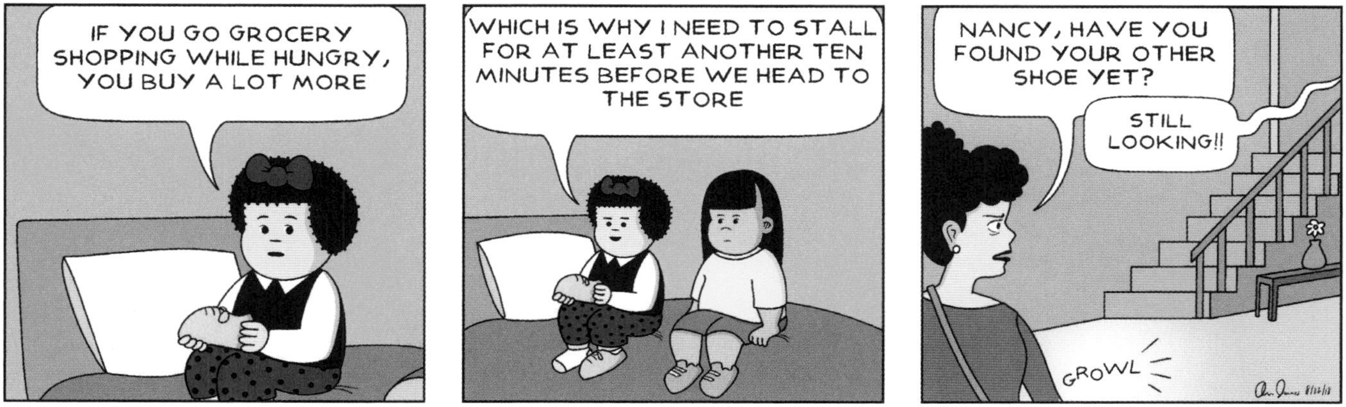
IF YOU GO GROCERY SHOPPING WHILE HUNGRY, YOU BUY A LOT MORE
WHICH IS WHY I NEED TO STALL FOR AT LEAST ANOTHER TEN MINUTES BEFORE WE HEAD TO THE STORE
NANCY, HAVE YOU FOUND YOUR OTHER SHOE YET?
STILL LOOKING!!
GROWL

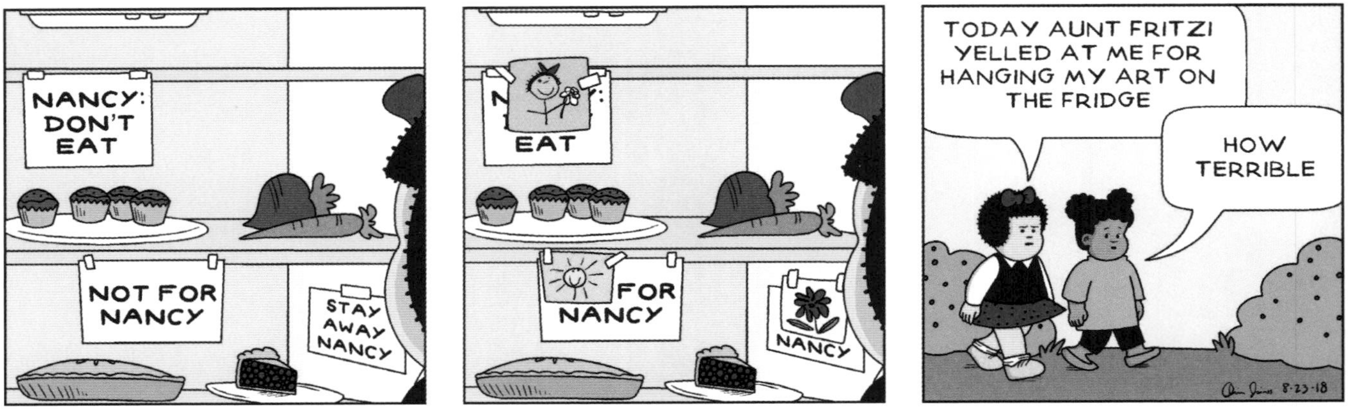
NANCY: DON'T EAT
NOT FOR NANCY
STAY AWAY NANCY
EAT
FOR NANCY
NANCY
TODAY AUNT FRITZI YELLED AT ME FOR HANGING MY ART ON THE FRIDGE
HOW TERRIBLE
8-23-18

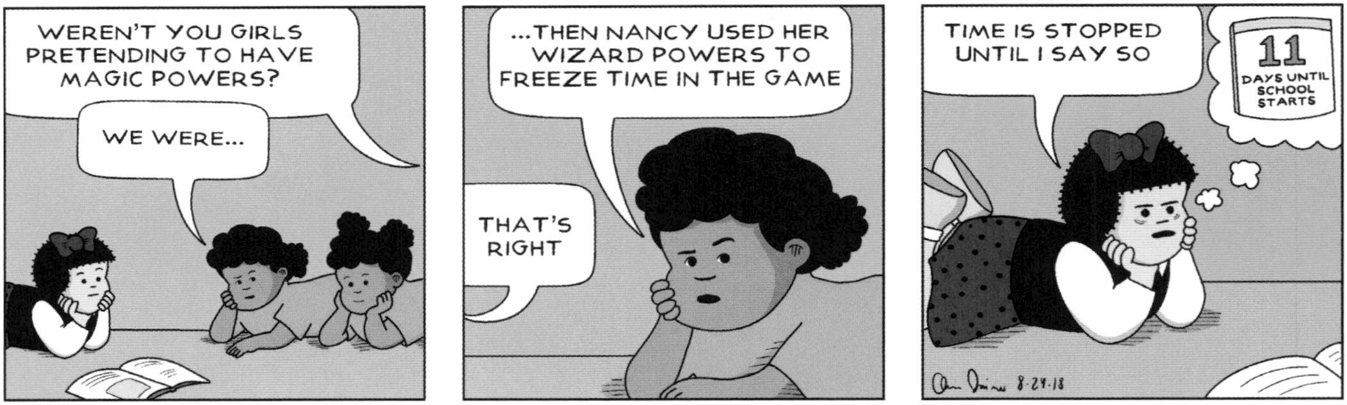
WEREN'T YOU GIRLS PRETENDING TO HAVE MAGIC POWERS?
WE WERE...
...THEN NANCY USED HER WIZARD POWERS TO FREEZE TIME IN THE GAME
THAT'S RIGHT
TIME IS STOPPED UNTIL I SAY SO
11
DAYS UNTIL SCHOOL STARTS
8-24-18

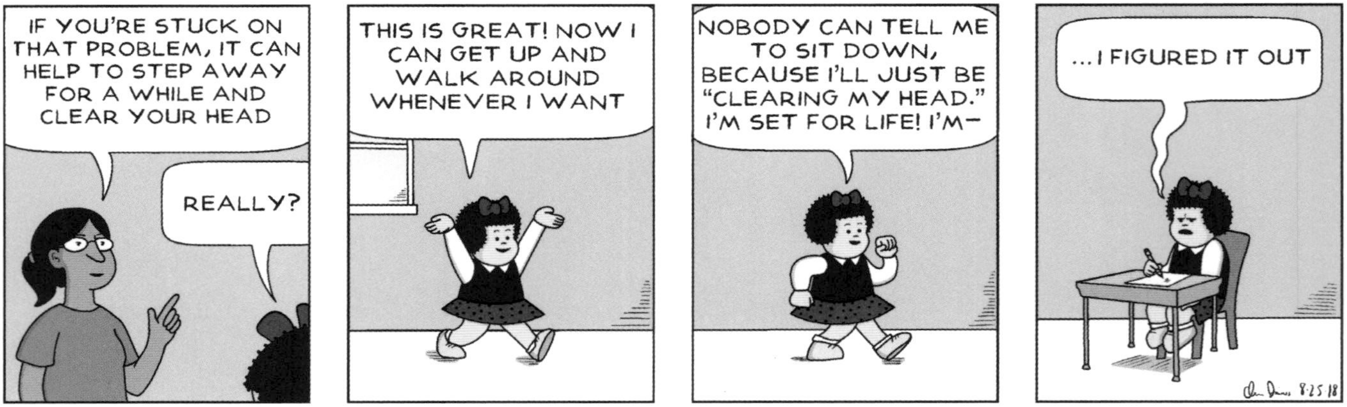
IF YOU'RE STUCK ON THAT PROBLEM, IT CAN HELP TO STEP AWAY FOR A WHILE AND CLEAR YOUR HEAD
REALLY?
THIS IS GREAT! NOW I CAN GET UP AND WALK AROUND WHENEVER I WANT
NOBODY CAN TELL ME TO SIT DOWN, BECAUSE I'LL JUST BE "CLEARING MY HEAD." I'M SET FOR LIFE! I'M—
...I FIGURED IT OUT
8-25-18

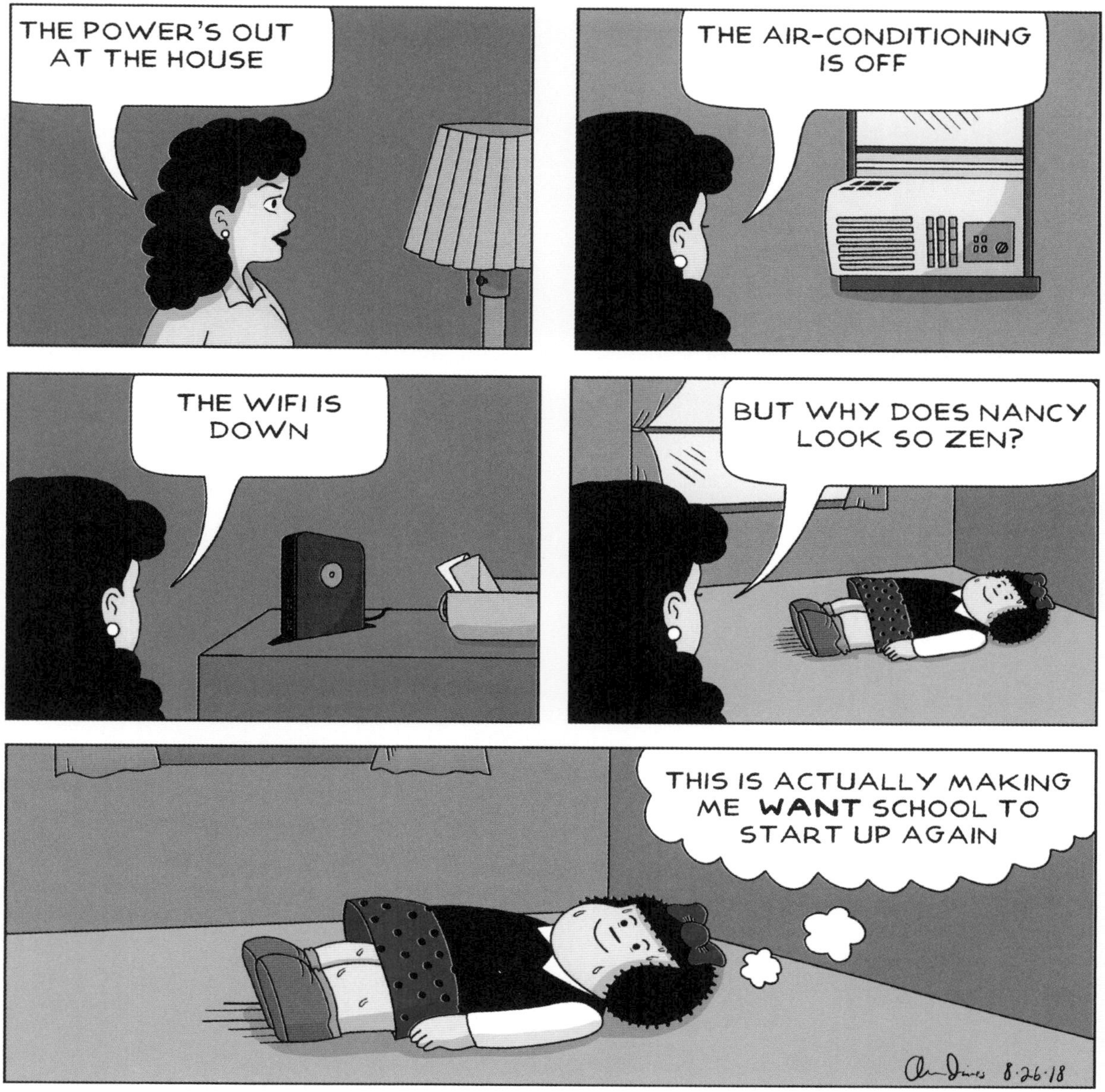
THE POWER'S OUT AT THE HOUSE
THE AIR-CONDITIONING IS OFF
THE WIFI IS DOWN
BUT WHY DOES NANCY LOOK SO ZEN?
THIS IS ACTUALLY MAKING ME **WANT** SCHOOL TO START UP AGAIN
8·26·18

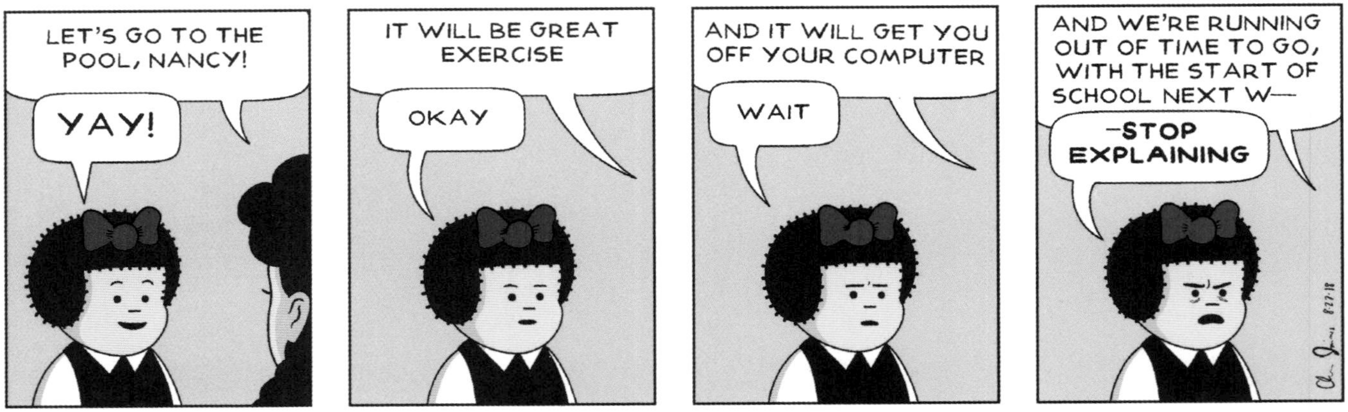

LET'S GO TO THE POOL, NANCY!
YAY!
IT WILL BE GREAT EXERCISE
OKAY
AND IT WILL GET YOU OFF YOUR COMPUTER
WAIT
AND WE'RE RUNNING OUT OF TIME TO GO, WITH THE START OF SCHOOL NEXT W—
—STOP EXPLAINING

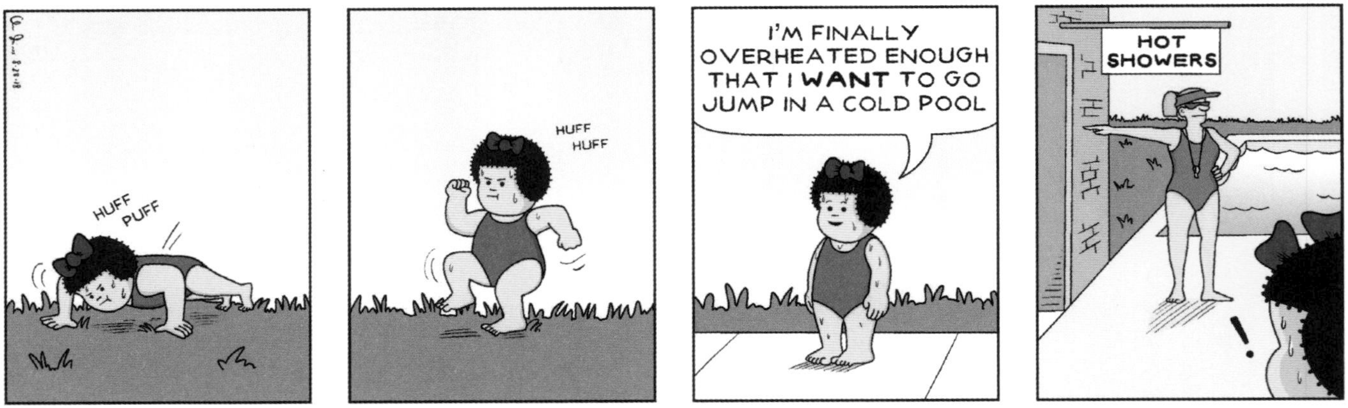

HUFF PUFF
HUFF HUFF
I'M FINALLY OVERHEATED ENOUGH THAT I WANT TO GO JUMP IN A COLD POOL
HOT SHOWERS

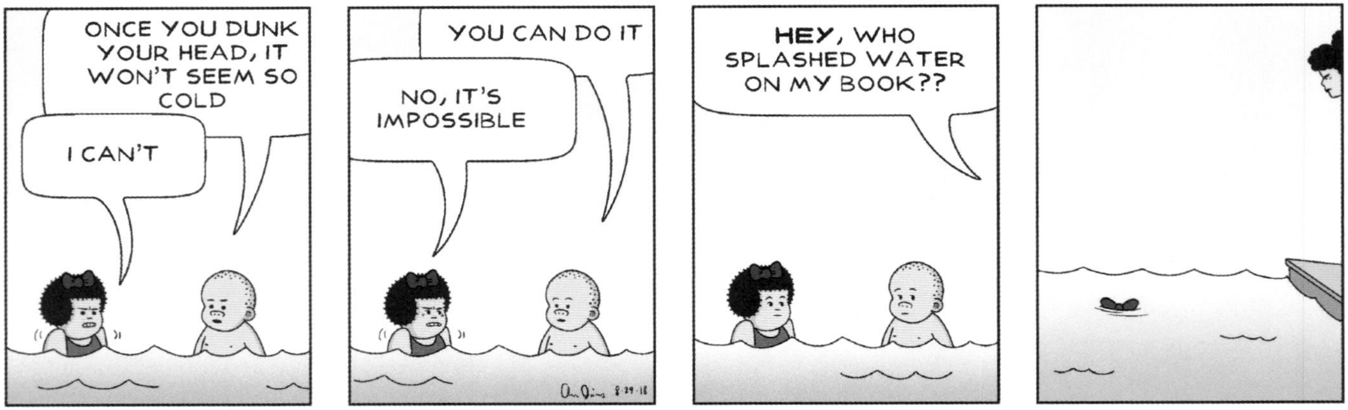

ONCE YOU DUNK YOUR HEAD, IT WON'T SEEM SO COLD
I CAN'T
YOU CAN DO IT
NO, IT'S IMPOSSIBLE
HEY, WHO SPLASHED WATER ON MY BOOK??

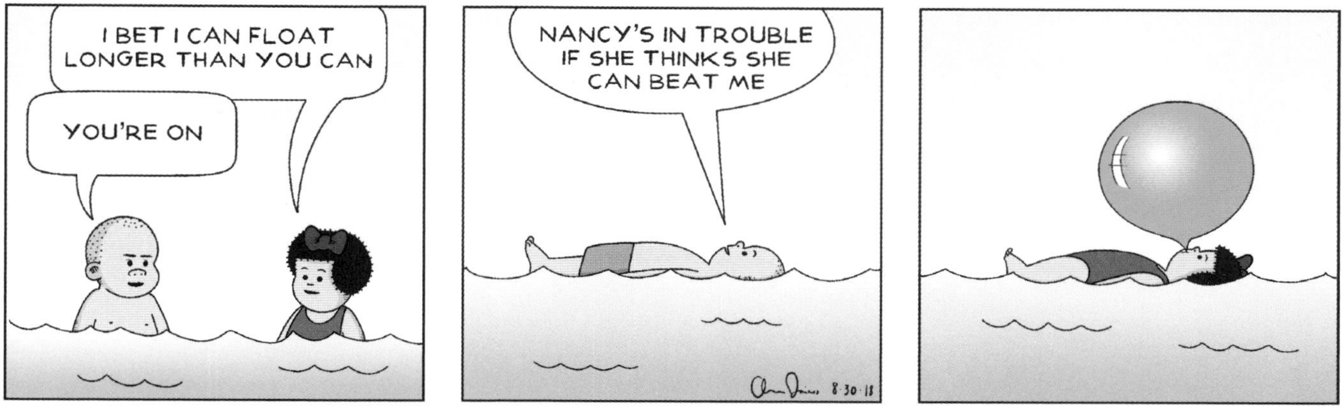
I BET I CAN FLOAT LONGER THAN YOU CAN
YOU'RE ON
NANCY'S IN TROUBLE IF SHE THINKS SHE CAN BEAT ME

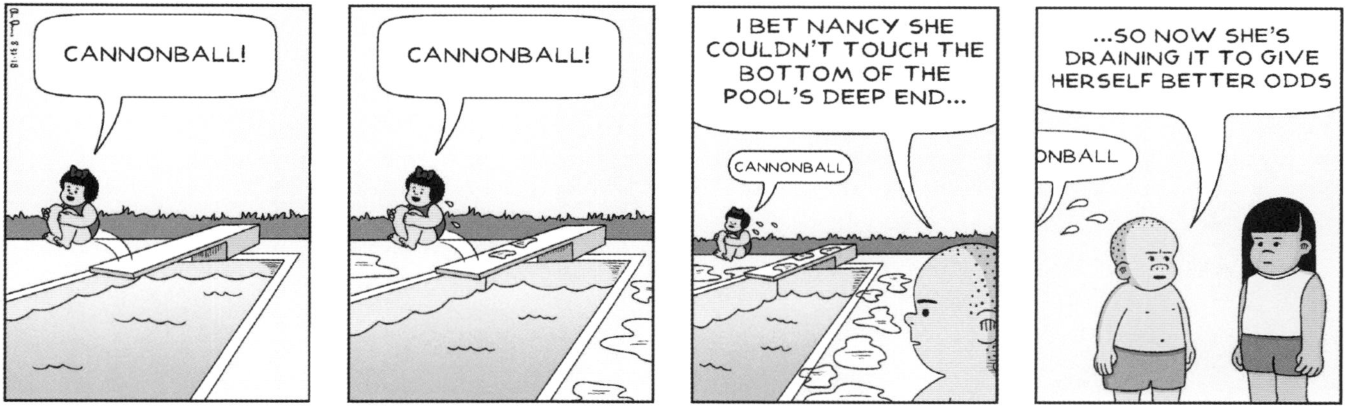
CANNONBALL!
CANNONBALL!
I BET NANCY SHE COULDN'T TOUCH THE BOTTOM OF THE POOL'S DEEP END...
CANNONBALL
...SO NOW SHE'S DRAINING IT TO GIVE HERSELF BETTER ODDS
ONBALL

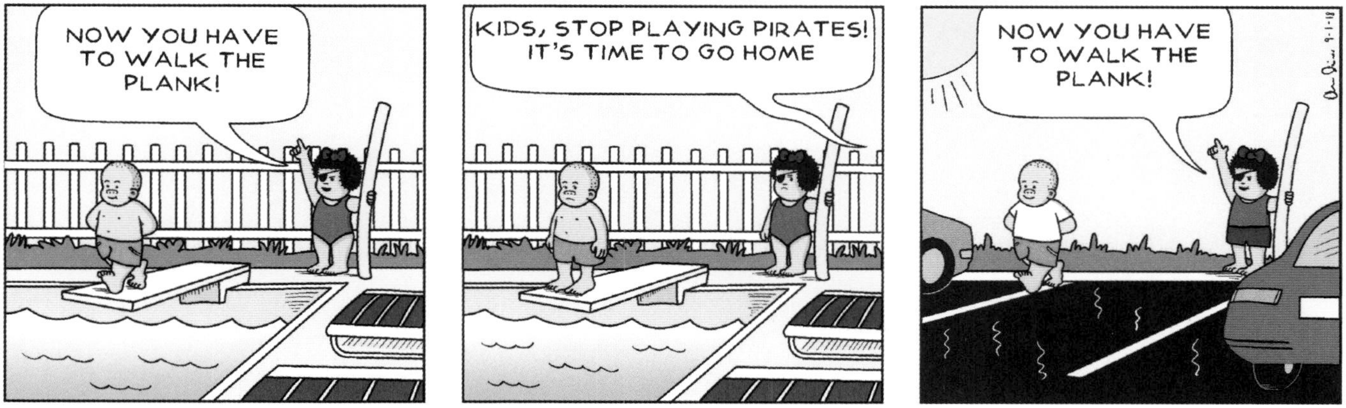
NOW YOU HAVE TO WALK THE PLANK!
KIDS, STOP PLAYING PIRATES! IT'S TIME TO GO HOME
NOW YOU HAVE TO WALK THE PLANK!

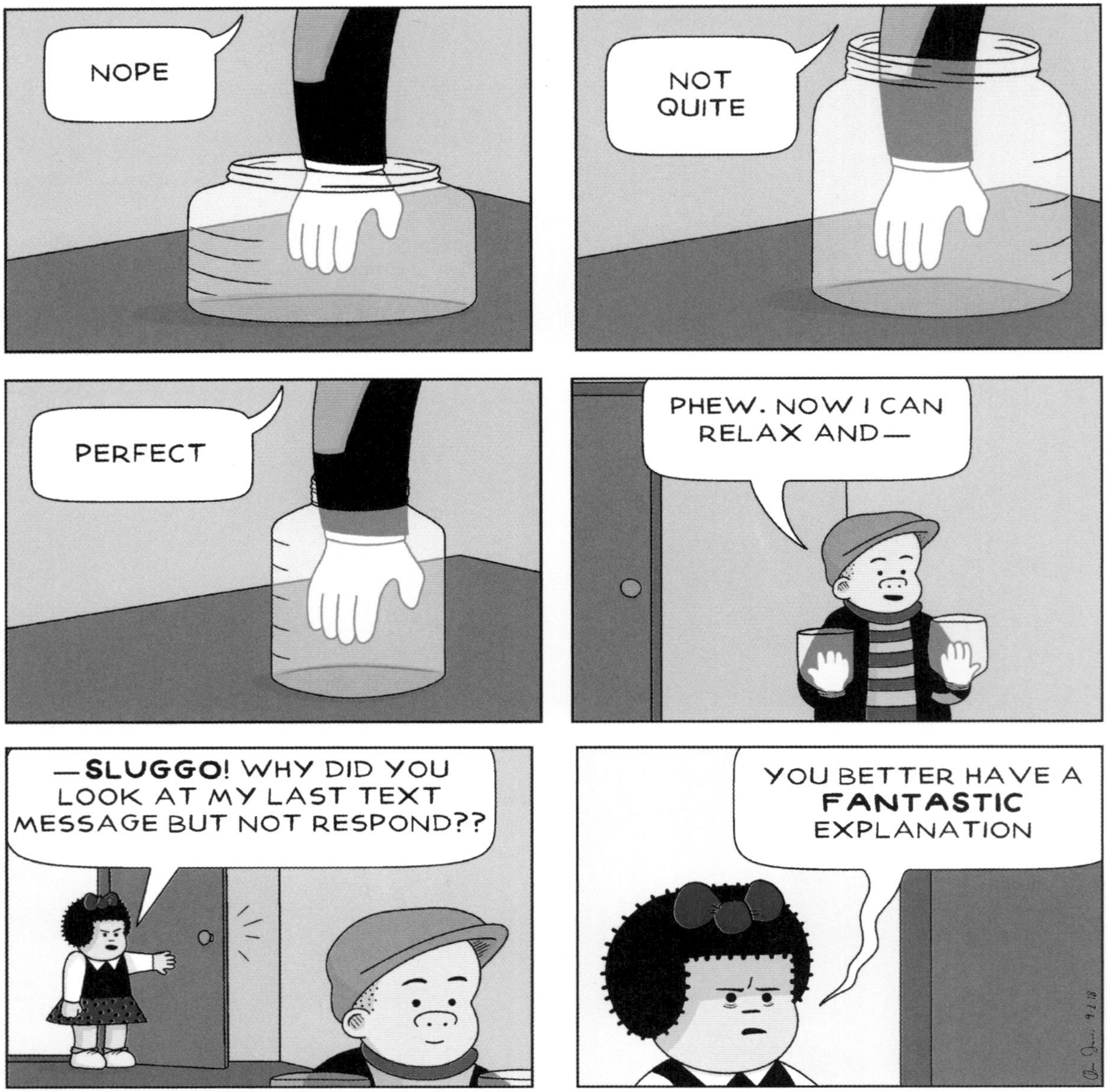

NOPE
NOT QUITE
PERFECT
PHEW. NOW I CAN RELAX AND—
—SLUGGO! WHY DID YOU LOOK AT MY LAST TEXT MESSAGE BUT NOT RESPOND??
YOU BETTER HAVE A FANTASTIC EXPLANATION

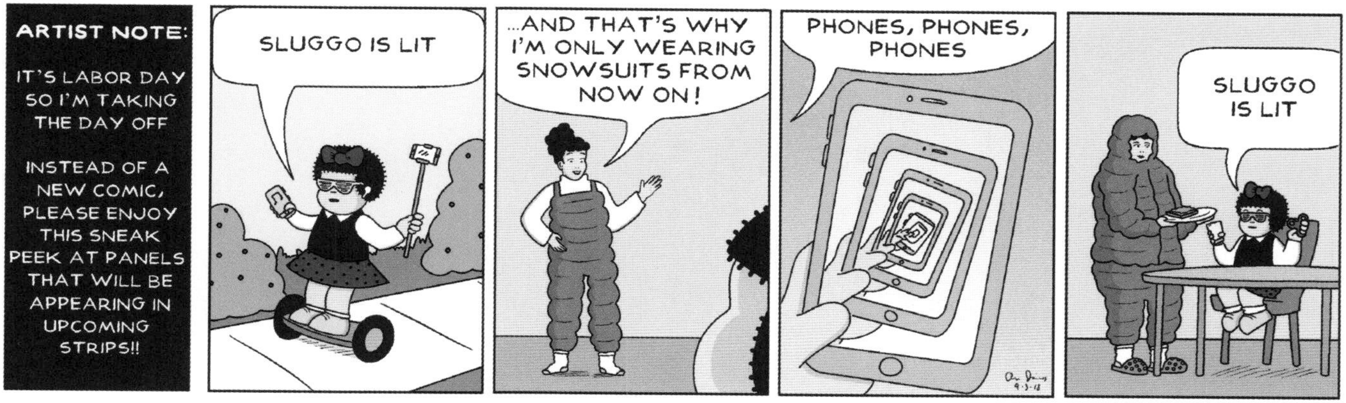
ARTIST NOTE:
IT'S LABOR DAY SO I'M TAKING THE DAY OFF
INSTEAD OF A NEW COMIC, PLEASE ENJOY THIS SNEAK PEEK AT PANELS THAT WILL BE APPEARING IN UPCOMING STRIPS!!
SLUGGO IS LIT
...AND THAT'S WHY I'M ONLY WEARING SNOWSUITS FROM NOW ON!
PHONES, PHONES, PHONES
SLUGGO IS LIT

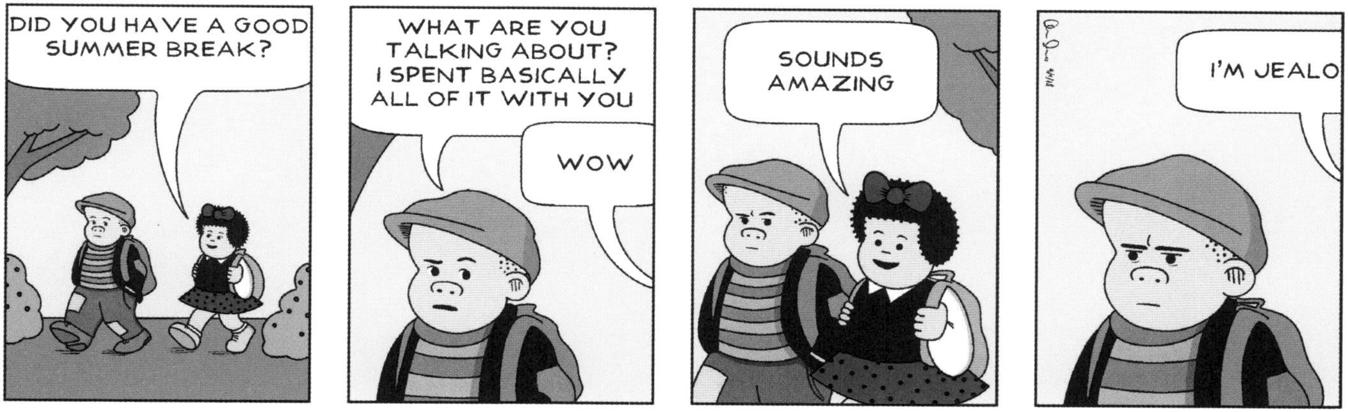
DID YOU HAVE A GOOD SUMMER BREAK?
WHAT ARE YOU TALKING ABOUT? I SPENT BASICALLY ALL OF IT WITH YOU
WOW
SOUNDS AMAZING
I'M JEALO

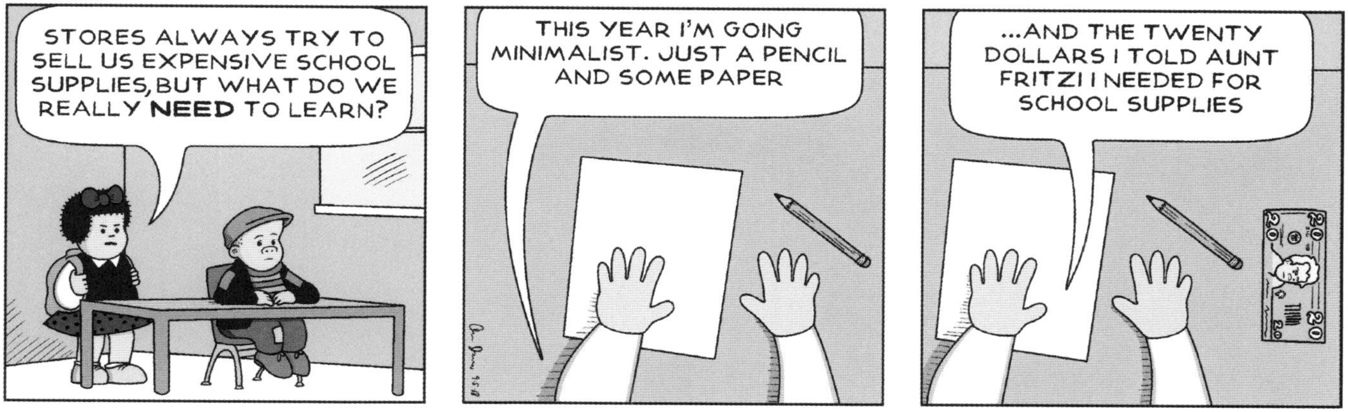
STORES ALWAYS TRY TO SELL US EXPENSIVE SCHOOL SUPPLIES, BUT WHAT DO WE REALLY NEED TO LEARN?
THIS YEAR I'M GOING MINIMALIST. JUST A PENCIL AND SOME PAPER
...AND THE TWENTY DOLLARS I TOLD AUNT FRITZI I NEEDED FOR SCHOOL SUPPLIES

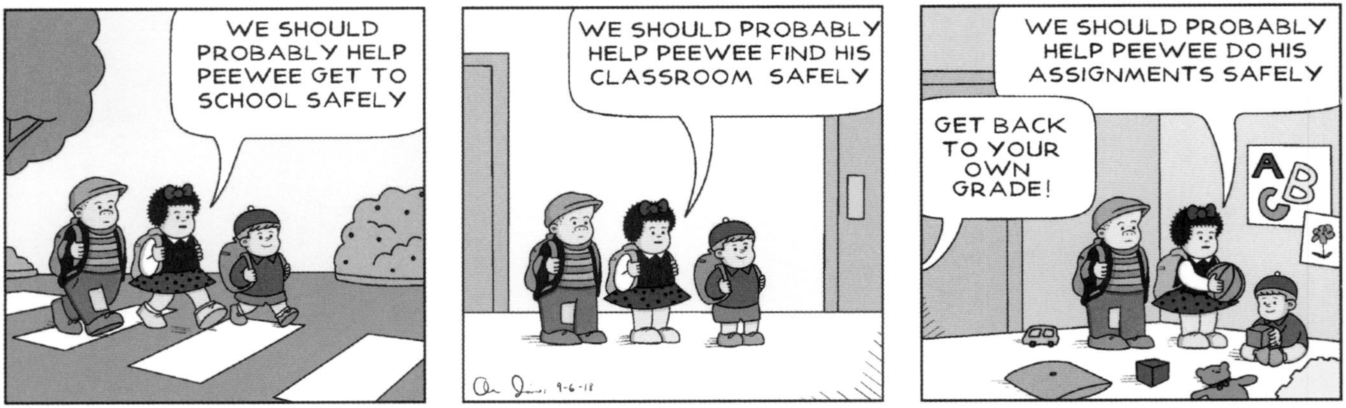
WE SHOULD PROBABLY HELP PEEWEE GET TO SCHOOL SAFELY
WE SHOULD PROBABLY HELP PEEWEE FIND HIS CLASSROOM SAFELY
WE SHOULD PROBABLY HELP PEEWEE DO HIS ASSIGNMENTS SAFELY
GET BACK TO YOUR OWN GRADE!
A B C

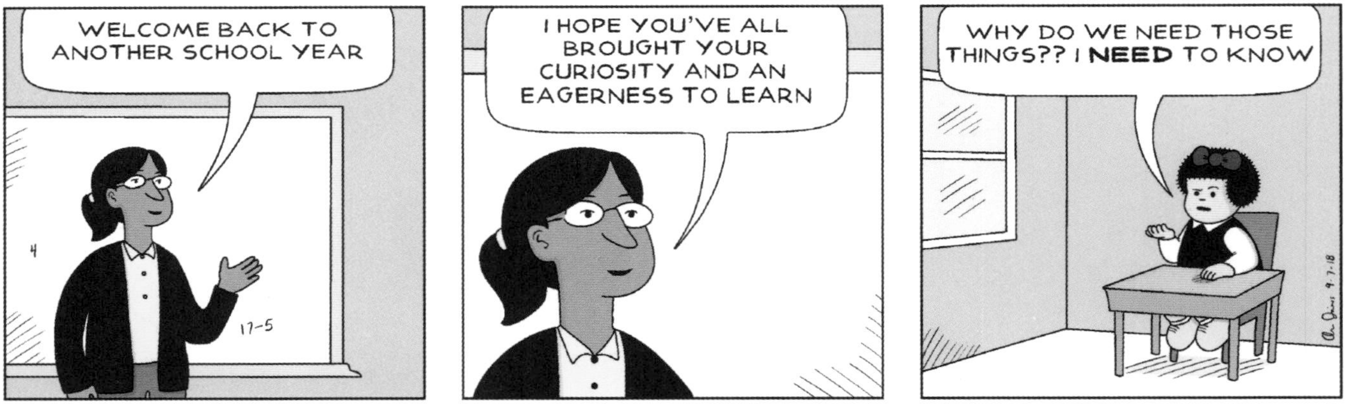
WELCOME BACK TO ANOTHER SCHOOL YEAR
I HOPE YOU'VE ALL BROUGHT YOUR CURIOSITY AND AN EAGERNESS TO LEARN
WHY DO WE NEED THOSE THINGS?? I **NEED** TO KNOW

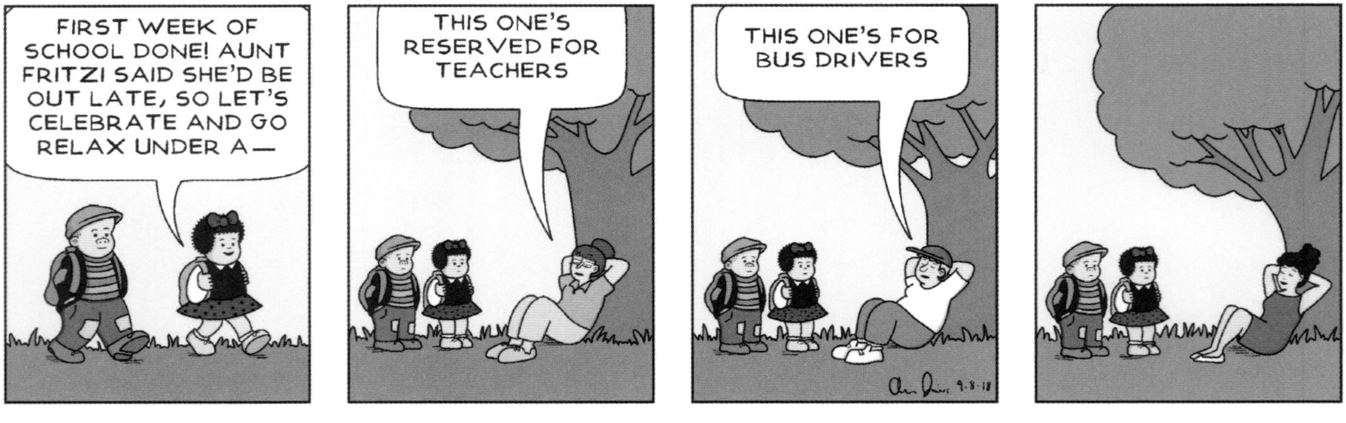
FIRST WEEK OF SCHOOL DONE! AUNT FRITZI SAID SHE'D BE OUT LATE, SO LET'S CELEBRATE AND GO RELAX UNDER A—
THIS ONE'S RESERVED FOR TEACHERS
THIS ONE'S FOR BUS DRIVERS

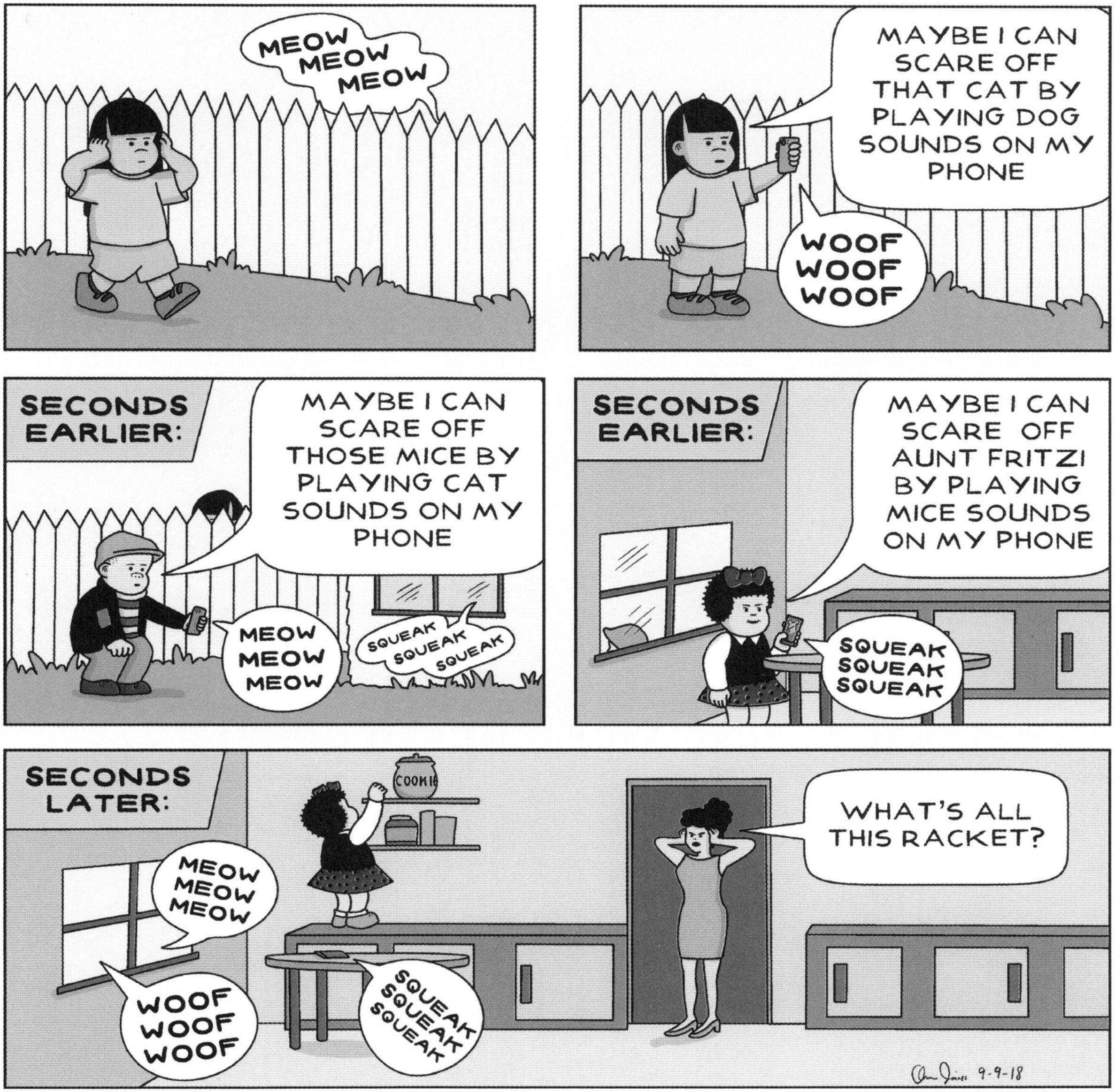
MEOW MEOW MEOW
MAYBE I CAN SCARE OFF THAT CAT BY PLAYING DOG SOUNDS ON MY PHONE
WOOF WOOF WOOF
SECONDS EARLIER:
MAYBE I CAN SCARE OFF THOSE MICE BY PLAYING CAT SOUNDS ON MY PHONE
MEOW MEOW MEOW
SQUEAK SQUEAK SQUEAK
SECONDS EARLIER:
MAYBE I CAN SCARE OFF AUNT FRITZI BY PLAYING MICE SOUNDS ON MY PHONE
SQUEAK SQUEAK SQUEAK
SECONDS LATER:
COOKIE
MEOW MEOW MEOW
WHAT'S ALL THIS RACKET?
WOOF WOOF WOOF
SQUEAK SQUEAK SQUEAK
9-9-18

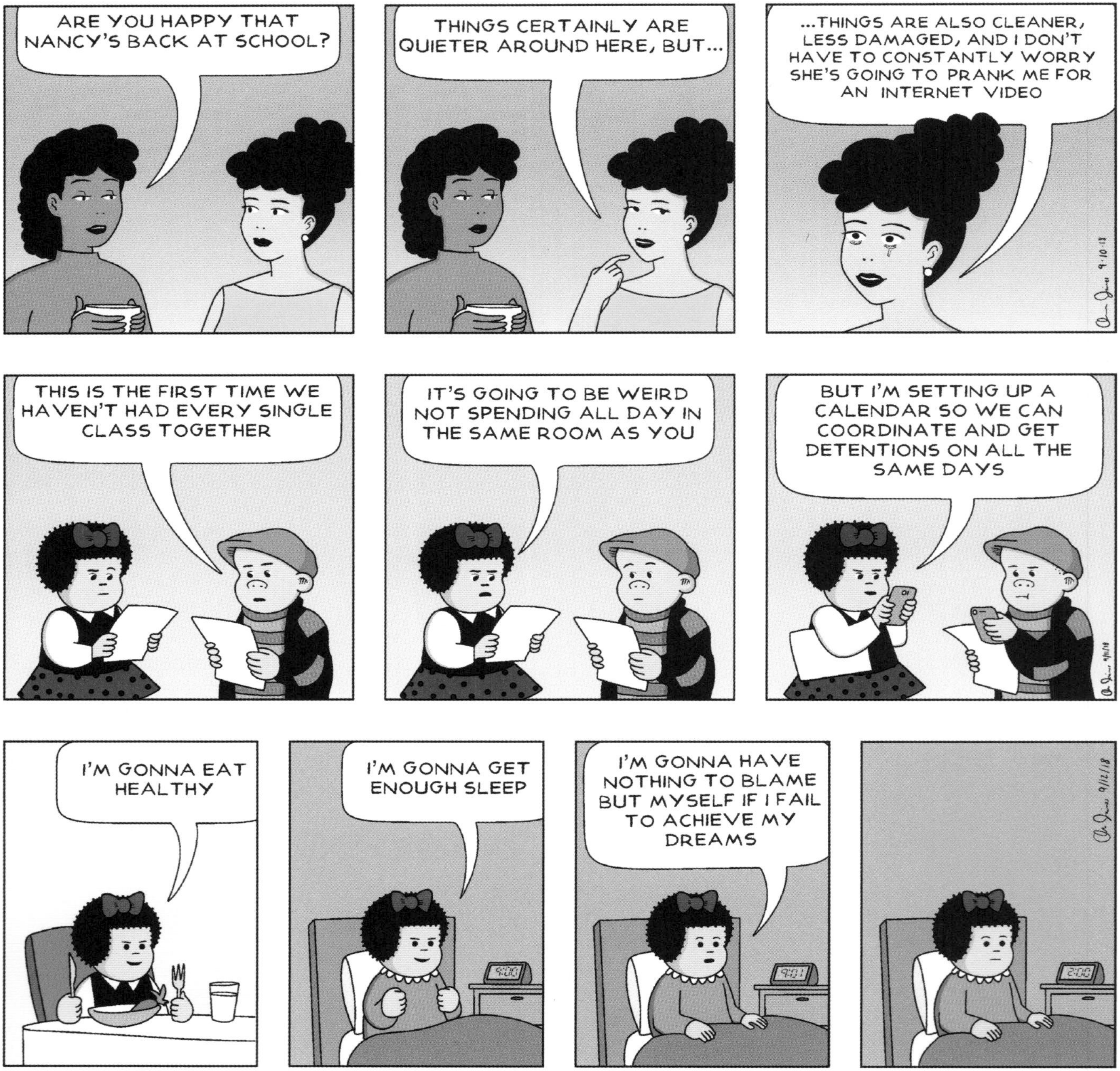
ARE YOU HAPPY THAT NANCY'S BACK AT SCHOOL?
THINGS CERTAINLY ARE QUIETER AROUND HERE, BUT...
...THINGS ARE ALSO CLEANER, LESS DAMAGED, AND I DON'T HAVE TO CONSTANTLY WORRY SHE'S GOING TO PRANK ME FOR AN INTERNET VIDEO
9-10-18
THIS IS THE FIRST TIME WE HAVEN'T HAD EVERY SINGLE CLASS TOGETHER
IT'S GOING TO BE WEIRD NOT SPENDING ALL DAY IN THE SAME ROOM AS YOU
BUT I'M SETTING UP A CALENDAR SO WE CAN COORDINATE AND GET DETENTIONS ON ALL THE SAME DAYS
9/11/18
I'M GONNA EAT HEALTHY
I'M GONNA GET ENOUGH SLEEP
9:00
I'M GONNA HAVE NOTHING TO BLAME BUT MYSELF IF I FAIL TO ACHIEVE MY DREAMS
9:01
2:00
9/12/18

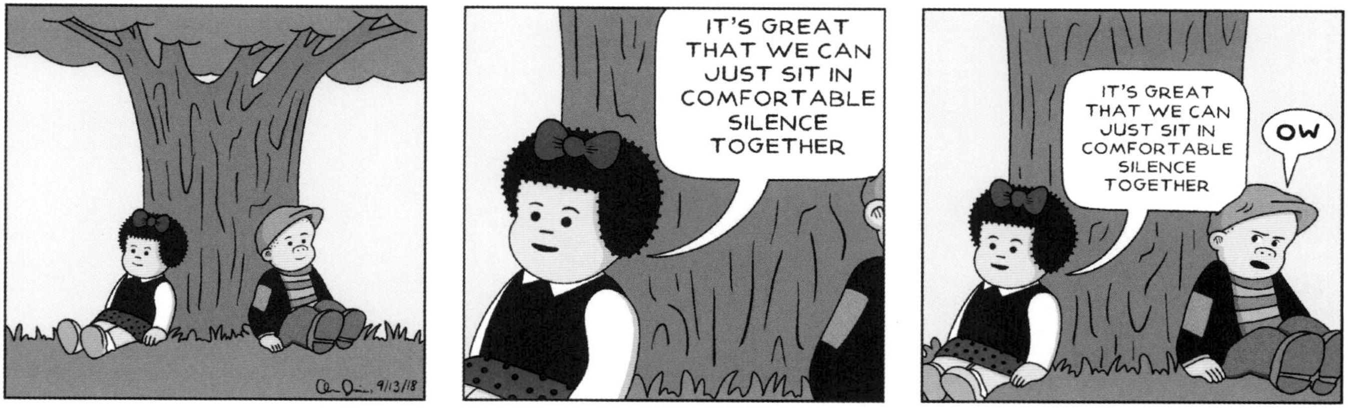
9/13/18
IT'S GREAT THAT WE CAN JUST SIT IN COMFORTABLE SILENCE TOGETHER
IT'S GREAT THAT WE CAN JUST SIT IN COMFORTABLE SILENCE TOGETHER
OW

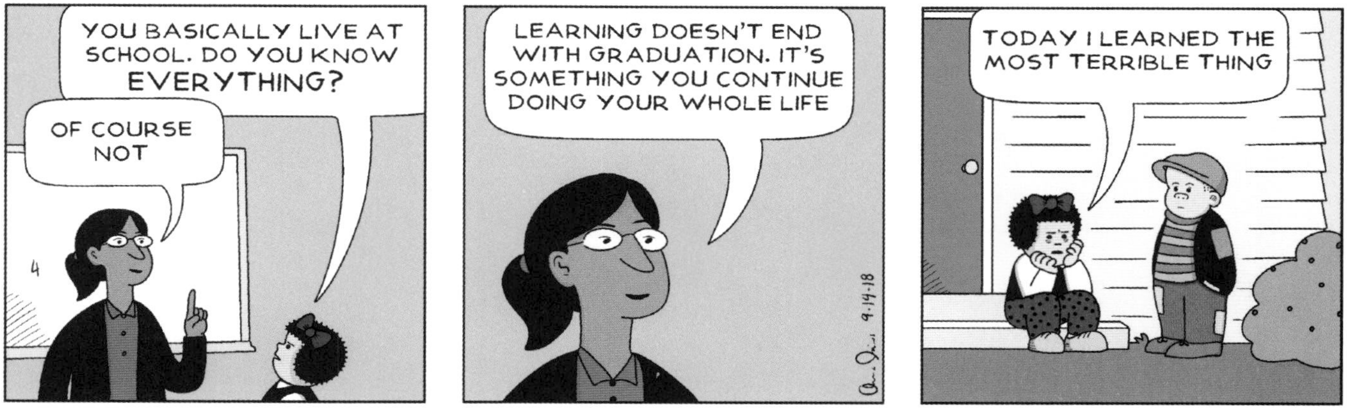
YOU BASICALLY LIVE AT SCHOOL. DO YOU KNOW EVERYTHING?
OF COURSE NOT
LEARNING DOESN'T END WITH GRADUATION. IT'S SOMETHING YOU CONTINUE DOING YOUR WHOLE LIFE
9-14-18
TODAY I LEARNED THE MOST TERRIBLE THING

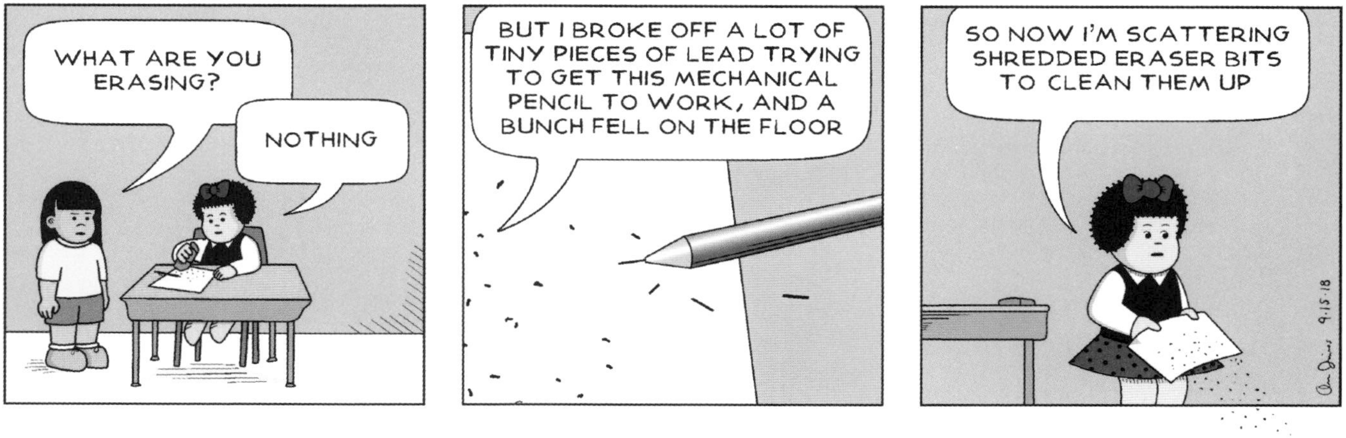
WHAT ARE YOU ERASING?
NOTHING
BUT I BROKE OFF A LOT OF TINY PIECES OF LEAD TRYING TO GET THIS MECHANICAL PENCIL TO WORK, AND A BUNCH FELL ON THE FLOOR
SO NOW I'M SCATTERING SHREDDED ERASER BITS TO CLEAN THEM UP
9-15-18

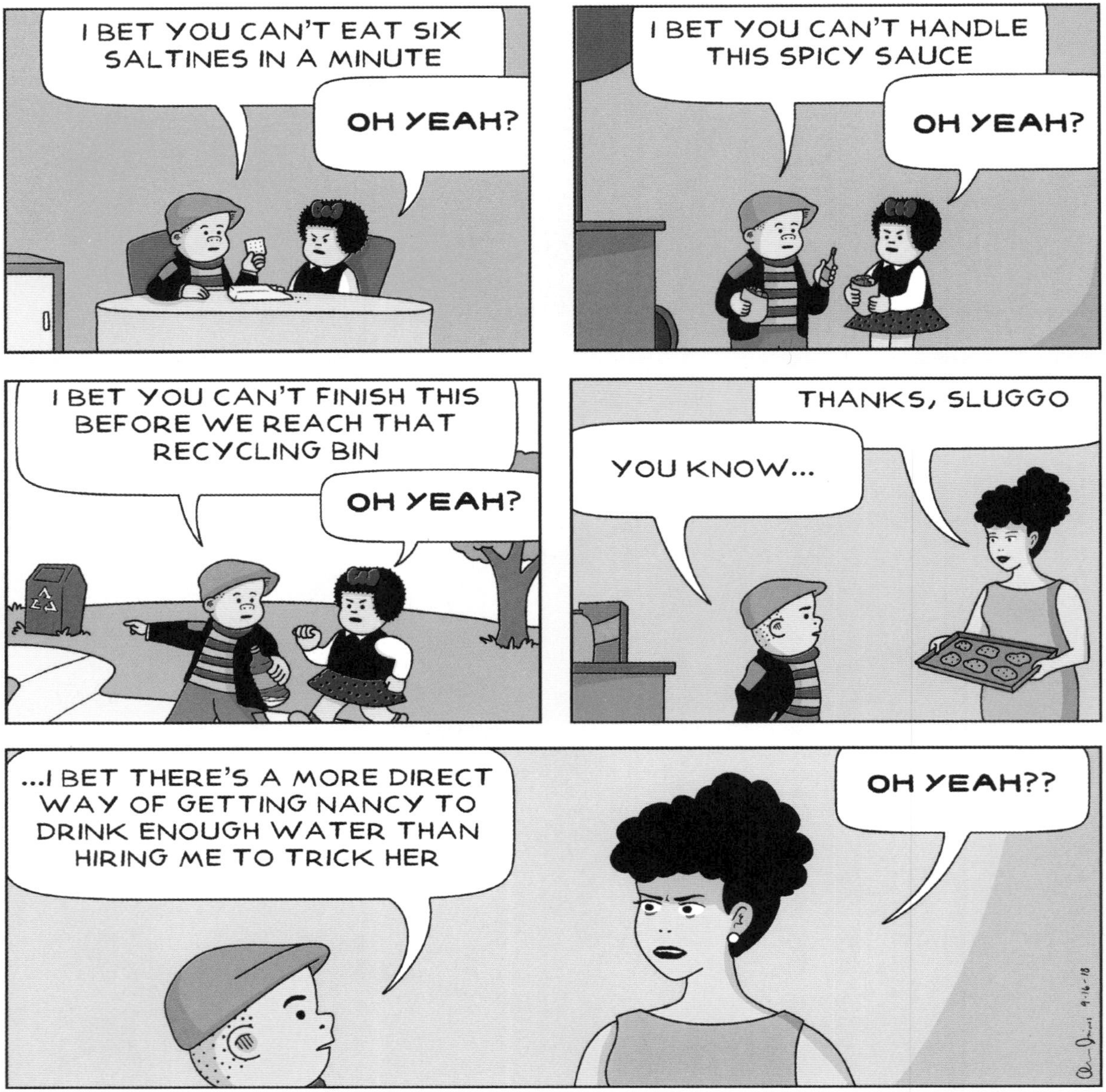
I BET YOU CAN'T EAT SIX SALTINES IN A MINUTE
OH YEAH?
I BET YOU CAN'T HANDLE THIS SPICY SAUCE
OH YEAH?
I BET YOU CAN'T FINISH THIS BEFORE WE REACH THAT RECYCLING BIN
OH YEAH?
THANKS, SLUGGO
YOU KNOW...
...I BET THERE'S A MORE DIRECT WAY OF GETTING NANCY TO DRINK ENOUGH WATER THAN HIRING ME TO TRICK HER
OH YEAH??

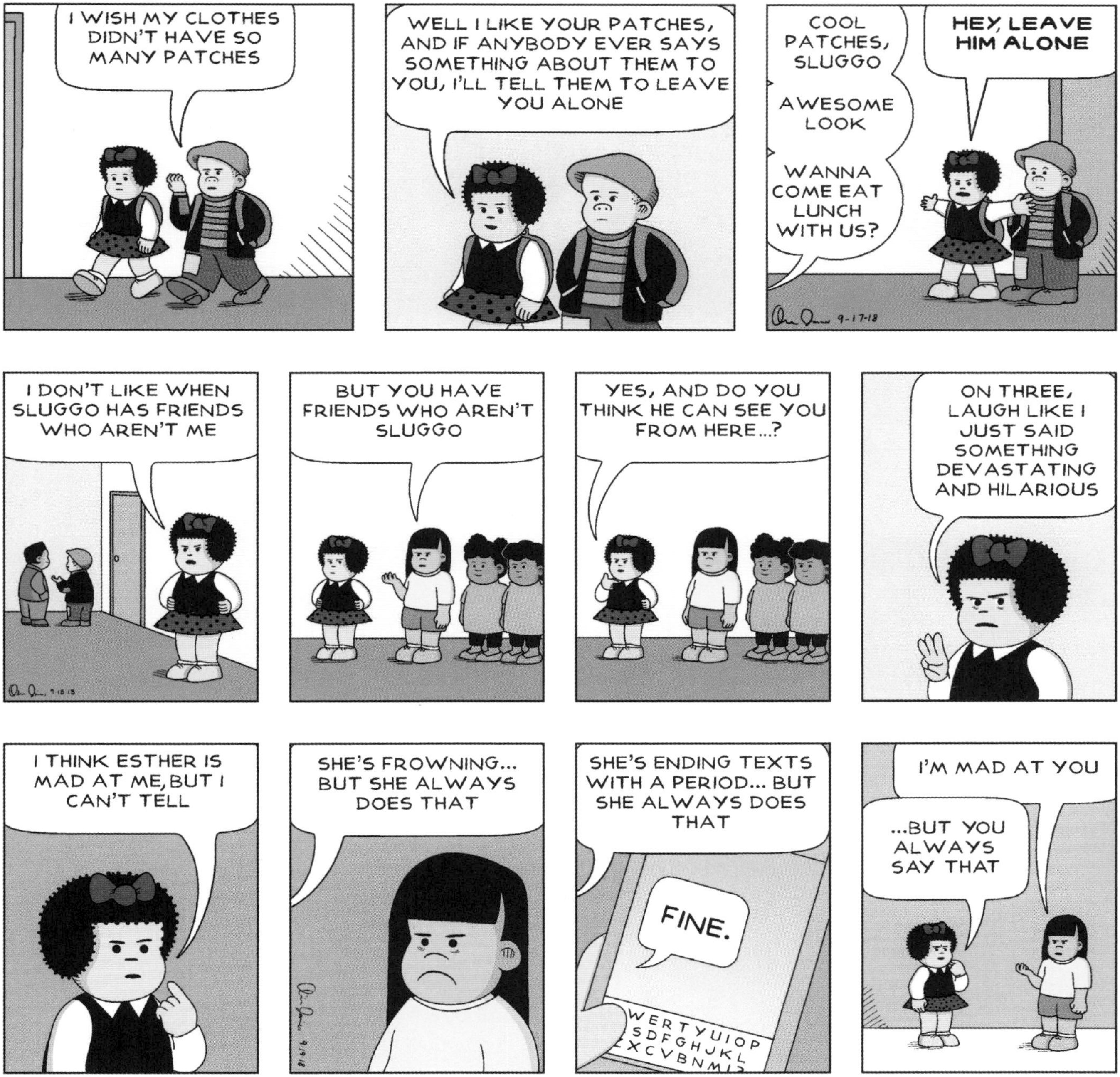
I WISH MY CLOTHES DIDN'T HAVE SO MANY PATCHES
WELL I LIKE YOUR PATCHES, AND IF ANYBODY EVER SAYS SOMETHING ABOUT THEM TO YOU, I'LL TELL THEM TO LEAVE YOU ALONE
COOL PATCHES, SLUGGO
AWESOME LOOK
WANNA COME EAT LUNCH WITH US?
HEY, LEAVE HIM ALONE
9-17-18
I DON'T LIKE WHEN SLUGGO HAS FRIENDS WHO AREN'T ME
BUT YOU HAVE FRIENDS WHO AREN'T SLUGGO
YES, AND DO YOU THINK HE CAN SEE YOU FROM HERE...?
ON THREE, LAUGH LIKE I JUST SAID SOMETHING DEVASTATING AND HILARIOUS
I THINK ESTHER IS MAD AT ME, BUT I CAN'T TELL
SHE'S FROWNING... BUT SHE ALWAYS DOES THAT
SHE'S ENDING TEXTS WITH A PERIOD... BUT SHE ALWAYS DOES THAT
FINE.
I'M MAD AT YOU
...BUT YOU ALWAYS SAY THAT

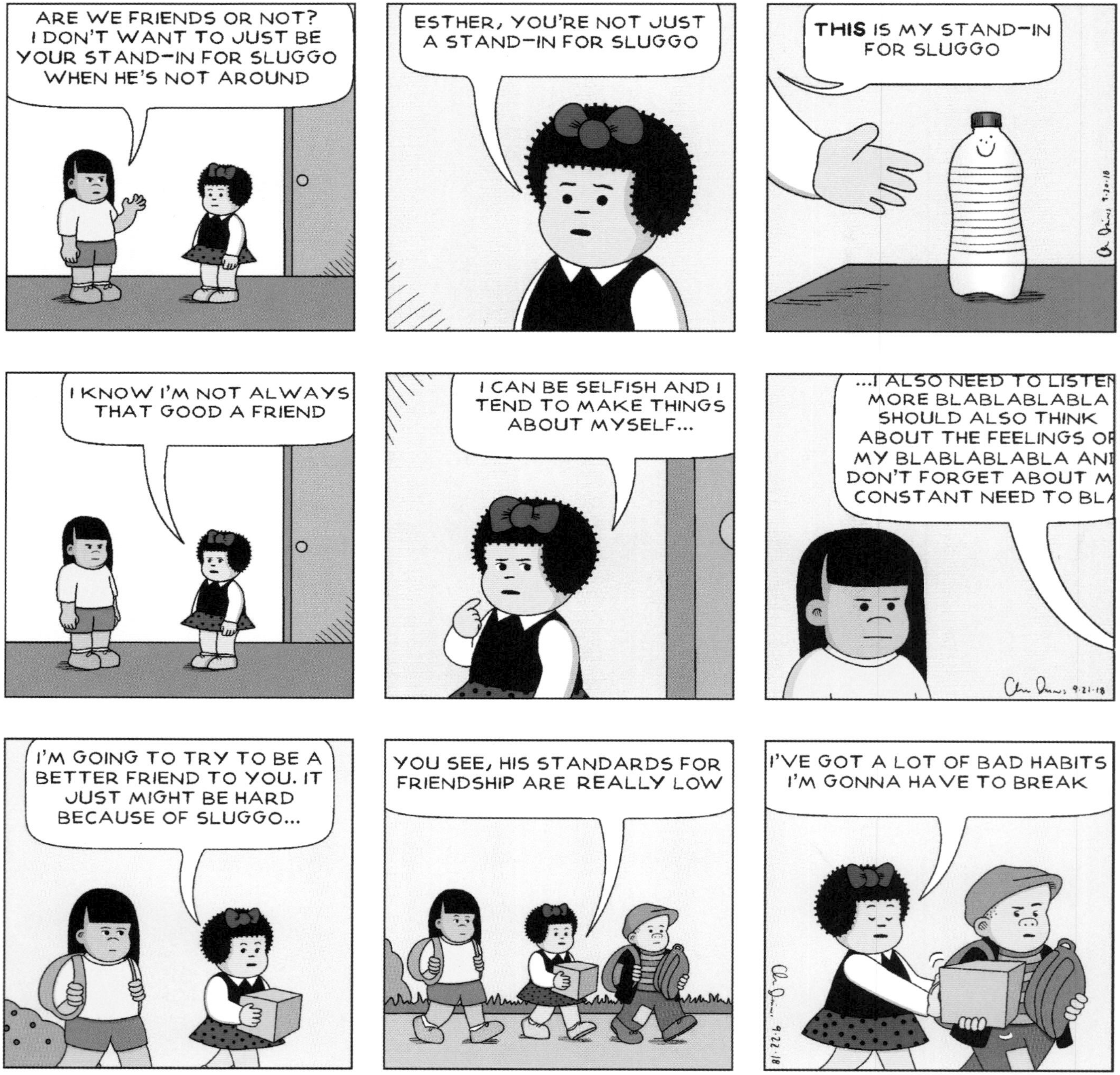
ARE WE FRIENDS OR NOT? I DON'T WANT TO JUST BE YOUR STAND-IN FOR SLUGGO WHEN HE'S NOT AROUND
ESTHER, YOU'RE NOT JUST A STAND-IN FOR SLUGGO
THIS IS MY STAND-IN FOR SLUGGO
I KNOW I'M NOT ALWAYS THAT GOOD A FRIEND
I CAN BE SELFISH AND I TEND TO MAKE THINGS ABOUT MYSELF...
...I ALSO NEED TO LISTE
MORE BLABLABLABLA
SHOULD ALSO THINK
ABOUT THE FEELINGS O
MY BLABLABLABLA AN
DON'T FORGET ABOUT M
CONSTANT NEED TO BL
I'M GOING TO TRY TO BE A BETTER FRIEND TO YOU. IT JUST MIGHT BE HARD BECAUSE OF SLUGGO...
YOU SEE, HIS STANDARDS FOR FRIENDSHIP ARE REALLY LOW
I'VE GOT A LOT OF BAD HABITS I'M GONNA HAVE TO BREAK

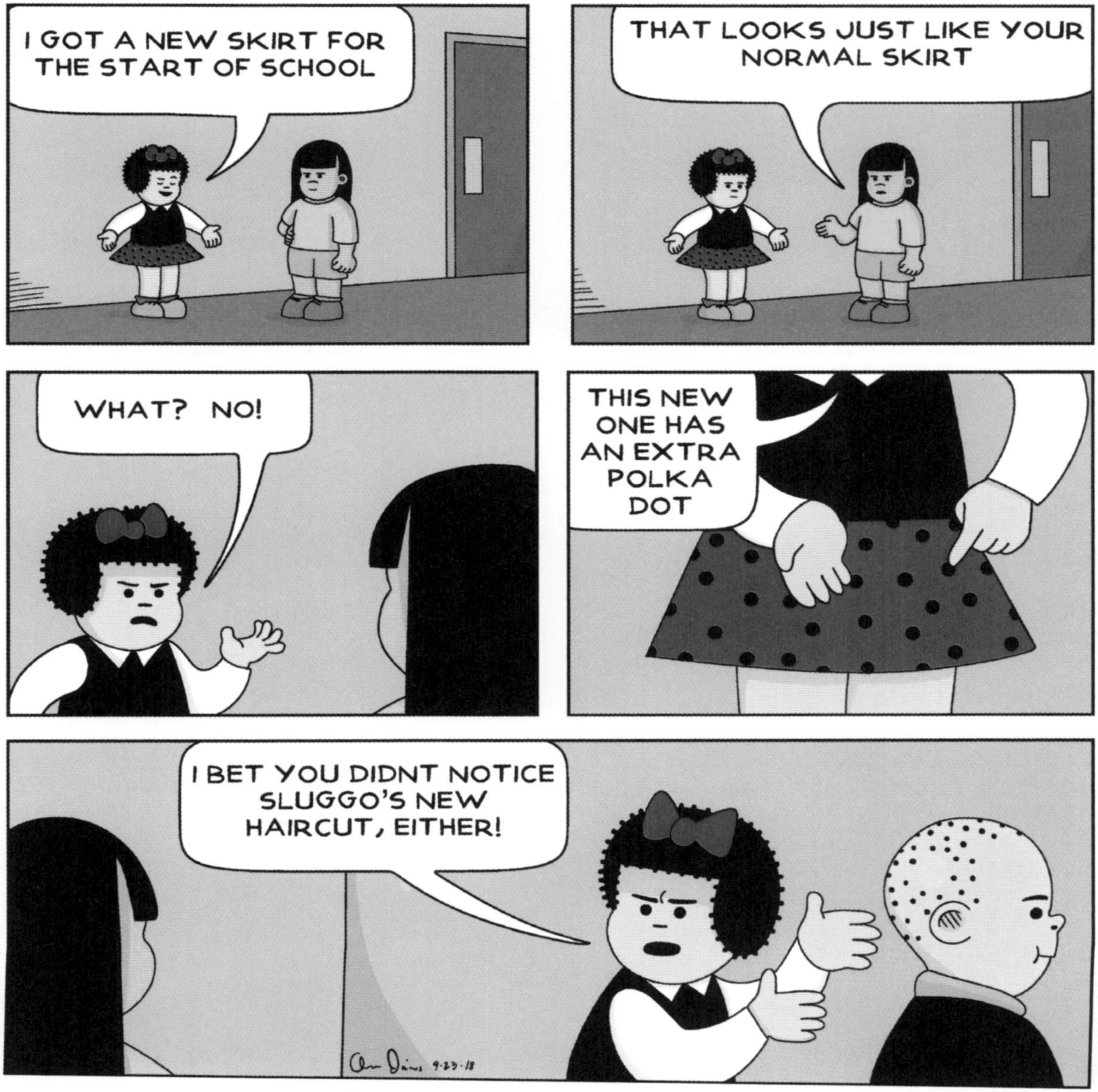
I GOT A NEW SKIRT FOR THE START OF SCHOOL
THAT LOOKS JUST LIKE YOUR NORMAL SKIRT
WHAT? NO!
THIS NEW ONE HAS AN EXTRA POLKA DOT
I BET YOU DIDNT NOTICE SLUGGO'S NEW HAIRCUT, EITHER!

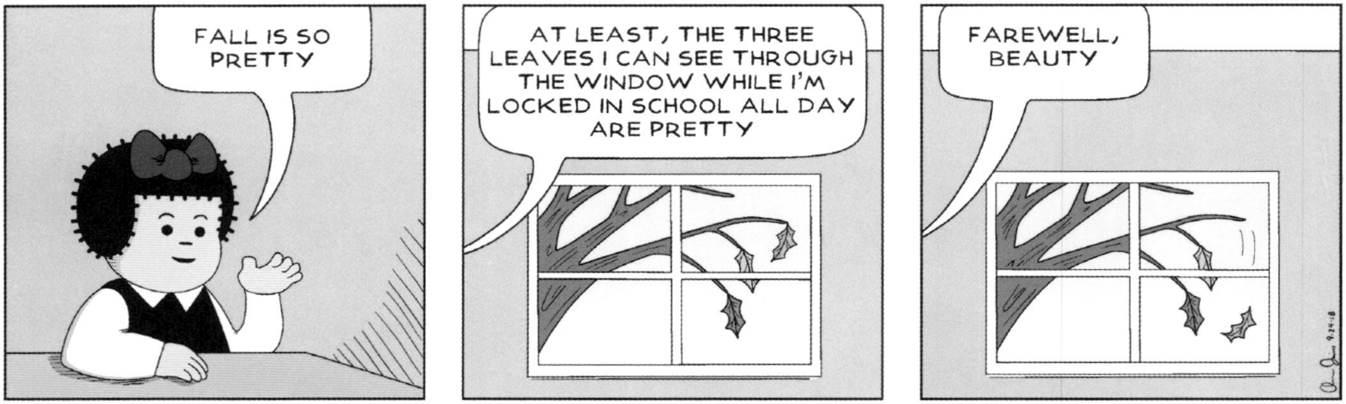
FALL IS SO PRETTY
AT LEAST, THE THREE LEAVES I CAN SEE THROUGH THE WINDOW WHILE I'M LOCKED IN SCHOOL ALL DAY ARE PRETTY
FAREWELL, BEAUTY

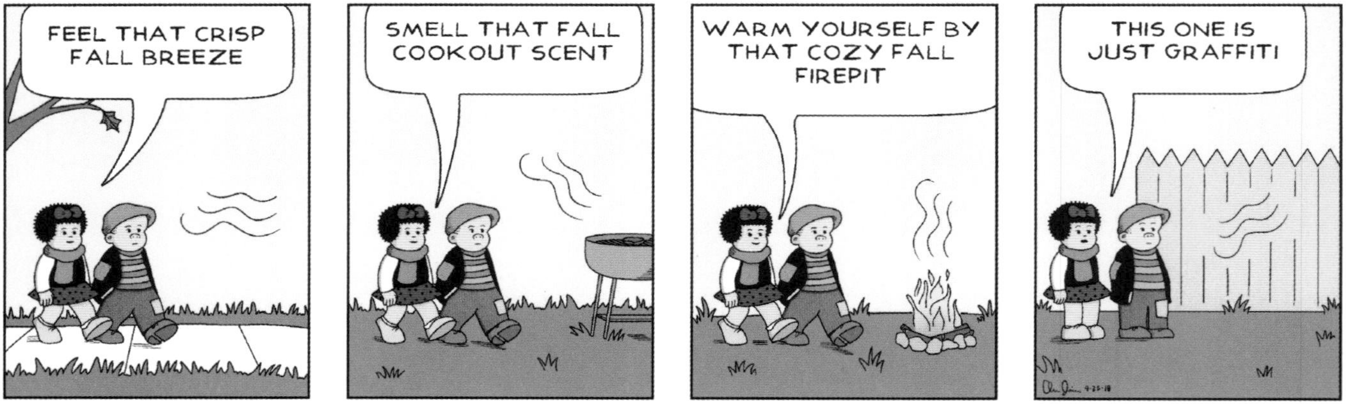
FEEL THAT CRISP FALL BREEZE
SMELL THAT FALL COOKOUT SCENT
WARM YOURSELF BY THAT COZY FALL FIREPIT
THIS ONE IS JUST GRAFFITI

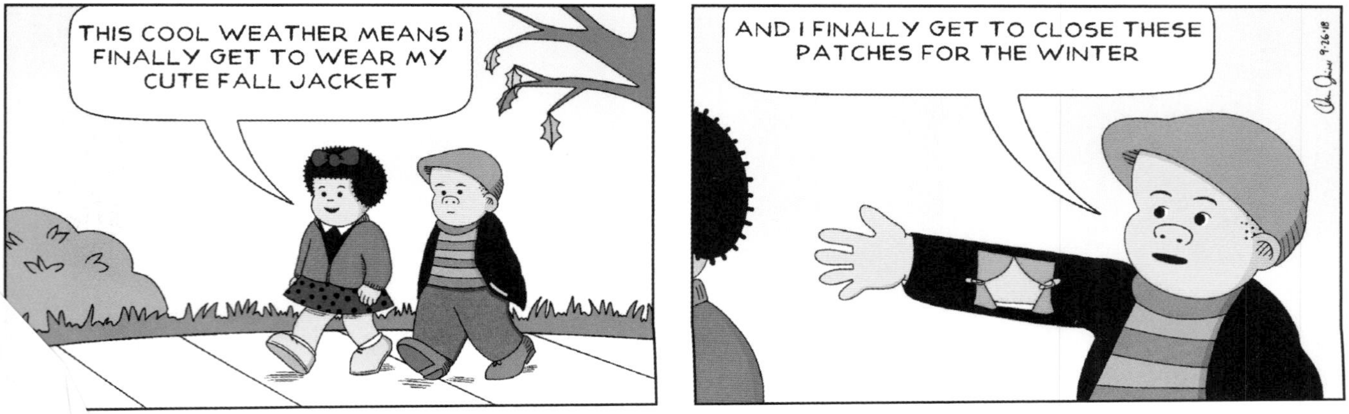
THIS COOL WEATHER MEANS I FINALLY GET TO WEAR MY CUTE FALL JACKET
AND I FINALLY GET TO CLOSE THESE PATCHES FOR THE WINTER

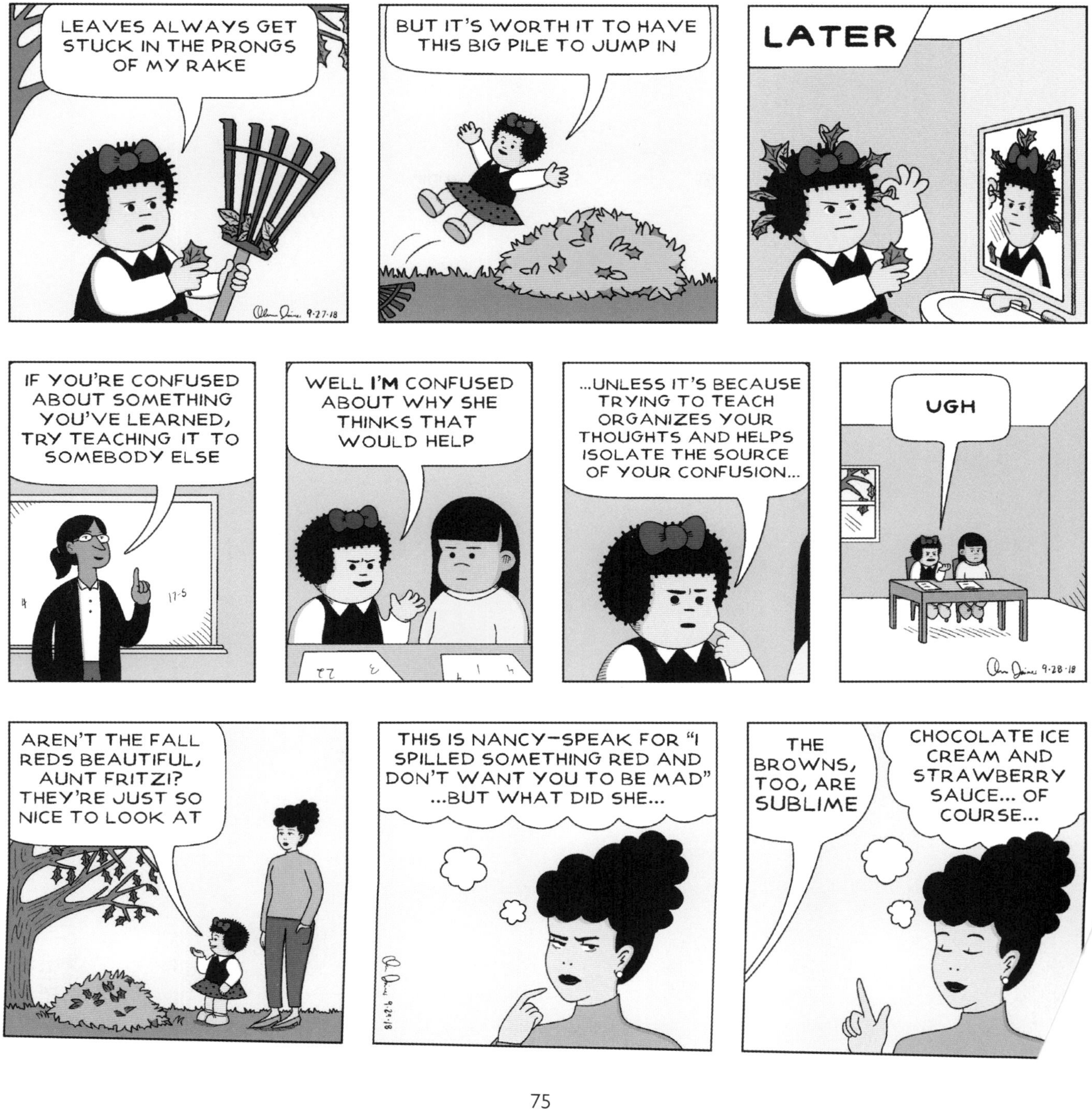
LEAVES ALWAYS GET STUCK IN THE PRONGS OF MY RAKE
BUT IT'S WORTH IT TO HAVE THIS BIG PILE TO JUMP IN
LATER
IF YOU'RE CONFUSED ABOUT SOMETHING YOU'VE LEARNED, TRY TEACHING IT TO SOMEBODY ELSE
WELL I'M CONFUSED ABOUT WHY SHE THINKS THAT WOULD HELP
...UNLESS IT'S BECAUSE TRYING TO TEACH ORGANIZES YOUR THOUGHTS AND HELPS ISOLATE THE SOURCE OF YOUR CONFUSION...
UGH
AREN'T THE FALL REDS BEAUTIFUL, AUNT FRITZI? THEY'RE JUST SO NICE TO LOOK AT
THIS IS NANCY—SPEAK FOR "I SPILLED SOMETHING RED AND DON'T WANT YOU TO BE MAD" ...BUT WHAT DID SHE...
THE BROWNS, TOO, ARE SUBLIME
CHOCOLATE ICE CREAM AND STRAWBERRY SAUCE... OF COURSE...

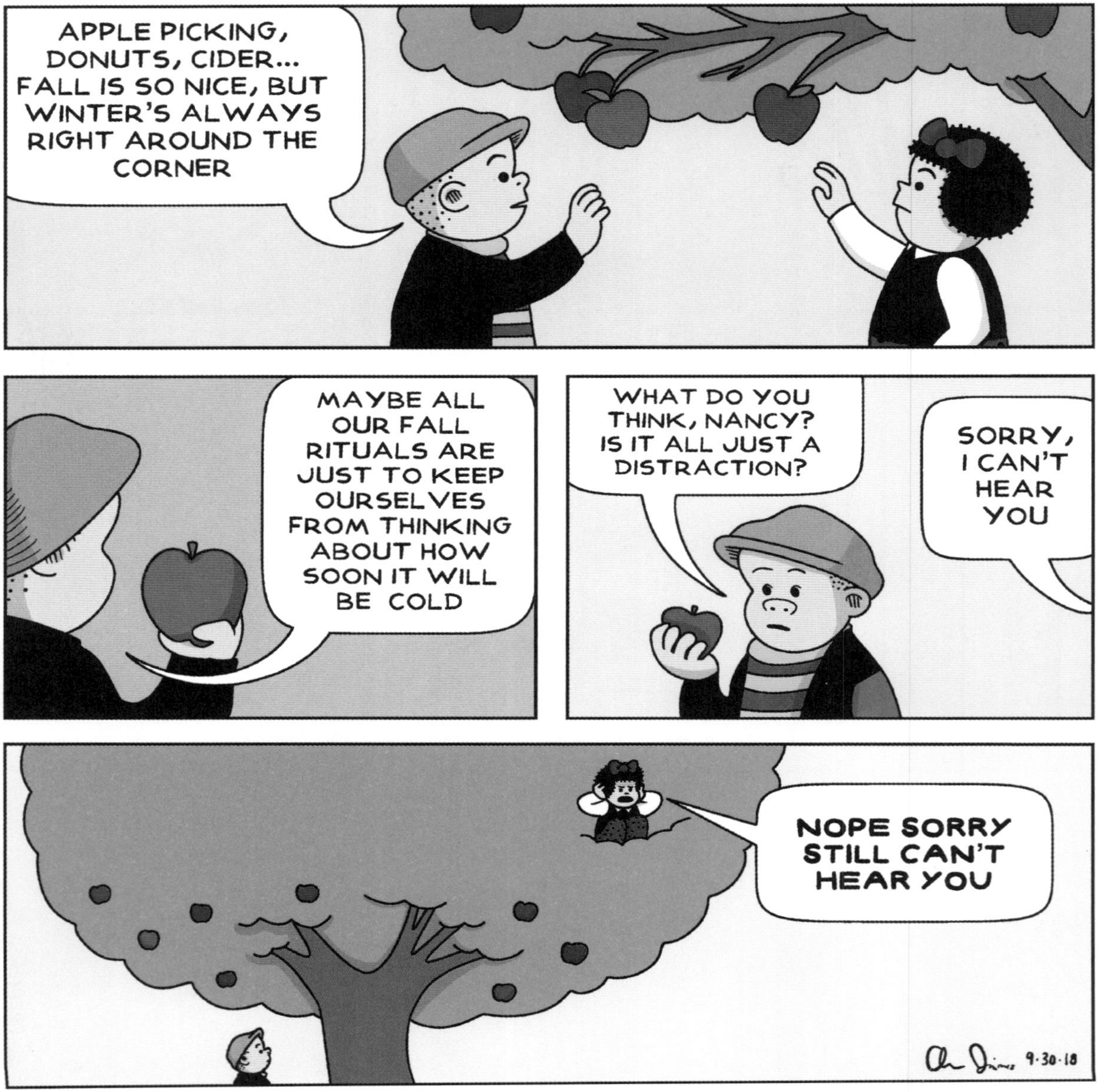
APPLE PICKING, DONUTS, CIDER... FALL IS SO NICE, BUT WINTER'S ALWAYS RIGHT AROUND THE CORNER
MAYBE ALL OUR FALL RITUALS ARE JUST TO KEEP OURSELVES FROM THINKING ABOUT HOW SOON IT WILL BE COLD
WHAT DO YOU THINK, NANCY? IS IT ALL JUST A DISTRACTION?
SORRY, I CAN'T HEAR YOU
NOPE SORRY STILL CAN'T HEAR YOU
9·30·18

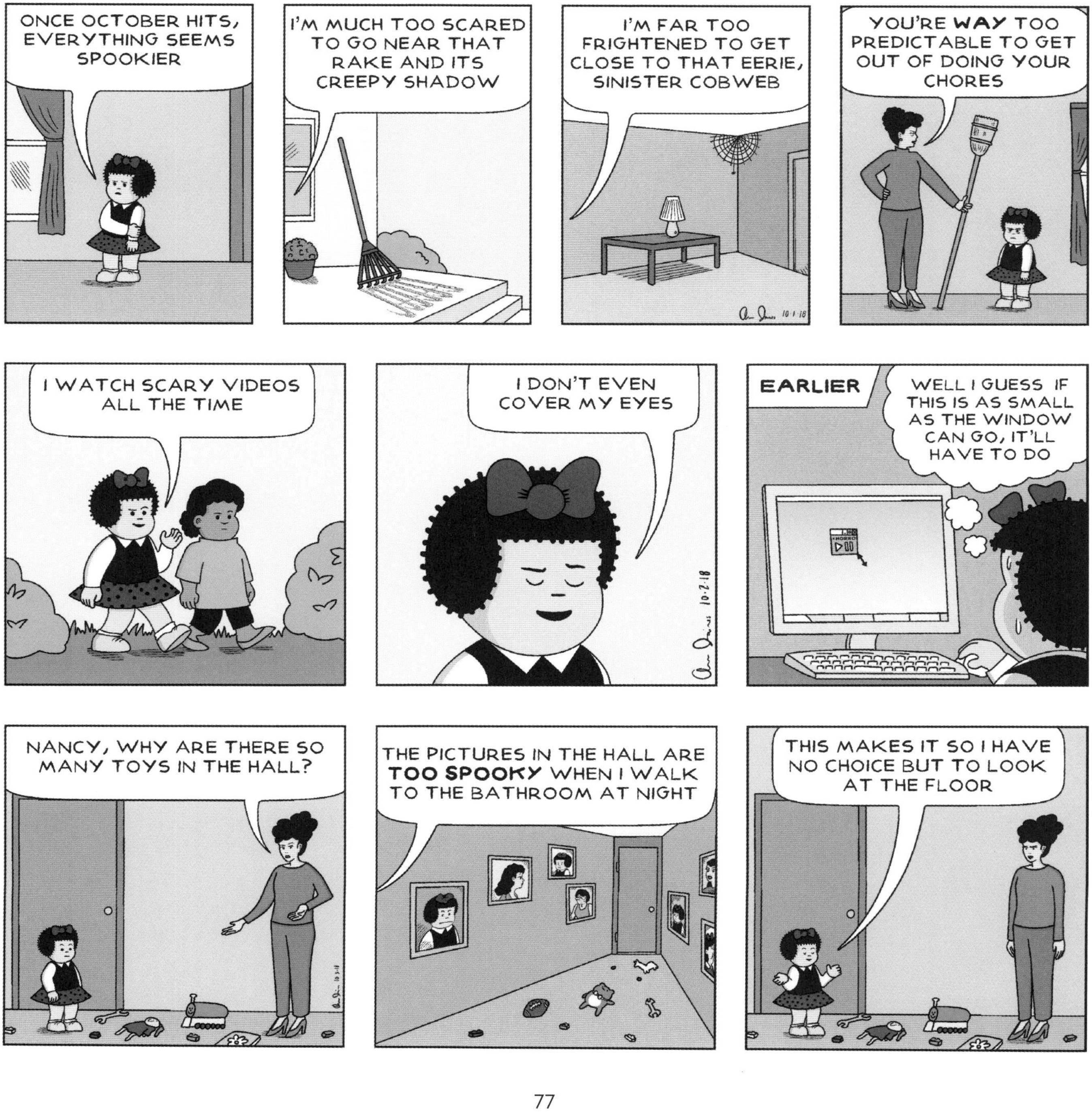
ONCE OCTOBER HITS, EVERYTHING SEEMS SPOOKIER
I'M MUCH TOO SCARED TO GO NEAR THAT RAKE AND ITS CREEPY SHADOW
I'M FAR TOO FRIGHTENED TO GET CLOSE TO THAT EERIE, SINISTER COBWEB
YOU'RE **WAY** TOO PREDICTABLE TO GET OUT OF DOING YOUR CHORES
I WATCH SCARY VIDEOS ALL THE TIME
I DON'T EVEN COVER MY EYES
EARLIER
WELL I GUESS IF THIS IS AS SMALL AS THE WINDOW CAN GO, IT'LL HAVE TO DO
NANCY, WHY ARE THERE SO MANY TOYS IN THE HALL?
THE PICTURES IN THE HALL ARE **TOO SPOOKY** WHEN I WALK TO THE BATHROOM AT NIGHT
THIS MAKES IT SO I HAVE NO CHOICE BUT TO LOOK AT THE FLOOR

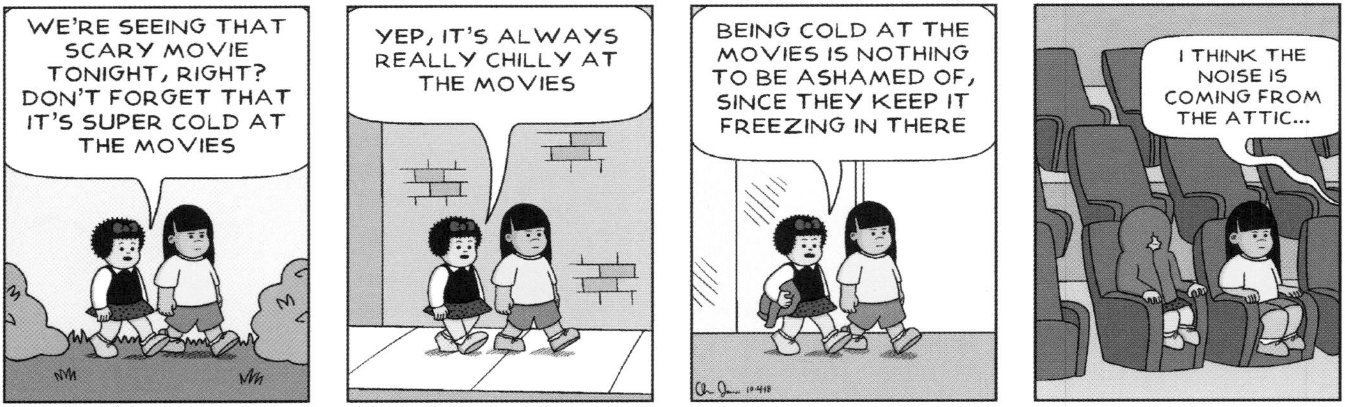
WE'RE SEEING THAT SCARY MOVIE TONIGHT, RIGHT? DON'T FORGET THAT IT'S SUPER COLD AT THE MOVIES
YEP, IT'S ALWAYS REALLY CHILLY AT THE MOVIES
BEING COLD AT THE MOVIES IS NOTHING TO BE ASHAMED OF, SINCE THEY KEEP IT FREEZING IN THERE
I THINK THE NOISE IS COMING FROM THE ATTIC...

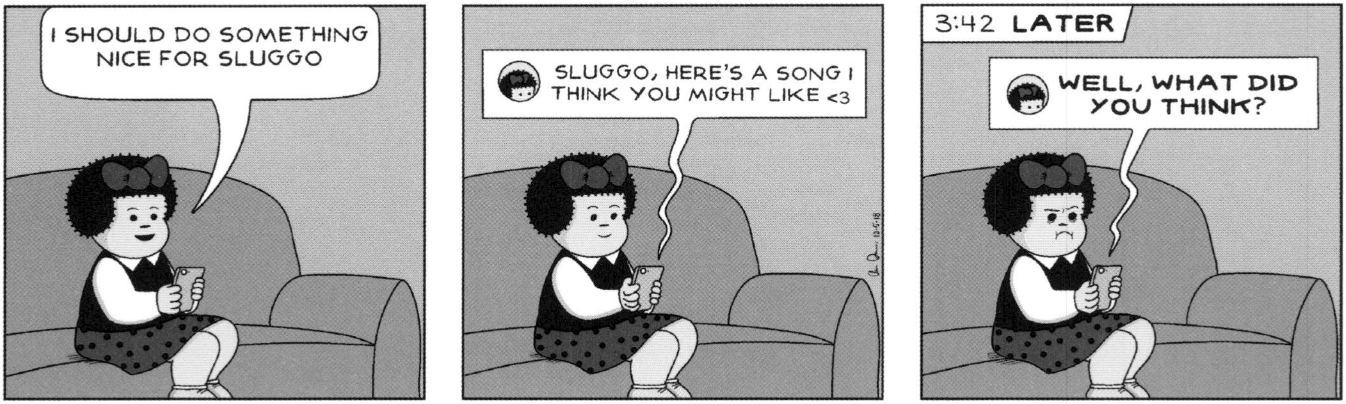
I SHOULD DO SOMETHING NICE FOR SLUGGO
SLUGGO, HERE'S A SONG I THINK YOU MIGHT LIKE <3
3:42 LATER
WELL, WHAT DID YOU THINK?

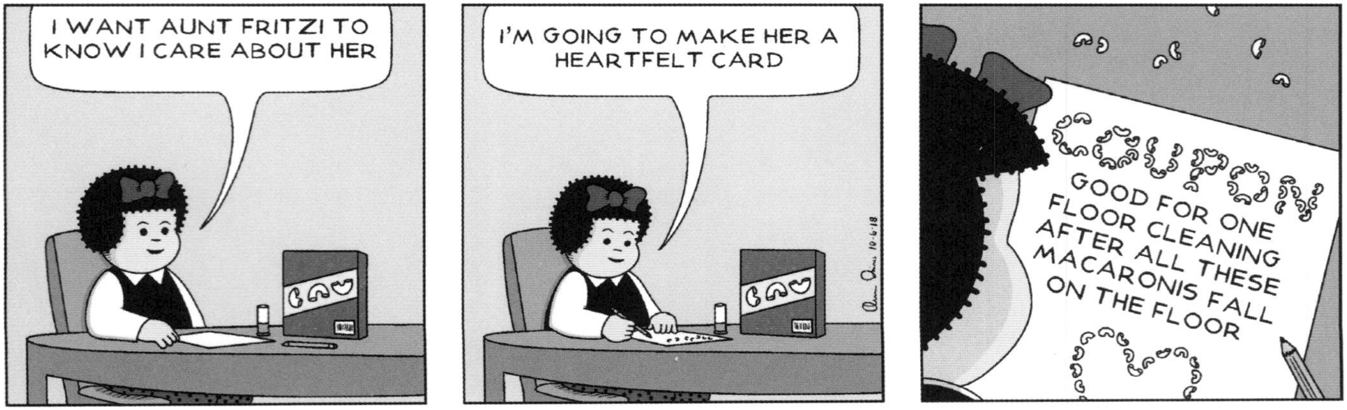
I WANT AUNT FRITZI TO KNOW I CARE ABOUT HER
I'M GOING TO MAKE HER A HEARTFELT CARD
COUPON
GOOD FOR ONE FLOOR CLEANING AFTER ALL THESE MACARONIS FALL ON THE FLOOR

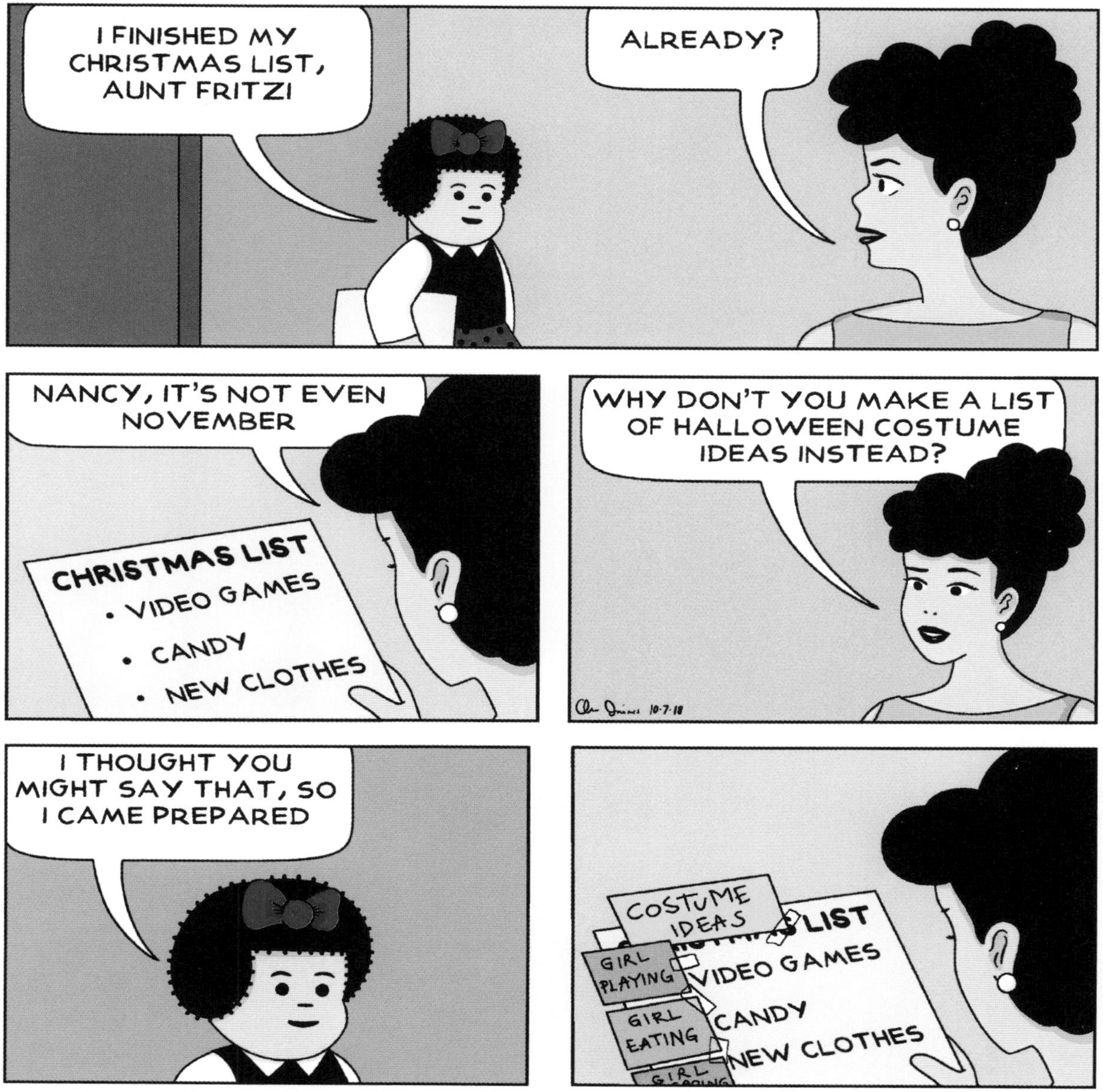

I FINISHED MY CHRISTMAS LIST, AUNT FRITZI
ALREADY?
NANCY, IT'S NOT EVEN NOVEMBER
CHRISTMAS LIST
• VIDEO GAMES
• CANDY
• NEW CLOTHES
WHY DON'T YOU MAKE A LIST OF HALLOWEEN COSTUME IDEAS INSTEAD?
10-7-18
I THOUGHT YOU MIGHT SAY THAT, SO I CAME PREPARED
COSTUME IDEAS
LIST
GIRL PLAYING
VIDEO GAMES
GIRL EATING
CANDY
NEW CLOTHES

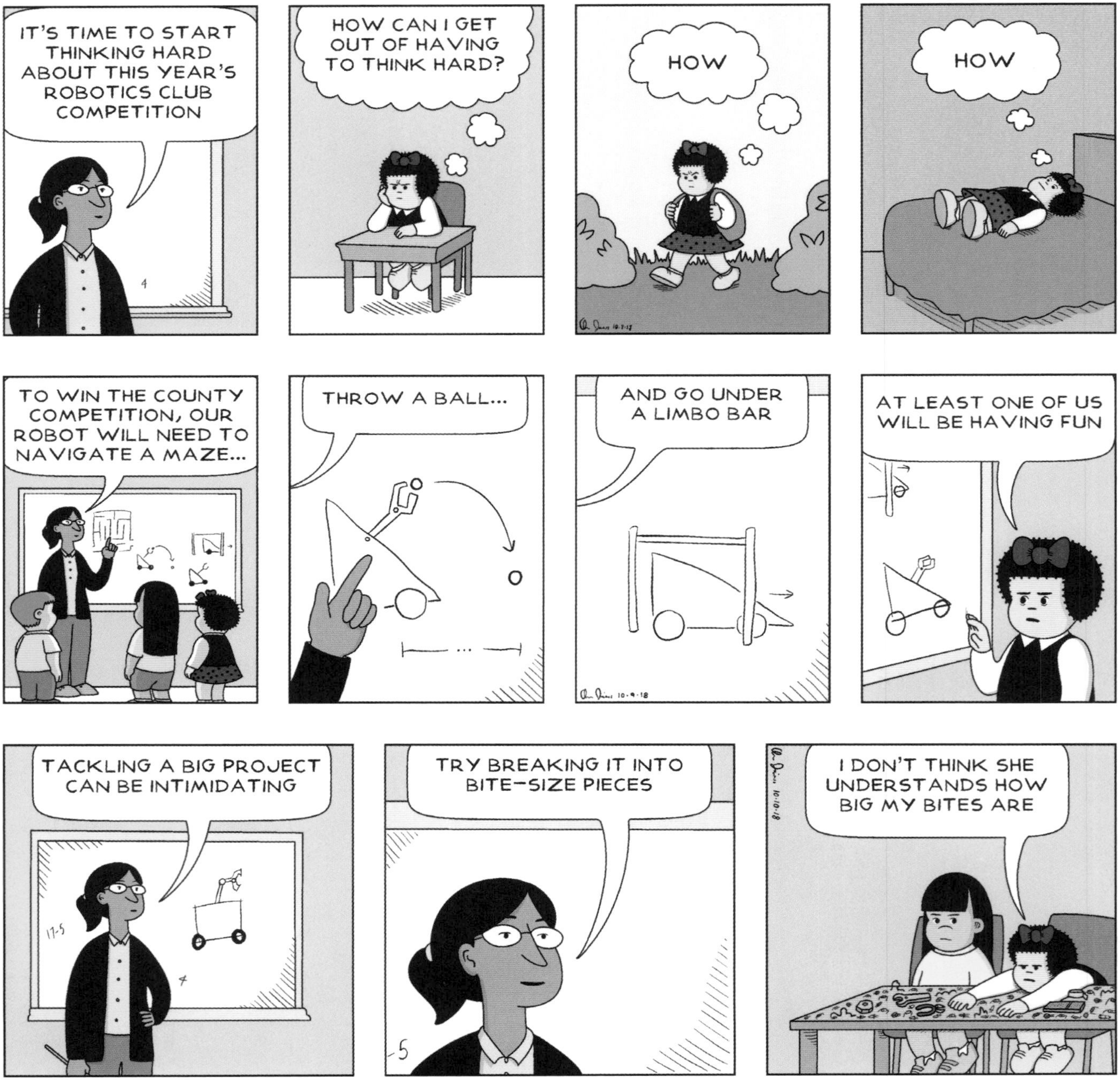
IT'S TIME TO START THINKING HARD ABOUT THIS YEAR'S ROBOTICS CLUB COMPETITION
HOW CAN I GET OUT OF HAVING TO THINK HARD?
HOW
HOW
TO WIN THE COUNTY COMPETITION, OUR ROBOT WILL NEED TO NAVIGATE A MAZE...
THROW A BALL...
AND GO UNDER A LIMBO BAR
AT LEAST ONE OF US WILL BE HAVING FUN
TACKLING A BIG PROJECT CAN BE INTIMIDATING
TRY BREAKING IT INTO BITE-SIZE PIECES
I DON'T THINK SHE UNDERSTANDS HOW BIG MY BITES ARE

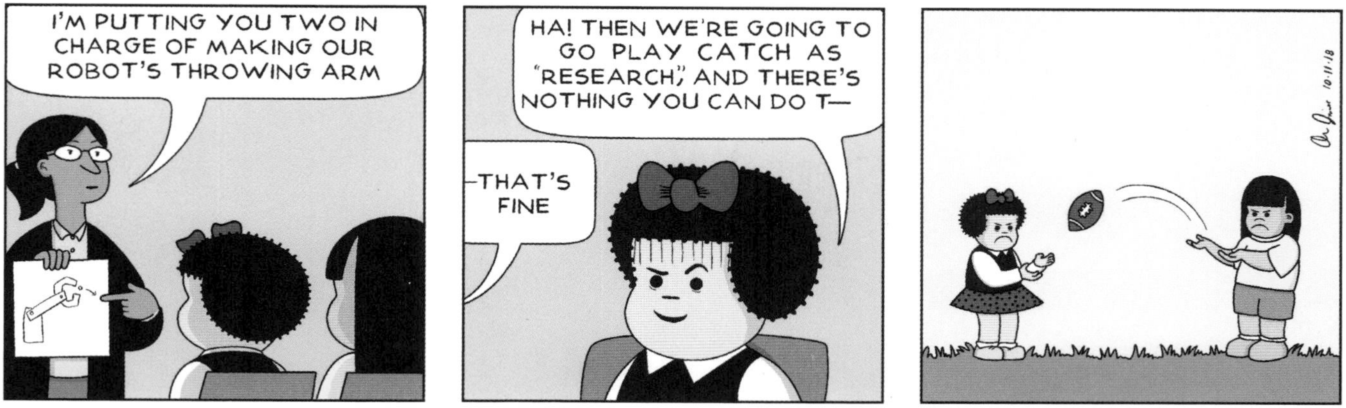
I'M PUTTING YOU TWO IN CHARGE OF MAKING OUR ROBOT'S THROWING ARM
HA! THEN WE'RE GOING TO GO PLAY CATCH AS "RESEARCH," AND THERE'S NOTHING YOU CAN DO T—
—THAT'S FINE

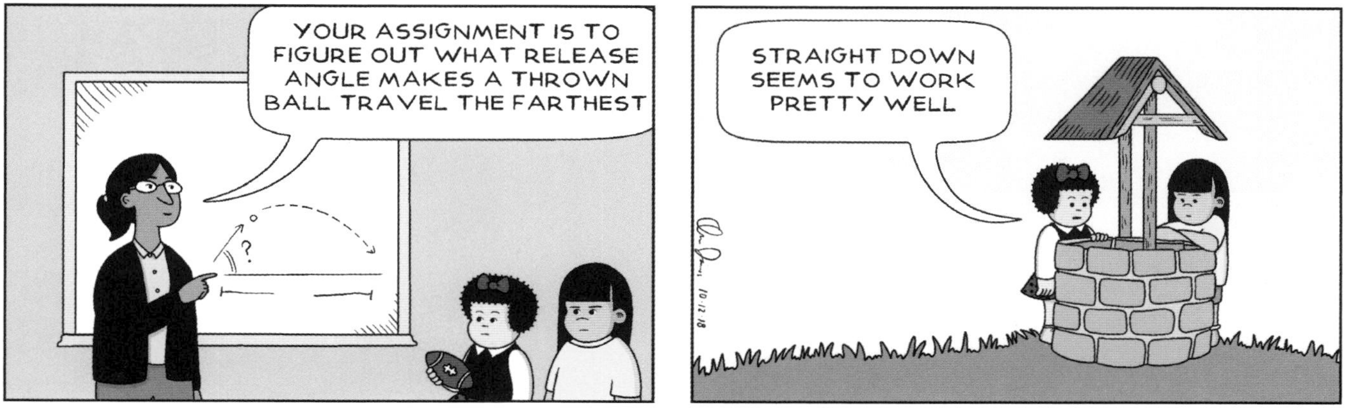
YOUR ASSIGNMENT IS TO FIGURE OUT WHAT RELEASE ANGLE MAKES A THROWN BALL TRAVEL THE FARTHEST
STRAIGHT DOWN SEEMS TO WORK PRETTY WELL

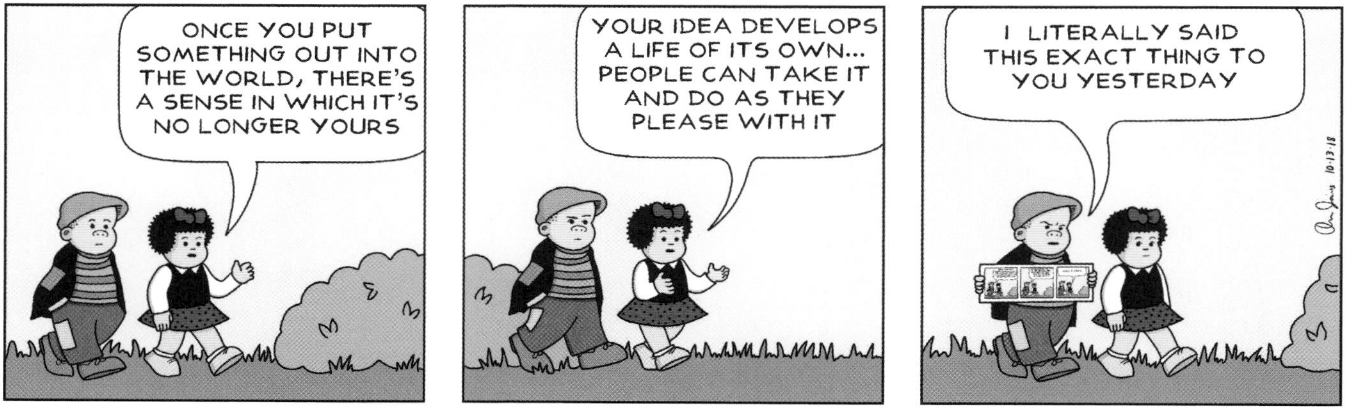
ONCE YOU PUT SOMETHING OUT INTO THE WORLD, THERE'S A SENSE IN WHICH IT'S NO LONGER YOURS
YOUR IDEA DEVELOPS A LIFE OF ITS OWN... PEOPLE CAN TAKE IT AND DO AS THEY PLEASE WITH IT
I LITERALLY SAID THIS EXACT THING TO YOU YESTERDAY

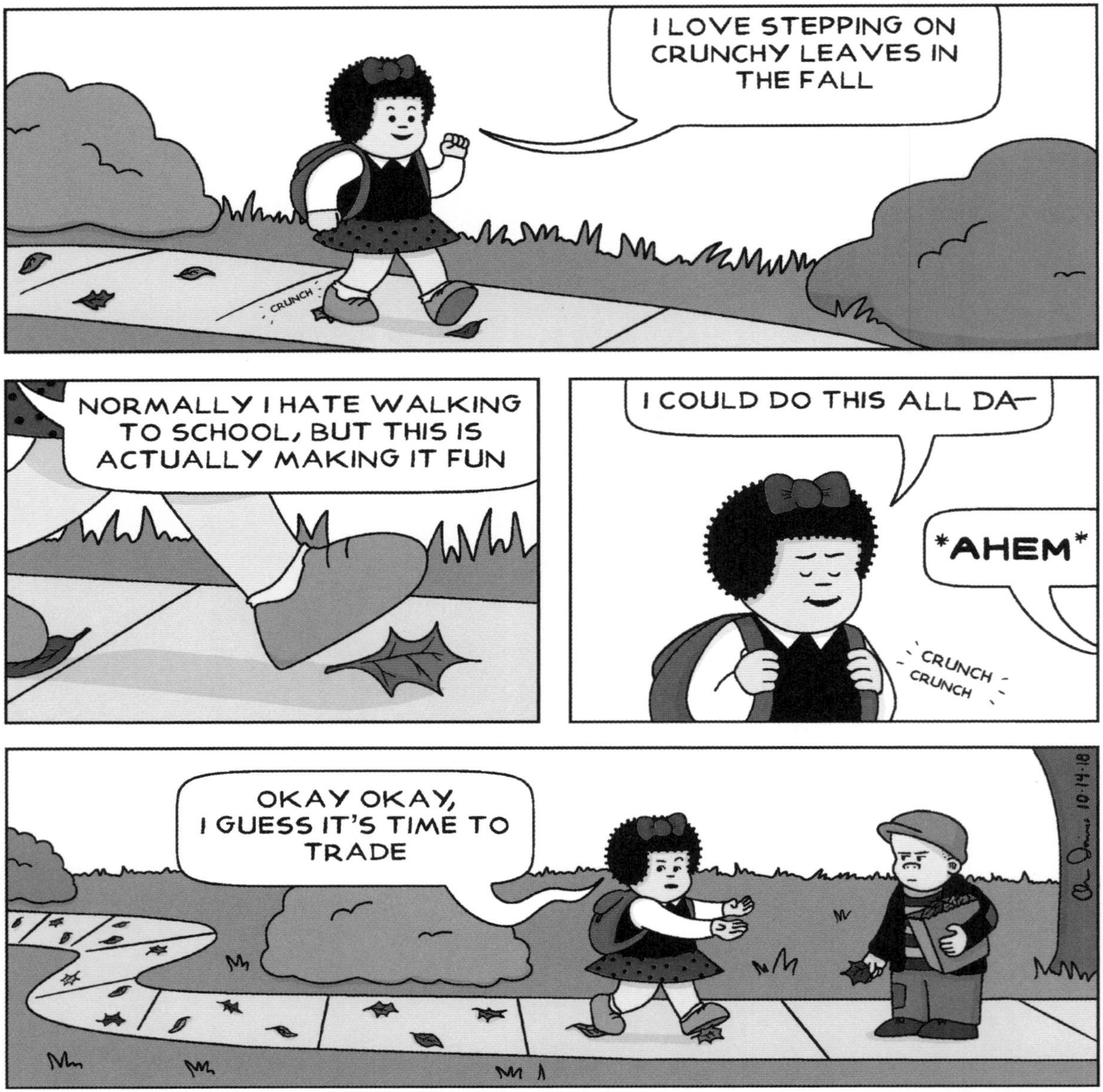
I LOVE STEPPING ON CRUNCHY LEAVES IN THE FALL
CRUNCH
NORMALLY I HATE WALKING TO SCHOOL, BUT THIS IS ACTUALLY MAKING IT FUN
I COULD DO THIS ALL DA—
AHEM
CRUNCH
CRUNCH
OKAY OKAY, I GUESS IT'S TIME TO TRADE

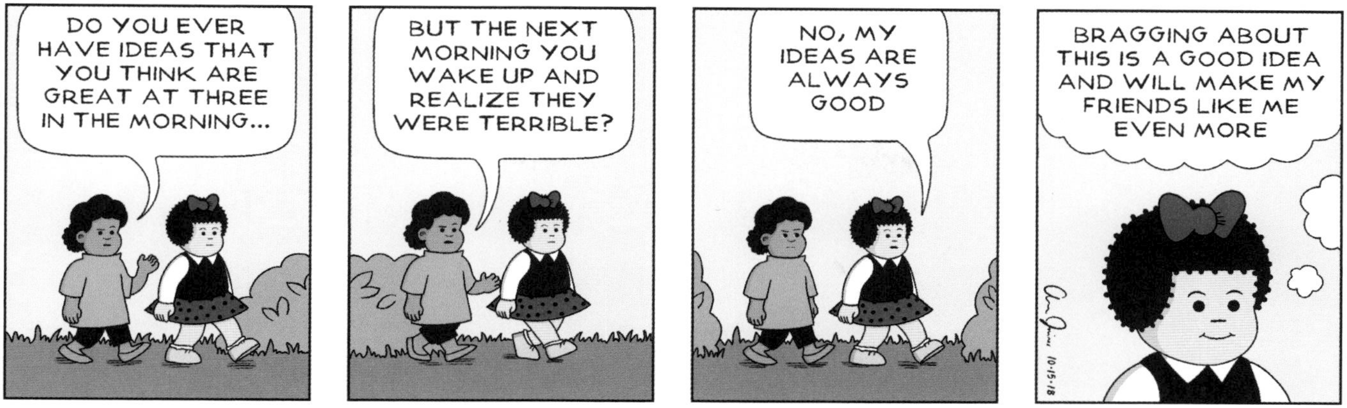
DO YOU EVER HAVE IDEAS THAT YOU THINK ARE GREAT AT THREE IN THE MORNING...
BUT THE NEXT MORNING YOU WAKE UP AND REALIZE THEY WERE TERRIBLE?
NO, MY IDEAS ARE ALWAYS GOOD
BRAGGING ABOUT THIS IS A GOOD IDEA AND WILL MAKE MY FRIENDS LIKE ME EVEN MORE

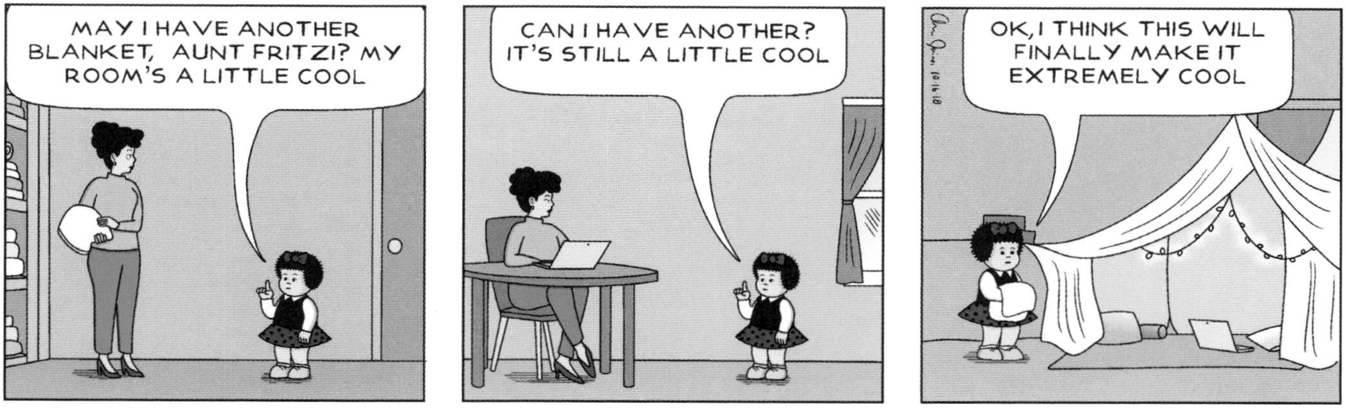
MAY I HAVE ANOTHER BLANKET, AUNT FRITZI? MY ROOM'S A LITTLE COOL
CAN I HAVE ANOTHER? IT'S STILL A LITTLE COOL
OK, I THINK THIS WILL FINALLY MAKE IT EXTREMELY COOL

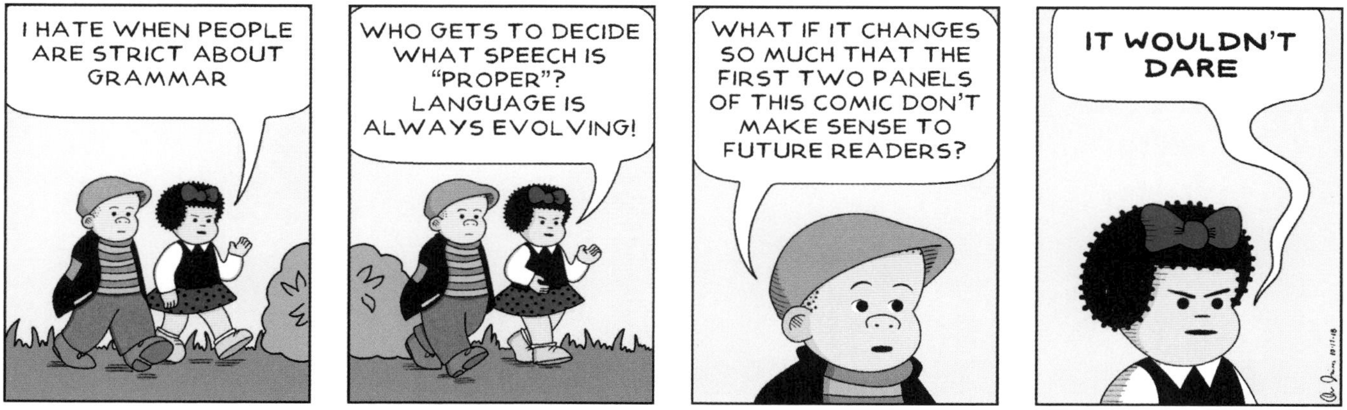
I HATE WHEN PEOPLE ARE STRICT ABOUT GRAMMAR
WHO GETS TO DECIDE WHAT SPEECH IS "PROPER"? LANGUAGE IS ALWAYS EVOLVING!
WHAT IF IT CHANGES SO MUCH THAT THE FIRST TWO PANELS OF THIS COMIC DON'T MAKE SENSE TO FUTURE READERS?
IT WOULDN'T DARE

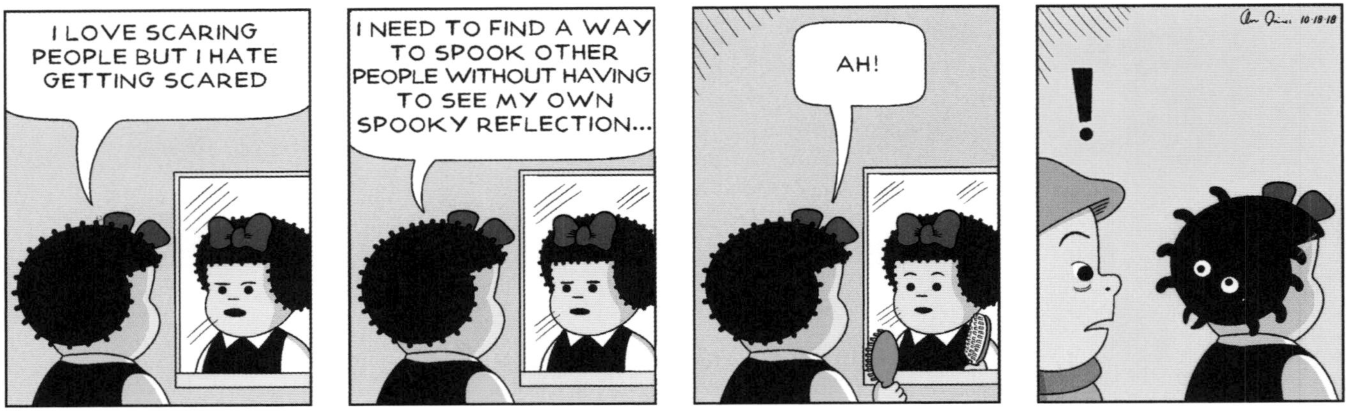
I LOVE SCARING PEOPLE BUT I HATE GETTING SCARED
I NEED TO FIND A WAY TO SPOOK OTHER PEOPLE WITHOUT HAVING TO SEE MY OWN SPOOKY REFLECTION...
AH!
!

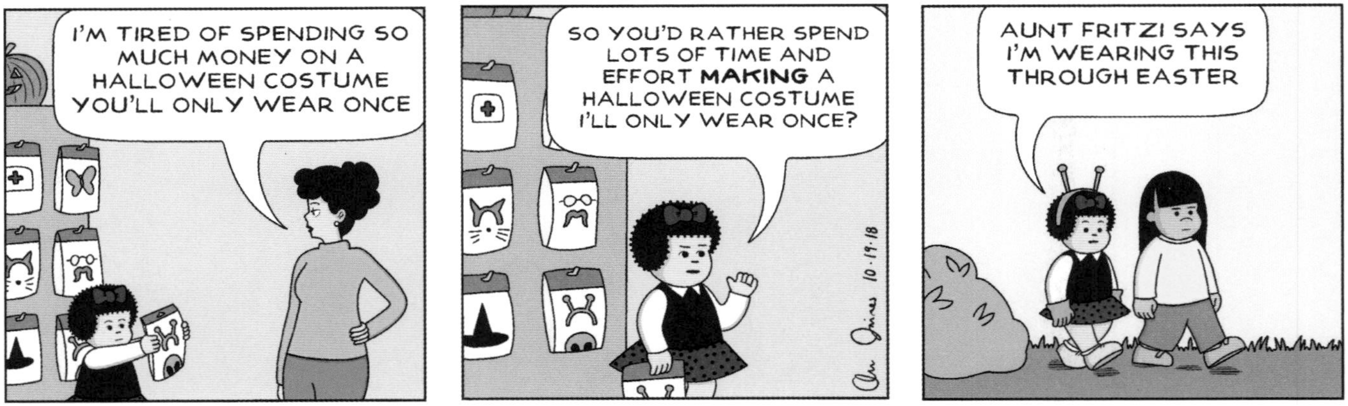
I'M TIRED OF SPENDING SO MUCH MONEY ON A HALLOWEEN COSTUME YOU'LL ONLY WEAR ONCE
SO YOU'D RATHER SPEND LOTS OF TIME AND EFFORT **MAKING** A HALLOWEEN COSTUME I'LL ONLY WEAR ONCE?
AUNT FRITZI SAYS I'M WEARING THIS THROUGH EASTER

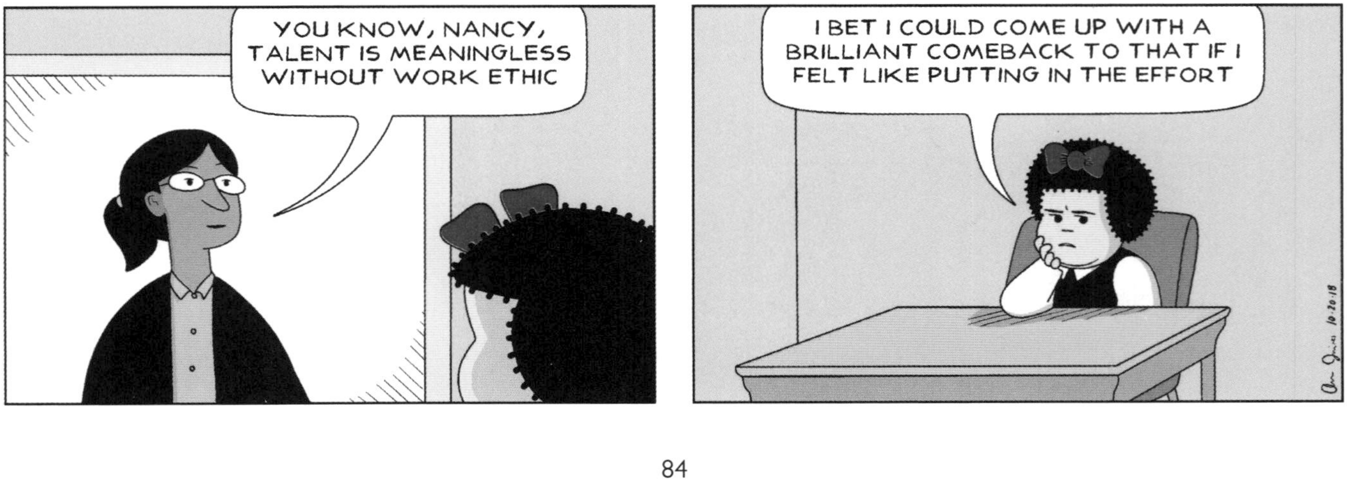
YOU KNOW, NANCY, TALENT IS MEANINGLESS WITHOUT WORK ETHIC
I BET I COULD COME UP WITH A BRILLIANT COMEBACK TO THAT IF I FELT LIKE PUTTING IN THE EFFORT

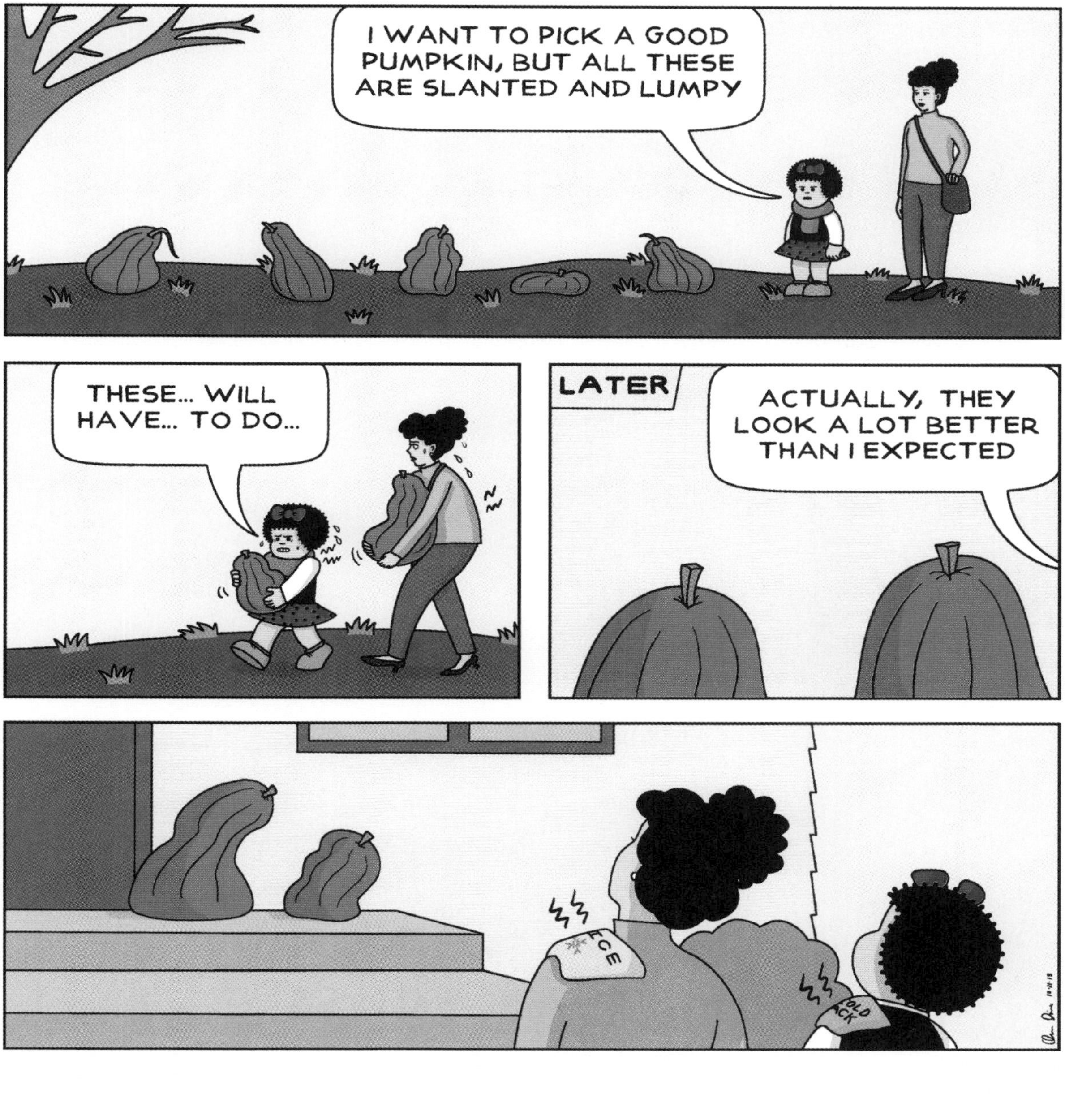
I WANT TO PICK A GOOD PUMPKIN, BUT ALL THESE ARE SLANTED AND LUMPY
THESE... WILL HAVE... TO DO...
LATER
ACTUALLY, THEY LOOK A LOT BETTER THAN I EXPECTED

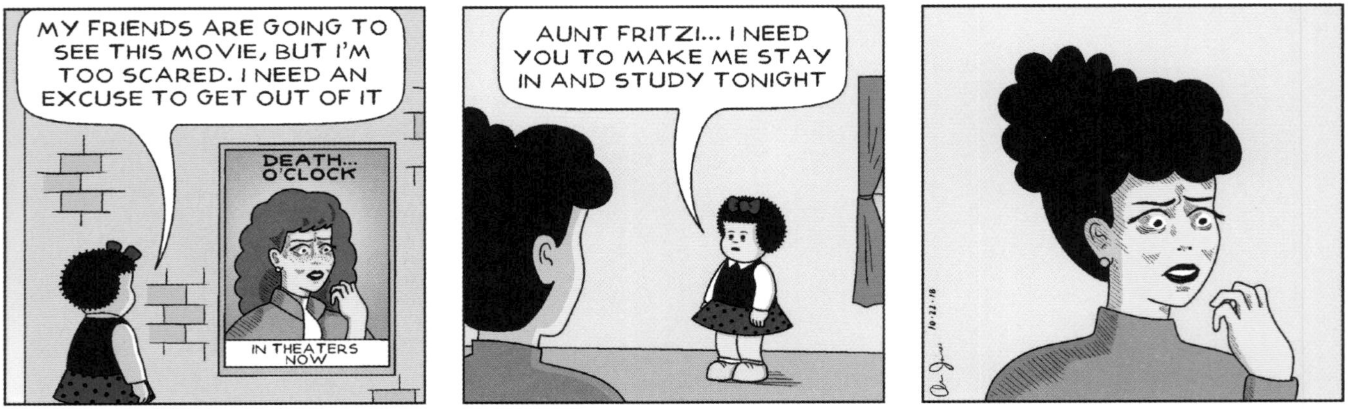
MY FRIENDS ARE GOING TO SEE THIS MOVIE, BUT I'M TOO SCARED. I NEED AN EXCUSE TO GET OUT OF IT
DEATH... O'CLOCK
IN THEATERS NOW
AUNT FRITZI... I NEED YOU TO MAKE ME STAY IN AND STUDY TONIGHT
10-22-18

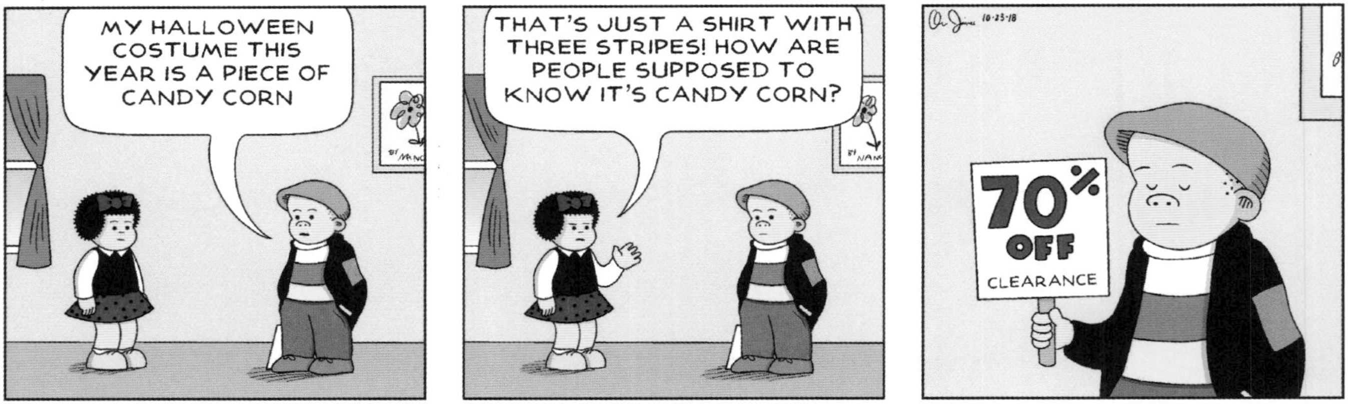
MY HALLOWEEN COSTUME THIS YEAR IS A PIECE OF CANDY CORN
THAT'S JUST A SHIRT WITH THREE STRIPES! HOW ARE PEOPLE SUPPOSED TO KNOW IT'S CANDY CORN?
10-23-18
70% OFF
CLEARANCE

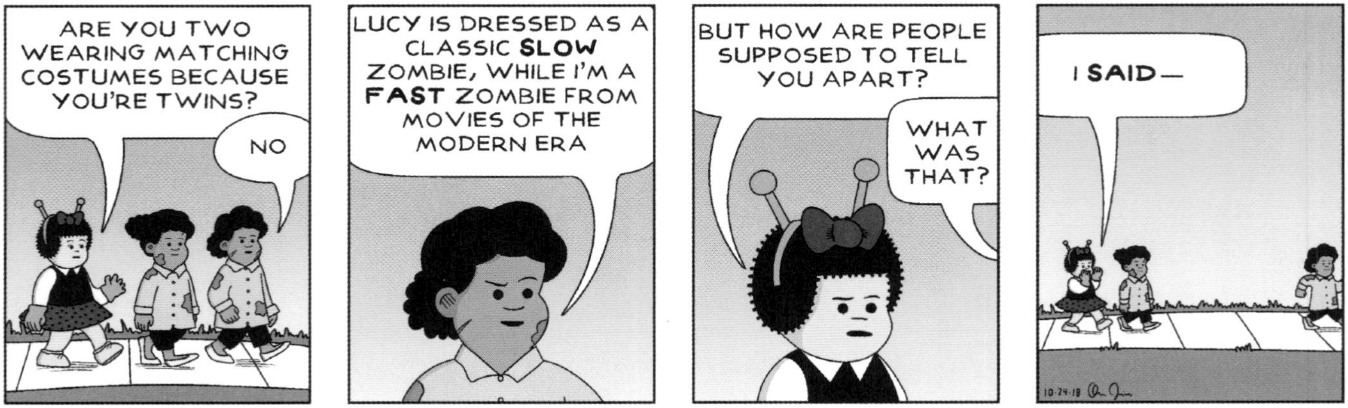
ARE YOU TWO WEARING MATCHING COSTUMES BECAUSE YOU'RE TWINS?
NO
LUCY IS DRESSED AS A CLASSIC **SLOW** ZOMBIE, WHILE I'M A **FAST** ZOMBIE FROM MOVIES OF THE MODERN ERA
BUT HOW ARE PEOPLE SUPPOSED TO TELL YOU APART?
WHAT WAS THAT?
I **SAID**—
10-24-18

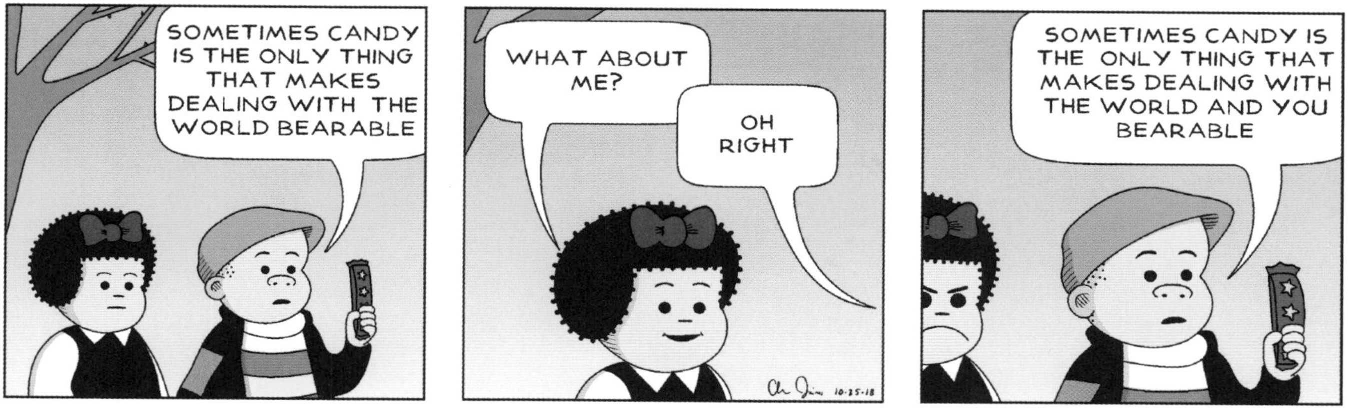
SOMETIMES CANDY IS THE ONLY THING THAT MAKES DEALING WITH THE WORLD BEARABLE
WHAT ABOUT ME?
OH RIGHT
SOMETIMES CANDY IS THE ONLY THING THAT MAKES DEALING WITH THE WORLD AND YOU BEARABLE

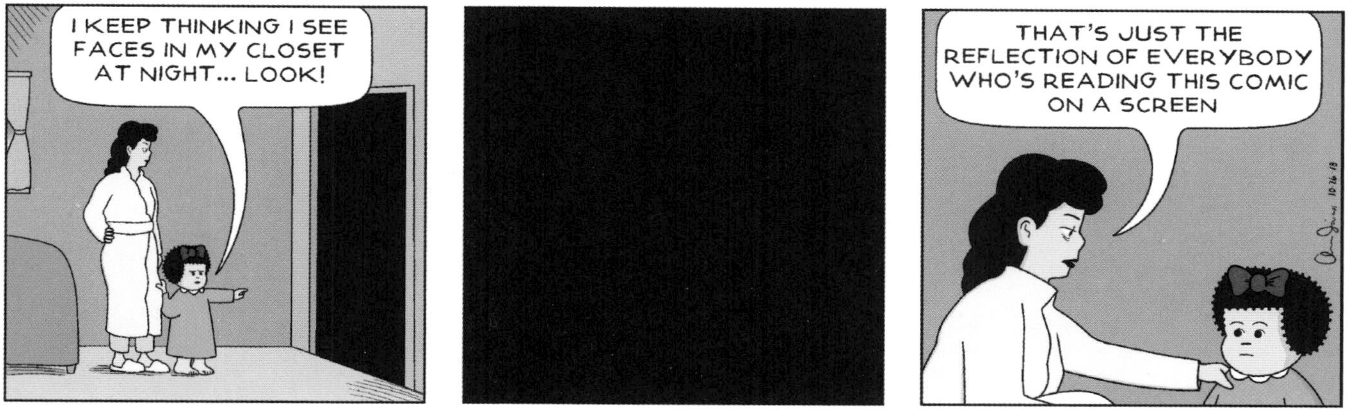
I KEEP THINKING I SEE FACES IN MY CLOSET AT NIGHT... LOOK!
THAT'S JUST THE REFLECTION OF EVERYBODY WHO'S READING THIS COMIC ON A SCREEN

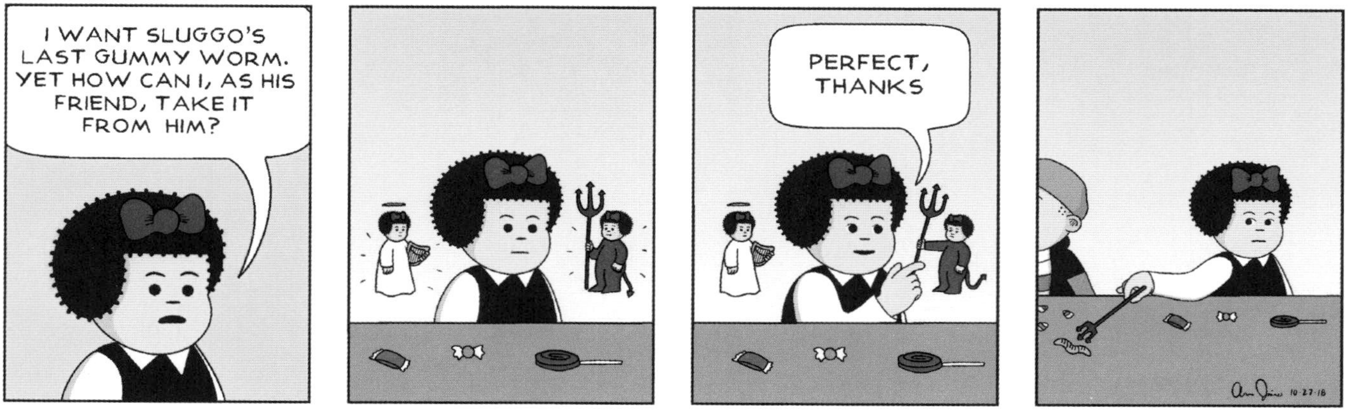
I WANT SLUGGO'S LAST GUMMY WORM. YET HOW CAN I, AS HIS FRIEND, TAKE IT FROM HIM?
PERFECT, THANKS

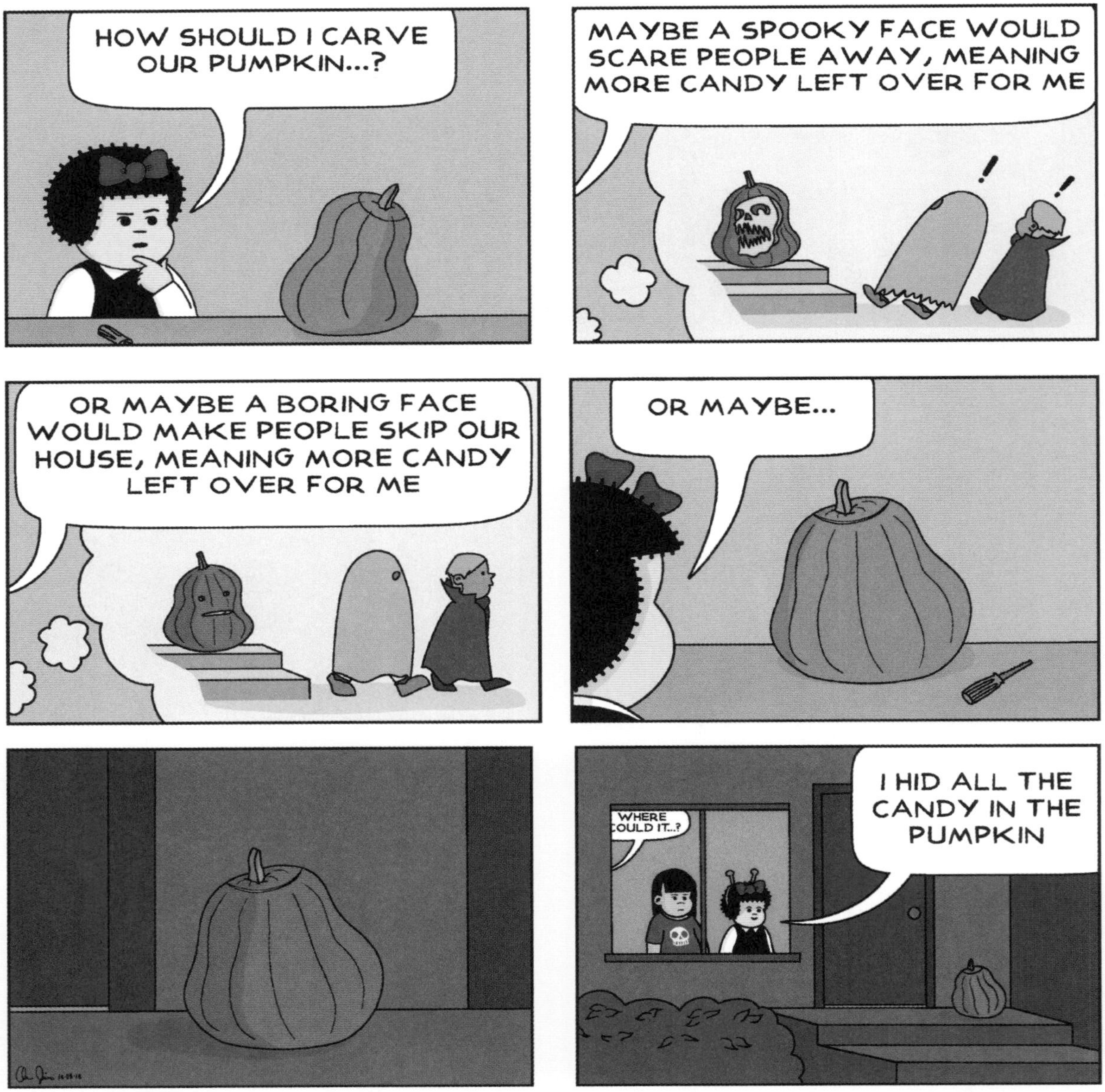
HOW SHOULD I CARVE OUR PUMPKIN...?
MAYBE A SPOOKY FACE WOULD SCARE PEOPLE AWAY, MEANING MORE CANDY LEFT OVER FOR ME
!
!
OR MAYBE A BORING FACE WOULD MAKE PEOPLE SKIP OUR HOUSE, MEANING MORE CANDY LEFT OVER FOR ME
OR MAYBE...
WHERE COULD IT...?
I HID ALL THE CANDY IN THE PUMPKIN

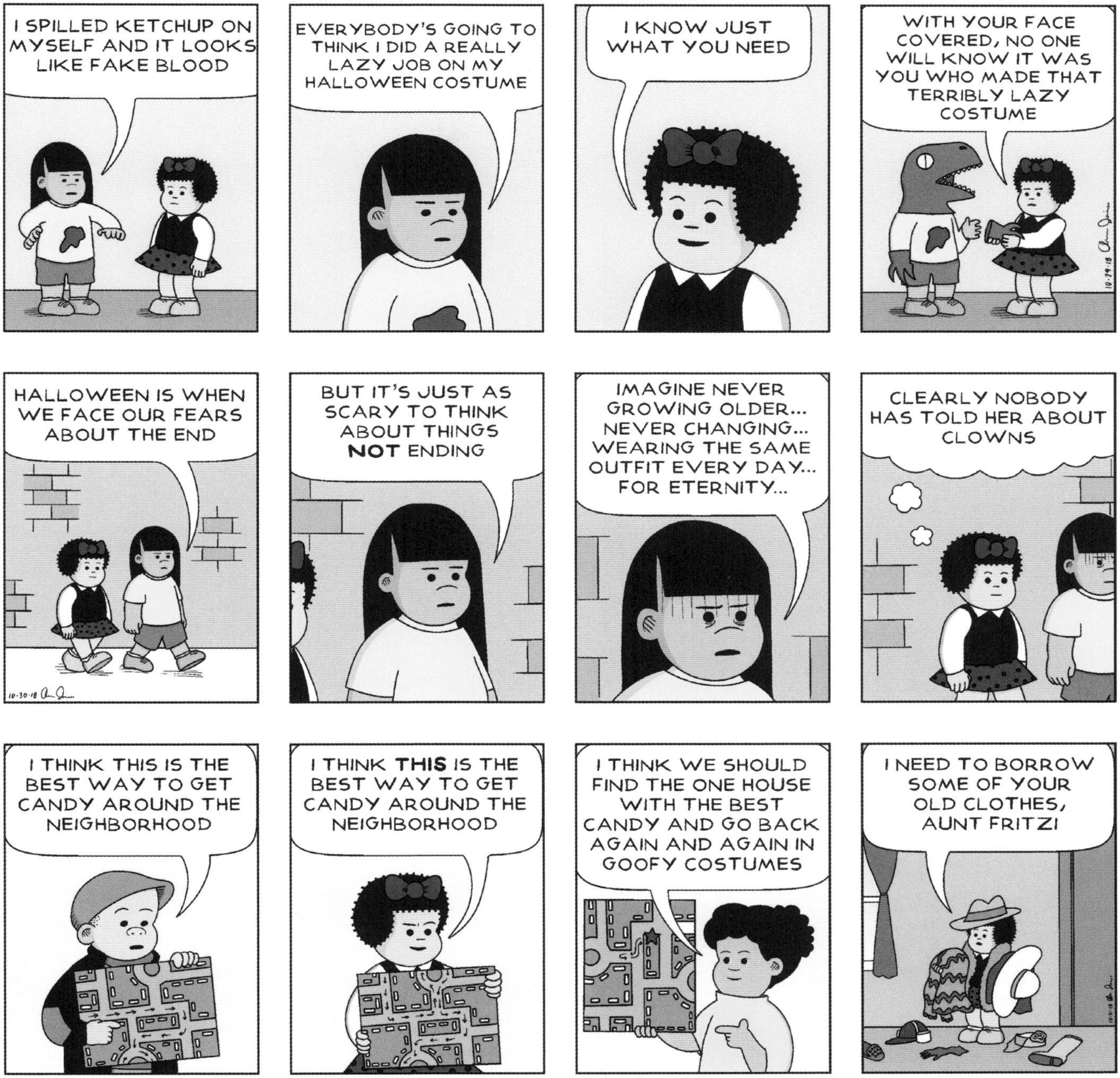
I SPILLED KETCHUP ON MYSELF AND IT LOOKS LIKE FAKE BLOOD
EVERYBODY'S GOING TO THINK I DID A REALLY LAZY JOB ON MY HALLOWEEN COSTUME
I KNOW JUST WHAT YOU NEED
WITH YOUR FACE COVERED, NO ONE WILL KNOW IT WAS YOU WHO MADE THAT TERRIBLY LAZY COSTUME
10-29-18
HALLOWEEN IS WHEN WE FACE OUR FEARS ABOUT THE END
BUT IT'S JUST AS SCARY TO THINK ABOUT THINGS **NOT** ENDING
IMAGINE NEVER GROWING OLDER... NEVER CHANGING... WEARING THE SAME OUTFIT EVERY DAY... FOR ETERNITY...
CLEARLY NOBODY HAS TOLD HER ABOUT CLOWNS
10-30-18
I THINK THIS IS THE BEST WAY TO GET CANDY AROUND THE NEIGHBORHOOD
I THINK **THIS** IS THE BEST WAY TO GET CANDY AROUND THE NEIGHBORHOOD
I THINK WE SHOULD FIND THE ONE HOUSE WITH THE BEST CANDY AND GO BACK AGAIN AND AGAIN IN GOOFY COSTUMES
I NEED TO BORROW SOME OF YOUR OLD CLOTHES, AUNT FRITZI

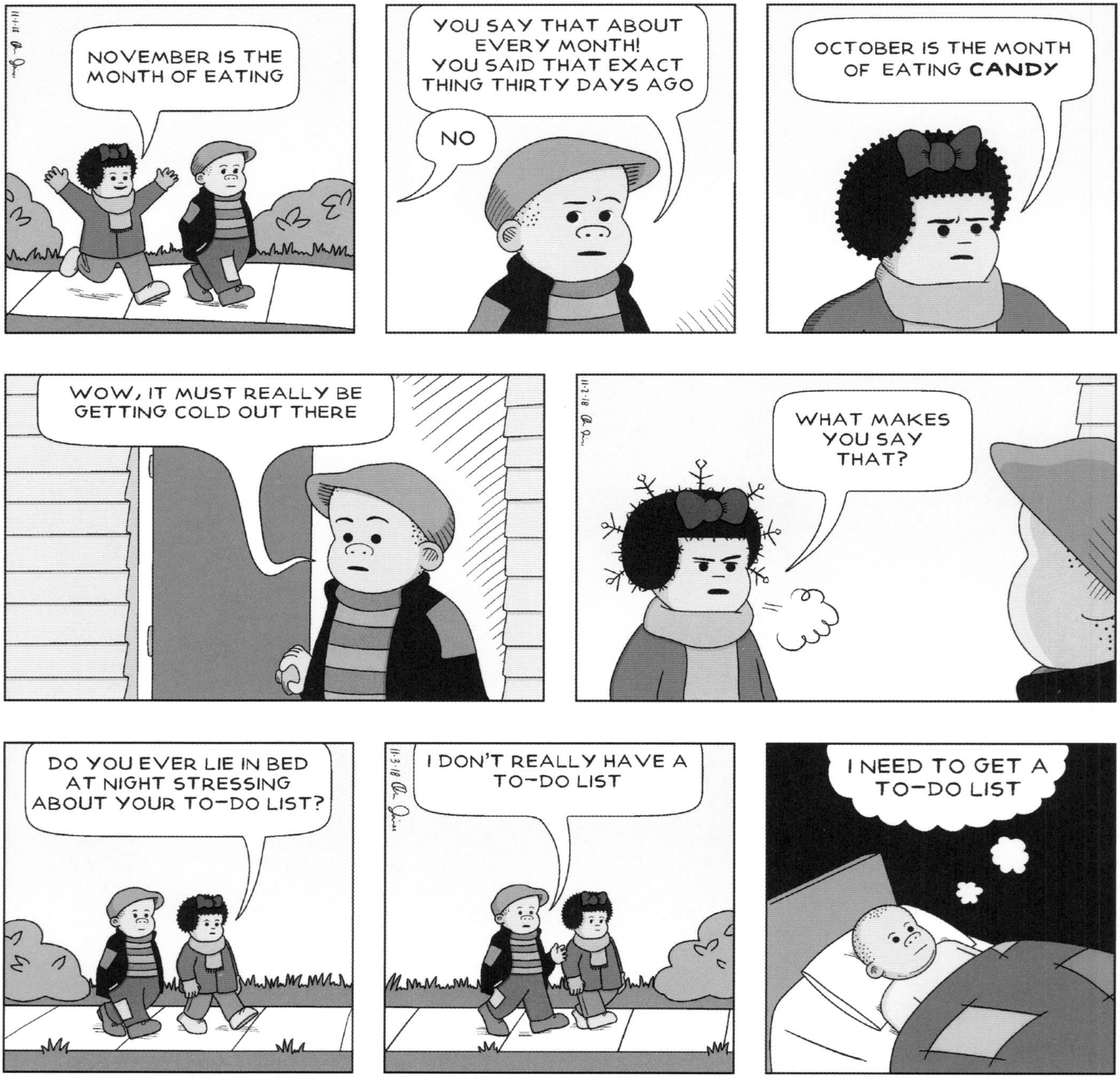
NOVEMBER IS THE MONTH OF EATING
YOU SAY THAT ABOUT EVERY MONTH! YOU SAID THAT EXACT THING THIRTY DAYS AGO
NO
OCTOBER IS THE MONTH OF EATING **CANDY**
WOW, IT MUST REALLY BE GETTING COLD OUT THERE
WHAT MAKES YOU SAY THAT?
DO YOU EVER LIE IN BED AT NIGHT STRESSING ABOUT YOUR TO-DO LIST?
I DON'T REALLY HAVE A TO-DO LIST
I NEED TO GET A TO-DO LIST

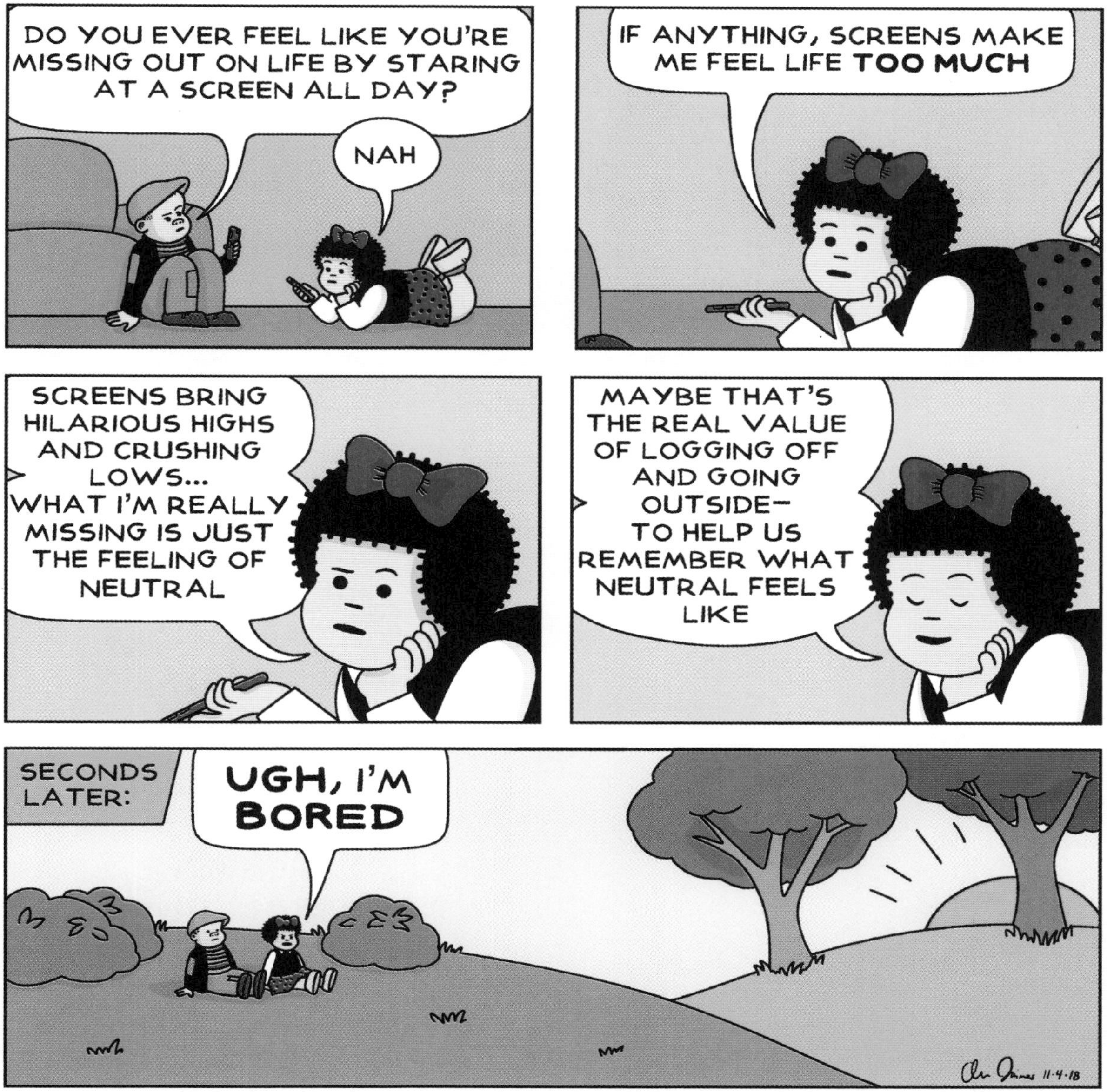
DO YOU EVER FEEL LIKE YOU'RE MISSING OUT ON LIFE BY STARING AT A SCREEN ALL DAY?
NAH
IF ANYTHING, SCREENS MAKE ME FEEL LIFE **TOO MUCH**
SCREENS BRING HILARIOUS HIGHS AND CRUSHING LOWS... WHAT I'M REALLY MISSING IS JUST THE FEELING OF NEUTRAL
MAYBE THAT'S THE REAL VALUE OF LOGGING OFF AND GOING OUTSIDE— TO HELP US REMEMBER WHAT NEUTRAL FEELS LIKE
SECONDS LATER:
UGH, I'M BORED
11·4·18

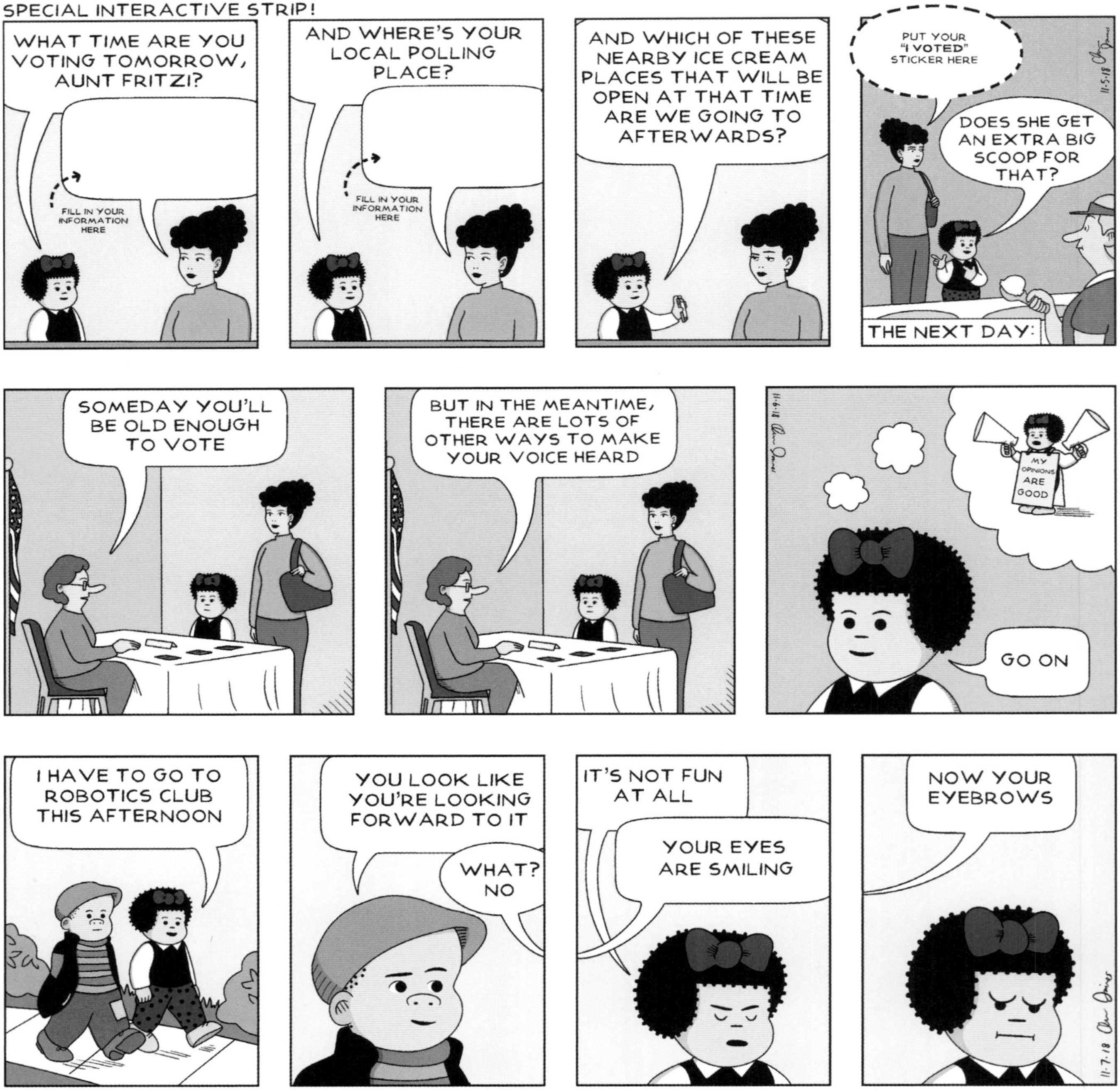
SPECIAL INTERACTIVE STRIP!
WHAT TIME ARE YOU VOTING TOMORROW, AUNT FRITZI?
FILL IN YOUR INFORMATION HERE
AND WHERE'S YOUR LOCAL POLLING PLACE?
FILL IN YOUR INFORMATION HERE
AND WHICH OF THESE NEARBY ICE CREAM PLACES THAT WILL BE OPEN AT THAT TIME ARE WE GOING TO AFTERWARDS?
PUT YOUR "I VOTED" STICKER HERE
11-5-18
DOES SHE GET AN EXTRA BIG SCOOP FOR THAT?
THE NEXT DAY:
SOMEDAY YOU'LL BE OLD ENOUGH TO VOTE
11-6-18
BUT IN THE MEANTIME, THERE ARE LOTS OF OTHER WAYS TO MAKE YOUR VOICE HEARD
MY OPINIONS ARE GOOD
GO ON
I HAVE TO GO TO ROBOTICS CLUB THIS AFTERNOON
YOU LOOK LIKE YOU'RE LOOKING FORWARD TO IT
WHAT? NO
IT'S NOT FUN AT ALL
YOUR EYES ARE SMILING
NOW YOUR EYEBROWS
11-7-18

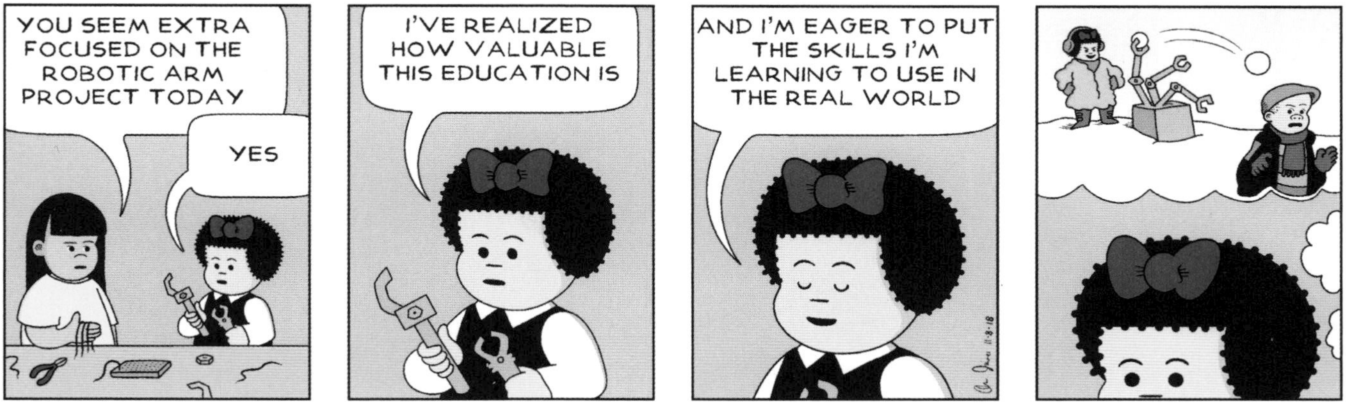
YOU SEEM EXTRA FOCUSED ON THE ROBOTIC ARM PROJECT TODAY
YES
I'VE REALIZED HOW VALUABLE THIS EDUCATION IS
AND I'M EAGER TO PUT THE SKILLS I'M LEARNING TO USE IN THE REAL WORLD

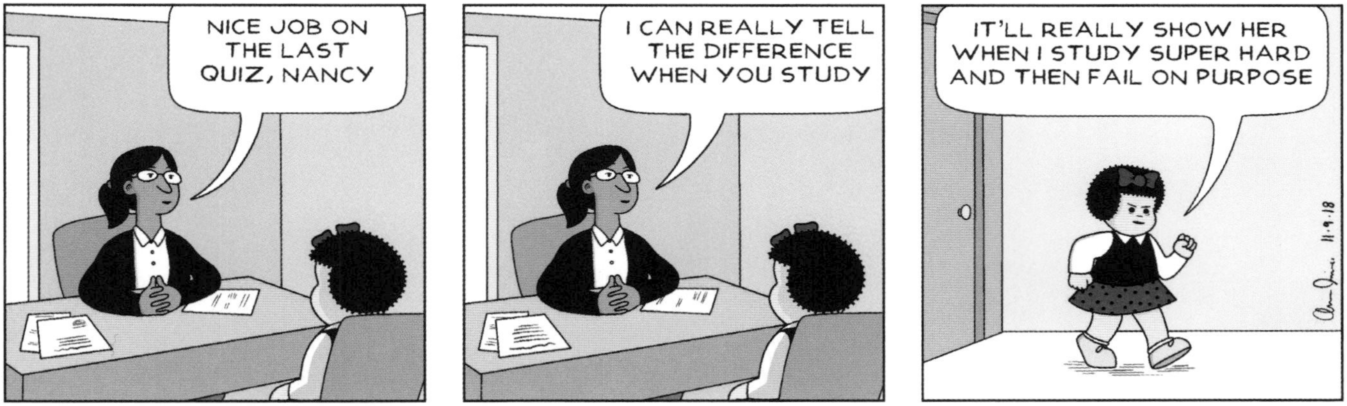
NICE JOB ON THE LAST QUIZ, NANCY
I CAN REALLY TELL THE DIFFERENCE WHEN YOU STUDY
IT'LL REALLY SHOW HER WHEN I STUDY SUPER HARD AND THEN FAIL ON PURPOSE

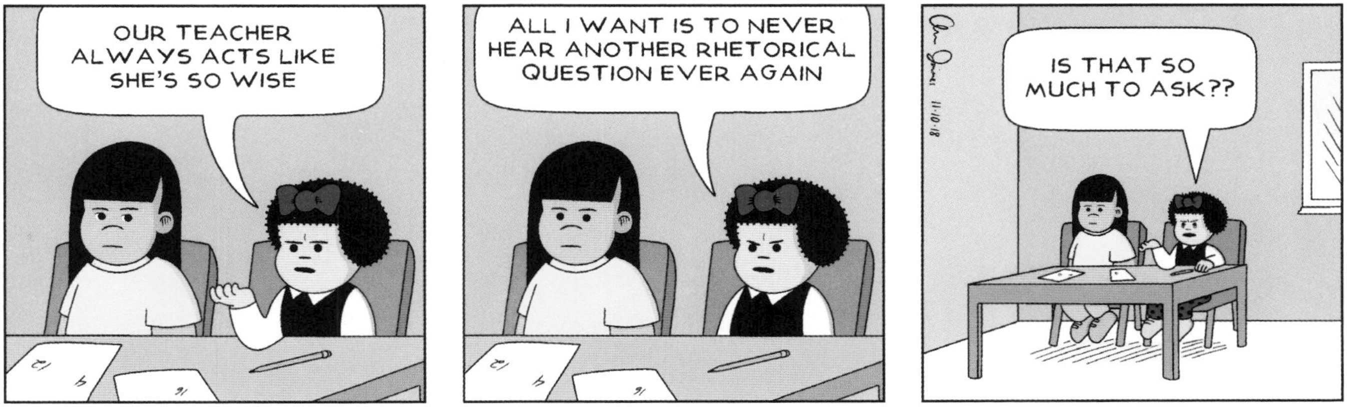
OUR TEACHER ALWAYS ACTS LIKE SHE'S SO WISE
ALL I WANT IS TO NEVER HEAR ANOTHER RHETORICAL QUESTION EVER AGAIN
IS THAT SO MUCH TO ASK??

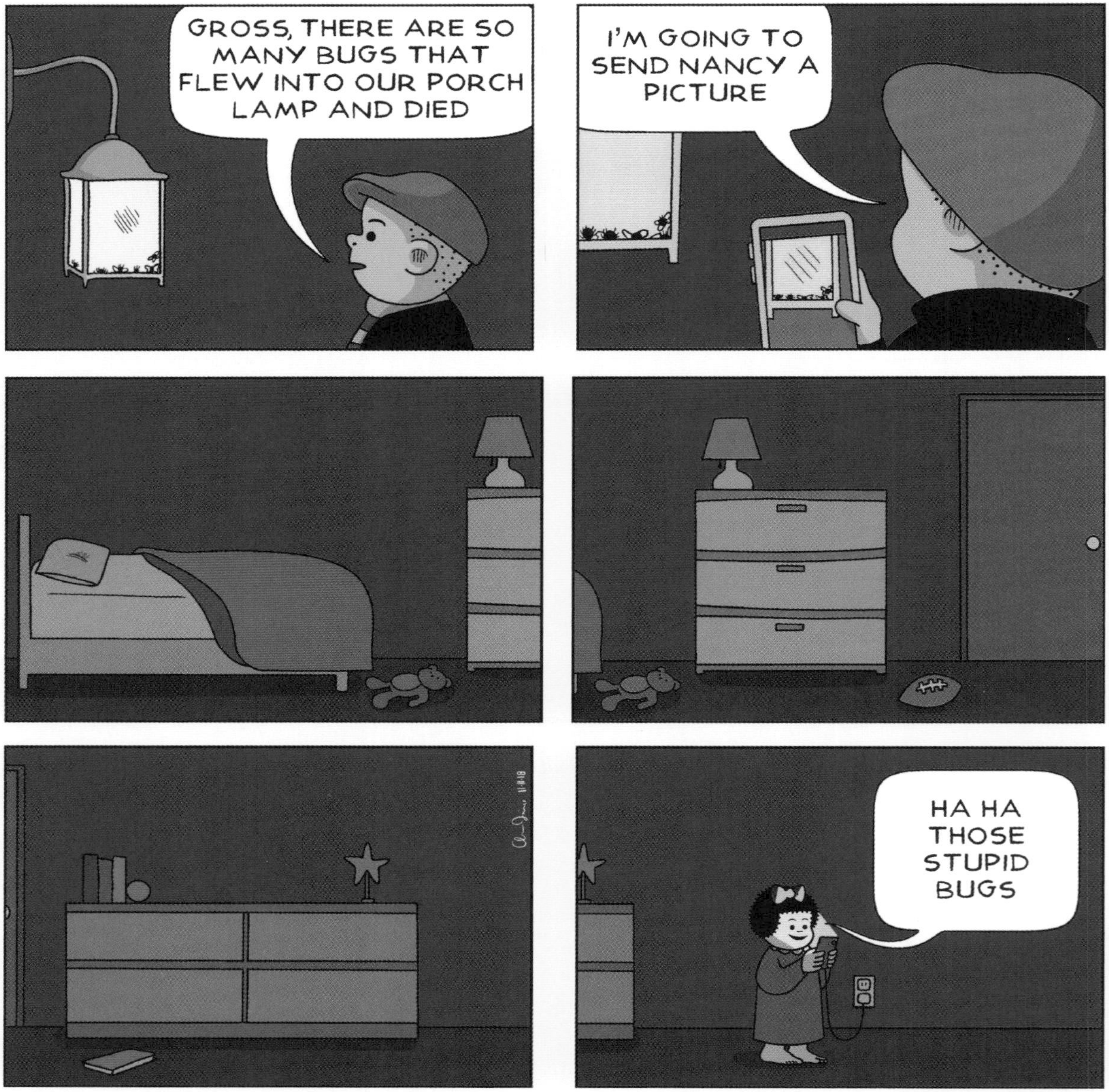
GROSS, THERE ARE SO MANY BUGS THAT FLEW INTO OUR PORCH LAMP AND DIED
I'M GOING TO SEND NANCY A PICTURE
HA HA THOSE STUPID BUGS

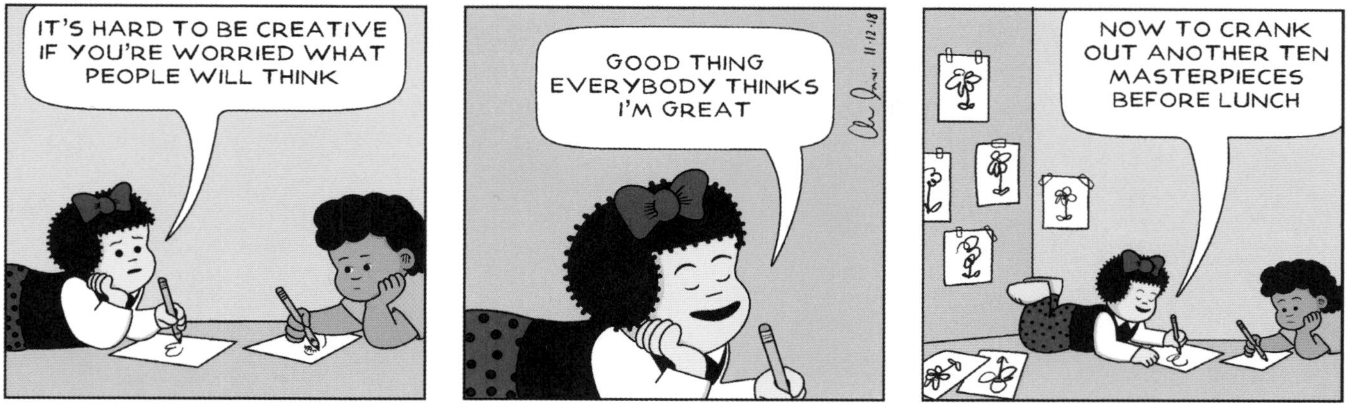
IT'S HARD TO BE CREATIVE IF YOU'RE WORRIED WHAT PEOPLE WILL THINK
GOOD THING EVERYBODY THINKS I'M GREAT
NOW TO CRANK OUT ANOTHER TEN MASTERPIECES BEFORE LUNCH

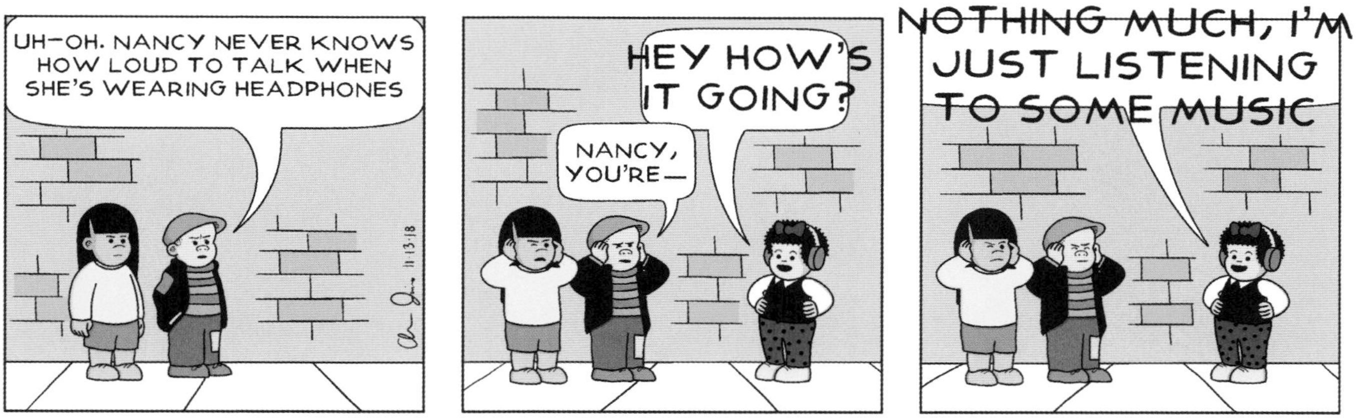
UH-OH. NANCY NEVER KNOWS HOW LOUD TO TALK WHEN SHE'S WEARING HEADPHONES
HEY HOW'S IT GOING?
NANCY, YOU'RE—
NOTHING MUCH, I'M JUST LISTENING TO SOME MUSIC

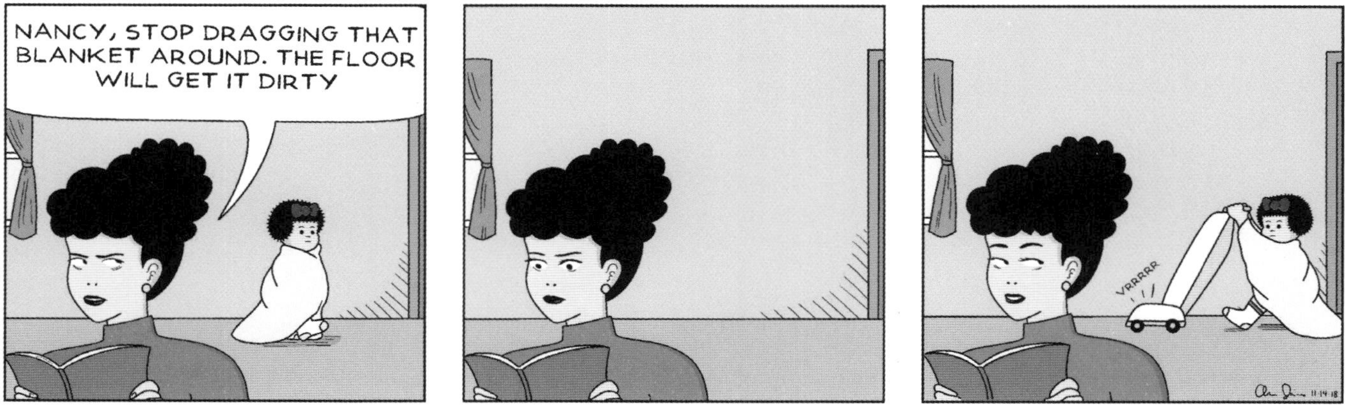
NANCY, STOP DRAGGING THAT BLANKET AROUND. THE FLOOR WILL GET IT DIRTY

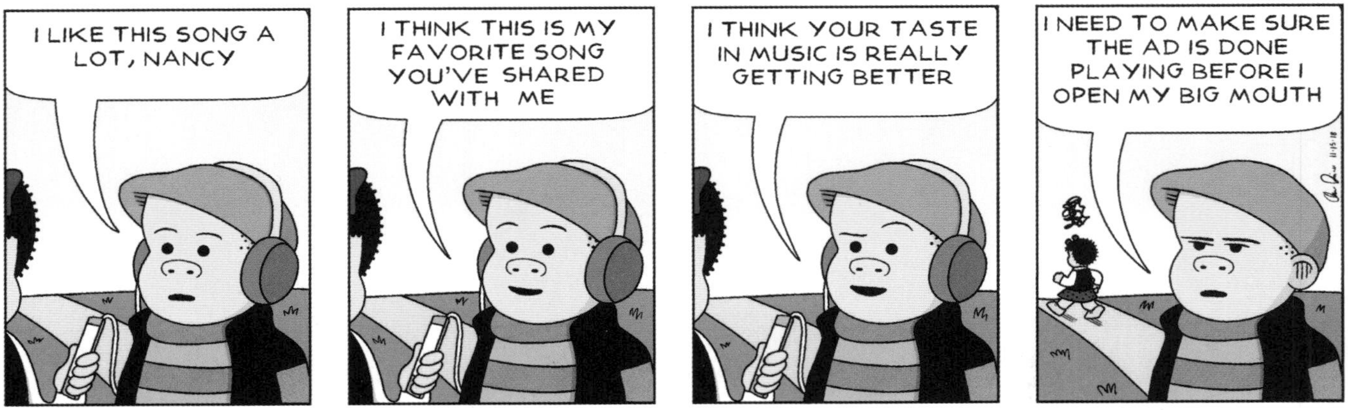
I LIKE THIS SONG A LOT, NANCY
I THINK THIS IS MY FAVORITE SONG YOU'VE SHARED WITH ME
I THINK YOUR TASTE IN MUSIC IS REALLY GETTING BETTER
I NEED TO MAKE SURE THE AD IS DONE PLAYING BEFORE I OPEN MY BIG MOUTH

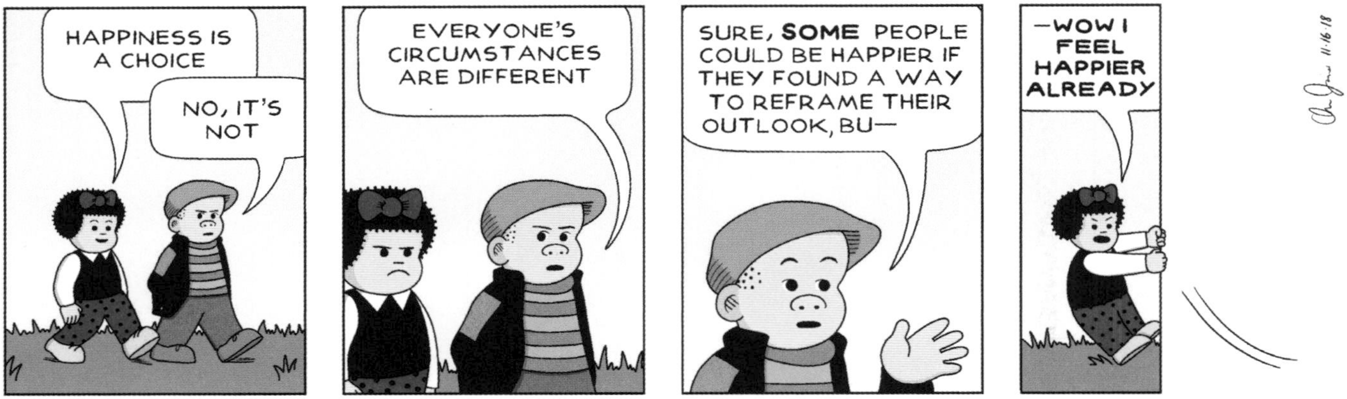
HAPPINESS IS A CHOICE
NO, IT'S NOT
EVERYONE'S CIRCUMSTANCES ARE DIFFERENT
SURE, **SOME** PEOPLE COULD BE HAPPIER IF THEY FOUND A WAY TO REFRAME THEIR OUTLOOK, BU—
—WOW I FEEL HAPPIER ALREADY

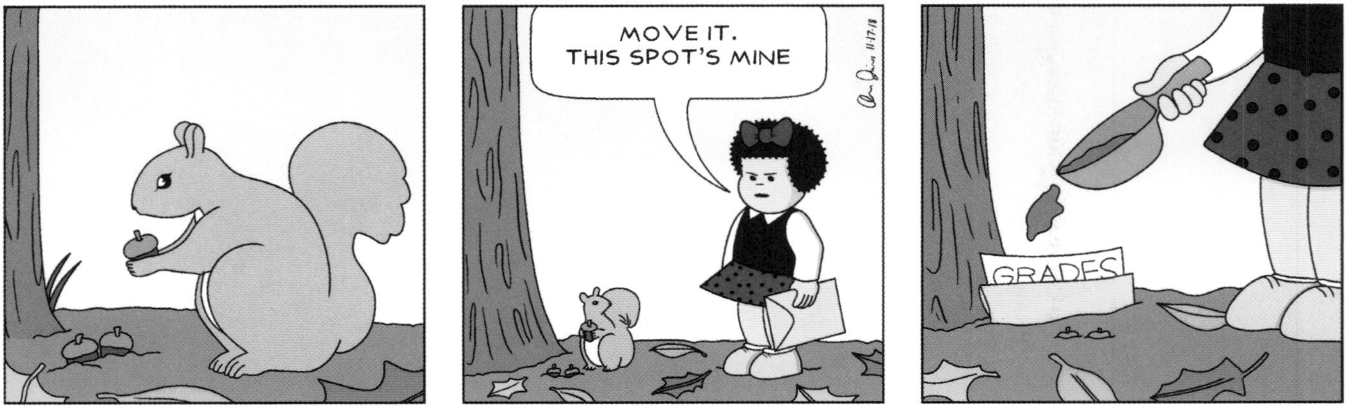
MOVE IT. THIS SPOT'S MINE
GRADES

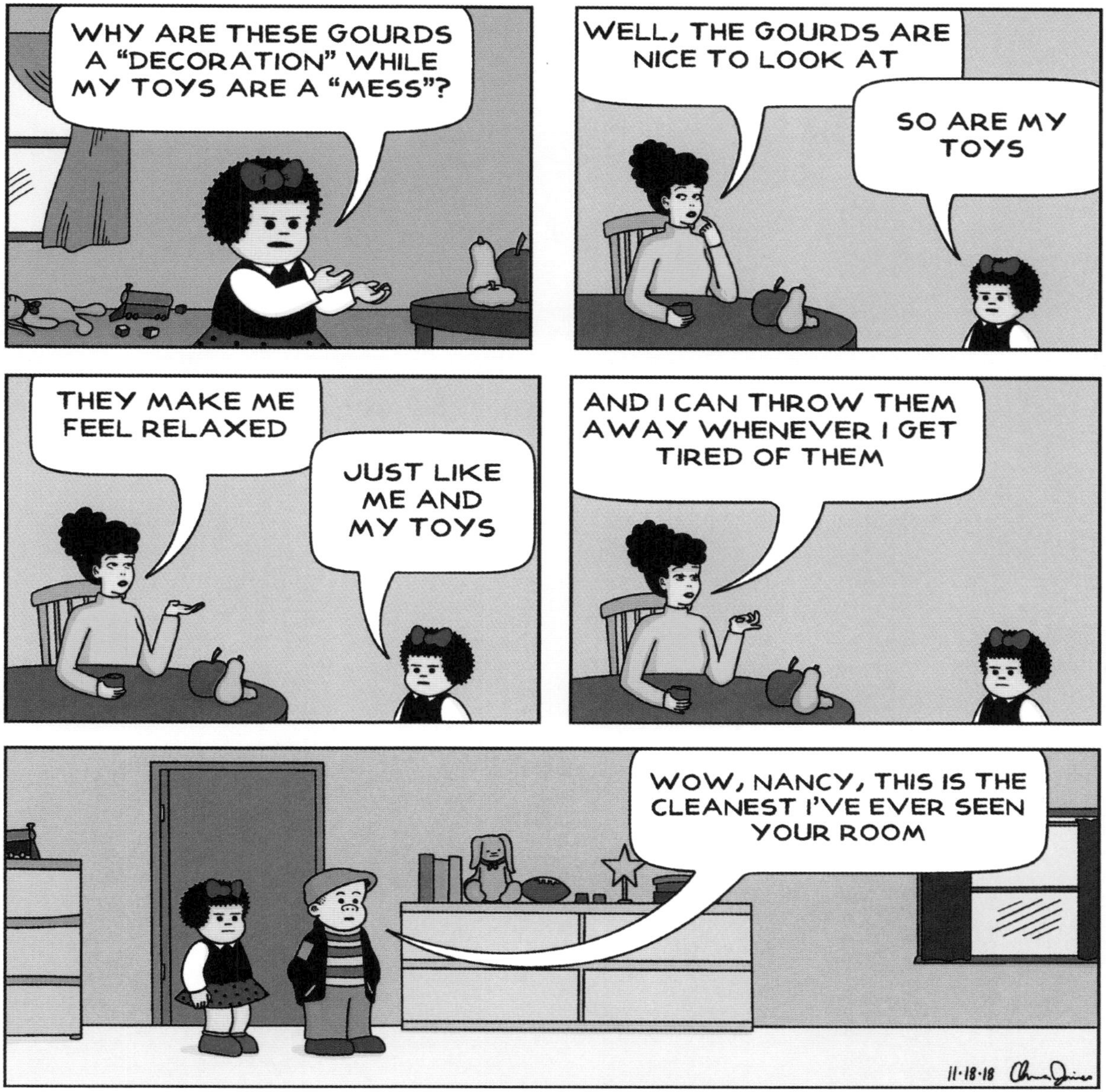
WHY ARE THESE GOURDS A "DECORATION" WHILE MY TOYS ARE A "MESS"?
WELL, THE GOURDS ARE NICE TO LOOK AT
SO ARE MY TOYS
THEY MAKE ME FEEL RELAXED
JUST LIKE ME AND MY TOYS
AND I CAN THROW THEM AWAY WHENEVER I GET TIRED OF THEM
WOW, NANCY, THIS IS THE CLEANEST I'VE EVER SEEN YOUR ROOM
11·18·18

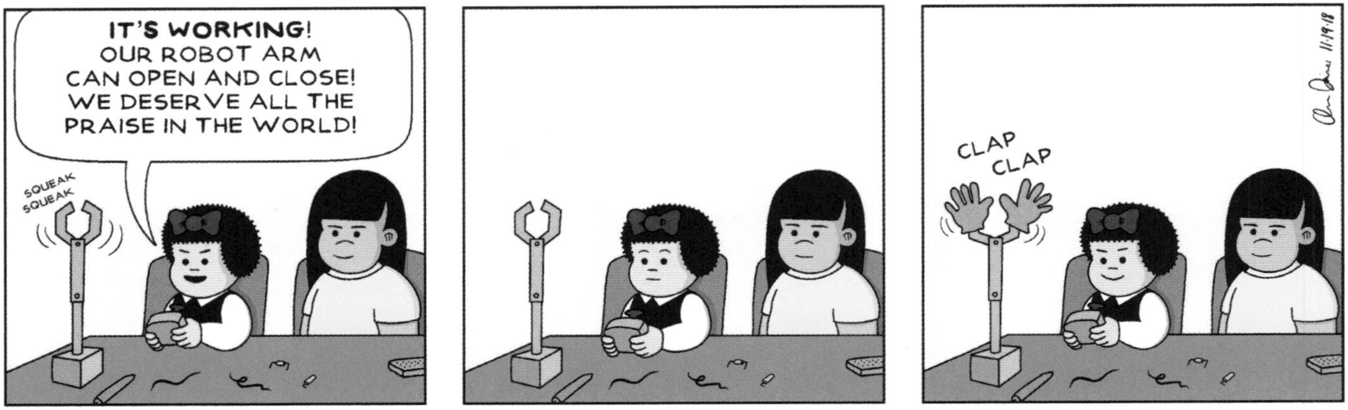
IT'S WORKING! OUR ROBOT ARM CAN OPEN AND CLOSE! WE DESERVE ALL THE PRAISE IN THE WORLD!
SQUEAK SQUEAK
CLAP CLAP
11-19-18

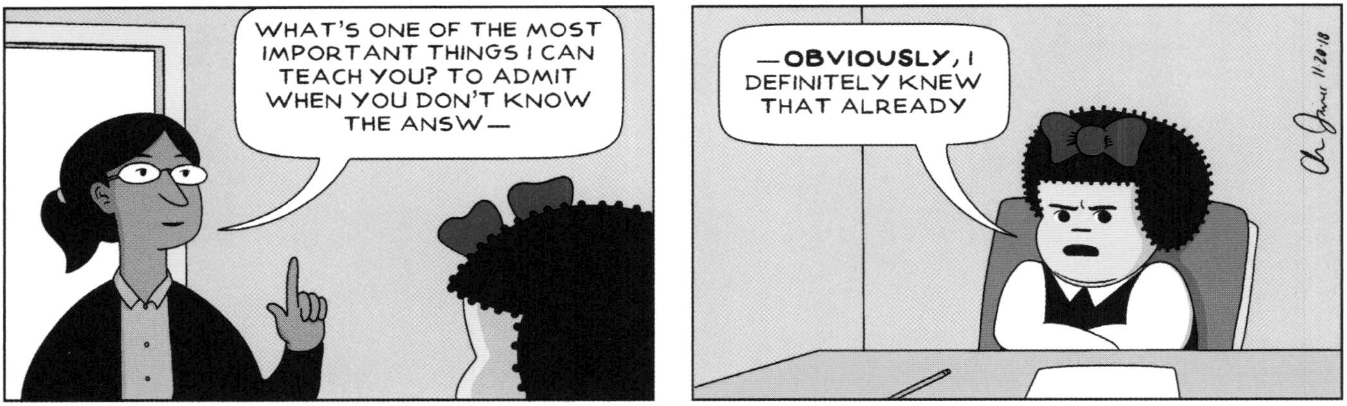
WHAT'S ONE OF THE MOST IMPORTANT THINGS I CAN TEACH YOU? TO ADMIT WHEN YOU DON'T KNOW THE ANSW—
—OBVIOUSLY, I DEFINITELY KNEW THAT ALREADY
11-20-18

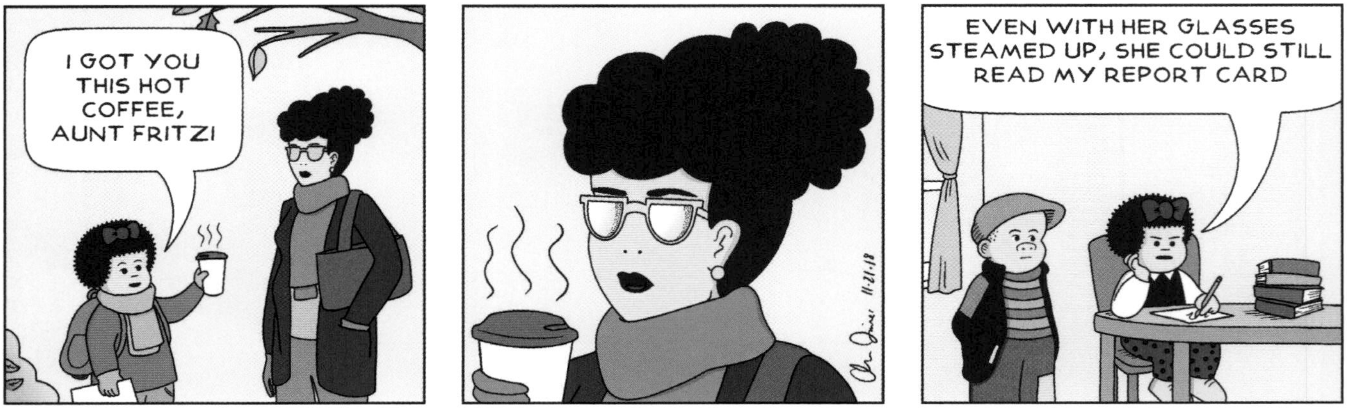
I GOT YOU THIS HOT COFFEE, AUNT FRITZI
11-21-18
EVEN WITH HER GLASSES STEAMED UP, SHE COULD STILL READ MY REPORT CARD

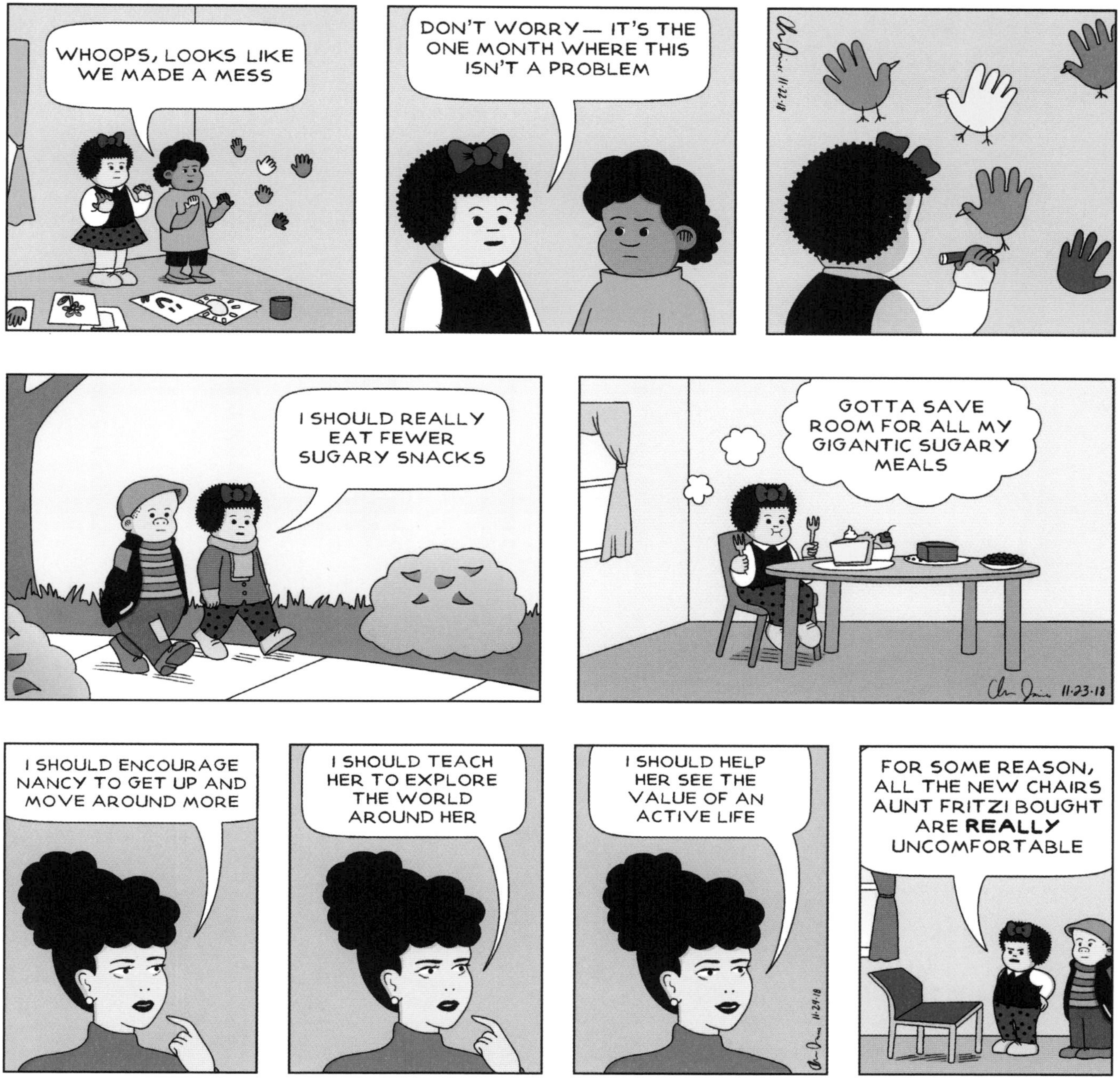

WHOOPS, LOOKS LIKE WE MADE A MESS
DON'T WORRY— IT'S THE ONE MONTH WHERE THIS ISN'T A PROBLEM
11-22-18
I SHOULD REALLY EAT FEWER SUGARY SNACKS
GOTTA SAVE ROOM FOR ALL MY GIGANTIC SUGARY MEALS
11-23-18
I SHOULD ENCOURAGE NANCY TO GET UP AND MOVE AROUND MORE
I SHOULD TEACH HER TO EXPLORE THE WORLD AROUND HER
I SHOULD HELP HER SEE THE VALUE OF AN ACTIVE LIFE
11-24-18
FOR SOME REASON, ALL THE NEW CHAIRS AUNT FRITZI BOUGHT ARE **REALLY** UNCOMFORTABLE

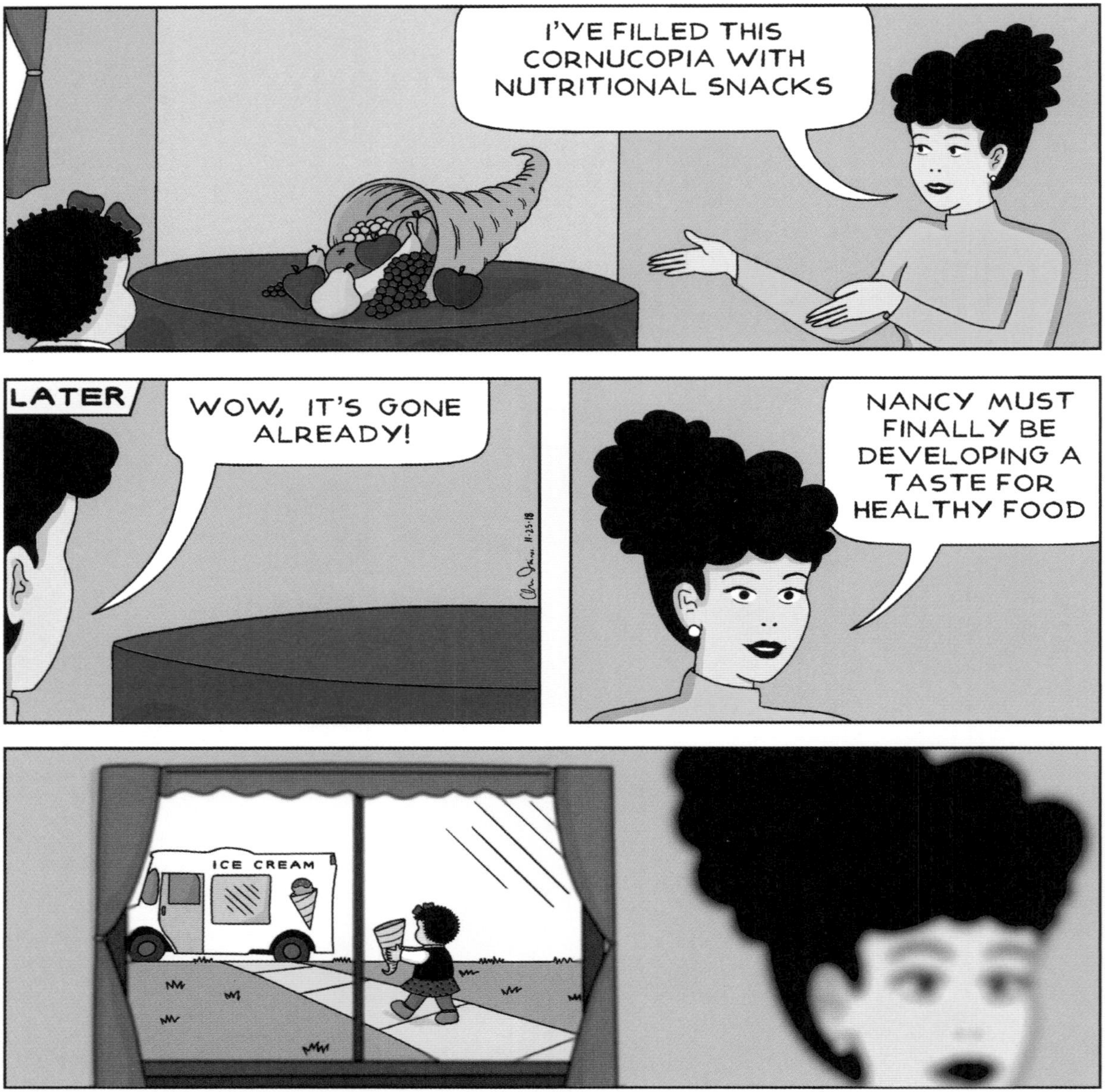
I'VE FILLED THIS CORNUCOPIA WITH NUTRITIONAL SNACKS
LATER
WOW, IT'S GONE ALREADY!
NANCY MUST FINALLY BE DEVELOPING A TASTE FOR HEALTHY FOOD
ICE CREAM

EVERY YEAR WE MAKE TOO MUCH FOOD FOR THANKSGIVING...

...AND EVERY YEAR WE'RE STUCK EATING LEFTOVERS FOR THE NEXT TWO WEEKS

..AND EVERY YEAR WE GET SO SICK OF THOSE LEFTOVER DISHES THAT WE DON'T COOK THEM FOR ANOTHER YEAR

WHICH IS WHY I MADE SURE EVERYTHING WE ATE FOR THANKSGIVING THIS YEAR CONTAINED KALE

IT'S SO HARD TO STAY AWAKE IN CLASS AFTER THANKSGIVING BREAK

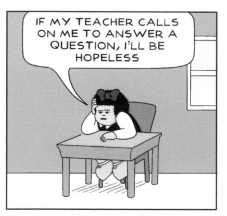

IF MY TEACHER CALLS ON ME TO ANSWER A QUESTION, I'LL BE HOPELESS

FIFTEEN SECONDS LATER:

...IF I DO WHAT?

NANCY'S BEEN HANGING CHRISTMAS LIGHTS FOR HOURS!

NOTHING LIKE THE HOLIDAYS TO GET HER UP AND MOVING

AT LAST I CAN GET SNACKS AND PLAY VIDEO GAMES WITHOUT EVER HAVING TO LEAVE THIS COMFY CHAIR

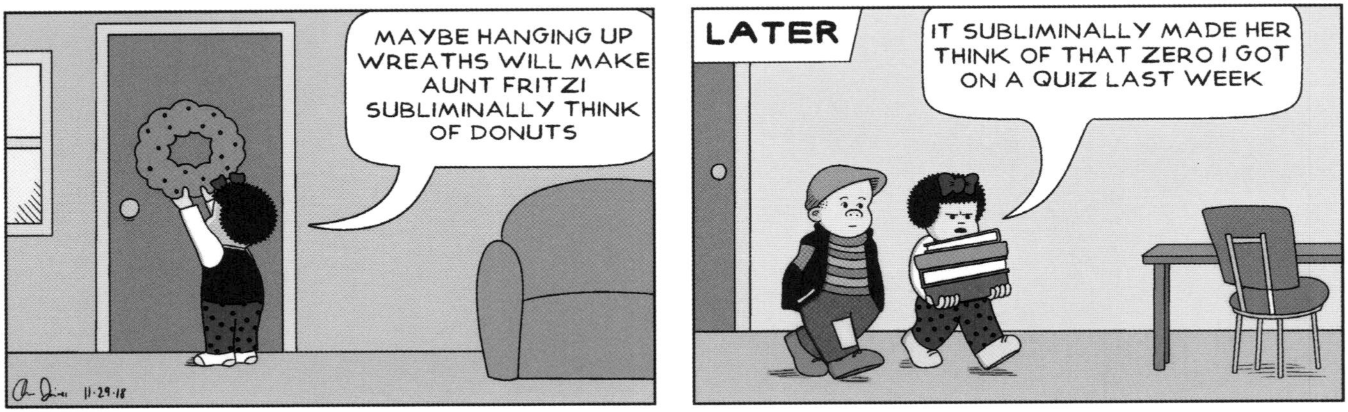
MAYBE HANGING UP WREATHS WILL MAKE AUNT FRITZI SUBLIMINALLY THINK OF DONUTS
LATER
IT SUBLIMINALLY MADE HER THINK OF THAT ZERO I GOT ON A QUIZ LAST WEEK

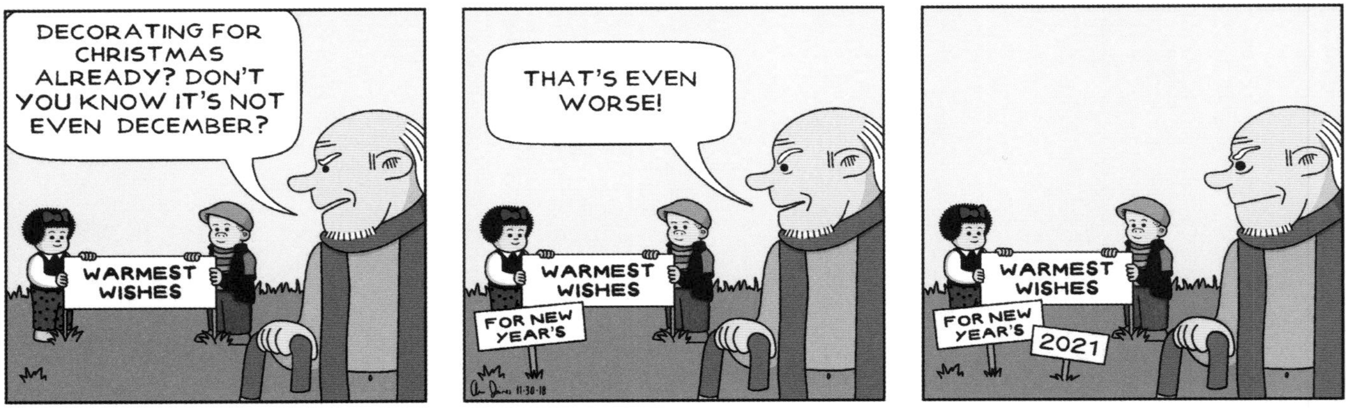
DECORATING FOR CHRISTMAS ALREADY? DON'T YOU KNOW IT'S NOT EVEN DECEMBER?
WARMEST WISHES
THAT'S EVEN WORSE!
WARMEST WISHES
FOR NEW YEAR'S
WARMEST WISHES
FOR NEW YEAR'S
2021

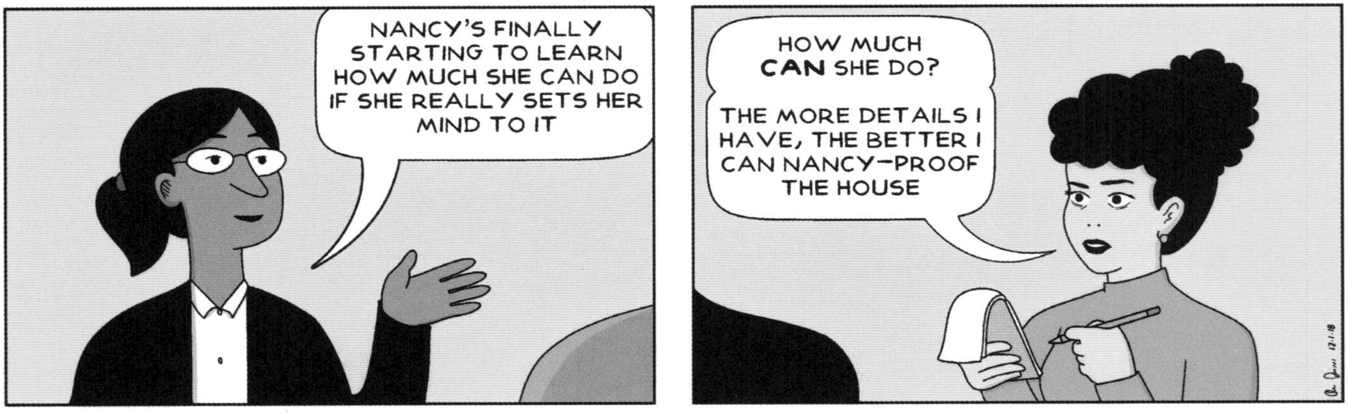
NANCY'S FINALLY STARTING TO LEARN HOW MUCH SHE CAN DO IF SHE REALLY SETS HER MIND TO IT
HOW MUCH **CAN** SHE DO?
THE MORE DETAILS I HAVE, THE BETTER I CAN NANCY-PROOF THE HOUSE

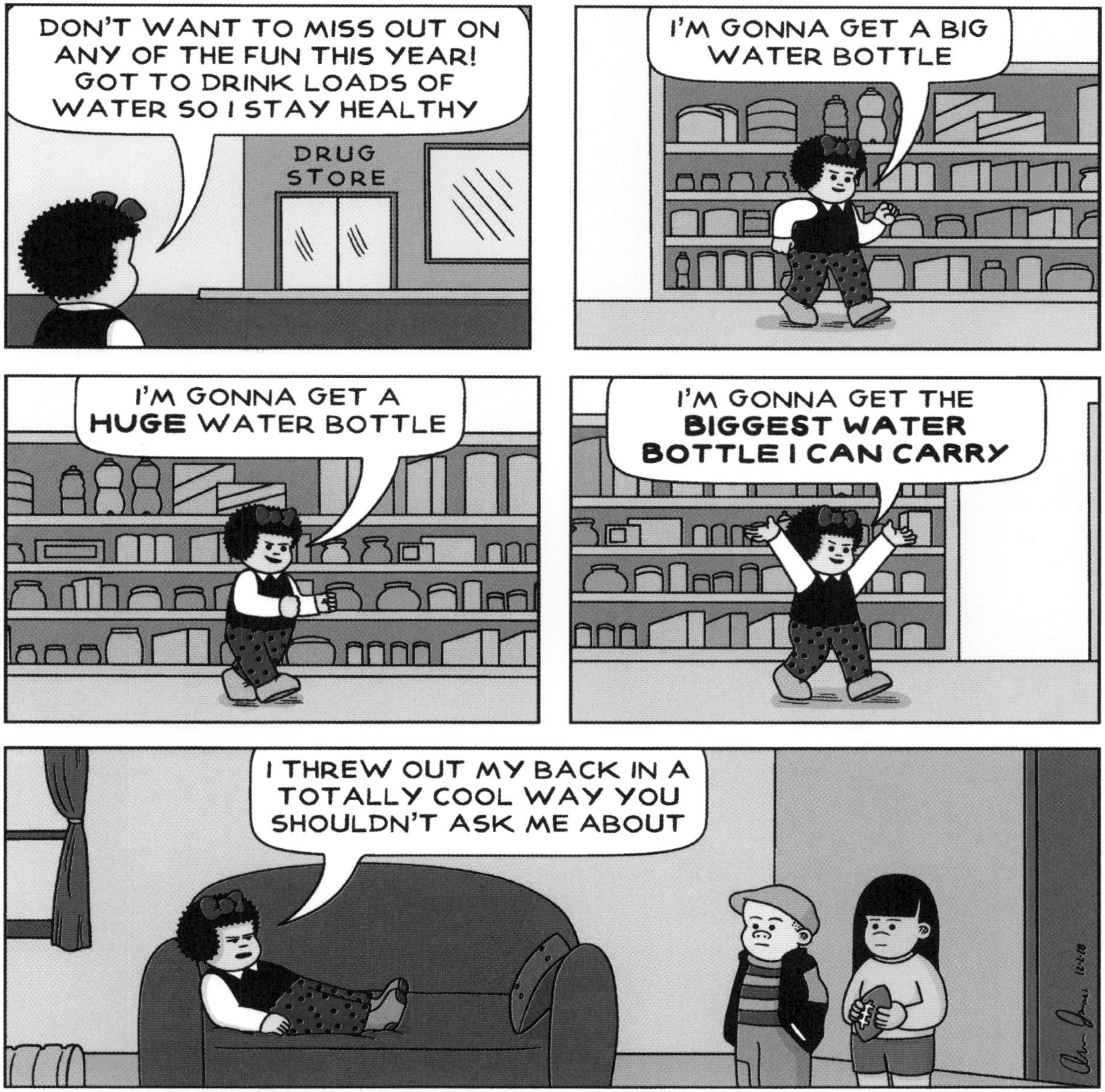
DON'T WANT TO MISS OUT ON ANY OF THE FUN THIS YEAR! GOT TO DRINK LOADS OF WATER SO I STAY HEALTHY
DRUG STORE
I'M GONNA GET A BIG WATER BOTTLE
I'M GONNA GET A **HUGE** WATER BOTTLE
I'M GONNA GET THE **BIGGEST WATER BOTTLE I CAN CARRY**
I THREW OUT MY BACK IN A TOTALLY COOL WAY YOU SHOULDN'T ASK ME ABOUT

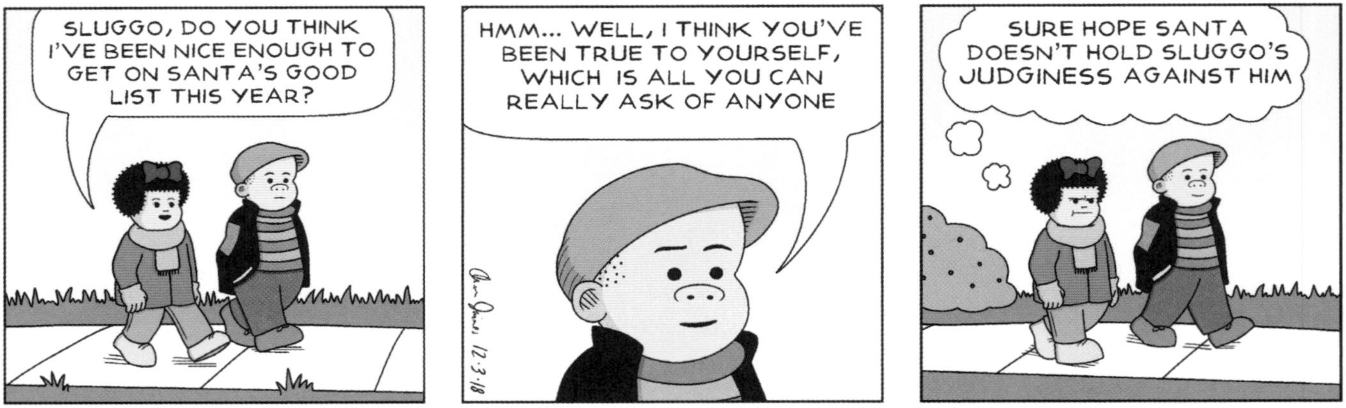
SLUGGO, DO YOU THINK I'VE BEEN NICE ENOUGH TO GET ON SANTA'S GOOD LIST THIS YEAR?
HMM... WELL, I THINK YOU'VE BEEN TRUE TO YOURSELF, WHICH IS ALL YOU CAN REALLY ASK OF ANYONE
12·3·18
SURE HOPE SANTA DOESN'T HOLD SLUGGO'S JUDGINESS AGAINST HIM

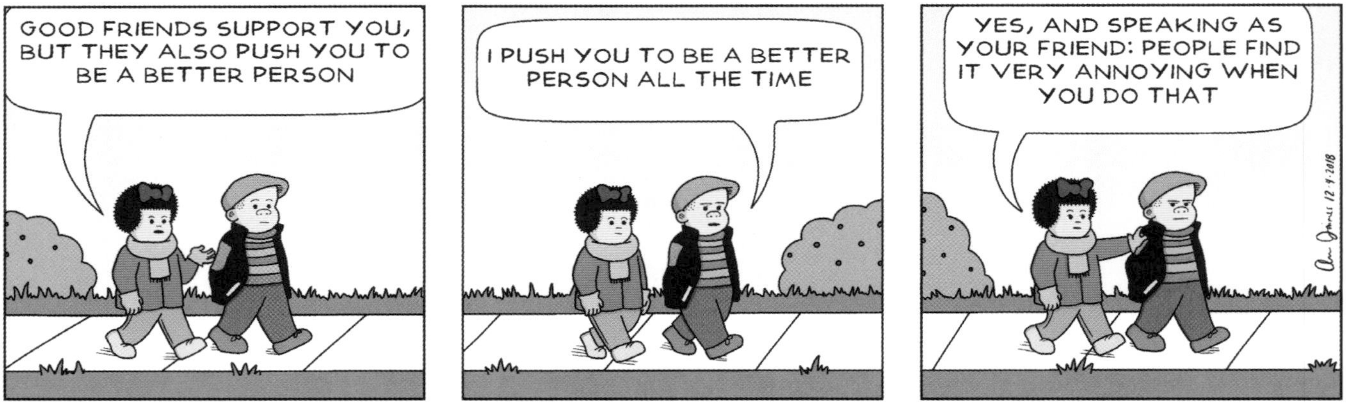
GOOD FRIENDS SUPPORT YOU, BUT THEY ALSO PUSH YOU TO BE A BETTER PERSON
I PUSH YOU TO BE A BETTER PERSON ALL THE TIME
YES, AND SPEAKING AS YOUR FRIEND: PEOPLE FIND IT VERY ANNOYING WHEN YOU DO THAT
12·4·2018

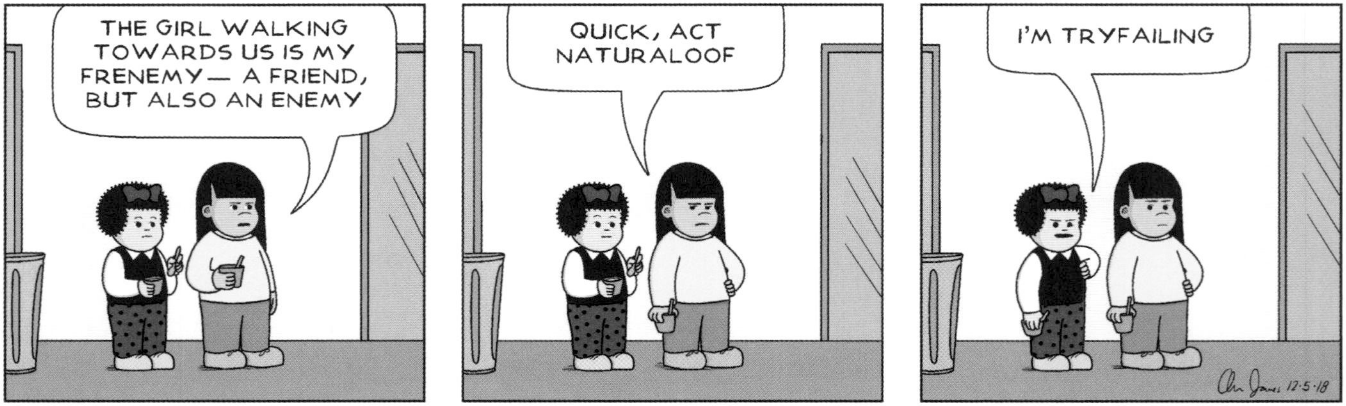
THE GIRL WALKING TOWARDS US IS MY FRENEMY— A FRIEND, BUT ALSO AN ENEMY
QUICK, ACT NATURALOOF
I'M TRYFAILING
12·5·18

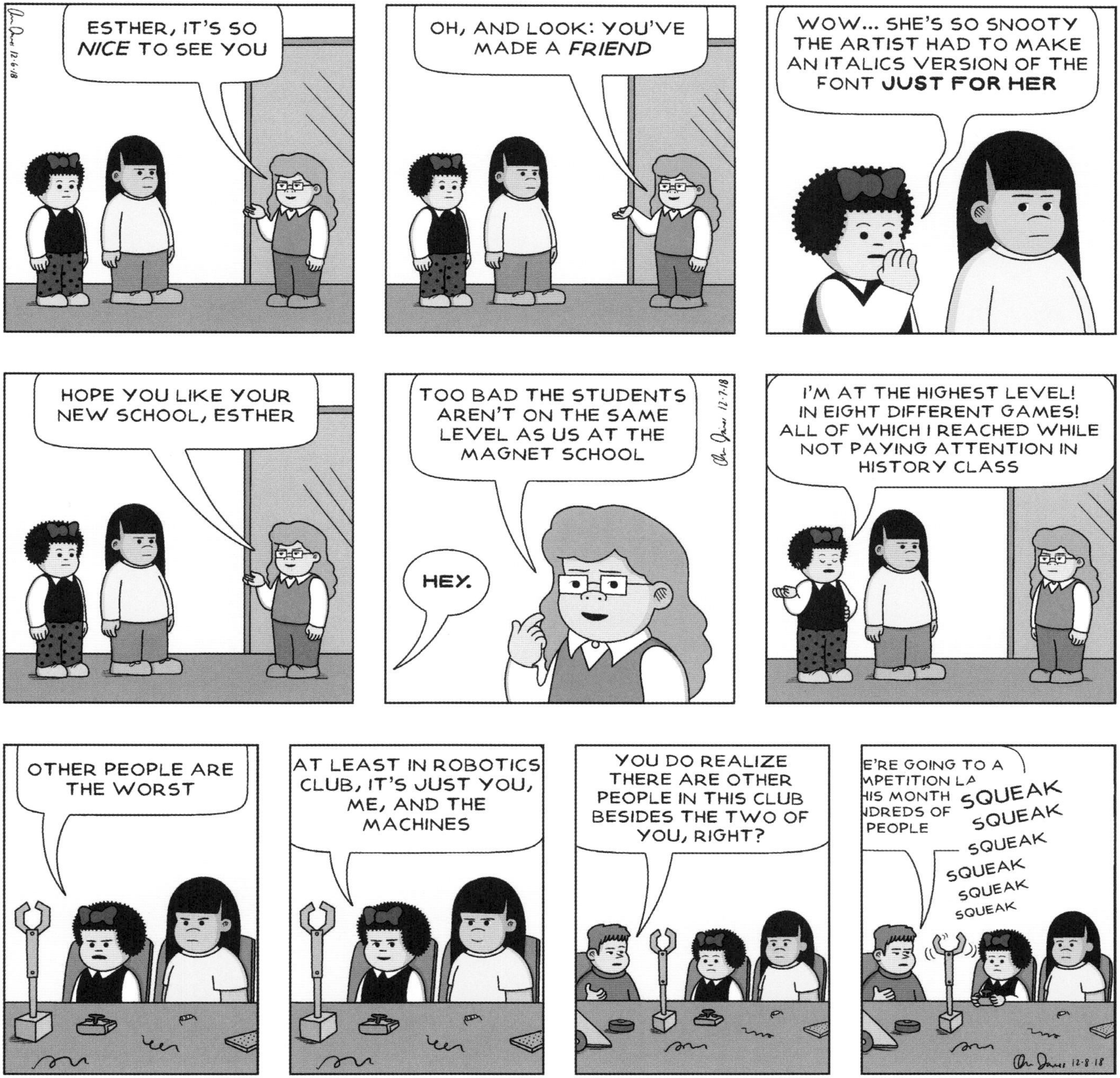
ESTHER, IT'S SO *NICE* TO SEE YOU
OH, AND LOOK: YOU'VE MADE A *FRIEND*
WOW... SHE'S SO SNOOTY THE ARTIST HAD TO MAKE AN ITALICS VERSION OF THE FONT **JUST FOR HER**
HOPE YOU LIKE YOUR NEW SCHOOL, ESTHER
TOO BAD THE STUDENTS AREN'T ON THE SAME LEVEL AS US AT THE MAGNET SCHOOL
HEY.
I'M AT THE HIGHEST LEVEL! IN EIGHT DIFFERENT GAMES! ALL OF WHICH I REACHED WHILE NOT PAYING ATTENTION IN HISTORY CLASS
OTHER PEOPLE ARE THE WORST
AT LEAST IN ROBOTICS CLUB, IT'S JUST YOU, ME, AND THE MACHINES
YOU DO REALIZE THERE ARE OTHER PEOPLE IN THIS CLUB BESIDES THE TWO OF YOU, RIGHT?
E'RE GOING TO A MPETITION LA HIS MONTH NDREDS OF PEOPLE
SQUEAK
SQUEAK
SQUEAK
SQUEAK
SQUEAK
SQUEAK

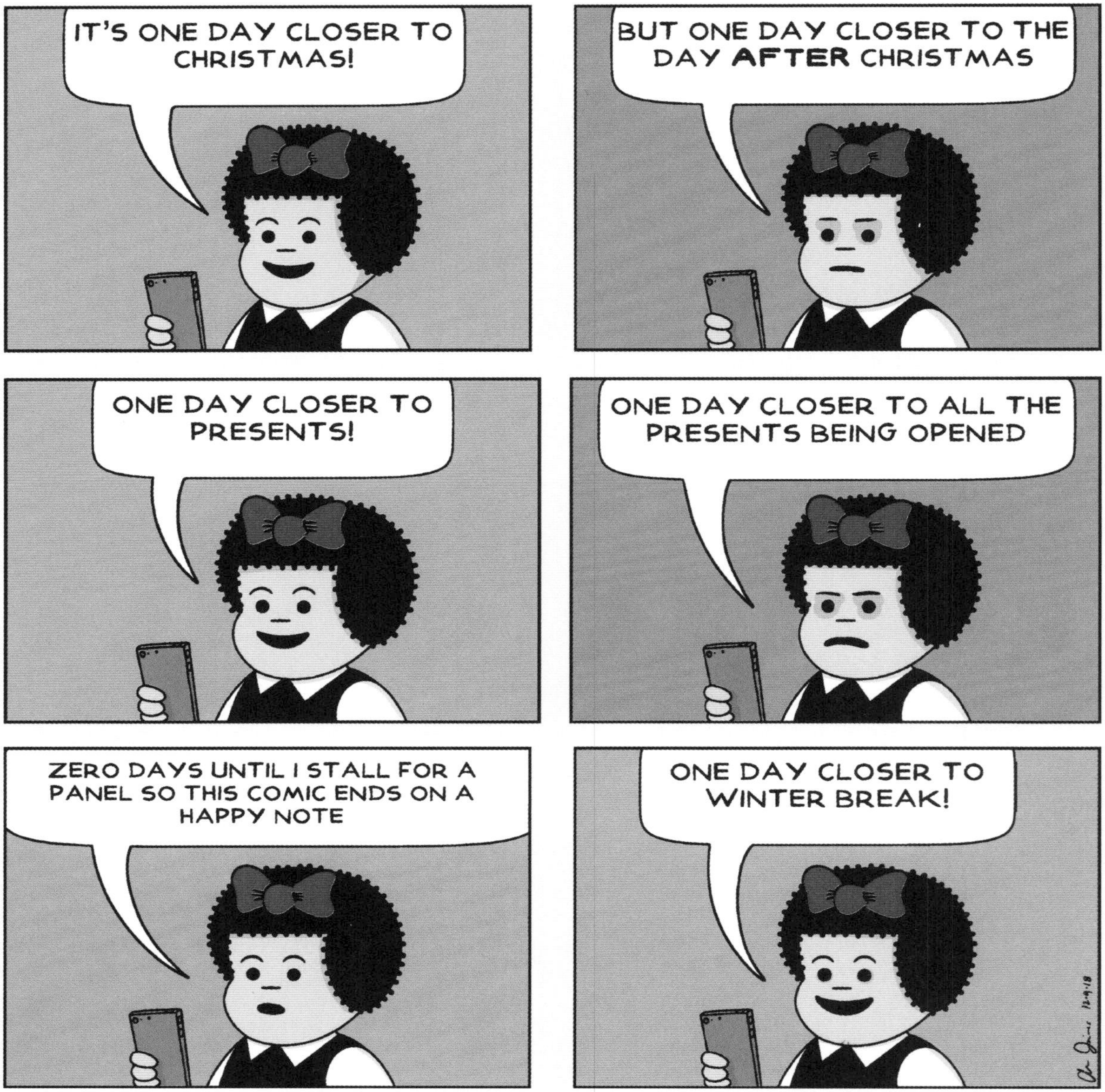
IT'S ONE DAY CLOSER TO CHRISTMAS!
BUT ONE DAY CLOSER TO THE DAY **AFTER** CHRISTMAS
ONE DAY CLOSER TO PRESENTS!
ONE DAY CLOSER TO ALL THE PRESENTS BEING OPENED
ZERO DAYS UNTIL I STALL FOR A PANEL SO THIS COMIC ENDS ON A HAPPY NOTE
ONE DAY CLOSER TO WINTER BREAK!

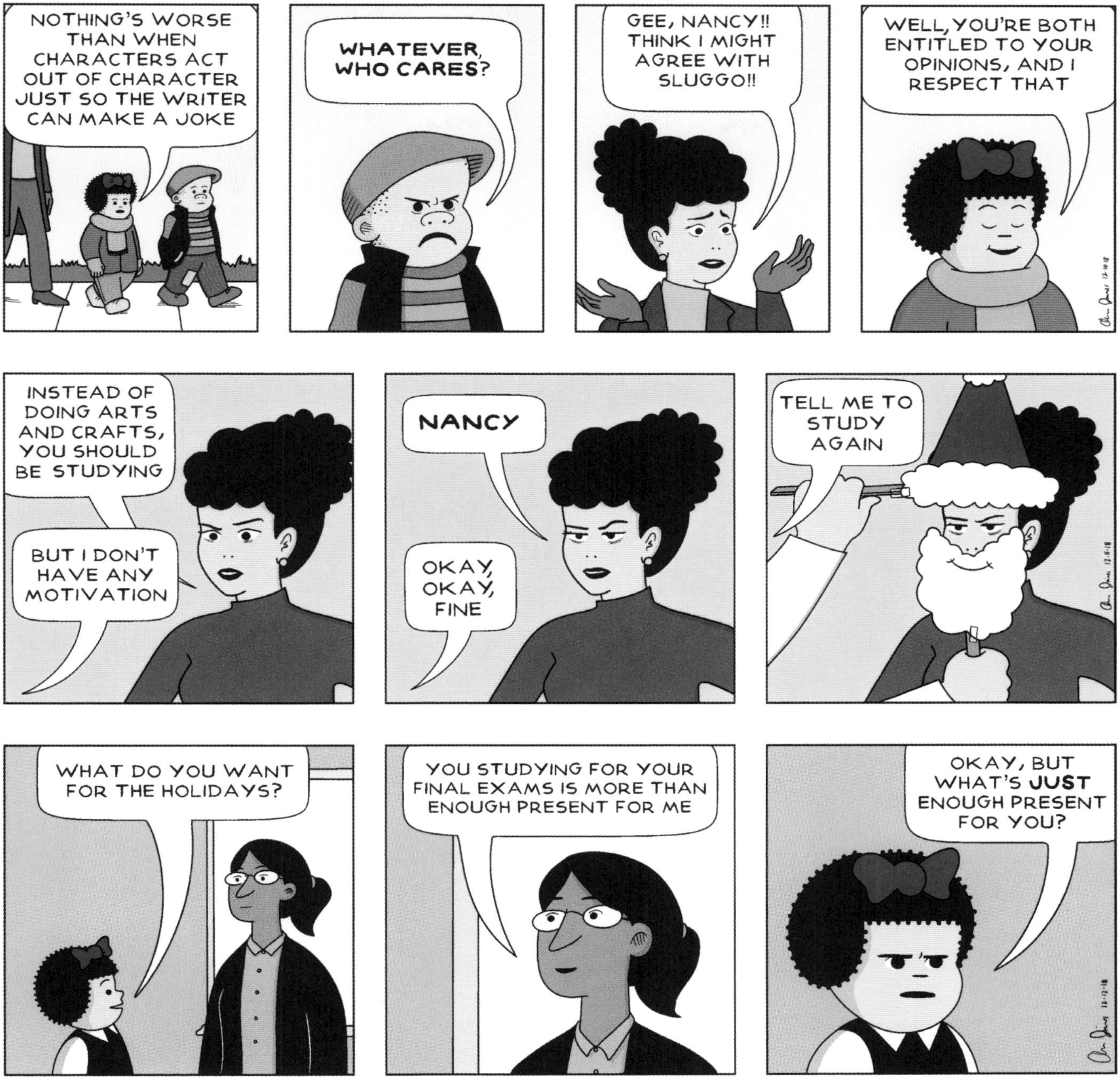
NOTHING'S WORSE THAN WHEN CHARACTERS ACT OUT OF CHARACTER JUST SO THE WRITER CAN MAKE A JOKE
WHATEVER, WHO CARES?
GEE, NANCY!! THINK I MIGHT AGREE WITH SLUGGO!!
WELL, YOU'RE BOTH ENTITLED TO YOUR OPINIONS, AND I RESPECT THAT
INSTEAD OF DOING ARTS AND CRAFTS, YOU SHOULD BE STUDYING
BUT I DON'T HAVE ANY MOTIVATION
NANCY
OKAY, OKAY, FINE
TELL ME TO STUDY AGAIN
WHAT DO YOU WANT FOR THE HOLIDAYS?
YOU STUDYING FOR YOUR FINAL EXAMS IS MORE THAN ENOUGH PRESENT FOR ME
OKAY, BUT WHAT'S JUST ENOUGH PRESENT FOR YOU?

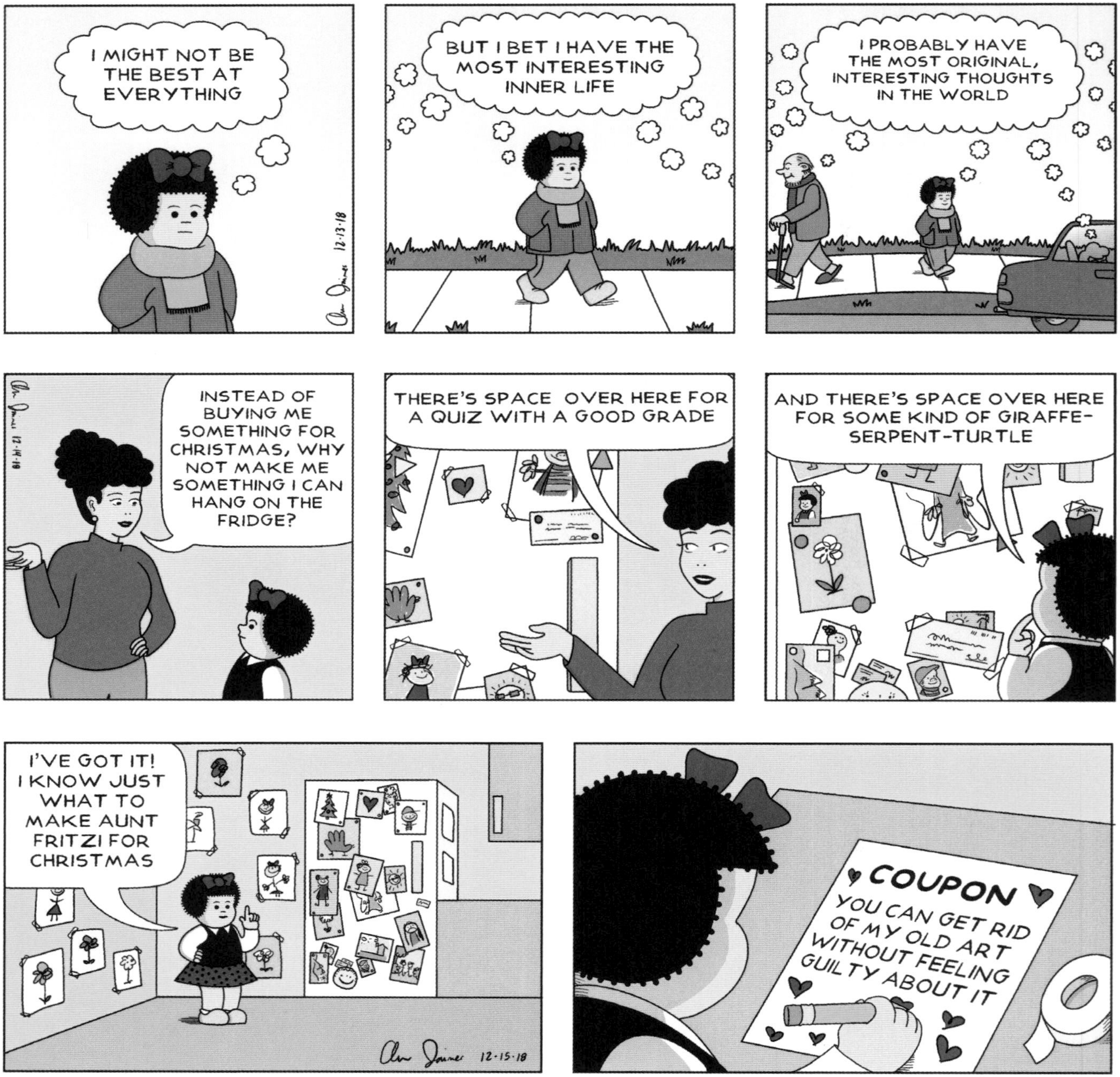
I MIGHT NOT BE THE BEST AT EVERYTHING
12-13-18
BUT I BET I HAVE THE MOST INTERESTING INNER LIFE
I PROBABLY HAVE THE MOST ORIGINAL, INTERESTING THOUGHTS IN THE WORLD
12-14-18
INSTEAD OF BUYING ME SOMETHING FOR CHRISTMAS, WHY NOT MAKE ME SOMETHING I CAN HANG ON THE FRIDGE?
THERE'S SPACE OVER HERE FOR A QUIZ WITH A GOOD GRADE
AND THERE'S SPACE OVER HERE FOR SOME KIND OF GIRAFFE-SERPENT-TURTLE
I'VE GOT IT! I KNOW JUST WHAT TO MAKE AUNT FRITZI FOR CHRISTMAS
12-15-18
COUPON
YOU CAN GET RID OF MY OLD ART WITHOUT FEELING GUILTY ABOUT IT

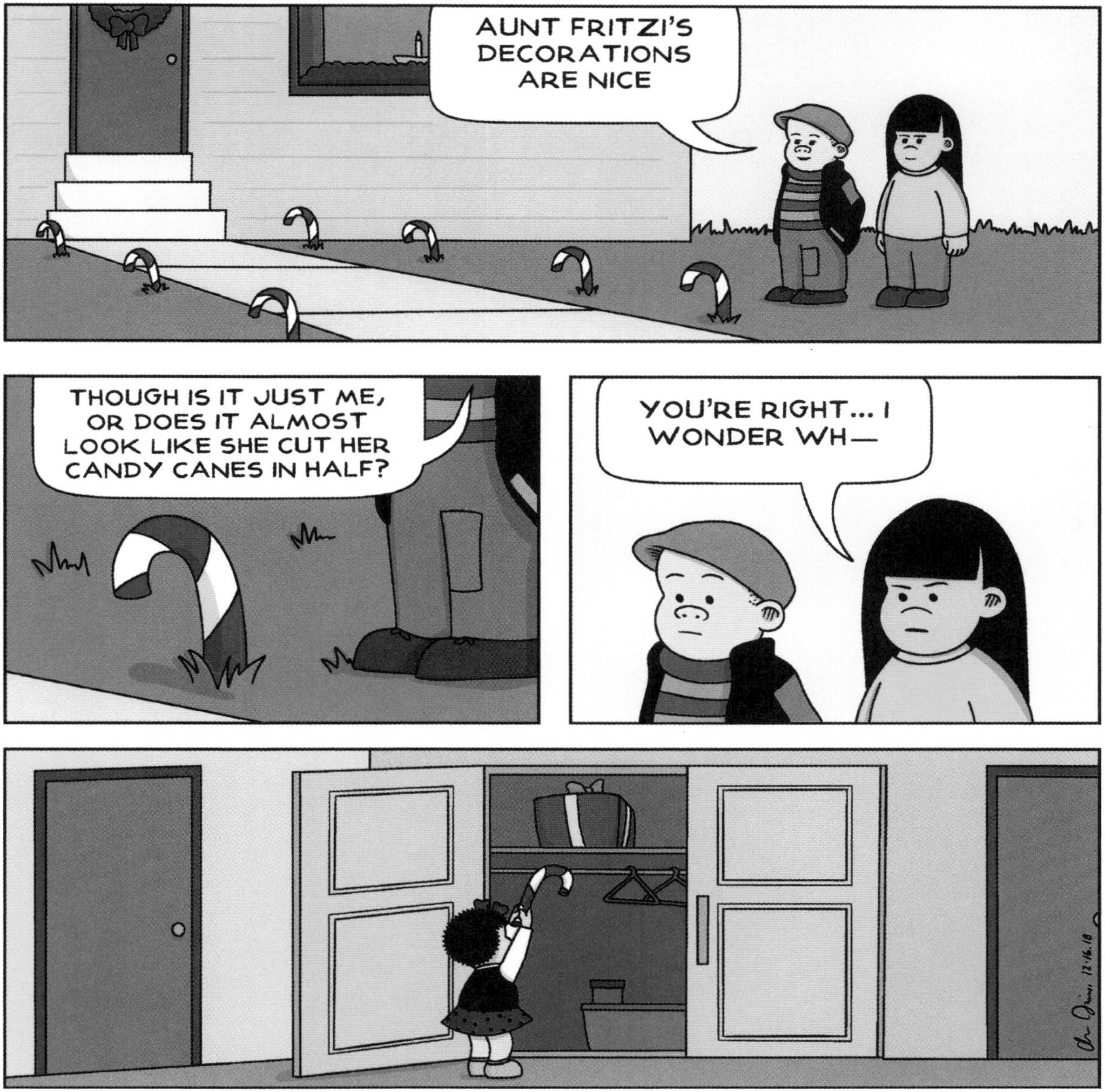
AUNT FRITZI'S DECORATIONS ARE NICE
THOUGH IS IT JUST ME, OR DOES IT ALMOST LOOK LIKE SHE CUT HER CANDY CANES IN HALF?
YOU'RE RIGHT... I WONDER WH—

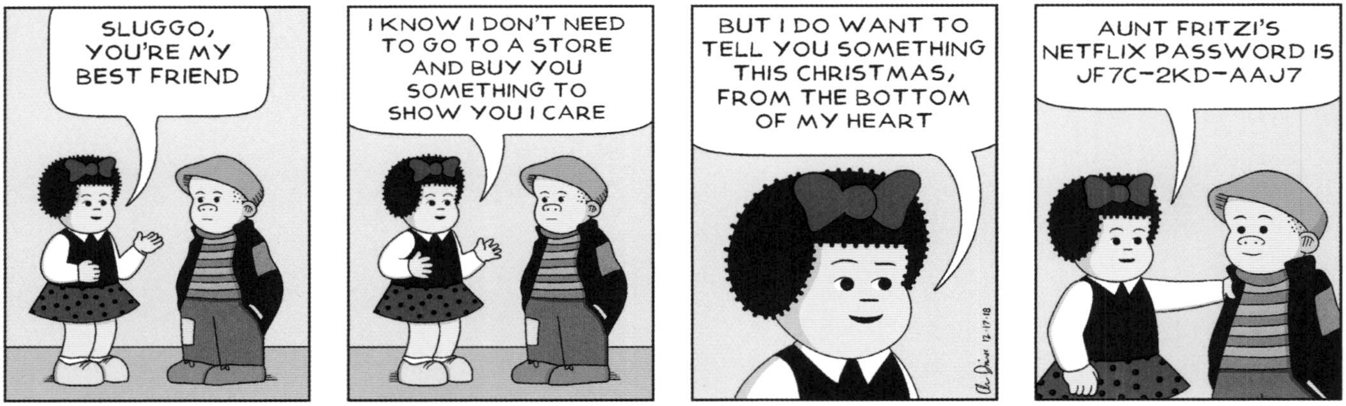
SLUGGO, YOU'RE MY BEST FRIEND
I KNOW I DON'T NEED TO GO TO A STORE AND BUY YOU SOMETHING TO SHOW YOU I CARE
BUT I DO WANT TO TELL YOU SOMETHING THIS CHRISTMAS, FROM THE BOTTOM OF MY HEART
AUNT FRITZI'S NETFLIX PASSWORD IS JF7C-2KD-AAJ7

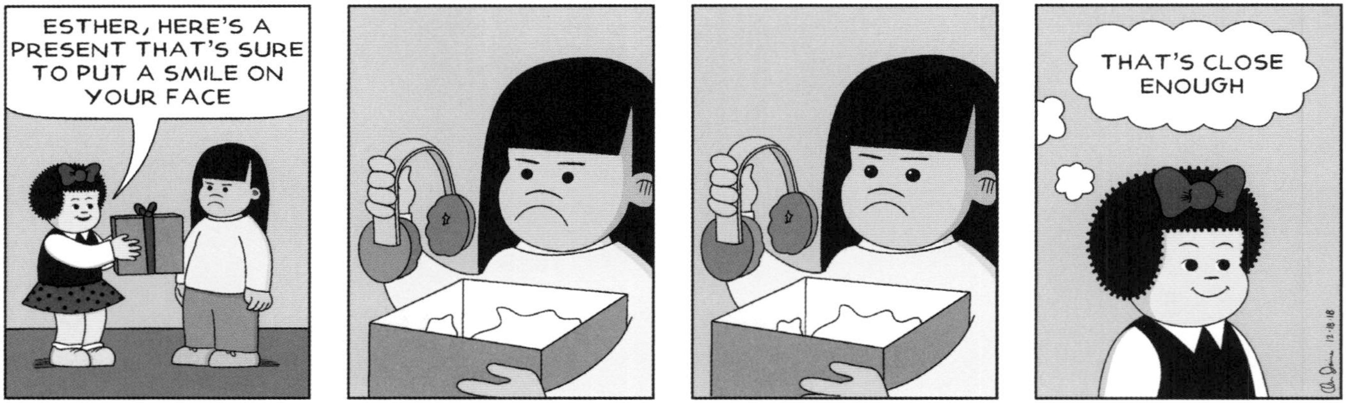
ESTHER, HERE'S A PRESENT THAT'S SURE TO PUT A SMILE ON YOUR FACE
THAT'S CLOSE ENOUGH

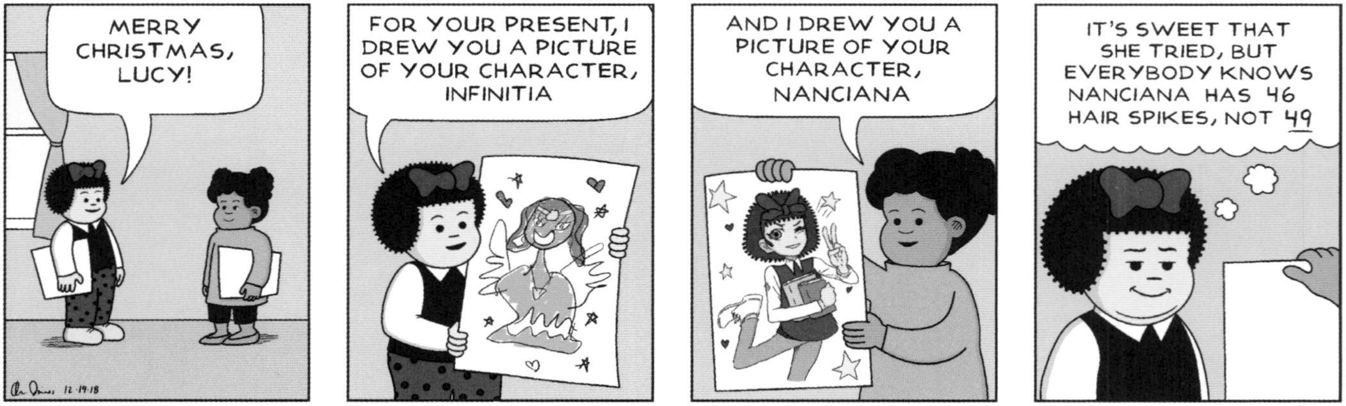
MERRY CHRISTMAS, LUCY!
FOR YOUR PRESENT, I DREW YOU A PICTURE OF YOUR CHARACTER, INFINITIA
AND I DREW YOU A PICTURE OF YOUR CHARACTER, NANCIANA
IT'S SWEET THAT SHE TRIED, BUT EVERYBODY KNOWS NANCIANA HAS 46 HAIR SPIKES, NOT 49

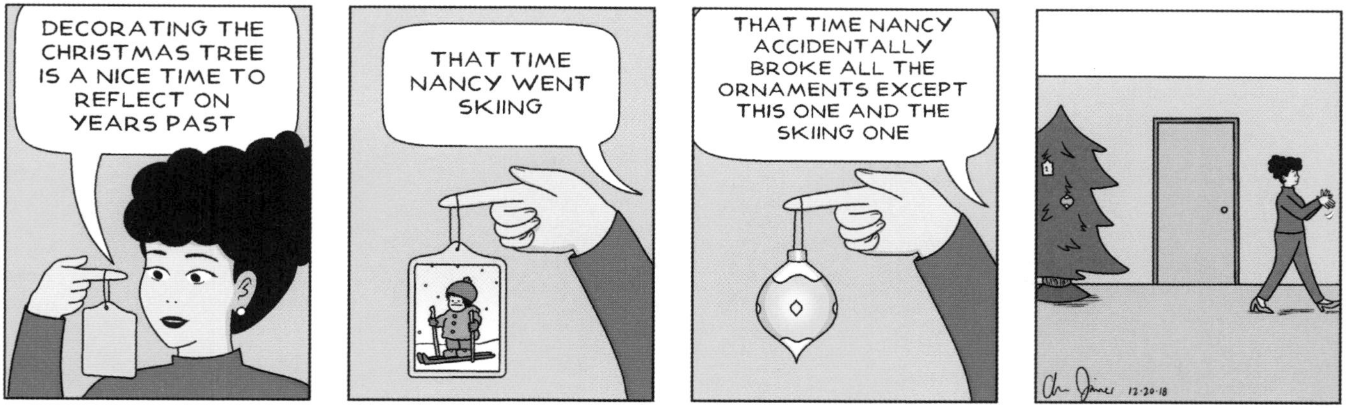
DECORATING THE CHRISTMAS TREE IS A NICE TIME TO REFLECT ON YEARS PAST
THAT TIME NANCY WENT SKIING
THAT TIME NANCY ACCIDENTALLY BROKE ALL THE ORNAMENTS EXCEPT THIS ONE AND THE SKIING ONE
12·20·18

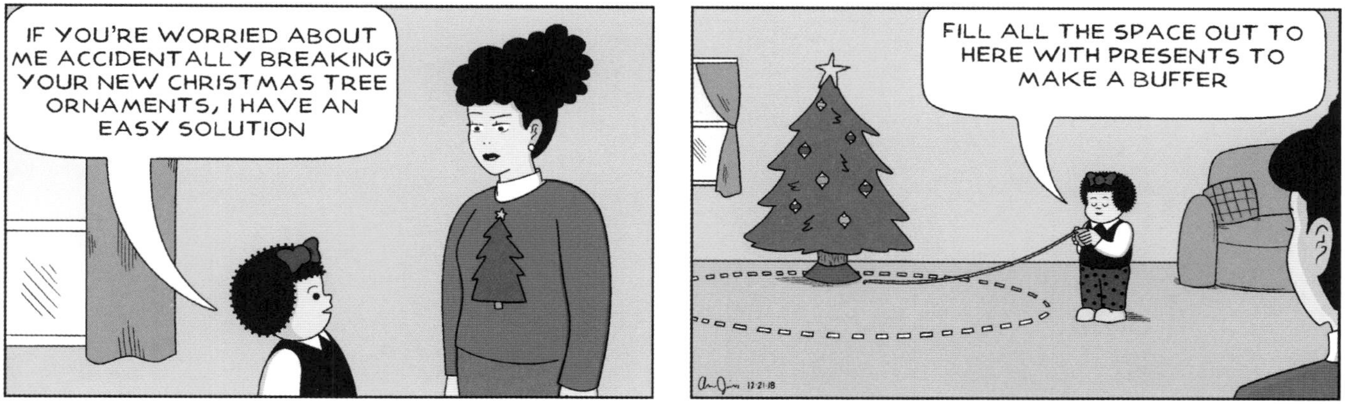
IF YOU'RE WORRIED ABOUT ME ACCIDENTALLY BREAKING YOUR NEW CHRISTMAS TREE ORNAMENTS, I HAVE AN EASY SOLUTION
FILL ALL THE SPACE OUT TO HERE WITH PRESENTS TO MAKE A BUFFER
12·21·18

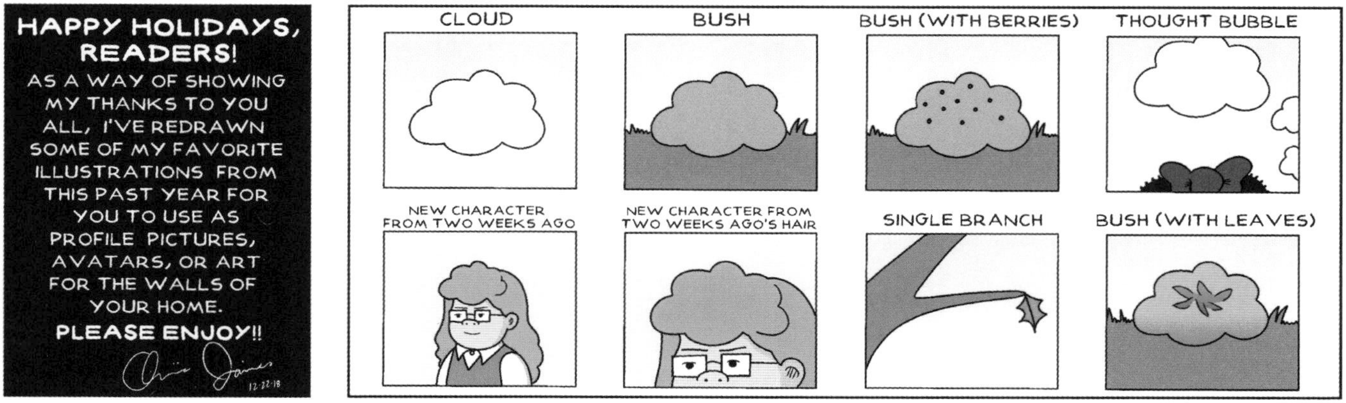
HAPPY HOLIDAYS, READERS!
AS A WAY OF SHOWING MY THANKS TO YOU ALL, I'VE REDRAWN SOME OF MY FAVORITE ILLUSTRATIONS FROM THIS PAST YEAR FOR YOU TO USE AS PROFILE PICTURES, AVATARS, OR ART FOR THE WALLS OF YOUR HOME.
PLEASE ENJOY!!
12·22·18
CLOUD
BUSH
BUSH (WITH BERRIES)
THOUGHT BUBBLE
NEW CHARACTER FROM TWO WEEKS AGO
NEW CHARACTER FROM TWO WEEKS AGO'S HAIR
SINGLE BRANCH
BUSH (WITH LEAVES)

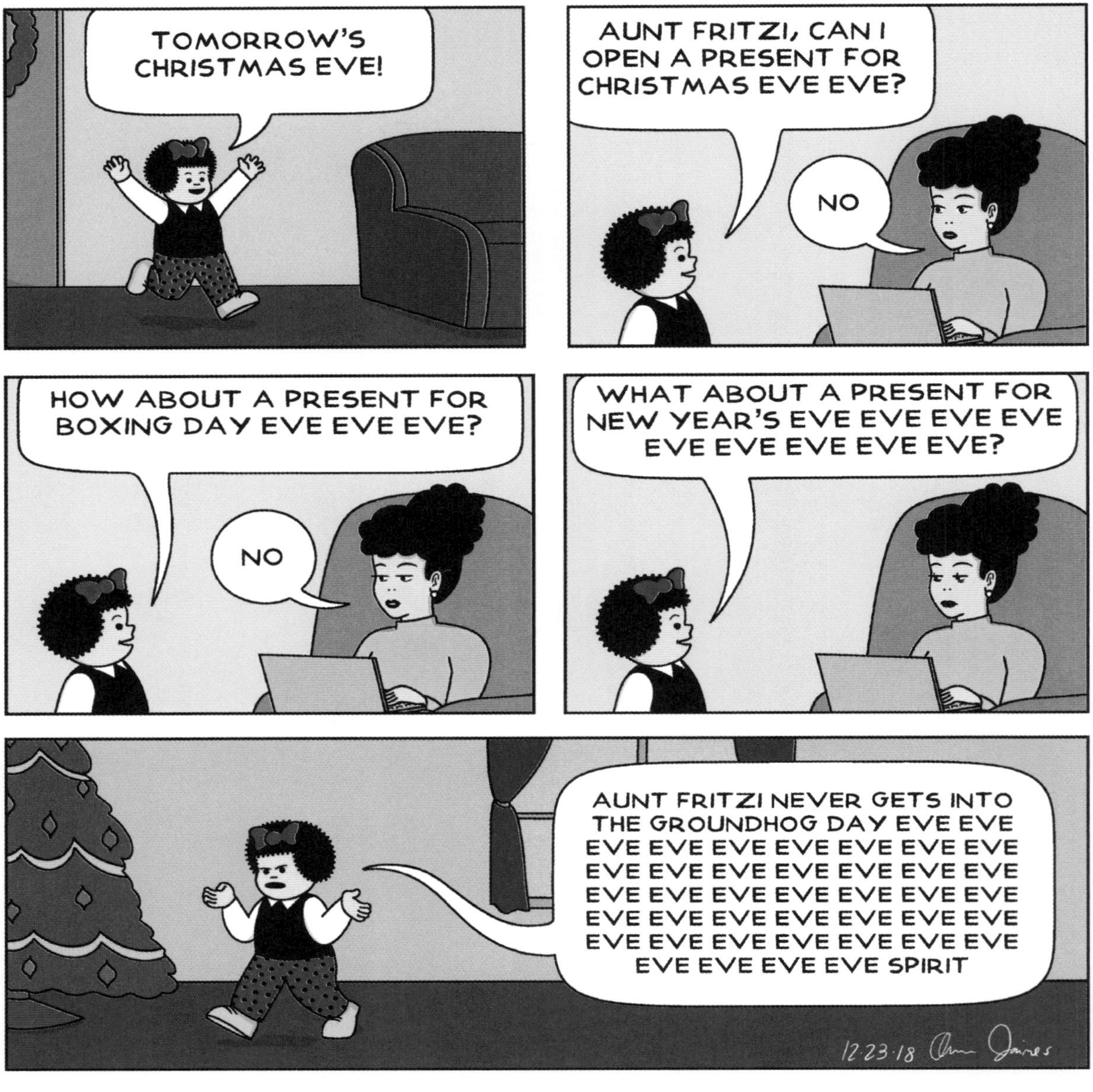
TOMORROW'S CHRISTMAS EVE!
AUNT FRITZI, CAN I OPEN A PRESENT FOR CHRISTMAS EVE EVE?
NO
HOW ABOUT A PRESENT FOR BOXING DAY EVE EVE EVE?
NO
WHAT ABOUT A PRESENT FOR NEW YEAR'S EVE EVE EVE EVE EVE EVE EVE EVE EVE?
AUNT FRITZI NEVER GETS INTO THE GROUNDHOG DAY EVE EVE EVE EVE EVE EVE EVE EVE EVE EVE EVE EVE EVE EVE EVE EVE EVE EVE EVE EVE EVE EVE EVE EVE EVE EVE EVE EVE EVE EVE EVE EVE EVE EVE EVE EVE EVE EVE EVE EVE EVE EVE EVE EVE EVE EVE EVE SPIRIT
12·23·18

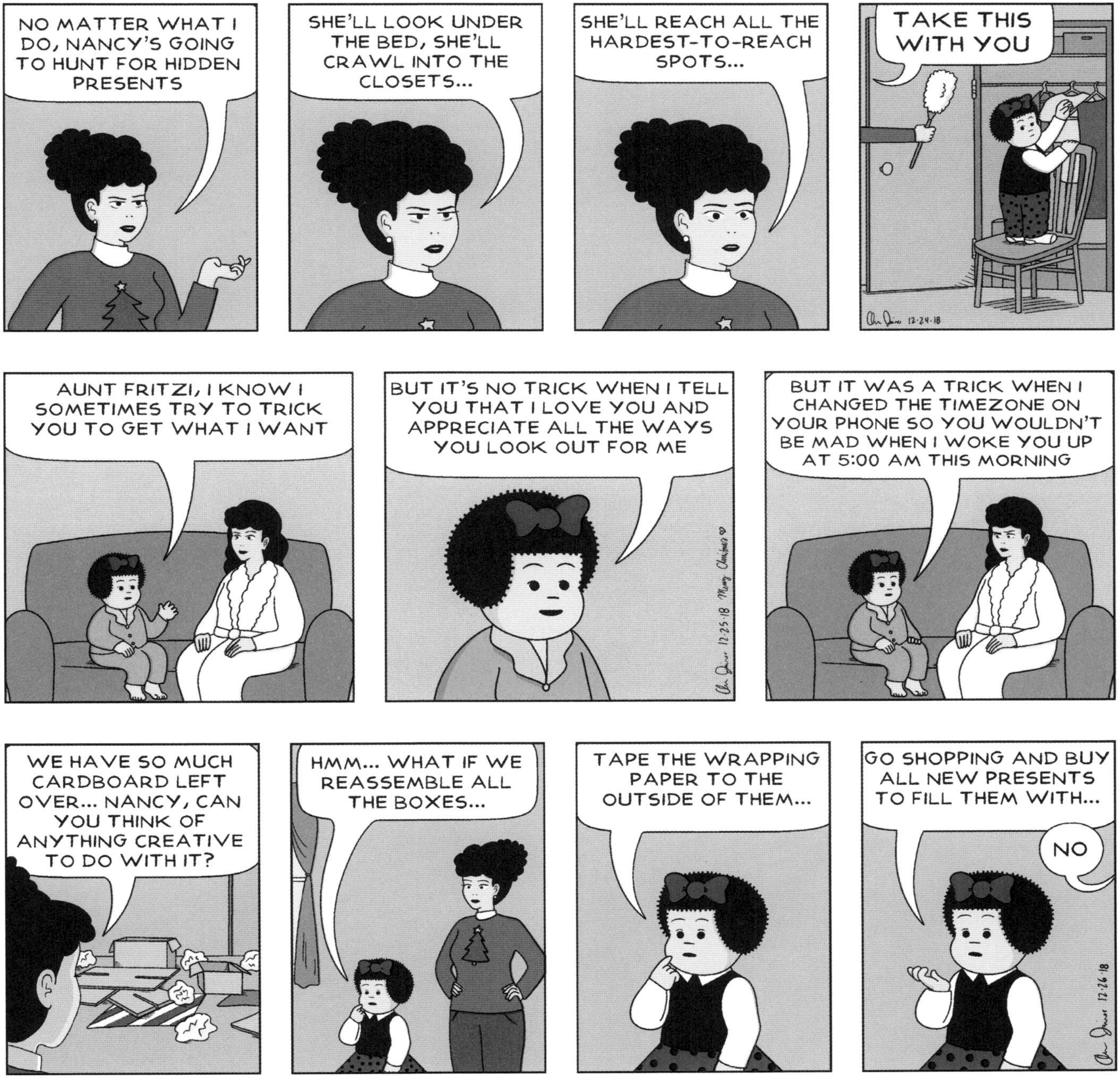
NO MATTER WHAT I DO, NANCY'S GOING TO HUNT FOR HIDDEN PRESENTS
SHE'LL LOOK UNDER THE BED, SHE'LL CRAWL INTO THE CLOSETS...
SHE'LL REACH ALL THE HARDEST-TO-REACH SPOTS...
TAKE THIS WITH YOU
AUNT FRITZI, I KNOW I SOMETIMES TRY TO TRICK YOU TO GET WHAT I WANT
BUT IT'S NO TRICK WHEN I TELL YOU THAT I LOVE YOU AND APPRECIATE ALL THE WAYS YOU LOOK OUT FOR ME
BUT IT WAS A TRICK WHEN I CHANGED THE TIMEZONE ON YOUR PHONE SO YOU WOULDN'T BE MAD WHEN I WOKE YOU UP AT 5:00 AM THIS MORNING
WE HAVE SO MUCH CARDBOARD LEFT OVER... NANCY, CAN YOU THINK OF ANYTHING CREATIVE TO DO WITH IT?
HMM... WHAT IF WE REASSEMBLE ALL THE BOXES...
TAPE THE WRAPPING PAPER TO THE OUTSIDE OF THEM...
GO SHOPPING AND BUY ALL NEW PRESENTS TO FILL THEM WITH...
NO

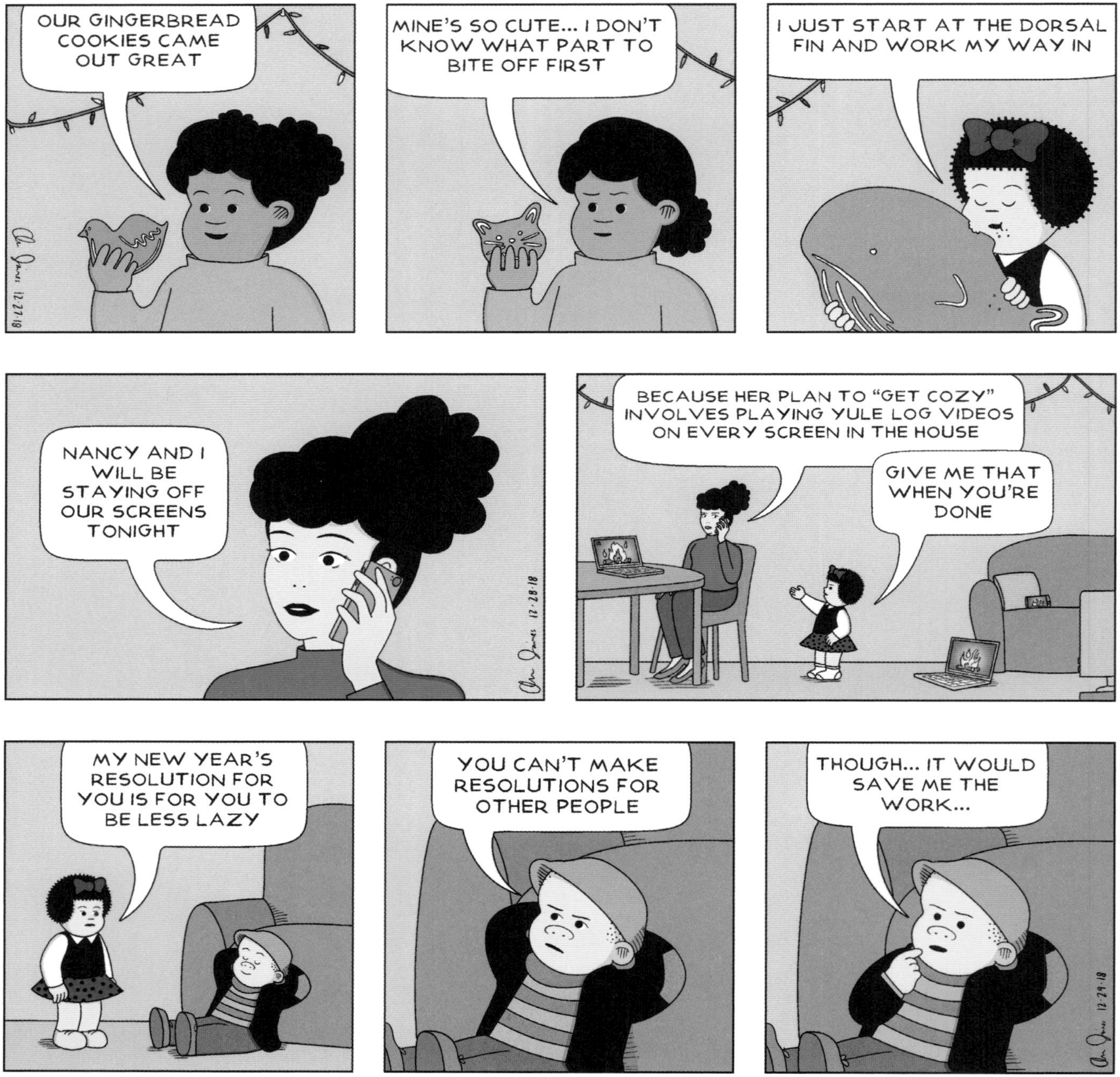
OUR GINGERBREAD COOKIES CAME OUT GREAT
12-27-18
MINE'S SO CUTE... I DON'T KNOW WHAT PART TO BITE OFF FIRST
I JUST START AT THE DORSAL FIN AND WORK MY WAY IN
NANCY AND I WILL BE STAYING OFF OUR SCREENS TONIGHT
12-28-18
BECAUSE HER PLAN TO "GET COZY" INVOLVES PLAYING YULE LOG VIDEOS ON EVERY SCREEN IN THE HOUSE
GIVE ME THAT WHEN YOU'RE DONE
MY NEW YEAR'S RESOLUTION FOR YOU IS FOR YOU TO BE LESS LAZY
YOU CAN'T MAKE RESOLUTIONS FOR OTHER PEOPLE
THOUGH... IT WOULD SAVE ME THE WORK...
12-29-18

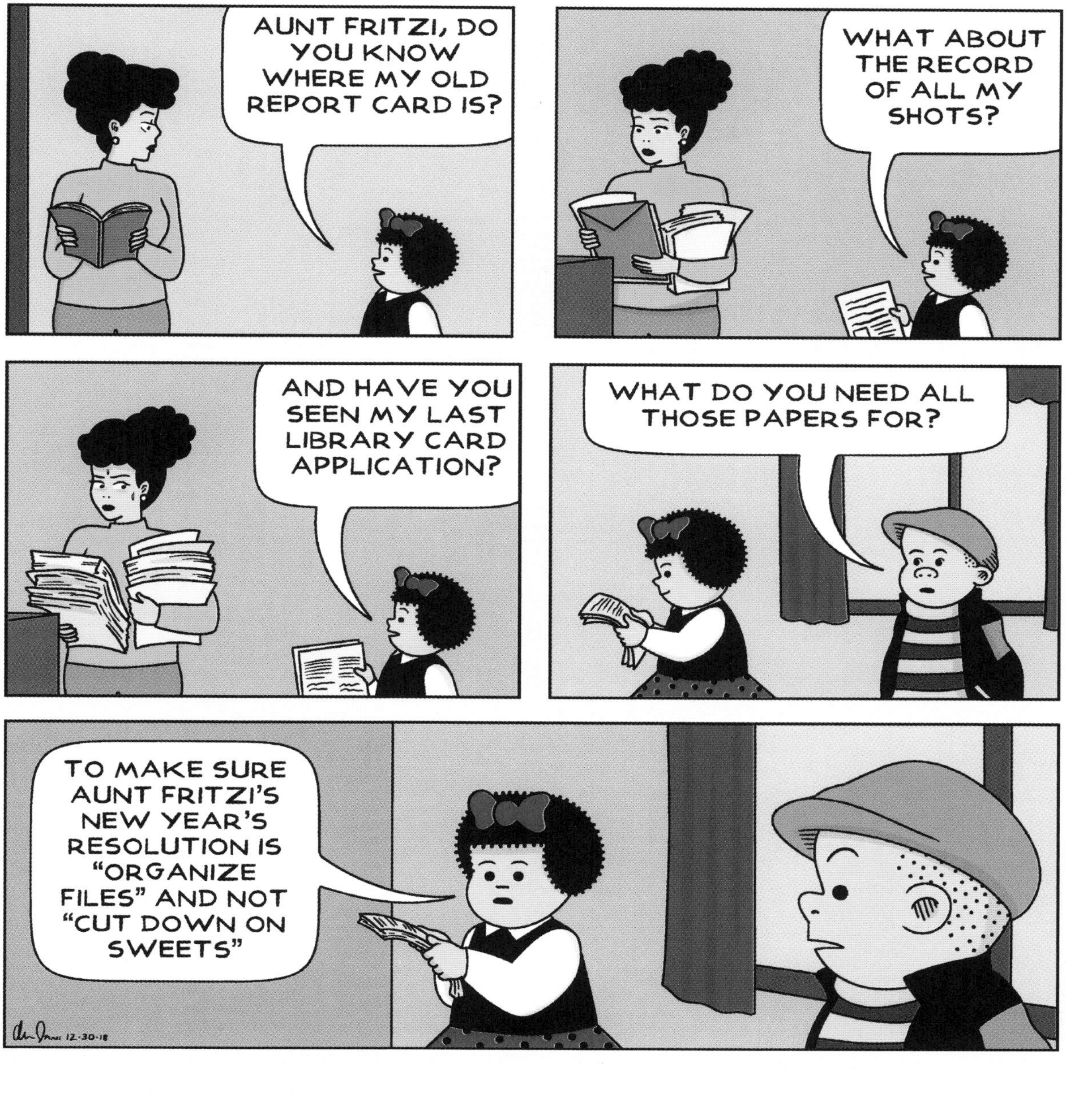
AUNT FRITZI, DO YOU KNOW WHERE MY OLD REPORT CARD IS?
WHAT ABOUT THE RECORD OF ALL MY SHOTS?
AND HAVE YOU SEEN MY LAST LIBRARY CARD APPLICATION?
WHAT DO YOU NEED ALL THOSE PAPERS FOR?
TO MAKE SURE AUNT FRITZI'S NEW YEAR'S RESOLUTION IS "ORGANIZE FILES" AND NOT "CUT DOWN ON SWEETS"
12-30-18

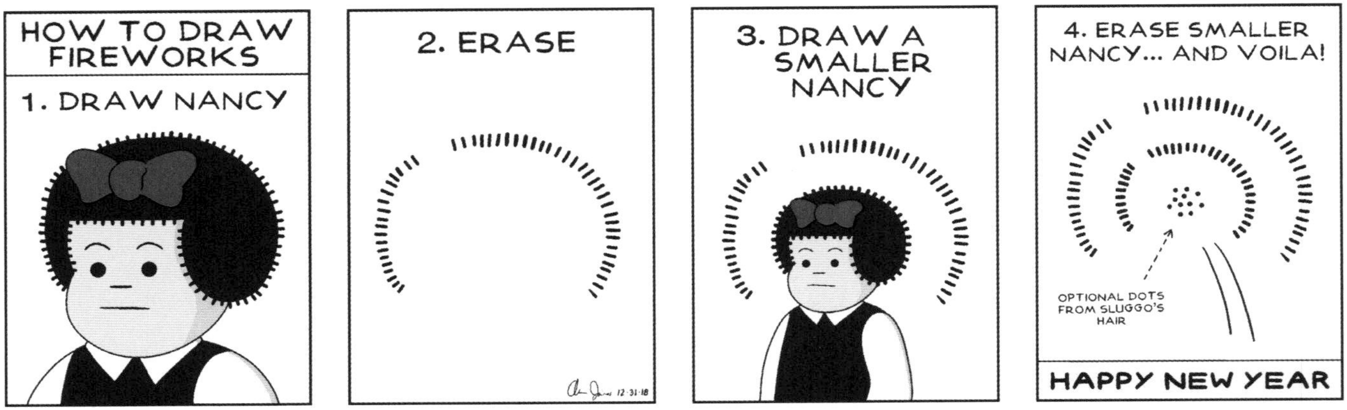
HOW TO DRAW FIREWORKS
1. DRAW NANCY
2. ERASE
3. DRAW A SMALLER NANCY
4. ERASE SMALLER NANCY... AND VOILA!
OPTIONAL DOTS FROM SLUGGO'S HAIR
HAPPY NEW YEAR

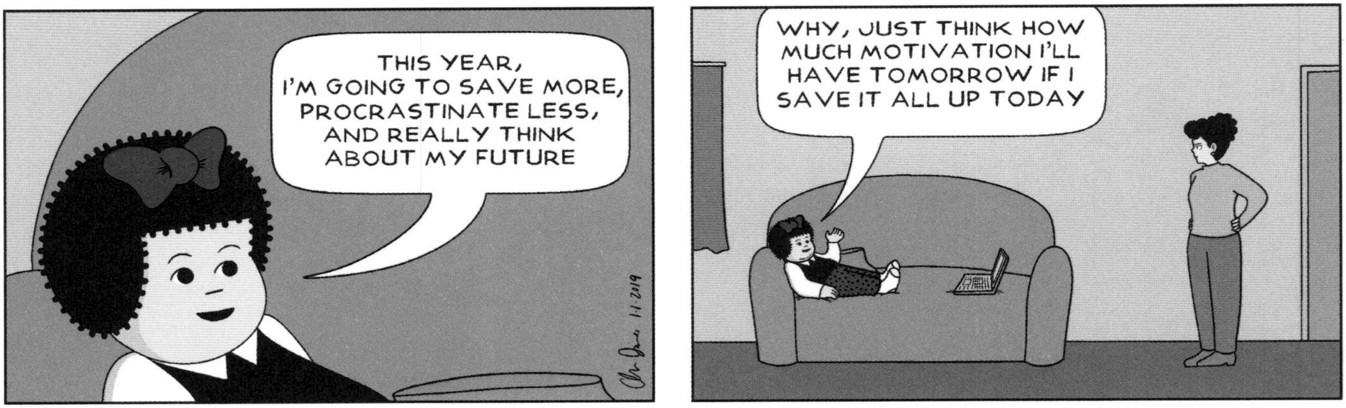
THIS YEAR, I'M GOING TO SAVE MORE, PROCRASTINATE LESS, AND REALLY THINK ABOUT MY FUTURE
WHY, JUST THINK HOW MUCH MOTIVATION I'LL HAVE TOMORROW IF I SAVE IT ALL UP TODAY

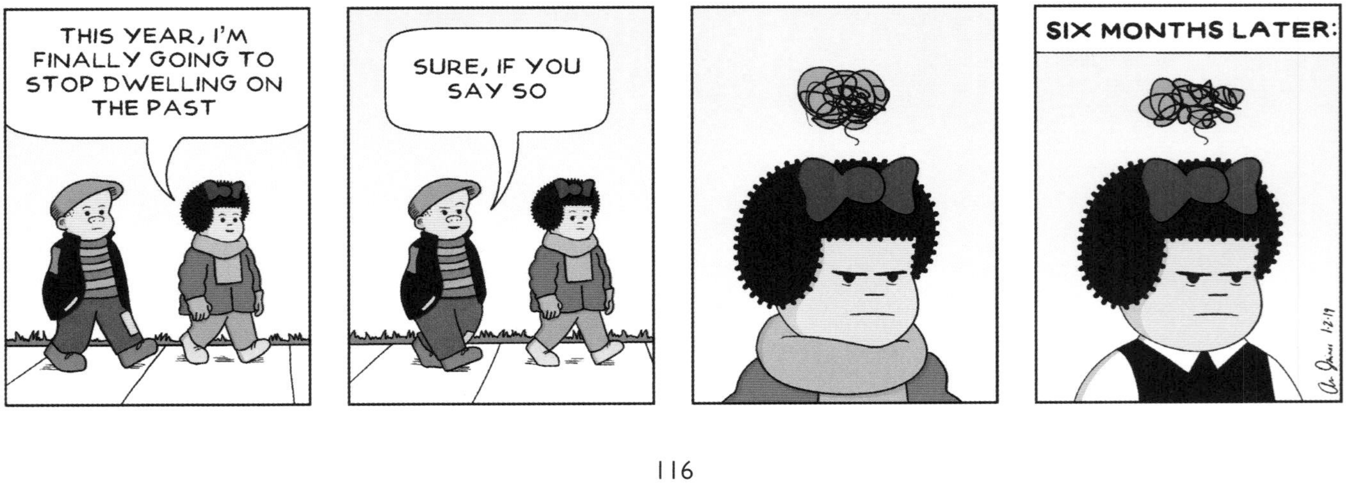
THIS YEAR, I'M FINALLY GOING TO STOP DWELLING ON THE PAST
SURE, IF YOU SAY SO
SIX MONTHS LATER:

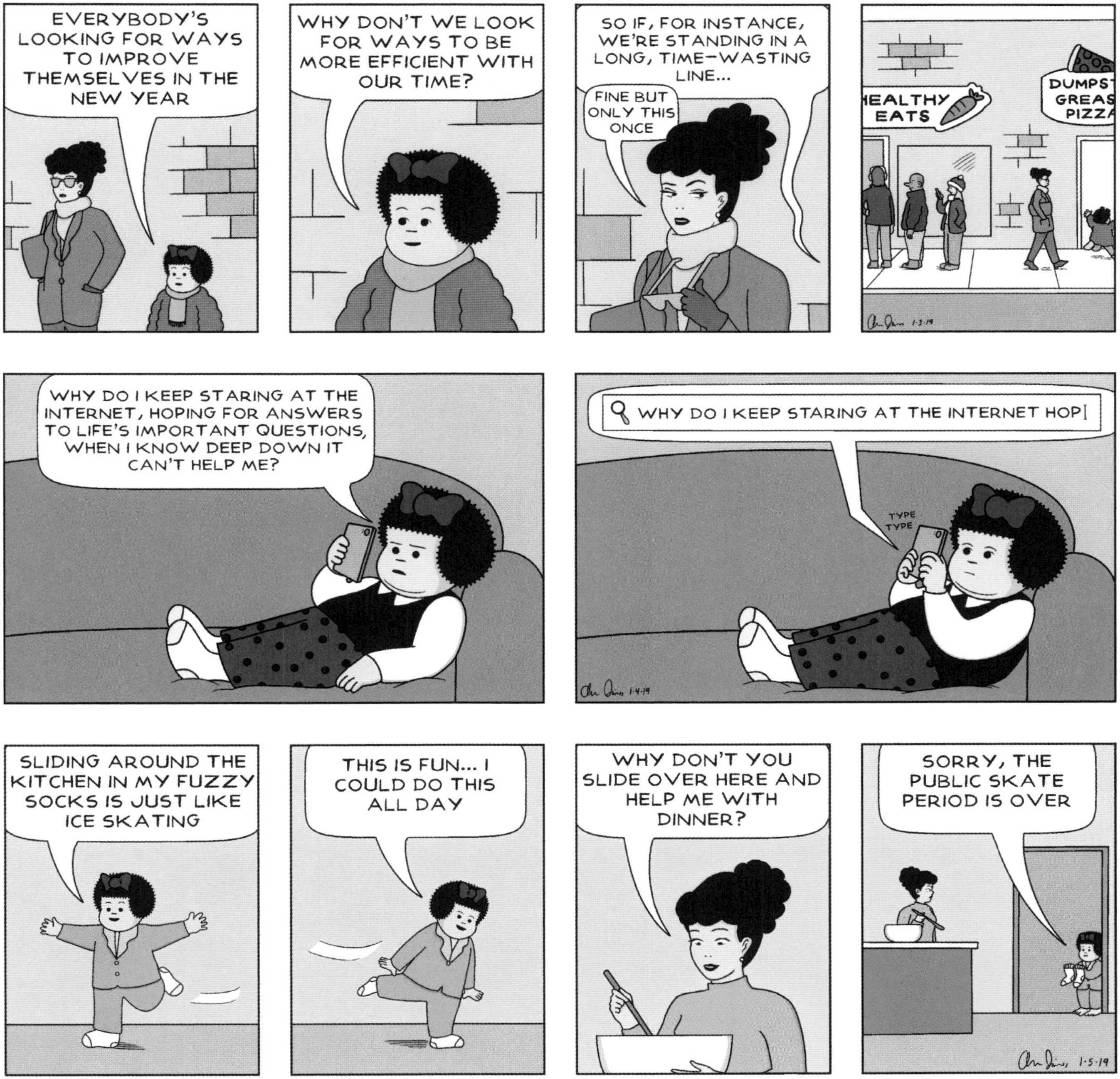
EVERYBODY'S LOOKING FOR WAYS TO IMPROVE THEMSELVES IN THE NEW YEAR
WHY DON'T WE LOOK FOR WAYS TO BE MORE EFFICIENT WITH OUR TIME?
SO IF, FOR INSTANCE, WE'RE STANDING IN A LONG, TIME-WASTING LINE...
FINE BUT ONLY THIS ONCE
HEALTHY EATS
DUMPST GREAS PIZZA
WHY DO I KEEP STARING AT THE INTERNET, HOPING FOR ANSWERS TO LIFE'S IMPORTANT QUESTIONS, WHEN I KNOW DEEP DOWN IT CAN'T HELP ME?
WHY DO I KEEP STARING AT THE INTERNET HOP
TYPE TYPE
SLIDING AROUND THE KITCHEN IN MY FUZZY SOCKS IS JUST LIKE ICE SKATING
THIS IS FUN... I COULD DO THIS ALL DAY
WHY DON'T YOU SLIDE OVER HERE AND HELP ME WITH DINNER?
SORRY, THE PUBLIC SKATE PERIOD IS OVER

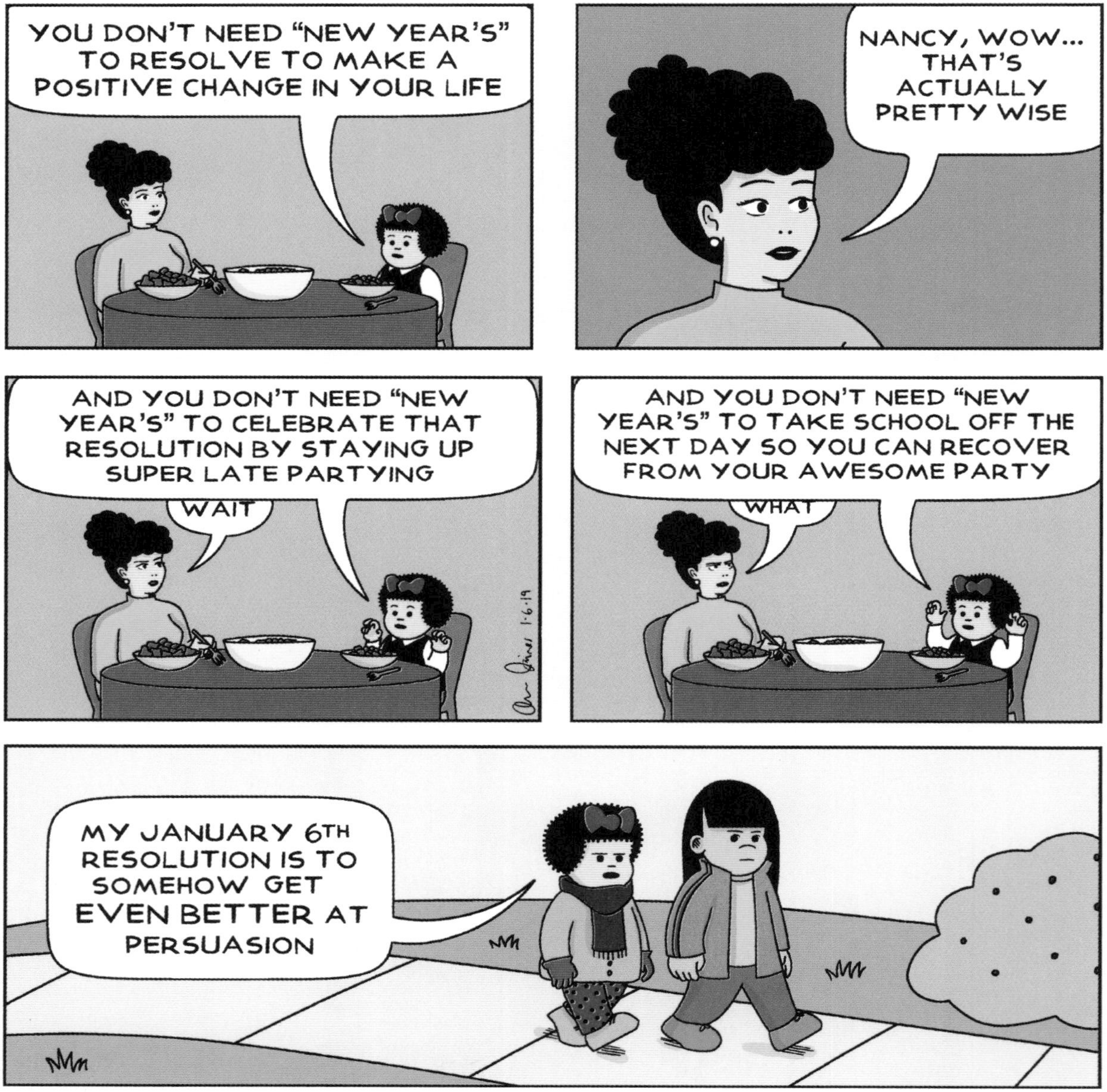
YOU DON'T NEED "NEW YEAR'S" TO RESOLVE TO MAKE A POSITIVE CHANGE IN YOUR LIFE
NANCY, WOW... THAT'S ACTUALLY PRETTY WISE
AND YOU DON'T NEED "NEW YEAR'S" TO CELEBRATE THAT RESOLUTION BY STAYING UP SUPER LATE PARTYING
WAIT
1-6-19
AND YOU DON'T NEED "NEW YEAR'S" TO TAKE SCHOOL OFF THE NEXT DAY SO YOU CAN RECOVER FROM YOUR AWESOME PARTY
WHAT
MY JANUARY 6TH RESOLUTION IS TO SOMEHOW GET EVEN BETTER AT PERSUASION

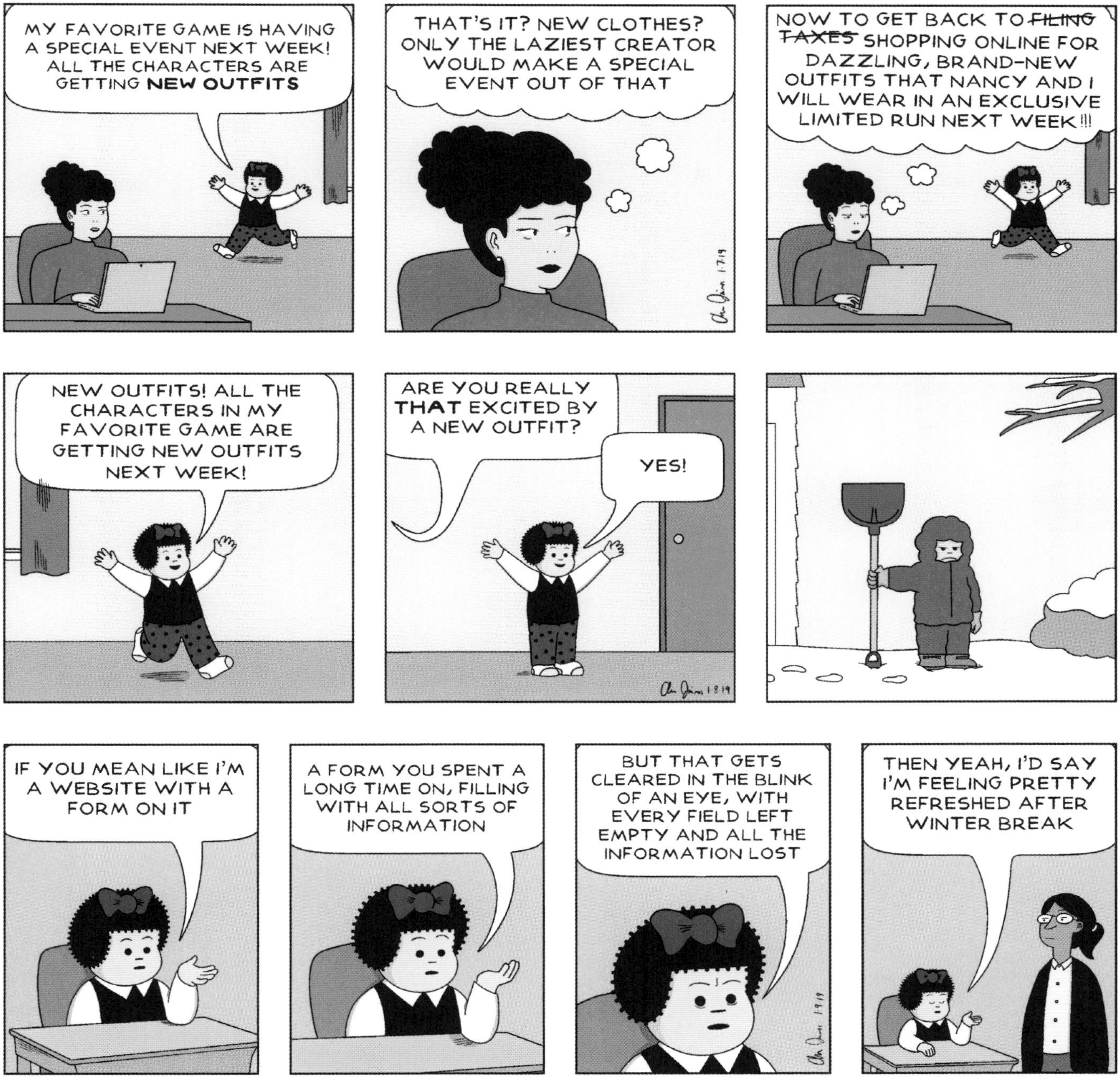
MY FAVORITE GAME IS HAVING A SPECIAL EVENT NEXT WEEK! ALL THE CHARACTERS ARE GETTING **NEW OUTFITS**
THAT'S IT? NEW CLOTHES? ONLY THE LAZIEST CREATOR WOULD MAKE A SPECIAL EVENT OUT OF THAT
NOW TO GET BACK TO ~~FILING TAXES~~ SHOPPING ONLINE FOR DAZZLING, BRAND-NEW OUTFITS THAT NANCY AND I WILL WEAR IN AN EXCLUSIVE LIMITED RUN NEXT WEEK!!!
NEW OUTFITS! ALL THE CHARACTERS IN MY FAVORITE GAME ARE GETTING NEW OUTFITS NEXT WEEK!
ARE YOU REALLY **THAT** EXCITED BY A NEW OUTFIT?
YES!
IF YOU MEAN LIKE I'M A WEBSITE WITH A FORM ON IT
A FORM YOU SPENT A LONG TIME ON, FILLING WITH ALL SORTS OF INFORMATION
BUT THAT GETS CLEARED IN THE BLINK OF AN EYE, WITH EVERY FIELD LEFT EMPTY AND ALL THE INFORMATION LOST
THEN YEAH, I'D SAY I'M FEELING PRETTY REFRESHED AFTER WINTER BREAK

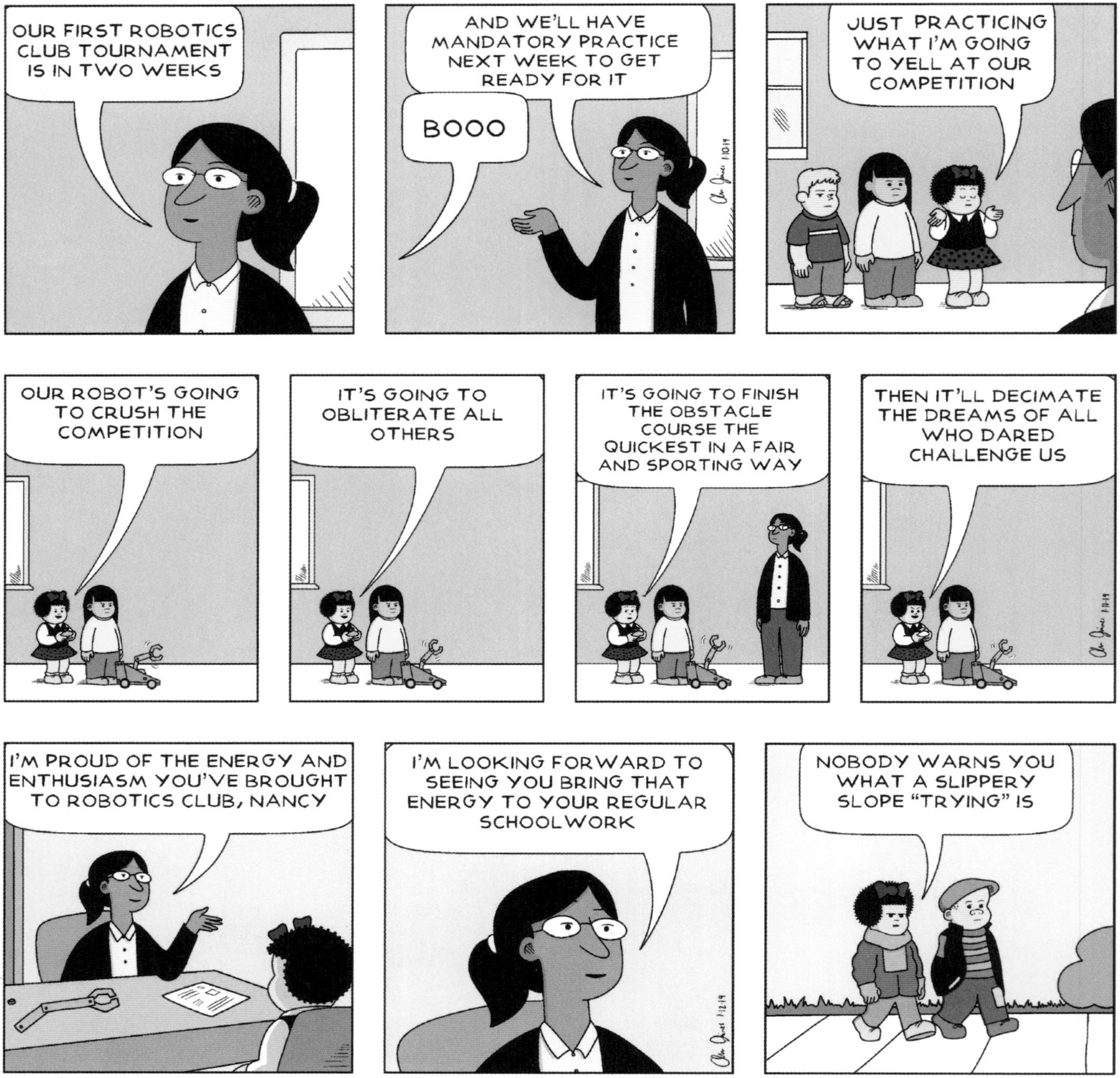
OUR FIRST ROBOTICS CLUB TOURNAMENT IS IN TWO WEEKS
AND WE'LL HAVE MANDATORY PRACTICE NEXT WEEK TO GET READY FOR IT
BOOO
JUST PRACTICING WHAT I'M GOING TO YELL AT OUR COMPETITION
OUR ROBOT'S GOING TO CRUSH THE COMPETITION
IT'S GOING TO OBLITERATE ALL OTHERS
IT'S GOING TO FINISH THE OBSTACLE COURSE THE QUICKEST IN A FAIR AND SPORTING WAY
THEN IT'LL DECIMATE THE DREAMS OF ALL WHO DARED CHALLENGE US
I'M PROUD OF THE ENERGY AND ENTHUSIASM YOU'VE BROUGHT TO ROBOTICS CLUB, NANCY
I'M LOOKING FORWARD TO SEEING YOU BRING THAT ENERGY TO YOUR REGULAR SCHOOLWORK
NOBODY WARNS YOU WHAT A SLIPPERY SLOPE "TRYING" IS

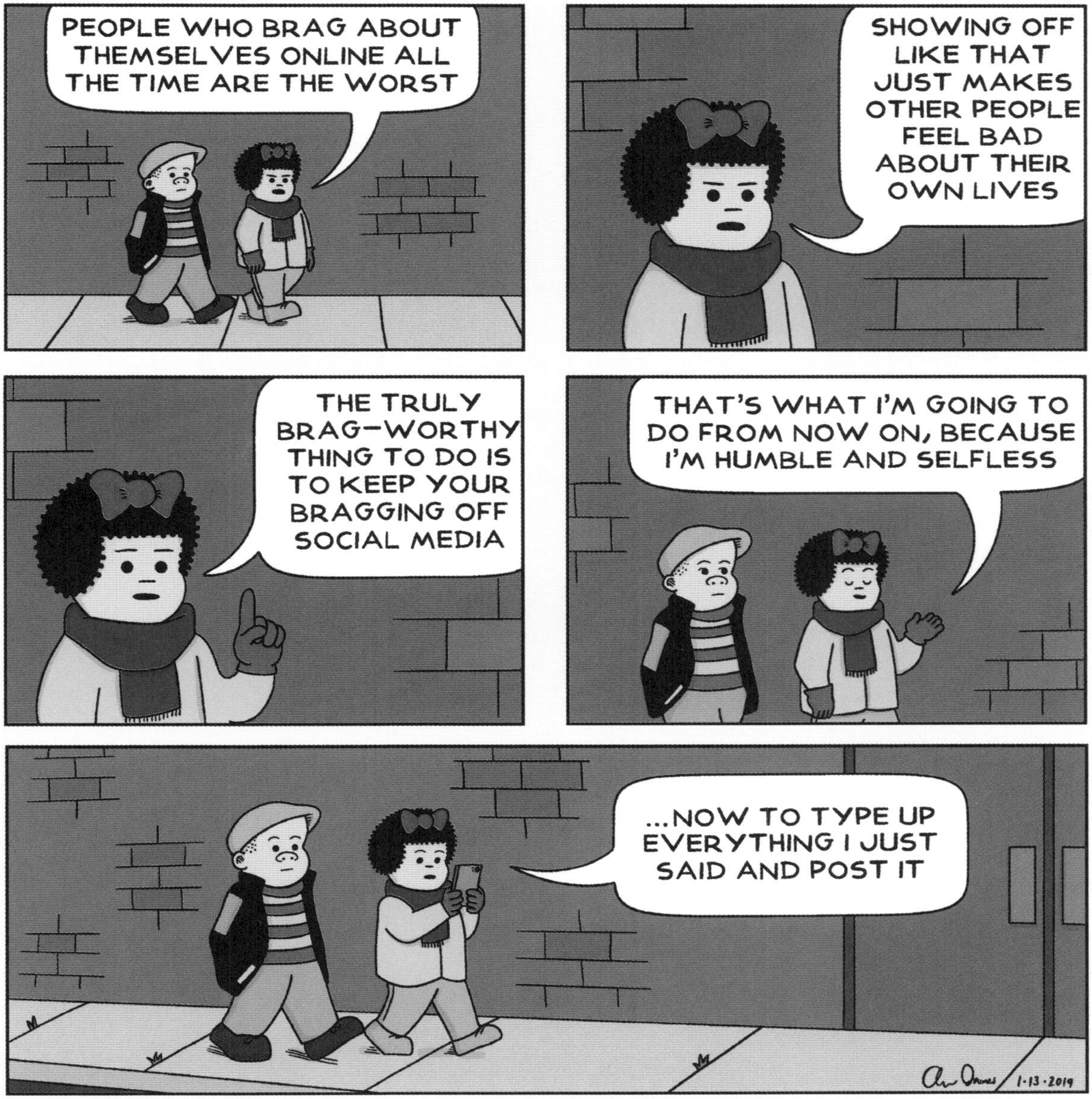
PEOPLE WHO BRAG ABOUT THEMSELVES ONLINE ALL THE TIME ARE THE WORST
SHOWING OFF LIKE THAT JUST MAKES OTHER PEOPLE FEEL BAD ABOUT THEIR OWN LIVES
THE TRULY BRAG-WORTHY THING TO DO IS TO KEEP YOUR BRAGGING OFF SOCIAL MEDIA
THAT'S WHAT I'M GOING TO DO FROM NOW ON, BECAUSE I'M HUMBLE AND SELFLESS
...NOW TO TYPE UP EVERYTHING I JUST SAID AND POST IT
1-13-2019

Olivia Jaimes, the Mysterious Cartoonist Behind *Nancy*, Gives Rare Interview

by Abraham Riesman

Originally published on Vulture.com, Nov. 26, 2018

Rarely in the history of comics has there been a turnaround as abrupt and pronounced as that of *Nancy*. As of just a few months ago, no discerning critic paid the long-running comic strip any mind. Sure, the strips made back in the day by original creator Ernie Bushmiller were held up as revered objects by comics nerds, but he'd died long ago and his successors had never garnered his level of fame. Then came Olivia Jaimes. Or perhaps we should say "Olivia Jaimes," for that name is a pseudonym. Since April 2018, she's been the cartoonist behind *Nancy*, cranking out shockingly funny material about the titular 8-year-old, her slothful pal, Sluggo, and her glamorous aunt, Fritzi, as well as a few new characters Jaimes has thrown into the mix. Virtually nothing is known about Jaimes, so it came as a surprise when she agreed to an extended, unmediated phone interview. Vulture caught up with the elusive draftswoman about the secret origin of her much-memed "Sluggo is lit" panel, the contents of her iPhone notes about strip ideas, and the overlap between *Nancy* and *The Good Place*.

Do you remember how you first got exposed to *Nancy*?

I read newspaper strips, so she was kind of in the air I was breathing. And my parents actually have an original *Nancy* in the house that I've read now, maybe, 10 million times. I'll describe it to you.

Please.

OK, so, panel one, Nancy's looking at Sluggo and she's like, "I really wish that guy would take a bath." And then in panel two, she's thinking really hard about soap, and her eyes are looking at him and there's a dashed line. And then in the third panel, he hasn't taken a bath, but instead, he's sitting on a soapbox, blowing soap bubbles, and listening to a soap opera. She has not succeeded in her goal. I was really more into Pokémon. When I was reading the newspaper strips, I was like, *No, what I gotta read is* Zits *and* Mutts *and other things that are cool for me, age 9*. It wasn't until I was in my early 20s that I really got into *Nancy*, and it was because there was a Tumblr that just posted panels out of context. Like, Nancy imagining a bank blowing up, or Nancy parading around banging something really loud. They were a gateway to more Nancy for me.

Ah, single-service Tumblrs. It was a better era. For how long in your life have you been an Extremely Online person?

Since I was 12, which is now old compared to the youths of today. They're just growing up with it the whole time, and I had 12 years of silence and disconnectedness before I just became one with the bits.

What was your online gateway drug?

I have to think about this. OK, give me one second because there are a lot of repressed memories here of embarrassing things I was doing on the internet. Oh, I know: Neopets. I'm gonna get a Kacheek, and I'm going to play Kiko Match for hours and hours.

I confess, I don't really know what Neopets is.

Neopets is exactly like Pokémon, except it's on your browser and you have a pet. I got into it, and then I had to make cool websites for my Neopets.

When did you start creating your own comics, roughly? Was that after you'd become an internet user, or have you been making comics since you were a wee person?

Since I've been a wee person. I found a bunch of old notebooks, not too long ago, with some really bad comics. No one would write essays being like, "Are these actually good?" They were written back in my predigital days, on paper.

And what kind of stuff did you find interesting to put in comics back then?

Dogs. I was like, *Yeah, I gotta draw some more dogs. This one will be a dog wearing a hat.* That was it. That was my content. My method was dogs. My jokes were dogs doing things dogs don't normally do.

About how long had you been putting comics online by the time you started doing *Nancy*?

I've been making comics in one form or another for so long. Ten years. Because, basically, as soon as I got on the internet, I just started putting things online. I mean, it might be like one thing a year. Not regularly, but for that long.

At what point in that 10 years did it start to become an obsession where you started doing it pretty regularly?

I don't know, maybe never. I mean, doing *Nancy* is the most regular I've ever been with comics.

That's a big step up, if you're all of a sudden doing a daily strip. How did you get from not doing *Nancy* to doing *Nancy*?

[Editor] Shena [Wolf] called me and was like, "Do you want to try out for *Nancy*?" And I was like, "Hahahaha, no way." Not that I wouldn't want it—it just seemed fake. And then I'm drawing the comics to submit for the test to be like, "Here's a couple weeks." And as I'm doing it, I'm like, "Hahahaha, no way, no way." In a very Nancy move, it wasn't like I was like, "No way they would pick me." I was just like, "*Obviously* they would pick me, if they have any taste at all, because these jokes are so great." But it didn't really even feel real as I was signing the contract. I was like, "Hahaha, what a funny joke this is." But, yeah, it worked out pretty good, and they've been really quite good in easing me into it, and giving me feedback, and having me go from not being a regular comic-maker to being "make one every day."

And is that how you do it, one a day? Or do you do big batches and front-load them?
I do big batches.

How many at a time? What's the most in one day that you've done?
I've done a week in a day.

Wow.
The writing of *Nancy* and the drawing of *Nancy* are such different skills for me that it's just like coming up with a joke and laying it out versus just being on autopilot while drawing. I feel like it's a lot easier to exhaust yourself writing—writing jokes or writing whatever—than it is to just draw Nancy's blob head and add little spikeys on it. I don't think I've ever come close to *writing* seven and then drawing all of them in one day.

Do you keep a little notebook and sketchbook around you at all times in case inspiration strikes, or is this more of a you sit down at your work desk and you bang it out?
The former one, except it's just the Notes app on my phone. Everybody I've talked to, every cartoonist, or the vast majority of us, have some notes program with ideas, and maybe a third of them are comprehensible and the rest you're like, *What was I thinking when I wrote this down?* Autocorrect is terrible for this. Autocorrect has probably killed hundreds of jokes for people, because they have a great idea and they write it down, but they spell it wrong, so it changes to something else, and then they're like, *What was this idea?*

I don't want you to give away anything that hasn't come out yet, but I'd love to have an example of what your notes look like.
Yeah, let me see. I'm opening the Notes app now. Hmmm, hmmm, hmmm. Hmmm, hmmm, hmmm. I have to go back a little way.

Take your time.
OK, so, there's one that's, "Coupon good for one floor clean of macaroni card." And that's one that came out, I think, sometime in the last month, where Nancy's doing something nice for Aunt Fritzi and she makes her a macaroni card coupon, with a coupon just to clean the floor when all the macaroni falls off. But then, other ones, it's not even jokes. It just says, "Nancy has been so bossy." And that's it. So I don't know what I was going for there. And then, underneath, I think I also have my to-do list of things to buy. It says "gloves." So, in the list of ideas, it's just like one bullet I have in lowercase letters, "gloves." And I haven't bought gloves yet, so it's really good that I remember. It's getting cold.

Why did you decide to lead off your run on the comic with the strip about Nancy eating corn bread?

I went back and I looked at the end of [previous *Nancy* cartoonist] Guy Gilchrist's run. Nancy as a character had drifted from where I envision her, in that the Nancy I know and love is a total jerk and also gluttonous and also has big feelings and voraciously consumes her world. And I was like, *I need to do a character-reset week*. Just kinda being like, *Here's who Nancy's gonna be right now*. And also, I love corn bread. So, that's it. That's the reason. I wanted to reset expectations and pay homage to my favorite food.

It's funny that you say the Nancy you know and love is a jerk because that plays into my thesis about why your version of the strip has caught on. We're living in this era of a curious sort of hedonism, where we're totally aware and ashamed that we're being slothful and vain and greedy, but we continue doing it all anyway. Nancy is our avatar, and we look at her and laugh because we see how terrible we, ourselves, are. Or maybe I'm off base.

No, that's so true! OK, so, yeah, I wanna talk more about this with you because I think you're really onto something. There's this thing in webcomics: #relatable. And #relatable can be used as a slur. To be like, "Uh, your comic is pandering to people." I'm almost always in the camp where . . . It's not like comics are easy, but I think it's great to be relatable, and I don't

want people to use relatable as an insult. I feel like Nancy *is* #relatable, except that she also isn't apologetic. So, there's the camp of #relatable, which is like, "I'm the worst person: I can't stop eating bread," or "I can't get out of bed," and, like, Nancy is that, but then she's also like, "So what?" The kind of self-hating type that often comes with relatable comics. The self-hating part that often comes with #relatable comics is being like, "Ohhhh, I procrastinated, I'm the worst." And *Nancy* adds one more panel to that, being like, "Who cares? I don't care. More corn bread for me."

So, tell me about Sluggo. What are the core tenets of Sluggo?

I'm kinda going in and tweaking Sluggo a little bit. This is something I've been thinking about a lot. Classic Sluggo, first of all, has his thick accent and he's like, "Noice." I originally sent in some strips where he was talking like that, but it was very forced, and anyone looking at it could tell. Shena was kind of like, "Just so you know, you don't have to have Sluggo keep his accent." I was like, *This is a huge relief*. He's just gonna have watched YouTube videos or something so that he now has changed his pronunciation to match generic midwestern Americans. Classic Sluggo also was kinda doing the thing where he's like, "Yowza, what a pretty girl!" Like, "Bow wow!" And they're 8 years old. I'm trying to keep him true to the spirit of that character, which is, he's kinda more passive and more go-with-the-flow than Nancy, who kinda wants to grab life by the shoulders and shake it violently. He's also somehow become wiser than Nancy, in a lot of ways.

How do the adult characters fit in? You've made Aunt Fritzi less sexualized than she was in the Gilchrist era, and you've introduced a new teacher character. How do they function in the *Nancy*-verse?

Fritzi I see as just Nancy, but Nancy who apologizes. Fritzi is like a Nancy who knows that she should do this or that and feels bad when she doesn't. She's dealing with the responsibilities of adulthood and caring for this child, who has come into her care for some reason. Which, actually, I don't know: Why is Nancy living with Aunt Fritzi? I've read a lot of the old strips; I've never seen this addressed. I need to do, like, a gritty *Riverdale*-style reboot where Nancy's parents mysteriously disappear and you don't find out what happens to them until the mid-season finale. Anyway, she's also a self-insert. I see a lot of myself in Nancy, but I'm really a lot more of a Fritzi because I feel bad if I step on people's toes. And then the teacher character is there, so Nancy has somebody who could push back on her and also maybe help her grow a little. I think of them maybe having some kind of development in some way. She doesn't grow up: like, doesn't turn 10 or go to college or anything. But she can learn something and have some kind of story line beyond just, "Sluggo's talking to another

girl! How dare he!" Young Olivia would have been like, *The second people start learning and growing, it's not gonna be funny anymore.* And there are more and more examples, nowadays, of shows where the characters do grow, and they do learn, and as long as they don't give up their fundamental characteristics, it's actually even more satisfying to see them change in ways that are productive. I think that's something the teacher character can do. Because Ernie Bushmiller's adults were almost always, I think, just pestering Nancy. Being like, "You have to do homework." "You have to do this." "I'm not gonna give you a bank loan." Nancy's not gonna become nice, but maybe she can begin to care about other people a little more. Maybe she can lay off Sluggo if he talks to other girls.

And you have her learning robotics.

Yeah! I realized that all of the nouns that Nancy used to have are being supplanted by a phone. Things that she would have lying around the house to make up a joke are gone. She uses megaphones for a ton of things in Bushmiller's strips, and I don't have megaphones lying around my house. So how, then, can Nancy solve problems, given that technology is advancing to the point where problems are being solved in really nonphysical ways? That's why I'm making her learn robotics. It opens up a wider range of visual gags to make down the line.

At what point in your conception of the strip did you sort of go, "I want to have these characters using their phones constantly"? It's remarkable how much you have them on their phones without it getting visually dull.

Oh, right away. Like, I'm on the phone with Shena and I'm like, "Obviously, they're gonna have to use their phones." We live in an environment where, especially now that Apple tracks how much time I use my phone, I know I spend a ton of time on it. All the time. If my favorite jokes are the ones that are on some level relatable, that people can see themselves in, then I'm basically cutting out a third of my life that people could relate to if I exclude phones. It's very nice of you to say that it's not visually boring to see the phones, because that's definitely something I worry about. It's not like my phone has no physical effect on me. It actually has a huge physical effect. Like, I dread when I see an email has come in but I can't see what it says. They're intensely emotional objects.

What was the note you wrote down for the famed "Sluggo is lit" Labor Day strip? Did you just write down "Sluggo is lit"?

No, actually, I had a couple of worse ideas for Labor Day because Labor Day is Nancy April Fools'. Ernie Bushmiller would always [jokingly] be like, "I'm not drawing Nancy today for X reason." My first ideas were to make it a do-it-yourself strip, like, "I'm not gonna write the joke, so here's a bunch of blank speech bubbles." Or one where there's just like a bunch of different scenes stolen from other

comics. And then I was like, *Actually, what are the panels that would most upset the person who likes me the least? The most upsetting panel to somebody who's like, "Nancy sucks now"?* I actually went to Shena because I don't read the comments. Shena was like, "Oh, definitely have a panel that's all phones." And then I'd been joking with her at the very beginning about how I was going to make Fritzi [who wore very formfitting outfits in the Gilchrist era] wear a parka, and she was like, "People would hate that." But then I was like, the incarnation of what I imagine my greatest hater would despise most is Nancy interacting with every piece of technology using words you don't understand. So, yeah, that's where that one came from.

Do you get royalties from the "Sluggo is lit" T-shirts?

Yeah. But I haven't yet. I don't know how much money I'm gonna get. So just keep buying T-shirts.

Let's talk about your live appearance at Cartoon Crossroads Columbus. How did that come together?

Shena put me in touch with the organizers and was like, "Hey, this is just something to consider." It was really just to toe the waters and see what this might be like, and also to put rumors to rest that I wasn't a woman or was a team of people. Also, it's in this context where Shena knows lots of people, and it can be something very limited. This does not mean that I wasn't terribly nervous. I was like, *Ohhh, what could happen?* I did spend two hours before I went on in a closet because it was in a library, and the room that I could come out of to go into the room we were in was a closet. I just hung out in there for two hours after I snuck into the library, watching *The Good Place*. That was part of the experience, just some good old-fashioned closet-sitting. It was nice, and I'm glad that I got to do it. I'm glad that I got to prove that I'm a real person. And I'm glad that nobody doxed me, which was also really nice.

And how did you pick out your outfit, the disguise?
It was very last minute. I had, like, eight different ideas, and one of them was a Skeletor mask. Then I was like, *I don't want to wear a Skeletor mask.* I had a couple options, but I ended up liking the one that we used best of all because Shena got a hat from somebody, and she got a hoodie from someone else, and I had a scarf and sunglasses. But she was like, "Also, wear this hat and this hoodie." And then she had lipstick from somebody else. It was like *The Fellowship of the Ring*, getting me a costume to put on: "And my ax!" Somebody sent me a screenshot where it was described as "Unabomber chic." I was like, *Yes! Yes!*

Did you have to go back into the closet after the panel was over?
The closet had a second door, so I did, but then we went out the back door of the closet and snuck out through the children's section. This closet, it had stuffed animals from children's programs at the library. So, I'm like, in the closet and drawing, and listening and watching *The Good Place*, and there are puppets everywhere. I'm like, *What if I go out and only talk through a puppet?* These are things you think about, for two hours, in a closet.

Do you have a 30-year plan for *Nancy*? Do you have arcs that you're thinking about? Do you see yourself doing this for a long time? What does the future look like?
I see myself doing it for a long time. I think the arcs that I have planned out right now, a lot of them are me trying to anticipate where technology is gonna go, so they're super sketchily planned. But just thinking about 10 years ago, I didn't have a smartphone and my life was very different. And I'm thinking, 10 years in the future, if that's the way things continue to grow, there are gonna be totally new annoyances related to technology that Nancy has to deal with or whine about. I want the strip to always match the time period in which it's occurring. And so, I want Nancy to be there to catch them on it.

You're going full *Black Mirror*.
This is my plan. *Nancy* is going to become *Black Mirror*.

This interview has been reprinted with the permission of Vulture.com and New York Media.

Self-portrait of the author, by Olivia Jaimes

Walking in Nancy's Shoes

The Long Mile from Ernie Bushmiller to Olivia Jaimes

by Hilary B. Price

Welcome to *Jeopardy!*
(This mock episode aired before April 2018.)

Category: Cartoons for $400

Question: Famous newspaper comics whose title is a female name?

What are . . . *Betty Boop, Blondie, Brenda Starr, Broom Hilda, Cathy, Little Orphan Annie, Luann, Mary Worth, Miss Peach, Momma, Nancy, Sally Forth, Sylvia, Rose Is Rose?*

Category: Cartoons for $600

Question: Famous newspaper comics whose title *AND* author are a female name?

What are . . . *Cathy, Sylvia,* and *Brenda Starr*?

It's not a scientific study*, but it highlights two things:

1. Female characters have flourished in the papers.
2. Female authors have not.

So, why is that?

Be warned, I am not a licensed comics historian. But I do have the cartoonist's callous on my finger from holding a pen, and I've had a strip for 25 years. Newspaper cartoons have been around for 125 years, so I've been in "the room where it happens" for the last 20 percent of its history.

The two opposing theories I've heard in my day and disagreed with:

1. Women are constitutionally wrong for the job. It's too _____.
(Pick an adjective, any adjective!)
Favorites: solitary/time-consuming/rigorous.

This is not an exhaustive list. It includes the most well known, by which I mean the most well known to me. *Little Lulu* is famous and originally authored by a woman, but it was gone from papers by the time I was born. *Mary Worth* was written and drawn by male authors from 1938 to 2004 but is presently written and drawn by two women. *Luann*'s creator now writes with his daughter. There's *Phoebe and Her Unicorn*, but that's a newer strip. Again, this is not scientific.

You get this tired, old saw every time there are a handful of women in a male-heavy field. (It also doesn't begin to explain why there are only a handful of people of color.)

2. There's an active conspiracy to keep female cartoonists and cartoonists of color out.

That has not been my experience in these last 25 years, either with my syndicate or my cohorts. (A syndicate is like a cartoonist's agent. They sell your strip to newspapers.) Syndicates want something exciting and different to sell. And my peers in the business, predominantly white, predominantly male, are truly kind, funny, helpful folks—what you'd expect from people who've found a way to doodle for a living.

So why is it that there are still so few female newspaper cartoonists?

Get comfortable. This is more than a sound bite.

Have you ever played Monopoly? Start by thinking about the comics page like a Monopoly game. For the first 60 years of newspaper comics, only a certain group was allowed to go around the board, collect their $200, and buy property. Empires were built. Fun fact: Did you know, until 1968 newspapers ran classified ads under "Jobs for Men" and "Jobs for Women"? And just three years before that, it became illegal to specify race in a job ad?

With the civil rights movement and the women's movement, more people started their journey around the Monopoly board. Except most of the properties were owned and occupied. Open a newspaper right now and a decent percent of the comic strips in it began before the game was open to all. The lopsided representation is baked in.

The comic strip syndication business plays an interesting role in this Monopoly game. Each competing syndicate looks at the newspaper page in terms of how many of their properties are on the newspaper page versus the other syndicates'. If there's a strip in a lot of papers, and the creator retires or dies, why would you stop the strip and lose all that revenue? Ever since its beginning, this medium was never fussy about who drew what. Hire a writer and an artist. Or, run repeats. When it's your property, you protect the old strip. When it's the competition's property, you fight to displace it with something fresh and new.

And finally, there are the newspapers themselves, who, on the one hand, want something different to attract new readers but, on the other hand, don't want to upset the readers who already subscribe by changing things up. It's an even stickier push-pull situation. Because there are plenty of female characters on the page, readers might not notice how few female creators there are. For cartoonists of color, there are rarely more than two minority-led strips per comics page. Editors tend to see race before they see genre, so a strip about a black family is seen as their black strip versus their family strip. With real estate scarce, the black strips are competing against each other for a place on the page. Editors are thinking about their readers—will their largely older, largely white readership want to or be able to identify with characters of color? They could be right about that. And perhaps the editors themselves have a hard time connecting with those characters.

Taken all together, gender and racial parity on the print newspaper comics page won't happen under the current conditions.

But why is it even important? I've gotten good as a reader at inserting myself in the creative worlds of white male authors. It's a muscle built over time. Meanwhile, the fellas don't get as much opportunity to build that muscle. If we value the importance of walking in another man's shoes, we need more than men's shoes.

So, as a young cartoonist, where do you go where the real estate is cheap and plentiful?

Hello, internet. That's where you'll find the new generation of female cartoonists. Heck, that's where you find the new generation of all cartoonists.

And that's where they found Olivia Jaimes.

For my generation, the internet is a place you visit. For Olivia's, it is a place you live. Your device is an extension of yourself. Olivia's work, aside from *Nancy*, is funny, smart, prolific, and exclusively online. She got her cartoonist's callous from an electronic pen. I wish I could share that with you, but she does her other work under a different name. Being known as the new *Nancy* invites unwanted attention, and the internet is not the safest neighborhood to live in.

Before there was Olivia "Nancy" Jaimes, there was, from the beginning, Ernie "Nancy" Bushmiller, Will "Nancy" Johnson, Al "Nancy" Plastino, Mark "Nancy" Lansky, Jerry "Nancy" Scott, and Guy and Brad "Nancy" Gilchrist. These guys came up through the newspaper business. It doesn't surprise me that the syndicate didn't ask a female cartoonist until *Nancy* was in her nineties. Old habits die hard.

After Ernie Bushmiller died, and in the 36 years before Olivia Jaimes took over, the guys in ties wanted the artists to keep *Nancy* "true" to her original creator. Do you get how impossible an ask that is? You are asking creative people to be creative every day but not from their own voice. No one could, or should, be Ernie Bushmiller.

For some reason, the newspaper comic strip world did not get the memo from the comic book world, where artists get to take their own spin on superheroes. There could be three different *Batman* titles running at the same time. There might be a favorite *Batman*, but there's no wrong *Batman*.

When do you dial down continuity and dial up ingenuity? That's the secret sauce to a more representative comics page, and involves creators, syndicates, and newspapers.

At the syndicates, some lasses with glasses joined the guys in ties, and one of them said to Olivia Jaimes: Here's Nancy. Go ahead and make her *your* Nancy.

So, who is this Nancy? Nancy is 100 percent geek, 0 percent meek. She is both a poster child for STEM and your average kid: addicted to video games, hungry for ice cream, and glued to her phone. (But not to call anybody. Did you seriously think that?) In short, Nancy is Olivia Jaimes's id having a field day.

Olivia Jaimes built her cartooning presence on the internet because real estate was cheap, it was open to all, and she spent most of her time there anyway. And now the newspaper comics business, which has yet to find a solid home in that digital world, has invited Olivia over to play.

We can now add *Nancy* to the *Jeopardy!* list of famous features with a female title and creator. Just in time, because *Brenda Starr*, *Cathy*, and *Sylvia* have all retired. It's you and *Mary Worth*.

Welcome, Olivia "Nancy" Jaimes.

Hilary B. Price, 2019
Rhymes with Orange

Fan Art of *Nancy*

by Olivia Jaimes

Nancy with a Pearl Earring

Untitled Nancy

Ecce Sluggo

Nancy Psycho 100

Nancy in the Style of "Cul de Sac"

Nancy's Aunt

Nancy and Cake

Princess Nancy

Sailor Nancy

Nancy is distributed internationally by Andrews McMeel Syndication.

Andrews McMeel Publishing
a division of Andrews McMeel Universal
1130 Walnut Street, Kansas City, Missouri 64106

www.andrewsmcmeel.com

19 20 21 22 23 SDB 10 9 8 7 6 5 4 3 2 1

ISBN: 978-1-5248-5325-9

Library of Congress Control Number: 2019932577

Nancy can be read online at GoComics.com/Nancy.

These strips appeared in newspapers from
April 9, 2018, to January 13, 2019.

Book Editor: Lucas Wetzel
Syndication Editor: Shena Wolf
Cover Design: David Douglass
Production Manager: Chuck Harper

Production Editor: Amy Strassner
Art Director: Spencer Williams
Title Page Design: Seth St. Pierre

ATTENTION: SCHOOLS AND BUSINESSES
Andrews McMeel books are available at quantity discounts with bulk purchase for
educational, business, or sales promotional use. For information, please e-mail the
Andrews McMeel Publishing Special Sales Department:
specialsales@amuniversal.com.

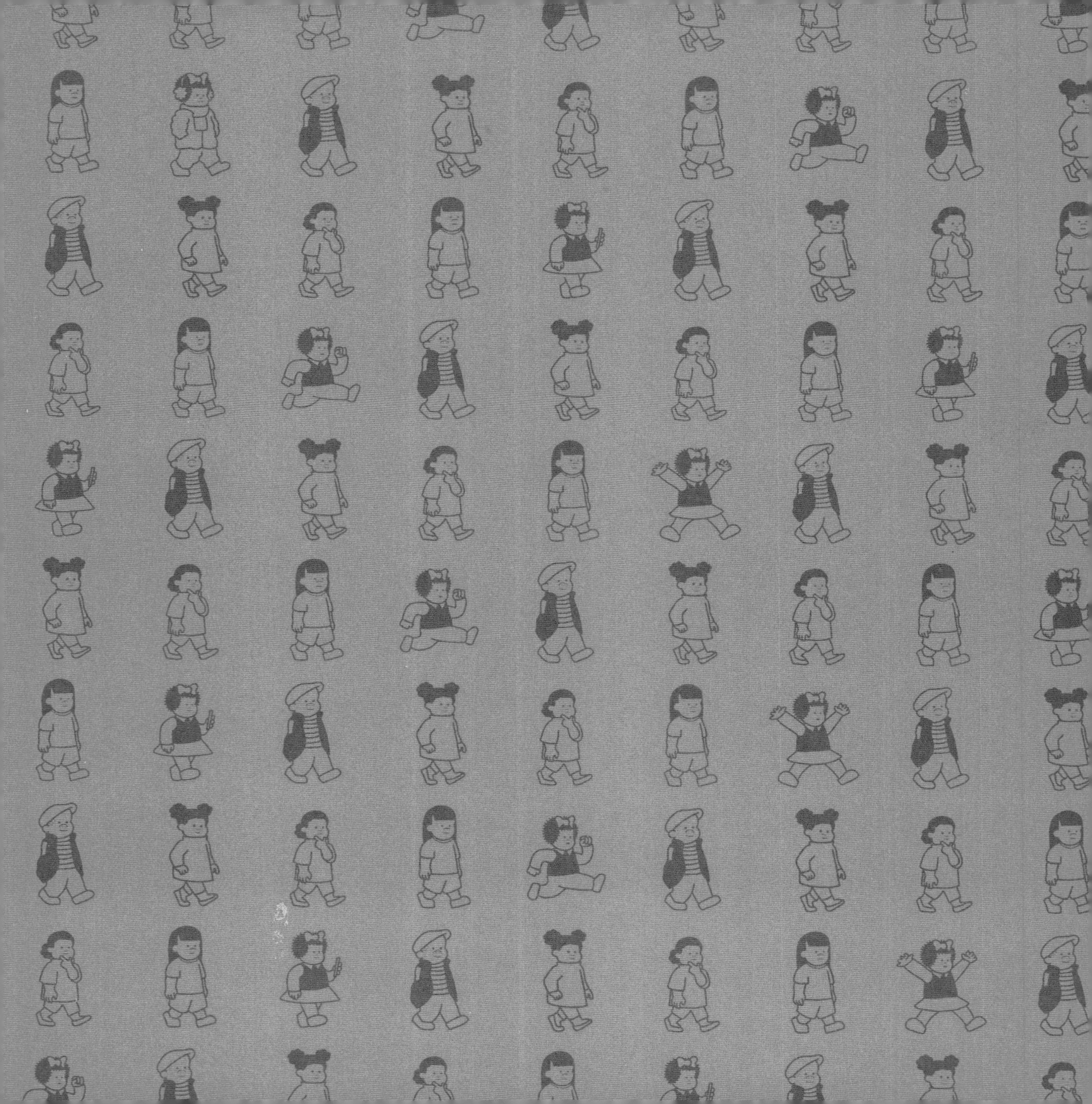